Problems of (
An Introducto:
of Ethi(

Durant Drake

Alpha Editions

This edition published in 2024

ISBN 9789362518217

Design and Setting By
Alpha Editions
www.alphaedis.com
Email - info@alphaedis.com

Contents

INTRODUCTORY - 1 -

PART I THE EVOLUTION OF MORALITY - 5 -

CHAPTER I THE ORIGIN OP PERSONAL MORALITY - 6 -

CHAPTER II THE ORIGIN OF SOCIAL MORALITY - 11 -

CHAPTER III OUTWARD DEVELOPMENT—MORALS - 17 -

CHAPTER IV INWARD DEVELOPMENT—CONSCIENCE - 25 -

CHAPTER V - 33 -

THE INDIVIDUALIZING OF CONSCIENCE - 33 -

CHAPTER VI CAN WE BASE MORALITY UPON
CONSCIENCE? - 40 -

PART II THE THEORY OF MORALITY - 46 -

CHAPTER VII THE BASIS OF RIGHT AND WRONG - 47 -

CHAPTER VIII THE MEANING OF DUTY - 54 -

CHAPTER IX THE JUDGMENT OF CHARACTER - 63 -

CHAPTER X THE SOLUTION OF PERSONAL PROBLEMS - 73 -

CHAPTER XI THE SOLUTION OP SOCIAL PROBLEMS - 81 -

CHAPTER XII OBJECTIONS AND
MISUNDERSTANDINGS - 90 -

CHAPTER XIII ALTERNATIVE THEORIES - 98 -

CHAPTER XIV THE WORTH OF MORALITY - 109 -

PART III PERSONAL MORALITY - 117 -

CHAPTER XV HEALTH AND EFFICIENCY - 118 -

CHAPTER XVI THE ALCOHOL PROBLEM - 128 -

CHAPTER XVII CHASTITY AND MARRIAGE
TEMPERANCE - 138 -

CHAPTER XVIII FELLOWSHIP, LOYALTY, AND LUXURY - 150 -

CHAPTER XIX TRUTHFULNESS AND ITS PROBLEMS - 160 -

CHAPTER XX - 170 -

CULTURE AND ART - 171 -

CHAPTER XXI - 182 -

THE MECHANISM OF SELF-CONTROL - 183 -

CHAPTER XXII THE ATTAINABILITY OF HAPPINESS - 191 -

I. HEARTY ALLEGIANCE TO DUTY. - 191 -

II. HEARTY ACQUIESCENCE IN OUR LOT. - 192 -

III. HEARTY APPRECIATION OF THE WONDER
AND BEAUTY IN LIFE. - 195 -

PART IV PUBLIC MORALITY - 200 -

CHAPTER XXIII PATRIOTISM AND WORLD-PEACE - 201 -

CHAPTER XXIV POLITICAL PURITY - 213 -

CHAPTER XXV SOCIAL ALLEVIATION - 226 -

III. COMMERCIALIZED VICE? - 233 -

CHAPTER XXVI INDUSTRIAL WRONGS - 240 -

II. TO INVENTORS? - 242 -

III. TO COMPETITORS? - 243 -

CHAPTER XXVII INDUSTRIAL RECONSTRUCTION - 250 -

II. PROFIT SHARING, COOPERATION, AND
CONSUMERS' LEAGUES? - 254 -

CHAPTER XXVIII LIBERTY AND LAW - 264 -

CHAPTER XXIX EQUALITY AND PRIVILEGE - 274 -

CHAPTER XXX THE FUTURE OF THE RACE - 288 -

INTRODUCTORY

What is the field of ethics?

To know what exists, in its stark reality, is the concern of natural science and natural philosophy; to know what matters, is the field of moral philosophy, or ethics. The one group of studies deals with facts simply as facts, the other with their values. Human life is checkered with the sunshine and shadow of good and evil, joy and pain; it is these qualitative differences that make it something more than a meaningless eddy in the cosmic whirl. Natural philosophy (including the physical and psychological sciences), drawing its impartial map of existence, is interesting and important; it informs us about our environment and ourselves, shows us our resources and our powers, what we can do and how to do it. Moral philosophy asks the deeper and more significant question, What SHALL we do? For the momentous fact about life is that it has differences in value, and, more than that, that we can MAKE differences in value. Caught as we are by the irresistible flux of existence, we find ourselves able so to steer our lives as to change the proportion of light and shade, to give greater value to a life that might have had less. This possibility makes our moral problem. What shall we choose and from what refrain? To what aims shall we give our allegiance? What shall we fight for and what against?

For the savage practically all of his activity is determined by his imperative needs, so that there is little opportunity for choice or reflection upon the aims of his life. He must find food, and shelter, and clothing to keep himself warm and dry; he must protect himself from the enemies that menace him, and rest when he is tired. Nor are most of us today far removed from that primitive condition; the moments when we consciously choose and steer our course are few and fleeting. Yet with the development of civilization the elemental burdens are to some extent lifted; men come to have superfluous strength, leisure hours, freedom to do something more than merely earn their living. And further, with the development of intelligence, new ways of fulfilling the necessary tasks suggest themselves, moral problems arise where none were felt before. Men learn that they have not made the most of their opportunities or lived the best possible lives; they have veered this way and that according to the moment's impulse, they have been misled by ingrained habits and paralyzed by inertia, they have wandered at random for lack of a clear vision of their goal. The task of the moralist is to attain such a clear vision; to understand, first, the basis of all preference, and then, in detail, the reasons for preferring this concrete act to that. Here are a thousand impulses and instincts drawing us, with infinite further possibilities suggesting themselves to reflection; the more developed our natures the more frequently do our desires conflict. Why is any one better than another? How can we decide between them? Or shall we perhaps disown them all for some other and better way.

Man's effort to solve these problems is revealed outwardly in a multitude of precepts and laws, in customs and conventions; and inwardly in the sense of duty and shame, in aspiration, in the instinctive reactions of praise, blame, contentment, and remorse. The leadings of these forces are, however, often divergent, sometimes radically so. We must seek a completer insight. There must be some best way of solving the problem of life, some happiest, most useful way of living; its pursuit constitutes the field of ethics. Nothing could be more practical, more vital, more universally human.

Why should we study ethics?

(1) The most obvious reason for the study of ethics is that we may get more light for our daily problems. We are constantly having to choose how we shall act and being perplexed by opposing advantages. Decide one way or the other we must. On what grounds shall we decide? How shall we feel assured that we are following a real duty, pursuing an actual good, and not being led astray by a mere prejudice or convention? The alternative is, to decide on impulse, at haphazard, after some superficial and one-sided reflection; or to think the matter through, to get some definite criteria for judgments, and to face the recurrent question, what shall we do? In the steady light of those principles. [Footnote: Cf. Matthew Arnold, Essays in Criticism, vol. i: "Marcus Aurelius," opening paragraph: "The object of systems of morality is to take possession of human life, to save it from being abandoned to passion or allowed to drift at hazard, to give it happiness by establishing it in the practice of virtue; and this object they seek to attain by presenting to human life fixed principles of action, fixed rules of conduct. In its uninspired as well as in its inspired moments, in its days of languor or gloom as well as in its days of sunshine and energy, human life has thus always a clue to follow, and may always be making way towards its goal."]

(2) In addition to the fact that we all have unavoidable problems which we must solve one way or another, a little familiarity with life, an acquaintance with the biographies of great and good men, should lead us to suspect that beyond the horizon of these immediate needs lie whole ranges of beautiful and happy living to which comparatively few ever attain. There are better ways of doing things than most of us have dreamed. The study of ethics should reveal these vistas and stimulate us to a noble discontent with our

inferior morals. [Footnote: Cf. Emerson, in a letter to Fraulein Gisela von Arnim: "In reading your letter, I felt, as when I read rarely a good novel, rebuked that I do not use in my life these delicious relations; or that I accept anything inferior or ugly."] Such a forward look and development of ideals not only adds greatly to the worth of life but prepares a man to meet perplexities and temptations which may some day arise. It pays to educate one's self for future emergencies by meditating not only upon present problems but upon the further potentialities of conduct, right and wrong, that may lie ahead, and building up a code for one's self that will make life not only richer but steadier and more secure.

(3) Another advantage of a systematic study of ethics is that it can make clearer to us WHY one act is better than another; why duty is justified in thwarting our inclinations and conscience is to be obeyed. Not only is this an intellectual gain, but it is an immense fortification to the will. There comes a time in the experience of every thinking man when a command not reinforced by a reason breeds distrust, and when until he can intelligently defend an ideal he will hesitate to give it his allegiance. Morality, to be depended upon, must be not a mere matter of breeding and convention, or of impulse and emotion, but the result of rational insight and conscious resolve. To many people morality seems nothing but convention, or an arbitrary tyranny, or a mysterious and awful necessity, something extraneous to their own desires, from which they would like to escape. To be able to refute these skeptics, expose the sophisms and specious arguments by which they support their wrongdoing, and show that they have chosen the lesser good, is a valuable help to the community and to one's own integrity of conduct. Too often the people perish for lack of vision; an understanding of the naturalness and enormous desirability of morality, together with an appreciation of its main injunctions, would enlist upon its side many restless spirits who now chafe under a sense of needless restraint and seek some delusory freedom which leads to pain and death. Morality is simply the best way of living; and the more fully men realize that, the more readily will they submit themselves to the sacrifices it requires.

(4) Finally, a study of ethics should help us to see what are the prevalent sins and moral dangers of our day, and thus arouse us to put the weight of our blame and praise where they are needed. Widespread public opinion is a force of incalculable power, which is largely unused. Politics and business, and to a far greater extent than now private life, will become clean and honest and kind just so soon as a sufficient number of people wake up and demand it. We have the power to make sins which are now generally tolerated and respectable, so odious, so infamous, that they will practically disappear. There are certain of the older forms of sin which the race in its

long struggle upward has so effectually blacklisted that only a few perverts now lapse into them; we have execrated out of existence whole classes of cruelty and vice. But with the changing and ever more complex relations of society new forms of sin continually creep in; these we have not yet come to brand with the odium they deserve. Leaders of society and pillars of the church are often, and usually without disturbance of conscience, guilty of wrongdoing as grave in its effects, or graver, than many of the faults we relentlessly chastise. On the other hand, many really useful reforms are blocked because they awaken old prejudices or cross silly and meaningless conventions. The air is full of proposals, invectives, causes, movements; how shall we know which to espouse and which to reject, or where best to lend a hand? We need a consistent and well-founded point of view from which to judge. To get such a sane and far-sighted moral perspective; to see the acts of our fellow men with a proper valuation; to be able to point out the insidious dangers of conduct which is not yet as generally rebuked as it ought to be; and at the same time to emancipate ourselves and others from the mistaken and merely arbitrary precepts that are intermingled with our genuine morality, and so attain the largest possible freedom of action, such should be the outcome of a thorough study of ethical principles and ideals.

PART I
THE EVOLUTION OF MORALITY

CHAPTER I
THE ORIGIN OP PERSONAL MORALITY

In almost any field it is wise to precede definition by an impartial survey of the subject matter. So if we are to form an unbiased conception of what morality is, it will be safest to consider first what the morals of men actually have been, how they came into being, and what function they have served in human life. Thus we shall be sure that our theory is in touch with reality, and be saved from mere closet-philosophies and irrelevant speculations. Our task in this First Part will be not to criticize by reference to any ethical standards, but to observe and describe, as a mere bit of preliminary sociology, what it is in their lives to which men have given the name "morality," of what use it has been, and through the action of what forces it has tended to develop. With these data in mind, we shall be the better able, in the Second Part, to formulate our criteria for judging the different codes of morality; we shall find that we are but making explicit and conscious the considerations that, unexpressed and unrealized, have been the persistent and underlying factors in their development. How early in the evolutionary process did personal morality of some sort emerge? Of course the words (in any language) and the explicit conceptions "morality," "duty," "right," "wrong," etc, are very late in appearance, presupposing as they do a power of reflection and abstraction which develops only in man and with a considerable civilization. Even in the Homeric poems, which reflect a degree of mental cultivation in some respects equal to our own, these concepts hardly appear. But ages earlier, far back in the course of animal evolution, there emerged phenomena which we may consider rudimentary forms of morality; and all early human history was replete writh unanalyzed and unformulated moral struggles. Concretely, we mean by personal morality courage, industriousness, self-control, prudence, temperance, and other similar phenomena, which have this in common, that they involve a crossing of earlier-developed impulses and redirection of the individual's conduct, with the result, normally, that his welfare is enhanced. Exceptions to this result will be considered later; but the point to be noted at the outset is that personal morality is not at first the outcome of reflection, or a purely human affair. If we were to take the term "morality" in a narrower sense, as meaning conscious obedience to a sense of duty or to the moral law, it would obviously be a late product. But morality in this sense is only an ultimate development of what in its less conscious and reflective forms dates far back in pre-human history.

Take courage, for example, which may be briefly defined as action in spite of the instinct of fear and contrary to its leading. Nearly all of the higher animals exhibit courage in greater or less degree, and there are many touching instances of it recorded to the credit of those we best know. Industriousness, again, is proverbial in the case of bees and ants "Go to the ant, thou sluggard!"—and noteworthy in the case of many birds, of beavers, and a long list of other animals. Prudence may be illustrated by the case of the camel who fills himself with water enough to last for many desert days, or that of the bird who builds her nest with remarkable ingenuity and pains out of the reach of invaders. Whether or not we shall attribute self-control to the lower animals is a mere matter of definition; in the looser sense we may credit with it the hungry fox who does not touch the bait whose dangerous nature he vaguely suspects. Temperance is probably one of the latest of the virtues, and is rather conspicuously absent in much of human history and biography; but perhaps students of animal psychology can guarantee instances to which the name might fairly be given.

In lesser degree, then, but unmistakably present, we find the same sort of conduct appearing in the animals to which we give in man the names courage, prudence, etc. Purely instinctive these acts usually are though we may see even in the animals the beginnings of mental conflicts, of reasoning, of reflection. But morality (if we keep to the wider sense of the term) is none the less morality when it is instinctive and natural. Morality is a general name for certain KINDS of conduct, certain redirections of impulse. These redirections appeared in animal life long before the emergence of what we may call man from his ape-like ancestry; and all of our self-conscious moral idealism is but a continuation and development of the process then begun. Any theory of right and wrong must take account of the fact that morality, unlike art, science, and religion, is not an exclusively human affair. In contrast with these late and purely human innovations, it is hoary with antiquity and the possession, in some rudimentary form or other, of nearly the whole realm of organic life.

What were the main causes that produced personal morality?

How did these germinal forms of courage, prudence, industriousness, etc, first come into existence? The answer to this question will also show what are the main underlying causes that promote these virtues today.

(1) They are in part due to certain organic needs and cravings which exist independently of the individual's environment. Hunger and thirst imperiously check the tendency to laziness, or heedlessness, and stimulate to industriousness and prudence. To this day the mere need of food and clothing and shelter is the main bulwark of these virtues. The acquisitive impulse, which is also rather early in appearance, has an increasing share in this sort of moralization. The craving for action, which is the natural result of abundant nervous and muscular energy, the combative instinct, the joy

of conquest and achievement, and the sexual impulse, go far in counteracting cowardice and inertia. The artistic impulse, when it emerges in man, long before the dawn of history, makes against caprice for orderliness, self-control, and patience. Ambition is a potent force in human affairs. The desire for the approval of others, which is prehuman, makes for all the virtues.

(2) But in addition to these inward springs of morality there is the constant pressure of a hostile environment. Cold, storms, rivers that block journeys, forests that must be felled, treacherous seas that lure with promise and exact toll for carelessness, arouse men out of their torpor and aid the development of the virtues we have been considering. The necessity of rearing some sort of shelter makes against laziness for industry and perseverance. The dangers of wind or flood check heedlessness in the choice of location for the home and foster prudence and foresight. In the harsher climates man is more goaded by nature; hence more moral progress has, probably, been effected in the temperate than in the tropical zones.

(3) A third and very important source lies in the mutual hostility of the animal species and of men. Slothfulness and recklessness mean for the great majority of animals the imminent risk of becoming the prey of some stronger animal. Among tribes of men the ceaseless struggles for supremacy have pricked cowardice into courage, demanded self-control instead of temper, supplanted gluttony and drunkenness by temperance. Cruel as has been the suffering caused by war, and deplorable as most of its effects, it did a great deal in the early stages of man's history to promote the personal virtues, alertness, moderation, caution, courage, and efficiency.

In the latest stages of man's development, conscious regard for law and custom, the fear of gods, the explicit recognition of duty and conscience, and the direct pursuit of ideals-all the reflective considerations that we may lump together under the word "conscientiousness"-play their ever increasing part and complicate the psychological situation. But even in modern civilized man the underlying animal forces count for far more. And without them the later self-conscious forces would not have come into play at all. There is a small class of people who are dominated throughout their activities by consciously present ideals or obedience to religious injunctions. But the average man still acts mainly under the pressure of the more primitive forces which we have enumerated.

How far has the moralizing process been blind and how far conscious?

(1) To a very large extent the moralizing process has been a merely mechanical one. Through slight differences in nerve-structure individuals have varied a little in their response to the pressure of inward cravings and outward perils. The braver, the more prudent, the more industrious have

had a better chance of survival. So by the process which we have come to call natural selection there has been a continual weeding-out of the relatively lazy, cowardly, reckless, and imprudent. Much of our morality is the result of tendencies thus long cultivated by the ruthless methods of nature; we inherit a complex nervous organization, the outcome of ages of molding and selection, which now instinctively and easily responds to stimuli with a certain degree of inbred morality. This is the case much more than is apparent upon the surface. The child seems very unmoral, the mere prey of passing impulses; but latent in his brain are many aptitudes and tendencies which will at the proper time ripen and manifest themselves. The period of adolescence is that during which the changes in mental structure which were effected during the later stages of evolution are being made in the mind of this new individual; he reenacts, as it were, in a few years, the history of the race, and emerges without any conscious effort, the possessor of the fruits of that long struggle of which he was always the heir.

(2) In all the later stages of animal evolution, however, moral development is largely conscious, or semi-conscious. Besides our inner inheritance of altered brain-paths there is a social inheritance of habits which each generation adopts by imitation of its predecessors. Without any deliberate intention, the young of every species imitate their parents, and then the older members of the flock or herd. "Suggestion" is said by some to be the chief means of moralization; we are brave or industrious because we see others practicing these virtues and naturally do as they do. At any rate, whichever are more important, the inherited tendencies or those acquired by contagion, both of these factors play a large part in the development of the individual's morals.

(3) The third method of moral development is that which we call "learning by experience." The pain or dissatisfaction which a wrong impulse brings in its train, the satisfaction which follows a moral act, are remembered, and recur with the recurrence of a similar situation, becoming perhaps the decisive factors in steering the animal or man toward his true welfare. Many animals quite low in the organic scale learn by experience; and though of course the degree of consciousness that accompanies these readjustments varies enormously, this method of moralization may be said to be always, like the preceding, a more or less conscious process. Learning by experience is subject, of course, to many mistaken judgments; the fallacy of post hoc propter hoc leads many learners to avoid perfectly innocent acts as supposedly involving some evil result with which they were once by chance connected; and the true causes of the evils are often overlooked. Even when dimly conscious readjustments become highly conscious deliberation, the results of that deliberation may be less forwarding morally than the unconscious and merciless grinding of natural selection.

More and more, of course, as men grew in power of reflection, did they consciously shape their morals; and this intelligent selection, which has as yet played a comparatively small role, is bound, as men become more and more rational, to supersede in importance the other factors in moral evolution. But in the later phases of evolution all three of these processes blend together; and it would be impossible for the keenest analyst to tell how much of his conduct was determined in each of these ways.

H. Spencer, Data of Ethics (also published as the first part of his Principles of Ethics), chap. I and chap. II, through sec. 4; or J. Fiske, Cosmic Philosophy, part II, chap, XXII, first half, to "We are now prepared to deal." L. T. Hobhouse, Morals in Evolution, part I, chap. I, secs. 1-4. I. King, Development of Religion, pp. 48-59 A great mass of concrete material will be found in E. Westermarck's Origin and Development of Moral Ideas, H. O. Taylor's Ancient Ideals, W. E. H. Leeky's History of European Morals.

CHAPTER II
THE ORIGIN OF SOCIAL MORALITY

How early was social morality developed?

By social morality we mean, concretely, such virtues as tender and fostering love, sympathy, obedience, subordination of selfish instincts to group-demands, the service of other individuals or of the group. These habits are later in development than some of the personal virtues, but long antedate the differentiation of man from the other animals. Instances of self-sacrificing devotion of parent to offspring among birds and beasts are too common to need mention. Devotion to the mate, though less developed, is early present in many species. The strict subordination of ants and bees to the common welfare is a well-known marvel, the latter enthusiastically and poetically described by Maeterlinck in his delightful Life of the Bees. The stern requirements of obedience to the unwritten laws of the herd, which make powerful so many species of animals individually weak, are graphically, though of course with exaggeration, set forth by Kipling in his Jungle Book. Many sorts of animals, such as deer and antelopes, might long ago have been exterminated but for their mutual cooperation and service. Affection and sympathy in high degree are evident in some sub-human species. When we come to man, we find his earliest recorded life based upon a social morality which, if crude, was in some respects stricter than that of today. It is a mistake to think of the savage as Rousseau imagined him, a freehearted, happy-go-lucky individualist, only by a cramping civilization bowed under the yoke of laws and conventions. Savage life is essentially group-life; the individual is nothing, the tribe everything. The gods are tribal gods, warfare is tribal warfare, hunting, sowing, harvesting, are carried on by the community as a whole. There are few personal possessions, there is little personal will; obedience to the tribal customs, and mutual cooperation, are universal. [Footnote: As an example of the solidarity of barbarous tribes, note how Abimelech, seeking election as king, says to "all the men of Shechem": "Remember that I am your bone and your flesh." (Judges IX, 2.) Later, "all the tribes of Israel" say to David, "Behold, we are thy bone and thy flesh." (2 Sam. V, 1.) Of savage life as observed in modern times we have many reports like this: "Many strange customs and laws obtain in Zululand, but there is no moral code in all the world more rigidly observed than that of the Zulus." (R. H. Millward, quoted by Myers, History as Past Ethics, p. 11.) Compare this: "A Kafir feels that the 'frame that binds him in' extends to the clan. The sense of solidarity of the family in Europe is thin and feeble compared to the full-blooded sense of corporate union of the Kafir clan. The claims of the clan entirely swamp the rights of the individual." (Kidd, Savage Childhood, p. 74.) An elaborate and stern social morality, then, long preceded verbally formulated laws; it was a matter of instinct and emotion long before it was a matter of calculation or conscience. The most primitive men acknowledge a duty to their neighbors; and the subsequent advance of social morality has consisted simply in more and more comprehensive answers to the questions, What is my duty? and Who is my neighbor? At first, the neighbor was the fellow tribesman only, all outsiders being deemed fair prey. Every member of the clan instinctively arose to avenge an injury to any other member, and rejoiced in triumphs over their common foes. We still have survivals of this primitive code in the Corsican vendettas and Kentucky feuds. With the growth of nations, the cooperative spirit came to embrace wider and wider circles; but even as yet there is little of it in international relations. The old double standard of morality persists in spite of the command to which we give theoretic allegiance-"Ye have heard that it hath been said, Thou shalt love thy neighbor, and hate thine enemy. But I say unto you, Love your enemies!" From the same lips came the final answer to the question, "Who is my neighbour?" It can be found in the tenth chapter of the Gospel according to Luke. By what means was social morality produced?

(1) The earliest source of social morality lies in the maternal instinct; the first animal that took care of its young stood at the beginning of this wonderful advance. The originating causes of the first slight care of eggs or offspring lay, no doubt, in some obscure physiological readjustments, due to forces irrelevant to morality. But the young that had even such slight care had a survival advantage over their rivals, and would transmit the rudimentary instinct to their offspring. Thus, given a start in that direction, natural selection, steadily favoring the more maternally disposed, produced species with a highly developed and long continuing maternal love. In similar manner but in lesser degree a paternal instinct was developed. The existence of these instincts implied the power of sympathy and altruistic action that is, action by one individual for another's welfare. From sympathy for offspring to sympathy for mate and other members of the group was but a step; and all sympathetic action may have its ultimate source in mother love.

(2) Not only was natural selection early at work in the rivalry for existence between individuals, protecting those stocks that had the stronger maternal and paternal instincts, but it played an important part in the struggle between groups. Those species that developed the ability to keep together for mutual protection or for advantage. And within a species those particular herds or flocks or tribes that cooperated best outlived the others.

With the strongest animals, such as lions and tigers, and with the weakest, such as rabbits and mice, the instinct to stand by one another is of no value and so was never fostered by natural selection. But in many species of animals of intermediate strength, that by cooperation might be able to resist attack or overcome enemies that they would singly be impotent against, the cooperative instinct became strongly developed. Notably in such case was man; and we find group consciousness, tribal loyalty, continually enhanced by the killing off of the tribes in which it was feebler. The dominant races in man's internecine struggles have been those of passionate patriotism and capacity for working together. Nature has socialized man by a repeated application of the method hinted at in the adage "United we stand, divided we fall." Successful war demands loyalty and obedience, self-forgetfulness and mutual service. It demands also the cessation of internal squabbling, the restraint of individual greed, lust, and caprice. At first instinctive, these virtues came with clearing consciousness to be deliberately cultivated by the tribe, in ways which we shall in a moment indicate.

(3) As in the development of personal morality, the hostility of inanimate nature, coupled with the urgency of inner needs, has also played its part in the socialization of man. The satisfying of hunger, protection against storm, flood, and other physical calamities, is greatly forwarded by cooperation. The rearing of a shelter, for example, that shall be at all comfortable and secure, demands the labor of several. With the development of civilization, mutual assistance and the division of labor become more and more imperative. As man developed more and more into a reflective animal, the comprehension of these advantages became clearer and clearer to him. Resentment against mere individualism grew keener; and any member whose laziness or passions led him to pull apart from the common good had to incur the anger of his fellows. Under these three heads—the selection of the maternal instinct, with its potentialities of universal sympathy, through the struggle between individuals; the selection of the various powers of loyalty and cooperation through the struggle between groups; and the production of cooperative habits through the struggle with inanimate nature-we may group the causes of social morality in man. How has morality been fostered by the tribe? Social morality, like personal morality, is passed on from generation to generation by heredity and by imitation. Both, in historic man, are also deliberately cultivated by the tribe. We have discriminated between the two aspects of morality for theoretic reasons which will later become apparent; but no discrimination is possible or needful for the savage. Courage and prudence and industriousness and temperance in its members are assets of the tribe, and are included among its requirements. We shall now consider in what ways the group brings pressure to bear upon the individual and influences his moral development.

(1) It needs no great powers of observation to convince the members of a tribe severally that immorality of any sort-laziness, cowardice, unrestrained lust, recklessness, quarrelsomeness, insubordination, etc. in another member is detrimental to him personally. His own security and the satisfaction of his needs are thereby in some degree decreased. Contentment at the morality of the other members of the group, and anger at their immorality, are therefore among the earliest psychological reactions. No men, however savage, are insensitive to these attitudes of their fellows; and the emotional response of others to their acts is from the beginning a powerful force for morality. When contentment becomes explicitly expressed, becomes praise, commendation, honor; when anger becomes openly uttered blame, contempt, ridicule, rebuke, their power is well nigh irresistible. A civilized man, with his manifold resources, may defy public opinion; the savage, who cannot with safety live alone and has few personal interests to fill his mind, is unavoidably subject to its sting. His impulses and passions lead him often to immoral conduct, but he is pretty sure to suffer from the condemnation of his fellows. The memory of that penalty in his own case, or the sight of it in the case of others, may be a considerable deterrent; while, on the other hand, the craving for applause and esteem may be a powerful incentive.

(2) Even among some of the animals, the resentment against the misconduct of a member of the herd finds expression in outward punishment maltreatment or death. Among men, punishments for the immoral and outward honors for the virtuous antedate history. Decorations, tattoos, songs, for the conspicuously brave and efficient, death or some lesser penalty for the cowardly, the traitorous, the insubordinate, figure largely in primitive life. These honors are capricious, uncertain, and transitory; but they are undoubtedly more stimulating to the savage, who lives in the moment, than they are in the more complex existence of the modern man. And while in general the savage is more callous to punishments, he has to fear much severer penalties than our humane conscience allows. They are inflicted, of course, with greatest frequency for those sins which instinctively arouse the hottest anger; that in turn varies with different types of men and various accidental circumstances that have determined the tribal points of view. But in general it is the virtues that most obviously benefit the tribe that are rewarded, and those that most obviously harm it that are punished.

(3) Another important means of securing morality in the tribe is the education of the young. This includes not only deliberate instruction, encouragement, and warning, but various symbolic rites and customs, whose value in impressing the plastic minds of the boys and girls of the tribe is only half realized. Initiation into manhood is accompanied in many

races of men by solemn ceremonies, which instill into the youth the necessity and glory of courage, endurance, self-control, and other virtues. The maidens are taught by equally solemn rites the obligatoriness of chastity. The lowest races studied by anthropologists which, however, represent, of course, the result of ages of evolution have commonly an elaborate provision for the guidance of the young into the paths of the tribal morals.

(4) Further, all occasions upon which the tribe gets together for common work or play strengthen the group loyalty and make the group welfare appeal to the member as his own good. Hunting expeditions and wars, the sowing and reaping of the communal harvest, births, marriages, and deaths, in which usually the group as a whole takes a keen interest, feasts and dances, bard recitals, in common undertakings, dangers, calamities, triumphs, and celebrations, merge the individuality of the separate members into a unity. In many primitive races these influences are so strong that the individual has scarcely any separate life, but lives from childhood till death for the tribe and its welfare.

(5) Religion is, until late in civilization, almost wholly a group affair. The gods are tribal gods, their commands are chiefly the more obvious duties to the tribe. The fear of their displeasure and the hope of their assistance are among the most powerful of the sanctions of early morality. Where a special set of men are set aside as priests, to foster the religious consciousness and insure obedience to the divine behests, he is rash who dares openly to transgress. The idea of "taboo" of certain acts which must not be done, certain objects which must not be touched, etc. i extraordinarily prominent among many early peoples. The taboo may not be clearly connected with a divine prohibition; but, whether vague and mysterious or explicit, it brings the awe of the supernatural to bear upon daily conduct. The worship of the gods is one of the most important of the common activities, covered by the preceding paragraph, which make for the unifying of a tribe; and the sense of their presence and jealous interest in its welfare one of the strongest motives that restrain the individual from cowardice or lust or any anti-social conduct.

(6) With the development of language, the moral experience of a people becomes crystallized into maxims, proverbs, and injunctions, which the elders pass on to the boys and girls together with their comments and personal instruction. Oral precepts thus condense the gist of recurrent experience for the benefit of each new generation. Such saws as "Honesty is the best policy," "Lies are short lived," "Ill gotten gains do not prosper," date, no doubt, well back toward the origin of articulate language. The gathering antiquity of this inherited counsel adds prestige to the personal authority of the old men who love to repeat it; and the customs once

instinctive and unconsciously imitated, or adopted from fear and the hope of praise, are now consciously cultivated as intrinsically desirable. There is, of course, very little realization of WHY some acts are commended and others prohibited; the mere fact that such and such are the tribal customs, that thus and so things have been done, is enough. Primitive peoples are highly innovation. So that the moral habits which were established before the age of reflection and articulate speech remain for the most part after they have become crystallized into precepts and commands, and by this articulating process become much more firmly entrenched. Then from the existence of miscellaneous maxims and prohibitions, taught by the elders and linked with whatever impulsive and haphazard punishments are customary, to the formulation of legal codes, with definite penalties attached to specific infringements, is an easy transition. With the invention of written language these laws could become still better fixed and more clearly known. The appointment of certain men of authority as judges, to investigate alleged cases of transgression and award the proper penalties, completes the evolution of a civilized legal system, the most powerful of all deterrents from flagrantly anti- social acts. Dewey and Tufts, Ethics, chaps. II, III. H. Spencer, Data of Ethics, chap. II, secs. 5, 6. J. Fiske, Cosmic Philosophy, part II, chap. XXII, second half. A. Sutherland, Origin and Growth of the Moral Instinct, vol. I. C. S. Wake, Evolution of Morality, vol. I, chaps. V, VI, VII. P. V. N. Myers, History as Past Ethics, chap. I. P. Kropotkin, Mutual Aid, chaps. I-IV. L. T. Hobhouse, Morals in Evolution, part I, chaps. I-III. Westermarck, op. cit, chap. XXXIV. J. Fiske, Through Nature to God, part II, "The Cosmic Roots of Love and Self-Sacrifice." C. Read, Natural and Social Morals, chap. III.

CHAPTER III
OUTWARD DEVELOPMENT—MORALS

What is the difference between morals and non-moral customs?

MORALITY, before it is a matter of legal prescription or of reflective insight, is a matter of instinctive and unconsciously imitated habit. That this is so is shown by the fact that many ethical terms are by their etymology connected with the idea of custom. "Morals" and "morality" are from the Latin mores, usually translated "customs," "ethics," from a Greek root of similar sense. The German Sitten has the same fused meanings. Most of our present-day morality is a matter of custom or convention; and there are those who make a complete identification of the two concepts, morality being simply to them conventional habits of conduct. But a little thought will show that there is a distinction in our common usage; the two categories overlap, but are not identical. On the one hand, our highest moral ideals have never become customary; we long, in our best moments, to make them habitual, but seldom actually attain them. The morals of Jesus, of Buddha, of Marcus Aurelius, have never become habits with any but the saints, yet we recognize them as the high-water mark of human morality. On the other hand, many of our customs have no moral aspect. I may have a fixed habit of going from my home to my office by a certain one out of a number of equally advantageous routes. All of the members of my set may habitually pronounce a given word in a certain way rather equally correct. But about such habits there is nothing moral or immoral. In a word, MORALS ARE CUSTOMS THAT MATTER, OR ARE SUPPOSED TO MATTER; standards to which each member of a group is expected by the other members to conform, and for the neglect of which he is punished, frowned upon, scorned, or blamed. Toward these standards he feels, therefore, a vague or definite pressure, the reflection in him of he feelings of his fellows.

The line between mere habits or manners and morals is differently drawn in different times and places, according to the differing ideas as to what matters. The same actions which are moral to one community (i.e, arouse feelings or judgments of commendation) may be immoral to another community (i.e., arouse reprobation or scorn) and non-moral to a third (i.e., arouse no such response at all). For example, in one tribe tattooing may be a mere matter of personal liking, of no importance and with no group-judgment upon it; yet certain habits with regard to it may become widespread. In another tribe certain tattoos may be thought to be enjoined by the god, and their neglect deemed a matter of serious importance to the tribe as a whole; tattooing may here be said to be a part of the tribal morals. To us moderns it is probably a morally indifferent affair; but if we should learn it to be seriously deleterious to the body, it would again become a moral matter. In short, morals are customs that affect, or are supposed to affect, a man's life or that of his tribe for weal or woe. Obviously, this discrimination is not consciously made by savages; indeed, to this day, such distinctions are enveloped in a haze for the average man. Men do not realize the raison d'etre of morals. They follow them because their fathers did or their fellows do; because they inherit instincts that drive them in their direction or inevitably imitate those who have formed the habits before; because they feel a pressure toward them and are uncomfortable if they hold out against it. When pressed for a justification of their conduct, they are usually surprised at the inquiry; such action seems obviously the thing to do, and that is the end of it. Or they will hit upon some of the secondary sanctions that have grown up about these habits the penalties of the law, the commandment of the gods, or what not. But with our resources of analysis and reflection, it is not difficult to discern that the various forces at work have been such as to preserve, in general, habits which made for the welfare of individual or tribe and discard the harmful ones. It is, then, not merely habits, but habits that matter, moral habits, with whose growth and alteration we are here concerned. What, in general, has been the direction of moral progress? We have noted the main causes at work in the production of morality; we now ask in what general direction these forces push. We have in mind the concrete virtues which have been developed; but what common function have these habits of conduct, so produced, had in human life? What has been the net result of the process? At first sight a generalized answer seems impossible. All sorts of chance causes bring about local alterations in morals. The momentary dominance of an impulse ordinarily weak, the whim of a ruler, the self-interest of classes, superstitious interpretation of omens, the attribution of some success to a prior act which may have had nothing to do with it such accidental and irrational sources of morals, and the resulting codes, are numberless. But as in the process of organic evolution the various obscure physiological alterations which produce variations of type are all overruled and guided in a few directions of value to the species by the law of natural selection, so in the evolution of in all directions are subject to the law of the survival of the fittest. It is really of comparatively little importance to discover how a given moral habit first arose; it may have arisen in a hundred different ways in a hundred different places; indeed, the precise origin of most of the cardinal virtues lies too far back in the mists of the past to be traced with assurance. But the important truth to observe is not the particular details of their haphazard origin but the causes of their survival. Overlaying the countless originating causes of moral ideals are two main preservation—causes, two constant factors which retain certain of the innumerable impulses for one reason or other momentarily dominant. These are of extreme significance for a comprehension of the function of morality in life.

(1) In the first place, a certain number of these blind, hit-or-miss experiments in conduct were, as we have seen, of use to individuals or the tribe in increasing their chances of survival in the ceaseless rivalry for life. The inclemency's of nature and the enmity of the beasts and other men kill more often the less moral than the more moral. So that in general and in the long run those that developed the higher moral habits outlived the others and transmitted their morals to the future. Even within historic times this same weeding-out process has been observable. On the whole, the races and the individuals with the more advanced moral standards survive, while those of lower standards perish. This law accounts, for instance, in some measure probably for the relatively greater increase of whites than of Negroes in the United States, in spite of the higher birth rate of the latter. Other causes are, to be sure, also at work in this competition for life; for one thing, the long period of intercommunication between European races has largely weeded out the stocks most liable to certain diseases, while the antecedent isolation of savage tribes, with no such elimination at work, allows them to fall victims in greater numbers to European diseases when mutual contact is established. But the degree of the moralization of a people has been certainly one of the criteria of survival; and thus by a purely mechanical elimination mankind has grown more and more moral. It hardly needs to be added that the conscious selection of codes that tend to preserve life is a factor of growing importance in insuring movement in this same direction. Altogether, moral progress consists primarily in an increasing adaptation of codes to the preservation of life.

(2) Morality, however, makes not only for life, thus insuring its own perpetuation; it makes also for happiness. Arbitrary and tyrannous rules, cruel or needlessly prohibitive customs, engender restlessness, and are not stable. Such barbarous morals may long persist, propped by the power of the rulers, the superstitions of the people, and all the forces of conservatism; but sooner or later they breed rebellion and are cast aside. On the other hand, more rational codes promote peace and security, banish fear and hatred, and make for all the benefits of civilization. Such codes are in relatively more stable equilibrium and gradually tend to replace the others. All morality is, of course, in one aspect, a restraint upon desire, a check upon impulse; rebelliousness against its decrees will be perpetually recurrent until human nature itself is completely refashioned and men have no inordinate and dangerous desires. But while all codes of conduct are repressive at the moment of passion, they vary widely in the degree in

which they satisfy or thwart man's deeper needs. Such institutions as the gladiatorial games of Rome, human sacrifice, or slavery, were fruitful of so much pain that they were bound in time to perish. In contrast with these cruel customs, the prohibitions of the Jewish law, the Ten Commandments, for example, were so humane, so productive of security and concord and a deep-rooted and lasting satisfaction, that they persisted and became the parent of much of our present day morality. An increasing part in this progress has been played by the conscious recognition of the advantages of code over code; but long before such explicit perception of advantage, the blind instincts and emotions of men were making for the gradual humanizing of morals, the selection of ideals and laws that make for human happiness. As civilization advances, the consideration of mere preservation counts for less, and that of happiness for more; the margin, the breathing space, for liberal interests, grows. Men become interested in causes for which they willingly risk their lives. But, except as these causes are fanatical, off the real track of moral progress, they make for human happiness. And the center of interest can never shift too far. For not only is premature death, an evil in itself, it precludes the cultivation of the humane pursuits that life might have allowed.

Men have to learn to find their happiness not in what saps health or invites death, but in what makes for health and life. What definition of morality emerges from this? The foregoing summary permits us to formulate a definition of morality. Historically, there has been a gradual, though not continuous, progress toward CODES OF CONDUCT WHICH MAKE FOR THE PRESERVATION OF LIFE AND FOR HAPPINESS. These codes have received an imaginative consecration, and all sorts of secondary sanctions; but it is their underlying utility that is of ultimate importance. Very simple and obvious causes have continually tended to destroy customs which made in the contrary direction and to select those which, however originating, made for either or both of these two ends. It is these customs, important for the welfare of the individual or tribe, which we call morality. If the original instincts of mankind had been delicately enough adjusted to their needs, there would have been no need of these secondary and overruling impulses, and the differentiation of impulse and duty, of the natural and the spiritual man, would never have arisen. But actually, mankind inherited from its brute ancestry instincts which, unguided, wrought great harm. Without the development of some system of checks men would forever have been the prey of overindulgence, sexual wantonness, civil strife, and apathy. They would have remained beasts and never won their dominance on the earth. Even rudimentary moral codes came as an amelioration of this dangerous and unhappy situation; they enabled men, by abstention from dangerous passions and from idleness, to make their lives efficient, interesting, and comparatively free from pain; by cooperation and mutual service to resist their enemies and develop a civilization. Morality thus has been the greatest instrument of progress, the most fundamental of man's achievements, the most important part of the wisdom of the race.

Is moral progress certain?

A measure of hopefulness is to be won from the observation that, quite apart from the conscious effort of men, natural laws have been making for moral progress. And unquestionably there has been a great advance in morality within historic times. We are forever past the age of cannibalism, of human torture, of slavery, of widespread infanticide. War is on the wane and may vanish within a few generations. Never before was there so much sympathy, so much conscious dedication to human service, in the world. We are apt to idealize the past; we sigh for a "return to nature," or to the golden age of Greece. And there is some justification in our regrets. Simplicity of living, hospitality, courage, patriotism one virtue or another has been more conspicuous in some particular age than ever before or since. Moral progress wavers, and not all that is won is retained. But on the whole there can be no doubt that we stand on a higher level morally than the Greeks who had vices and sins that we scarcely hear of today and incomparably higher than savage races. Even within a lifetime one can see the wave of moral advance push forward. Yet this observable progress is not so certain of continuance that we can lapse into inertia and trust it to go on of itself. With the softening of the struggle for existence among men, with the disappearance of danger from wild animals, and the increasing conquest over nature, the chief means of moral progress hitherto are being removed. More and more we must rely on man's conscious efforts on personal consecration and self-mastery, on improved and extended legislation, on the growth of a moralized public opinion, on organizations and institutions that shall work for specific causes. Moreover, with the changing situations in which man finds himself, and especially with the growing complexification of society, new opportunities for sin and new temptations continually arise. No sooner is one immoral habit stamped out than another begins insidiously, and perhaps unnoticed, to form. The battle-line moves on, but new foes constantly appear; it will not be an easy road to the millennium. On the whole, our material and intellectual advance has outrun our moral progress; at present our chief need is to catch up morally. [Footnote: Cf. Alfred Russel Wallace, in his last book, Social Environment and Moral Progress (p. 50): "This rapid growth of wealth and increase of our power over Nature put too great a strain upon our crude civilization and our superficial Christianity; and it was accompanied by various forms of social immorality, almost as amazing and unprecedented."] We may note several reasons for this eddy in the moralizing process, this counter-movement toward the development of new sins and the renascence of old ones.

(1) With the growth of large cities and the development of individual interests we come to live less and less in one another's eyes. In primitive life it is almost impossible for a man to indulge in any vice or sin without its being immediately known to his fellows; but today millions live such isolated lives in the midst of crowded communities that all sorts of immorality may flourish without detection. Under early conditions foodstuffs or other goods were consumed if not by the producer, at least by his neighbors; and any adulteration or sham was a dangerous matter. Today we seldom know who slaughtered the meat or canned the fruit we eat, who made the clothing or utensils we use; shoddy articles and unwholesome food can be sold in quantity with little fear of the consumer's anger. All sorts of intangible and hardly traceable injuries can be wrought today by malicious or careless men injuries to reputation, to credit, to success. In a city the criminal can hide and escape far more easily, can associate with his own kind, have a certain code of his own (cf. "honor among thieves"), and more completely escape the pangs of conscience, than under the surveillance of village life. In a hundred ways there are increased opportunities for doing evil with impunity. [Footnote: Cf. E. A. Ross, Sin and Society, pp. 32: "The popular symbol for the criminal is a ravening wolf; but alas, few latter day crimes can be dramatized with a wolf and a lamb as the cast! Your up-to-date criminal presses the button of a social mechanism, and at the other end of the land or the year innocent lives are snuffed out. As society grows complex, it can be harmed in more ways. Each advance to higher organization runs us into a fresh zone of danger, so there is more than ever need to be quick to detect and foil the new public enemies that present themselves. The public needs a victim to harrow up its feelings. The injury that is problematic, or general, or that falls in undefined ways upon unknown persons, is resented feebly, or not at all. The fiend who should rack his victim with torments such as typhoid inflicts would be torn to pieces. The villain who should taint his enemy's cup with fever germs would stretch] [Footnote continued from previous page: hemp. But think of it!-the corrupt boss who, in order to extort fat contracts for his firm, holds up for a year the building of a filtration plant designed to deliver his city from the typhoid scourge, and thereby dooms twelve hundred of his townspeople to sink to the tomb through the flaming abyss of fever, comes off scatheless."]

(2) With the gentler conditions of civilized life there is a general tendency toward the relaxing of social restraints. The harsh penalties of early days would shock us by their cruelty; and early codes are full of prohibitions and injunctions on matters which are now left to the individual conscience.

Needlessly cramping and cruel as these primitive laws often were, they were powerful deterrents, and their lapse has often been followed by greater moral laxity. The passionate pursuit of liberty, which has been so prominent in modern times, though on the whole of great advantage to man, has not been without its ill effects.

(3) The monotonously specialized and unnatural work, which confines a large proportion of our men, women, and youths today, promotes restlessness and the craving for excitement. The normal all-round occupations of primitive men tended to work off their energies and satisfy their natural impulses. But the dulled and tired worker released from eight or ten hours' drudgery in a factory is apt to be in a psychological state that demands variety, excitement, pleasure at any cost. It does not pay to repress human nature too much, or to try to make out of a red-blooded young man or woman a mere machine. Gambling, drunkenness, prostitution, and all sorts of pathological vices flourish largely as a reaction from the dullness and monotony of the day's work. We are paying this heavy penalty for our increase of material efficiency at the expense of normal human living.

(4) With the increased possibilities of undetected sin, above mentioned, and the opportunity which criminals now have of forming within a city a little community of their own which permits them fellowship without rebuke for their sins, there have arisen whole classes of vice-caterers. These men and women make their living by tempting others to sin; the allurements which they set before the young constitute a great check to moral advance, and even threaten continually a serious moral degeneration. The keepers of gambling houses, saloons, and houses of prostitution, the venders of vile pictures and exciting reading matter, the proprietors of indecent dance-halls and theaters, of the "shows" of all sorts that flourish chiefly through their offering of sexual stimulation these are the worst sinners of our times, for they cause thousands of others to sin, and deliberately undermine the moral structure so laboriously reared, and at such heavy cost. Conspicuous in commercialized vice-catering is the Casino of Monte Carlo, where thousands of lives have been ruined. The business of seducing and kidnapping girls-the "white slave trade" flourishes secretly in our great cities. Associations of liquor producers and sellers are very powerful social and political forces. One of the greatest problems before the race is how to exterminate these human beasts of prey that live at the expense of the moral deterioration and often utter ruin of their victims.

(5) While the older racial and national barriers between peoples are breaking down, so that the possibilities of human brotherhood and cooperation are laterally increasing, and the wretched fratricidal wars between peoples coming toward an end, [Footnote: As I read the proof sheets of this book (August, 1914), news comes of the outbreak of what may prove the

costliest and one of the least excusable wars of history. Nevertheless, the end of international wars draws near.] Other barriers, between upper and lower classes, are thickening, new antagonisms and antipathies that threaten yet much friction and unhappiness and a retardation of moral progress. Rich are becoming farther and farther consciousness is on the increase, class-wars in the form of strikes, riots, and sabotage, are ominous symptoms. Masses of the laboring class believe that a great class-war is not only inevitable but desirable. Such conflicts, however, besides their material losses, engender hatred, cruelty, lust, greed, and all sorts of other forms of immorality. No one can predict how far such struggles may go in the future toward undoing the socializing process which at best has so many obstacles to meet and moves so slowly. Many forces are at work, however, for moral uplift. The spread of education, teaching men to think, to discern evils, and to comprehend the reasons for right conduct, the increasing influence of public opinion through newspapers and magazines, the growing number of organizations working to eradicate evils, the gradual increase of wise legislation, the reviving moral pressure of the Christian Church such signs of the times should give us courage as well as show us where we can take hold to help. Morality is not static, a cut-and-dried system to be obeyed or neglected, but a set of experiments, being gradually worked out by mankind, a dynamic, progressive instrument which we can help ourselves to forge. There is room yet for moral genius; we are yet in the early and formative stage of human morality. We should not be content with past achievement, with the contemporary standards of our fellows. If we give our keenest thought and our earnest effort, there is no knowing what noble heights of morality we may be helping the future to attain.

Dewey and Tufts, Ethics, chap. IV. Hobhouse, op. cit, part II, chaps. II, VIII. Westermarck, op. cit, chap. VII. Sutherland, op. cit, vol. II, chaps. XIX-XXI. W. G. Sumner, Folkways, chaps. I, II, XI. Sir H. Maine, Village Communities. C. Darwin, Descent of Man, part I, chap. v. J. G. Schurman, Ethical Import of Darwinism. W. I. Thomas, Source Book for Social Origins, part VII. C. Read, Natural and Social Morals, chap. VI. I. King, Development of Religion, chap. XI. On the question of moral progress: Dewey and Tufts, Ethics, pp. 187-92. W. Bagehot, Physics and Politics, chap. VI. H. G. Wells, New Worlds for Old, chap.I, secs. 2-4. J. Bryce, in the Atlantic Monthly, vol. 100, p. 145. E. Root, The Citizen's Part in Government, pp. 96-123. J. S. Mackenzie, Manual of Ethics (2d ed.), chap. XV. A. R. Wallace, Social Environment and Moral Progress.

CHAPTER IV
INWARD DEVELOPMENT—CONSCIENCE

What are the stages in the history of moral guidance?

THERE may be said to be five stages in the history of moral guidance: guidance by instinct, by custom, by law and precept, by conscience, and by insight. No one of these guides is discarded with the development of the others; we rely today upon all of them in varying degree. Their evolution overlaps; the alteration of instinct still goes on, changing laws and customs still bring their pressure to bear from without upon the individual; while our conscience and our insight have their roots far back in the past. Yet the prominence of each of these factors in turn marks a successive stage in the evolution of moral control. Inherited instinct, and then custom, unconsciously passed on by imitation and to some extent taught with a dimly conscious purpose, shape the crude morality of the animals though the other means of guidance are not wholly absent even in them. Among savages legal codes, unwritten and perhaps not even clearly formulated, yet exacting and strictly enforced by penalties, come to form an important supplement to instinct, custom, and proverbial wisdom. But quite as important is the gradual development of an inward guide—those very various secondary impulses and inhibitions which we hump together because of their common function and call the moral sense or conscience. We shall now consider briefly the origin of this internal steering-apparatus. The latest and most mature guide of all, reflective insight, arises in marked degree only when abstraction and analysis. There is no problem connected with its origin except the general problems of the development of human reason. How moral insight may be trained and brought to bear upon conduct will, it is hoped, be clear to the student who patiently studies this volume.

Out of what has conscience developed?

The "conscience" of our moralizing and religious literature figures as a sharply defined and easily recognizable "faculty," like "will" or "reason." But this classification, though useful, is misleading by its simplicity. If we observe by introspection what goes on in our minds when we "will" or "reason" or "listen to conscience," we shall find all sorts of emotions, ideas, impulses, surging back and forth, altering from moment to moment, never twice the same. At another period of our lives, or in another man's mind, the psychological stuff pigeonholed under these names may be almost entirely different. A great many diverse mental elements have at one time or other taken the role of, or formed an ingredient in, the function we label "conscience." We will enumerate the more important:

(1) Experience quickly teaches her pupils that certain acts to which they feel a strong impulse will lead to an aftermath of pain or weariness, or will stand in the way of other goods which they more lastingly desire or more deeply need. The memory of these consequences of acts remains as a guide for future conduct, not so often in the form of a clearly recognized memory as in a dim realization that the dangerous act must be avoided, a vague pressure against the pull of momentary inclination, or an uncomprehended feeling of impulsion toward the less inviting path. This residuum of the moral experience of the individual is one ingredient in what we call his conscience.

(2) But there is much more than this. The individual is a member of a group. The customs and expectations of this group not only bear upon him from without but find a reflection in his own motor mechanism. He hears the voice of the community in his heart, an echo of the general condemnation and approval. This acquired response, the reverberation of the group judgment, may easily supplant his personal inclinations. Primitive man is sensitive to the judgments and emotional reactions of his fellows; the tribal point of view is unquestioned and authoritative over him. So important is this pressure in his mental life, though not understood or recognized for what it is, that conscience is denned by many moralists as the pressure of the judgment of the tribe in the mental life of its members, or in similar terms. Paulsen calls it "the existence of custom in the consciousness of the individual." This is to neglect unjustly the other sources of the sense of duty; but certainly the pulls and pushes arising from these two sources, which we may call the inner aspect of individual moral experience and of loyalty to the community-morals, reinforcing one another as they generally do, produce a very powerful form of conscience.

(3) A number of primitive emotions join forces with them. Sympathy is generally on their side, and the instinctive glow of patriotism or pride in the tribe's success. The shrinking from disapproval, the craving for esteem, the very early emotions of shame and vanity, help to pull away from the self-indulgent or selfish impulse. The spontaneous admiration of others for their virtues and anger at them for their sins is applied involuntarily by a man to himself; contempt for his own weakness and joy in his superiority according to the generally accepted code are powerful deterrents. The consciousness of the resentment that others will feel if he does evil, the instinctive application to himself of a trace of the resentment he would feel toward him or toward these fellow tribesmen of is-such complex states of mind complicate his mental processes and help check his primary instincts.

(4) To these ingredients we must early add the more or less conscious fear of the penalties of the tribal law, of the vengeance of chiefs or powerful members of the tribe, of the tribal gods and their jealous priests. These fears may be but dimly felt and not clearly discriminated; but however subconscious they may be in a given case of moral conflict, they play a large part. The peace of mind that accompanies a sense of conformity to the will of rulers or of gods, contrasted with the anxiety that follows infraction, gives a greatly increased weight to that growing pressure of counter instincts which comes so largely to override a man's animal nature. Most of the sources of conscience thus date far back beyond the dawn of history. But they can be pretty safely inferred from the earliest records, from a study of existing savage races, and from the study of childhood. The definite conception of "conscience" is very late, scarcely appearing until very modern times. And the fact that conscience itself, even in its rudimentary forms, was much later in growth than the underlying animal instincts which it developed to control and guide, is shown by its late development in the child-not, normally, until the beginning of the third year. The early life of the individual parallels the evolution of the race; and the later-developed faculties in the child are those which arose in the later stages of human progress. But the existence of our well-defined moral sense, with its significant role in modern life, needs no supernatural explanation. It has grown up and come to be what it is as naturally as have our language, our customs, and our physical organs.

What is conscience now? It is a valuable exercise in introspection to observe a case of "conscience" in one's own life and note of what mental stuff it is made. When a number write down their findings without mutual suggestion, the results are usually widely divergent. Any of the original ingredients hitherto mentioned may be discovered, or other personal factors. There may be present to consciousness only a vague uneasiness or restlessness, or there may be a sophisticated recurrence of the concepts of "conscience," "duty," etc. The one universal fact is that there is a conflict between some primitive impulse or passion and some maturer mental checks. Any sort of mental stuff that serves the purpose of controlling desire will do; we must define conscience in terms not of content but of function. There is no such unity in the material as the single name seems to imply; and whether or not that name shall be given to a given psychological state is a matter of usage in which there is considerable variation.

In general, we reserve the name "conscience" for the vaguer and more elusive restraints and leadings, the sense of reluctant necessity whose purpose we do not clearly see although we feel its pressure, the accumulated residuum of long inner experience and many influences from without. Our minds retain many creases whose origin we have forgotten;

we veer away from many a pleasant inclination without knowing why. These unanalyzed and residual inhibitions that grip us and will not let us go, form a contrasting background to our more explicit motives and often count for more in our conduct. The very lack of comprehension serves in less rational minds to enhance their prestige with an atmosphere of awe and mystery. These strange checks and promptings that well up in a man's heart are which he must not dare to disobey. The voice of God in our hearts we may, indeed, well conceive them to be. The attempt to analyze into its psychological elements and trace the natural genesis of conscience, as of morality in general must not be taken as an attempt to discredit it or to read God out of the world. For God works usually, if not universally, through natural laws; and the historical viewpoint, that sees everything in our developed life as the outcome of ages of natural evolution, is not only rich in fruitful insight, but entirely consistent with a deep religious feeling. For hortatory or inspirational purposes we do not need to make this analysis; it has, indeed, its practical dangers. It tends to rob the glory from anything to analyze it into its parts and study the natural causes that produced it. The loveliest painting is but a mess of pigments to the microscope, the loveliest face but a mess of cells and hairs and blood vessels. There is something gruesome and inhuman about embryology and all other studies of origins.

While we are analyzing an object, or tracing its genesis, we are not responding to it as a whole or feeling its beauty and power. The mystery, the spell, vanishes; we cease to thrill when we dissect. But knowledge proceeds by analysis, and gains by a study of origins and causes. And the temporary emotional loss should be more than balanced by the value of the insight won. We need not linger too long at our dissecting. The discovery that conscience is an explicable and natural development does not preclude a realization of the awfulness of obligation, the sacredness of duty, any more than a geologist must cease to thrill at the grandeur and beauty of the Grand Canyon because he has studied the composition of the rocks and understands the causes that have slowly, through the ages, wrought this miracle. So we need feel no sense of duty is not something imposed upon human nature from without; it is of its very substance, it has developed step by step with our other faculties, slowly crystallizing through millenniums of human and pre-human experience. In the abstract, then, we may say that conscience is a name for ANY SECONDARY IMPULSES OR INHIBITIONS WHICH CHECK AND REDIRECT MAN'S PRIMARY IMPULSES, FOR A GREATER GOOD; any later developed aversions or inclinations, judgments of value or feelings of constraint, which guide a man in the teeth of his animal nature toward a better way of life PROVIDED THAT THESE SUPERIMPOSED IMPULSES ARE NOT EXPLICIT ENOUGH TO BE CLASSIFIED UNDER SOME OTHER HEAD. For example, we may be pulled up sharply from a course of self-indulgence by a conscious realization of the harm we are doing to others thereby; this bridling state of mind, whether chiefly emotional or more intellectual, we may call sympathy, or an altruistic instinct, or love. But when we feel the pressure from these same mental states incipiently aroused, when our motor-mechanism half automatically steers us away from the selfish act, without our consciously formulating a specific name for the new impulse or recognizing any articulate motive, we are apt to give this mental push the more general name of conscience. So if we consciously reckon up, balance advantages, and decide on the less inviting act in recognition of its really greater worth to us, we say we act from prudence or insight, we are reasonable about it; while if the grumbling of the prudential motives remain subterranean, subconscious, they play the role of conscience. Conscience is, on such occasions, but inarticulate common sense. Usually, however, prudential and altruistic motives would both be discovered if the dumb driving of conscience were to be made articulate. The reverberation of parental teachings, of sermons heard and books read, of the opinions and emotions of our fellows, might be found, all bent and fused into a combined "suggestion," a mental push, a "must" or "ought," from whose influence we find it difficult to escape.

The detailed psychological analysis of cases of conscience and the study of its genesis are of no essential ethical interest, except as they show us that the sense of duty is not an ultimate, irreducible element in our consciousness, or make clearer to us its function and value. Conscience is the general name for coercion upon conduct from within the mind. The important thing to note is the useful purpose, which, in its so widely varying forms, it serves. Whatever its sources or its exact nature in contemporary man, it is one of the most valuable of our assets. To a more explicit statement of its value we must now turn. What is the value of conscience?

It would seem, at first glance, as if the development of reason should make conscience unnecessary. When we are able to discern the consequences of our acts, formulate and weigh our motives and aims, what need of these vague pre-rational promptings and inhibitions? Why not train men to supplant a blind sense of duty by a conscious insight, a rational valuation of ends and means? Is not reason, as it has been recently called, "the ultimate conscience"? [Footnote: G. Santayana, Reason in Science, p. 232; where also the following: "So soon as conscience summons its own dicta for revision in the light of experience and of universal sympathy, it is no longer called conscience, but reason."]

(1) Conscience is valuable on account of our ignorance. Individually we have not had experience enough to guide us in our crises; conscience is the representative in us of the wisdom of the race. In many cases we should

never reason out the right solution of a problem; we lack the data. But we can lean upon the racial experience. Many past experiences, now forgotten, have gone to the molding of this faculty. The need of action is often imminent, there is no time for the long study of the situation which alone could form a sure insight into the conduct it demands. We need readymade morals. Moreover, we are subject to bias, to individual one sidedness, and to the distortion of passion; in the stress of temptation we are not in a mood to reason judicially, even if we have the necessary data. Altogether, insight, though in the long run the critic of conscience, is not a practical substitute. What conscience tells us is more apt to be true than what at the moment seems a rational judgment.

(2) Conscience is also valuable in view of our rebelliousness. Conventional morality is external, and would continually arouse revolt, were it not reinforced by an inward prompting. If external motives and penalties alone bore upon us we should chafe under them, and under the stress of passion or longing throw them aside. Even if these external sanctions were reinforced by insight into the rationality of morality, that insight might still leave us rebellious and unpersuaded. Knowledge alone is feeble, marginal in our lives. We often sin in the full knowledge of the penalties awaiting us. We need something more dynamic, pressure as well as information. Conscience is such a driver. Its commands weigh upon us, and will not be stilled. Reason plays but a weak part in the best of us; and to counteract our incurable waywardness, our recurrent longings for what cannot be had without too great a cost, we need not only the presence of law and convention, not only the weak voice of knowledge, but the stern summons of this powerful psychological response. Nature was wise when she evolved this function as a bulwark against our weakness, a bit between our because of our forgetfulness. Over and over again we say, "I didn't stop to think." If our conscience had been properly acute, it would have made us stop. Insight, however comprehensive and clear, is apt to remain somewhere in a locked drawer in our minds when the hot blooded impulse appears. If we were but to pause and reflect, we should be sensible and kind. But our intellect is dulled by our emotions, it does not get working. We need a more instinctive, a deeper-rooted mechanism, an imperious "Halt!" at the brief moment between the thought of sin and the act. Conscience is not only a teacher and a driver, it is a sentinel. Its red flag stops us at the brink of many a disaster, and we have it to thank for many an otherwise forgotten duty performed.

To sum up: Instinct and desire are lacking in proper adjustment to the needs of life. Society seeks to control them by the pressure of law and custom. These powerful forces, however, are external, and, savoring more or less of tyranny, tend at times to awaken a rebellious spirit in the hotheaded. So a perpetual antinomy would exist between internal impulse and external constraint, were it not that that external constraint is reflected within the individual mind by a secondary and overlying set of inhibitions and promptings which we call variously the "moral sense," the "sense of duty," or "conscience." We often do not know or remember consciously at the moment of decision what the law ordains or the wisdom of the race teaches. But we have an inward monitor. We often hang back from a recognized duty. But we feel an inward push. When the wrong impulse is pungent and enticing, and the right one insipid and tame, when we would forget if we could the perils of sin, conscience surges up in us and saves us from ourselves. It is a mechanism of extreme value, which nature has evolved in us for imposing on our weak and vacillating wills action that makes for a truer good than we should otherwise choose. No wonder, then, if we reverence this saving power within us, and crown it with a halo as the divine spark in the midst of our grosser nature. The more we revere it, the brighter the glamour it has for us, the stronger it grows and the more it helps us. The apotheosis of conscience has been of immense use in leading men to heed its voice and obey its leading. Yet this blind allegiance has its dangers; conscience has often been a cruel tyrant. It is by no means an always-safe guide, as we shall presently note. And as men grow more and more adjusted by instinct and training to their real needs, they will have less and less need of this helmsman. After all, there is something wrong with a life that needs conscience; it is a transition help for the long period of man's maladjustment. Spencer looks forward, a little too hopefully, perhaps, to a time in the measurable future when we shall have outgrown the need of it, when we shall wish to do right and need no compulsion, outer or inner. And Emerson, in a well known passage, writes: "We love characters in proportion as they are impulsive and spontaneous. When we see a soul whose acts are all regal, graceful, and pleasant as roses, we must thank God that such things can be and are, and not turn sourly on the angel and say, 'Crump is a better man with his grunting resistance to all his native devils.'" A Chinese proverb says, "He who finds pleasure in vice and pain in virtue is still a novice in both." The saint is he who has learned really to love virtue, in its concrete duties, better than all the allurements of sin; to him we may say, as Virgil said to Dante, "Take thine own pleasure for thy guide henceforth." But until we are saints it is wise for us to cultivate conscientiousness, the habit of obedience, even when it costs, to that inward urging which is, on the whole, for most of us, our safest guide.

F. Paulsen, System of Ethics, book II, chap. V, secs. 1, 2, 5. H. Spencer, DATA OF ETHICS, chap. VII, secs. 44-46. S. E. Mezes, ETHICS, DESCRIPTIVE AND EXPLANATORY, chaps. V, VIII. Sutherland, op. cit, chap. XV. F. Thilly, INTRODUCTION TO ETHICS, chap. III. Westermarck, op. cit, chap. V. Darwin,

DESCENT OF MAN, partt. I, chap. III. J. H. Hyslop, ELEMENTS OF ETHICS, chaps. VI, VII. J. S. Mill, UTILITARIANISM, chap. v. H. W. Wright, SELF-REALIZATION, part. I, chap. IV.

CHAPTER V

THE INDIVIDUALIZING OF CONSCIENCE

Conscience as we have seen, is the result of a fusion of elements coming from personal experience and tribal judgment. In its early phases the latter elements predominate; conscience may be fairly called the inner side of custom. Primitive men have little individuality and involuntarily reflect the general attitude. But with widening experience and growing mental maturity, conscience, like man's other faculties, tends to become more individual and divergent, until we find, in civilized life, a man standing out for conscience' sake against the opinion of the world. The individualization of conscience, with the consequent clash of ideals, gives the study of morality much of its interest and difficulty; it will be worthwhile to note some of its causes. Why did not the individualizing of conscience occur earlier?

(1) In primitive man there is not much opportunity for the development of individuality. There are few personal possessions, there is little scope for the exercise of peculiar talents, there is little power of reflection, to develop strongly individual ideas. The self-assertive instincts are to considerable extent still dormant for lack of stimulus to call them forth. The individual is content to take his place in the group life, and it seldom occurs to him to question the group- judgment.

(2) In primitive life there is a drastic repression of any incipient rebelliousness, through the enforcement of custom or explicit law in the ways we have indicated; the fear of a heavy discouragement to any innovator. If men dared to defy the community morals, they were very likely to be put to death before the habit of free judgment had much time to spread. There was thus a sort of artificial selection for survival of the conventional type, and weeding-out of the freethinker and moral genius. Even in historic times this process has continued and been an enormous clog on human progress. The man of revolutionary moral insight has had to pay the penalty, if not of death as in the case of Socrates or of Jesus-at least of ridicule and ostracism, of excommunication and isolation as, in our own day, with Tolstoy. Many and many a saint who might have been a beacon-light to mankind has lived under the curses or sneers of his fellows and died in loneliness, to be soon forgotten. A few have, after years of opposition, obtained a following and accomplished great reforms, as did Buddha, Mohammed, St. Francis, and Luther. But none can count the potential reformers, the men of new insight, of individual moral judgment, who have

been crushed by the weight of group-opposition. Man has been the worst enemy of his own progress.

(3) There is another aspect to this selective process, noted before in another context- the struggle for existence between groups. So intense are these tribal struggles in early society that harmony within a group is absolutely necessary. Individualization means disorganization; and whatever communities developed free thought and divergent ideas were at a disadvantage when it came to action. Many such groups, ahead of their rivals in individual moral development, were wiped out by barbaric armies that gave unquestioning obedience to the tribal will and worked together like a machine. Up to a certain stage in human development individuality was an undesirable variation and was ruthlessly repressed, sometimes by the execution of the particular offenders, sometimes by the destruction of the group to which they belonged and which they by their divergence weakened. What forces made against custom-morality? Against these repressive forces, however, other forces were from early times urging men on to reject the tyranny of custom. Those inward promptings that we call conscience were continually tending to become less the echo of the group conventions and more the expression of the individual's needs and deepest desires.

(1) At bottom, of course, lay the natural restlessness and passions of men, the impatience of control, the longing for liberty, and the craving for self-expression. The combative instinct, pride, obstinacy, and notably the sex-instinct, were from earliest times spurring men on to a disregard of the conventional and the formation of individual standards.

(2) We may make special mention of the love of power over others, which has been one of the deep roots of the perpetual internecine struggles of man. There is a need of leadership in every group; and this need is felt more and more keenly as the groups increase in size. At first the authority of the elders suffices, or of strong men who push to the fore at times of crisis, as in the case of the so called judges, the military dictators, as we might better call them, of early Israel. But as Israel, grown in numbers, and feeling the need of greater unity and readiness, clamored for a king, so generally, at a certain stage of culture, permanent chiefs of some sort become necessary. Now the chief, enjoying his sense of power, usually imposed his will upon the people; his individuality, at least, had more or less free play. And thus, through the changing decrees of successive rulers, all sorts of varying standards became realized, and the rigidity of early custom was steadily loosened.

(3) In the hunting stage of primitive life, and even in the pastoral stage, there was little private property, and hence little opportunity for the

development of the acquisitive instinct. But with the transition to an agricultural life, and still more with the growth of commerce and the arts, private accumulation became possible. Individual initiative began to pay; the smarter and more ingenious could outstrip their fellows by breaking through the crust of custom, while those who were hidebound by a conventional conscience were at a disadvantage. To a large extent this lawlessness or innovation in conduct came into conflict with the individual's conscience. But the question "Why not?" would at once arise; if possible, a man would justify his act to himself. And to some degree those new ways of acting would swing conscience over to their side.

(4) In earliest times each tribe lived, very, much to itself and developed its own morals, under the stress of similar forces, but without much influence from the experience of other groups. It was thus exceedingly difficult for it to conceive of any other ways of doing things; the ancestral customs were accepted as inevitable, like the sun and the rain. Inter-tribal conflicts first gave, perhaps, a vantage point for mutual criticism. A clan that by some custom had an obvious advantage over its neighbors would naturally be imitated as soon as men became quick-witted enough to understand its superiority. The taking of prisoners, the exchange of hostages or envoys, friendly missions and journeys, would give insight into one another's life. With the development of commerce, this mutual criticism of morals would be greatly accelerated. So the authority of local conventions and standards would be discredited, custom would become more fluid, and individual judgment find freer play. Especially would the more observant, the more traveled, the more reflective, tend to vary from the ideals of their neighbors.

(5) In various other ways, apart from the mutual influence of divergent group-customs, the progress of civilization tends to produce variations in ideals. The increase of knowledge, the development of science and philosophy, bring floods of new ideas to burst the old dams; deepening insight reveals the irrationality of old ideas to the leaders of thought. The progress of the arts gives new interests and valuations. The spiritual seers and prophets see visions of a better order and proclaim new gospels. The development of classes and castes allows to the aristocracy more leisure to think and criticize; the institution of slavery, in particular, produced a class of slave-owners with ample time to dissect their inherited conceptions.

(6) Finally, where, under favoring conditions, the danger of war in which man has for the most part lived became less acute, custom generally grew laxer. It is the imperious necessity of selfpreservation that has been the greatest conservative force; warlike states have demanded strict allegiance and looked with suspicion upon deviations from the group ideals. But peoples that, whether from a fortunate geographical situation or because of their marked superiority in numbers and power over their neighbors have

escaped this need of perpetual self-defense could afford to relax their vigilance for conformity. And the very notable increase in individual variations in conduct and ideal during the past century has been largely owing to the era of comparative peace. We seem to be reaching the age when the advantage is to lie not with the nation that has the most rigid customs, but with the nation that shows the most individual initiative and progress.

Conservatism vs. radicalism

We have become forever emancipated from the tyranny of custom morality under which the majority of men have lived. Legislation is, to be sure, continually on the increase, shutting men out from the ever-new ways they discover to prey upon their fellows. But nevertheless, the freedom with which men may now live their own lives according to their own ideas is almost a new phenomenon upon the earth. When we compare the free range that our individuality has with the tyranny of public opinion even so recently as the lifetime of our Puritan grandparents, when we see the new experiments in personal life and social legislation which are being tried on every hand, when we read a few of the thousands of books and magazines and newspapers that are pouring a continual flood of new ideas into the world, we must realize the immense change from the stereotyped customs of nearly all past epochs. In each of our forty eight States different codes are showing their relative advantages; here woman's suffrage is on trial, there the initiative and referendum, there the recall. Almost every sort of possible marriage law, it would seem, is being tried somewhere. It is a time of moral confusion, of the unsettling of old conceptions and a groping, stumbling progress toward the new.

In such a situation it is no wonder that we have two types of thought, two sets of forces, at work. On the one hand we have the conservatives, the "stand-patters," the maintainers of the existing order; on the other hand are the progressives, the radicals, the reformers of the existing order. For the former the moral standards of their particular age and country tend to have an absolute and unconditional worth, which must not be criticized or questioned. The necessity of allegiance to morality has been so deeply stamped upon their minds that it has become a loyalty to the particular brand of morality they have grown up in, however flagrantly inadequate or tyrannous it may be. For the latter a commendable impatience with the imperfect is apt to foster a blindness to the value that almost always lies in ancient customs and a lack of regard for the need of stability and common agreement on some plane. These iconoclasts, vociferous in condemnation, are often most empty handed, giving us nothing wiser or more advantageous wherewith to replace the conventions they discard. So it is difficult to say whether humanity is more in danger from the red-handed radicalism which destroys the precious fruit of long experience, or from the obstinate obstructionists who by the dead weight of their apathy or the positive pull-back of their antagonism delay the remedying of existing evils. The ideal lies in keeping morality plastic while giving its approved forms our hearty allegiance. Widely different ideals are theoretically conceivable; but we live in a specific time and place and must defer to the code of our fellows; it is along these lines, and by gradual steps, that progress must be made. We must be on the alert for new suggestions, but slow to tear down till we can build better. The greatest of prophets, keenly as he saw the flaws in existing standards, proclaimed that he came not to destroy but to fulfill. It is evident enough to the impartial observer that our present chaos and mutual antagonism of conflicting view-points is not ideal; we need to work out of this disorder into some sane and stable order; when we can find the best way of life we must discard these manifold variations, most of which are foolish and ill-advised. The undesirability of this contemporary disagreement, which in some matters amounts to almost a complete moral anarchy, is enough to explain the pull back of the conservatives. And it is precisely the purpose of such a volume as this to help in the crystallizing of definite and universally accepted moral principles for personal and social life. But, on the other hand, this temporary chaos is more pregnant with promise than the older blind acquiescence in full light of criticism and experiment to bear upon the laws and customs of the past.

"New occasions teach new duties, Time makes ancient good uncouth."

We should reverence the great seers and lawmakers of the past; but their true disciples are not those who slavishly accept their dicta, they are rather those who think for themselves, as they did, and contribute, as they did, toward the slow progress of man.

What are the dangers of conventional morality?

The reasons why we cannot be content with our fathers' conservatism in morals, and our fathers' custom-bound conscience, may be summarized as follows:

(1) Conventional morality is almost necessarily too general; it is not elastic enough to fit the infinite variations in specific cases, not detailed enough to fit all needs. It therefore often causes needless and cruel repression; the most sensitive and aspiring spirits have often revolted from the morality of their times because of its harshness. It is well for the marriage-tie to be binding; divorce has generally been deemed unchristian. But if this judgment is rigidly enforced, special cases arise, very piteous, very pathetic, crying out for a more discriminating rule. Our forebears, with their grave realization of the dangers of frivolousness, forbade by law and a stern public opinion many innocent and wholesome diversions. Such injustices

are inevitable where custom has unchecked sway. The general aim and result may be very salutary, but the application is too sweeping, and brings suffering to many unfortunate individuals, or to the community as a whole, by its indiscrimination.

(2) But even in its general result custom may be harmful. Morals have developed blindly, as we have seen, through all sorts of irrational influences, swayed this way by class interest, by rulers or priests, veered that way by superstition, passion, and stupidity. Morality has not understood itself; and the natural forces which have developed it into its enormous usefulness have not always weeded out the baneful elements. The persecution of heretics was sheer mistake, but it was acceded to by practically the entire Church in the Middle Ages, and practiced with utter conscientiousness. The hostility of the Puritans to music and art was pure folly, though it seemed to them their grim duty.

(3) New situations are continually arising, new sins appearing. Conventional morality, while sometimes over-severe against old and well-recognized sins, lags far behind in its branding of the newer forms. The evils arising from the modern congestion of population, the unscrupulousness of modern business, the selfishness of politicians, the servility of newspapers to the "interests" and to advertisers, for example, find too little reprobation in our established moral codes. "Business is business" has been said by respectable church-members. A successful American boss, when asked if he was not in politics for his pocketbook, said, "Of course! Aren't you?" with no sense of shame. Probably he was very "moral" along the old lines, an excellent father, a kind husband, an agreeable neighbor; but his conventional code, shared by most of his contemporaries, did not include the reprobation of the practice of politics for private gain. In the upper classes are many people who are "good" by the old standards, but who are unhelpful and trivial-minded, mere parasites devoted to sport or society, with never a qualm of conscience for their selfishness. The old standards need the constant infusion of new blood; our consciences need to be adjusted to our new relations and deeper insight. [Footnote: Cf. Rosa, Sin and Society, p. 14: "One might suppose that an exasperated public would sternly castigate these modern sins. But the fact is, the very qualities that lull the conscience of the sinner blind the eyes of the onlookers. People are sentimental; and bastinado wrongdoing not according to its harmfulness, but according to the infamy that has come to attach to it. Undiscerning, they chastise with scorpions the old authentic sins, but spare the new. They do not see that blackmail is piracy, that embezzlement is theft, that speculation is gambling that deleterious adulteration is murder. The cloven hoof hides in patent leather; and today, as in Hosea's time, the people 'are destroyed for lack of knowledge.'"]

(4) Custom-morality tends to literalism, a mere formal observance of law or custom without the true spirit of service, without any inward sweetness or power. Christ's condemnation of the Pharisees will occur to every one; the parable of the Pharisee and publican, and that of the widow's mite, among others, are classic illustrations of a cut-and dried formalism in morality. Such a legalism Paul found could not save him. And forever the prophets and spiritual leaders of men have had to burst the bonds of tradition to awaken a real love of and devotion to the good. The letter killeth, and a punctilious observance of rules may choke out the aspirations of the soul.

(5) Finally, conflicts between customs inevitably arise. Which shall a man obey? The moral perplexity thus caused gives a great deal of its poignancy to the tragedy of life. When one accepted ideal pulls us one way, and another standard, to which we have given allegiance, calls us the other, when we cry out with Desdemona, "I do perceive here a divided duty," the only solution lies in the development of insight and a recognition of the transition-nature of much of our accepted code. If for no other reason, to avoid these conflicts of ideals we must comprehend the ultimate aims of morality and take existing standards with a sort of tentative allegiance. It should be clear, then, that the individualizing of conscience, which has been going on observably in recent times, is, in spite of its dangers, a necessary and desirable process. Dewey and Tufts, ETHICS, chaps, V. IX. W. Bagehot, PHYSICS AND POLITICS, chaps. II, VI. F. Paulsen, SYSTEM OF ETHICS, part II, chap. V, sec. 6. S. E. Mezes, ETHICS, chap, VII, pp. 164-83. J. H. Coffin, THE SOCIALIZED CONSCIENCE, pp. 12-23.

CHAPTER VI
CAN WE BASE MORALITY UPON CONSCIENCE?

What is the meaning of "moral intuitionism"?

With the growth of individualism in morals, the relaxing of the constraint of publicly accepted standards, there is, of course, a dangerous drift toward self-indulgence and moral nihilism. It becomes all the more necessary that conscience be strong and sensitive, that inner restraints take the place of outer. In the lack of a mature moral insight, which is one of the latest of mental developments, and indeed, where it exists, to reinforce its pale affirmations with greater impulsive power, a stern sense of duty is a veritable rock of salvation. Many a people have perished, many a brilliant hope of civilization been lost, because of its lack. So we cannot wonder when moralists put it forward as the foundation- stone of all morality and seek to build their systems upon it. To a man who has been bred to obey the inner voice, it seems the very source and basis of the right; it is so inescapable, so authoritative, that it cannot be deemed derived, or evolved by a mechanical process of selection. It figures as something ultimate and unanalyzable, if not frankly supernatural; that it is a mere instrument in the attainment of an ulterior end, to be used or rejected according to its observed usefulness is an abhorrent thought.

There has thus arisen a school of philosophers who base their justification of morality entirely upon the deliverances of conscience. Their theories vary in detail and have received sundry names; we will group them here for convenience under the general caption "moral intuitionism." As a rule they steer clear of the historic point of view; they refuse to believe that conscience has a natural history. Nor are they usually keen at psychological analysis; the numberless variations in form which conscience assumes in different individuals are, for their purposes, better ignored. Instead of analyzing the moral sense into its components and describing the mental stuff of which it is composed, instead of tracing its genesis and studying the forces that have produced it, they wax eloquent over its importance and universality. As preachers they are admirable. But the foundation they provide for morality is slippery. It amounts to saying, "We ought to do right because we know we ought!" When we ask how we can be sure, in view of the general fallibility of human conviction, that we are not mistaken in our assurance, and following a false light, they can but reiterate in altered phraseology that we know because we know.

To these intuitionists, and to the popular mind very often, the approval or disapproval of conscience is immediate, intuitive, and unerring. Its authority is absolute and not to be questioned. We have this faculty within us that tells us as surely what is right and what wrong as our color-sense tells us what is red and what green. Some people may, to be sure, be color-blind, or have defective consciences; but the great mass of unsophisticated people possess this innate guide and commandment, a quite sufficient warrant for all our distinctions of good and evil. Honest men do not really differ in their moral judgments. They may misunderstand one another's concepts and engage in verbal disputes; but at bottom their moral sense approves and disapproves the same acts. Our moral differences come mainly from the deluding effects of passion and the sophisticated ingenuities of the intellect. We should "return to nature," go by ourselves alone, and listen to the inner voice. If we sincerely listen and obey we shall always do right. [Footnote: "But truth and right, founded in the eternal and, is what every man can judge of, when laid before him. 'T is necessarily one and the same to every man's understanding, just as light is the same, to every man's eyes." (S. Clarke, Discourse upon Natural Religion, 1706.)]

We cannot but recognize a certain amount of practical truth in this picture. But it is over-simplified, and it is fundamentally unsatisfactory to the intellect. We shall now pass in review its most obvious inadequacies.

Do the deliverances of different people's consciences agree?

Nothing is more notorious to an unbiased observer than the conscientious differences between men. Even among members of a single community, with closely similar inheritance and environment, we find marked divergence in moral judgment. And when we compare widely different times and places we are apt to wonder if there is any common ground. It is only a very smug provincialism that can attribute the alien standards of other races and nations to a disregard of the light. Mohammedans and Buddhists have believed as firmly in, and fought as passionately for, their moral convictions as Christians have for theirs. When we survey the vast amount of material amassed by anthropologists, we find that, as has been often said, there is hardly a vice that has not somewhere been deemed a virtue, and hardly a virtue but has been branded as a vice. History is full of the pathos of havoc wrought by conscientious men, of foolish and ruinous acts which they have braced themselves to do for conscience' sake. One has but to think of the earnest and prayerful inquisitors and persecutors in the mediaeval Church, of the Puritans destroying the stained-glass windows and paintings of the Madonna, of the caliph who destroyed the great Alexandrian library, bereaving the world at one blow of that priceless culture-inheritance. Written biography, fiction which truly represents life, and individual memory are full of conscience have sundered those who truly loved and wrought irremediable pain and loss. Lately the newspapers told us of the heroic suicide of General Nogi and his wife, who felt it their duty not to survive their emperor. To a Catholic Christian this imperious dictate of the Japanese conscience would be a deadly sin. And so it goes. There is no need to multiply instances of what can be observed on every hand. Conscience reflects the traditions and influences amid which a man grows up.

But if the deliverances of different men's consciences conflict, how shall we know which to trust? If any particular command of the inner voice may be morally wrong, how can we trust it at all? There are obviously morbid and perverted consciences; but if conscience itself is the ultimate authority, and is not to be justified and criticized by some deeper test, what right have we to call any of its manifestations morbid or perverted? Is it not a species of egotism to hold one's own moral discernment as superior to another's; and if so, do we not need some criterion by which to judge between them? Surely the diversity of its judgments makes conscience an impossible foundation for morality; we should have as many codes as consciences and fall into a hopeless confusion. If conscience everywhere agreed in its dictates, could we base morality upon it? Even, however, if conscience led us all in the same direction, would that prove its authority? Perhaps we should all be following a will o' the wisp, and foolishly sacrificing our desires to an idol of the tribe, a universal superstition. Must it not show its credentials before it can legitimately command our allegiance? It is but one specific type of impulse among many; why should it be given the reins, the control over all? Do we say, because conscience makes for our best welfare? The answer would, in general, be true; but we should then be putting as our test and ultimate authority the attainment of our welfare, which would be to abandon the point of view we are discussing. Conscience claims authority. But that might conceivably be mere impudence and tyranny. Moreover, there are those who feel no call to follow conscience; how could we prove to them that they ought? Is it not the height of irrationality to bow down before an unexplained and mysterious impulse and allow it to sway our conduct without knowing why? If the "ought" is really shot out of the blue at us, if there is no justification, no imperious demand for morality but the existence of this inner push, why might we not raise our heads, refuse to be dominated by it, and live the life of free men, following the happy breezes of our desires? That is precisely what many have done, men who have reached maturity enough of mind to see the emptiness of following an ingrained impulse simply because it exists, but not a full enough maturity to see beyond to the real justification and significance of conscience.

A further realization of the inadequacy of the intuitive theory comes when we observe that conscience is by no means always clear in its dictates. It often leaves us in the lurch. Developed in us as it has been by circumstance and suggestion, it helps us usually only in certain recognized types of situation. When new cases arise, it is hopelessly at sea. As a practical working principle, conscientiousness is not only apt to be a perverted and provincial guide, it is insufficient for the solving of fresh and difficult problems. The science casnistry has been developed in great detail to supply this lack, to apply the well-recognized deliverances of a certain accepted type of conscience to the various possibilities of situation. These systems, however, reflect the idiosyncrasies of their makers, and have never won wide approbation. Morality must remain largely experimental, individual. Conscience will play a very useful role in spurring us to our recognized duty in the commoner situations, but for all the more delicate decisions we need a more ultimate touchstone. We must grasp the underlying principles of right conduct, and weigh the relative goods attainable by each possible act. A well-balanced and normal conscience will save us the recurrent reasoning out of typical perplexities, but it must be supplemented by an insight into the ends to be aimed for and kept rather strictly in its place.

What is the plausibility of moral intuitionism?

It is never wholly satisfactory merely to refute a theory; we must see its plausibility and understand its appeal if we are to be sure of doing it justice. In the case of the intuition-theory it is easy to discern the reasons that have kept it alive? though it has never been at all widespread among thinking men? in spite of the obvious objections that can be raised to it.

(1) Perhaps the original source of the doctrine was a certain sort of religious faith; it follows easily as a corollary to the belief in God. If God commands us to do right, it is felt, He must have given us some way to know what is right. The inner voice of conscience may be just such a God-given guide; therefore it is such a guide; therefore it is infallible. A natural piece of a priori reasoning, on a par with the Christian Scientist's syllogism: God is good; a good God would not permit evil to exist; therefore there is no evil. Unfortunately a priori reasoning has to yield to actual experience. Since we see that conscience is not infallible and evil does exist, there must be some fallacy in the arguments.

(2) Another source of the doctrine's strength lies in its simplicity. It is a great mental relief to drop the tangle of confusing considerations, to stop trying to reason out one's course of action, and follow a supposedly reliable guide. The intuition-theory goes naturally with a moral conservatism which dreads the chaos and uncertainty that follow upon the doubt of established moral habits. It is so much more comfortable to feel that one has already

the one divine and ultimate code, that one has always done right because one has steadily obeyed the inner light! It is reassuring to divide the world into the sheep and the goats? if one can believe one's self a sheep. But what O dismay! what if one were after all a goat! A great deal of mental anguish has been caused by the pseudo-simplicity of this dichotomy. There is no such clean-cut and clearly visible line between right and wrong; there is instead a bewildering maze of goods. Hardly any choice but involves a sacrifice, hardly any ideal but has its disadvantages. One learns with experience to be wary of these simple theories, these closet theories which collapse when they are brought out into the light of day.

(3) We must, however, be just. The fact of the reliability of conscience, and the wisdom of following its guidance, holds over a wide range of human experience and the experience which is most apparent upon the surface. For all ordinary cases we of Christendom agree without hesitation that murder is wrong, and lying, and stealing. It seems a waste of time to try to justify our instinctive verdict, and the attempt would only be bewildering to most men. It is only when brought face to face with some alien code that we see the need of digging below intuition. A missionary to the South Seas may be confronted with men to whom the killing of other tribesmen and the accumulation of skulls is a glorious and honorable feat, or to whom skillful lying is an enviable and proud accomplishment. But most of us live among neighbors whose conscience is comfortably like our own, and only occasionally become seriously perplexed. In the great mass of everyday occasions we do know our duty intuitively, and we do agree with one another. We recognize a duty at sight without realizing its teleology. It is not, indeed, an innate faculty; it was acquired during our formative years; it is not infallible. But the forces which have gone to the making of it are similar in all our lives, and the products are more alike than unlike.

(4) Finally, it is true that to obey conscience is, in a sense, to do right, to be moral, no matter how distorted conscience may be. Conscientiousness is in itself a virtue. To this point we shall later return. We need only say here that conscientiousness is not enough. Life is not so simple a matter as that. We need judgment, sanity, insight, as well as a strong sense of duty. We need to correct and train conscience, to adjust it to our real needs, to recognize that it is a means, not an end.

Our discussion, though rapid, should show that we cannot start with the "ought" of our conscience, or moral sense, and erect our moral theory upon that. Conscience itself needs to be explained. Its commands need to be justified by reference to some more ultimate criterion. It needs to be pruned of its fanaticism, developed where it is weak, and kept in line with our growing insight into what is best in conduct. Ruskin once summed the matter up by saying, "Obey thy conscience! But first be sure it is not the conscience of an ass!" Conscience may be a very dangerous guide. And even where it is normal and useful it must not be invested with any absolute and irrational authority.

Historical study, then, reveals the growth of personal and social morality through the action of forces, which tend to drive men into conduct that makes for their welfare more surely than did their primitive animal impulses. Conscience arises through these same forces. Though subject to perversion and infinitely variant in detail, community-morals and individual conscience have been the chief means of making man's life safe and wisely directed. The criterion that emerges from such a study is not, however, the bald existence of codes of morals, or of conscience, but the human welfare which those codes and that conscience exist to serve. To an exposition of the ways in which morality serves and should increasingly serve human welfare, we now turn.

Classic intuitional theories will be found developed in: Price, Review of the Chief Questions and Difficulties of Morals (1757), Shaftesbury, An Inquiry Concerning Virtue or Merit (1699). F. Hutcheson, An Inquiry Concerning Moral Good and Evil (1725). Joseph Butler, Fifteen Sermons upon Human Nature, II, III (1726). J. Martineau, Types of Ethical Theory (1885).

Criticisms of the intuitional theories will be found in: S. E. Mezes, Ethics, chap. III; Dewey and Tufts, Ethics, chap. XVI, sec. 3; F. Paulsen, System of Ethics, part II, chap. V, sec. 4; H. Spencer, Data of Ethics, chap. II, sec. 14; chap. IV, sec. 20; Muirhead, Elements of Ethics, secs. 32-35. H. Rashdall, The Theory of Good and Evil, book I, chap. IV. W. Fite, Introductory Study of Ethics,

PART II
THE THEORY OF MORALITY

CHAPTER VII
THE BASIS OF RIGHT AND WRONG

HISTORICAL knowledge without critical insight leads to moral nihilism, the conviction of the pre-Socratic Sophists that, since every time and people has its own standards, there is no real objective right and wrong. Morality is seen to be not a fixed code sent readymade from heaven, but a set of habits and intuitions that have had a natural origin and development. Our particular moral code is perceived to be but one out of many, our type of conscience psychologically on the same level with the strange, and to us perverted, sense of duty of alien races. How can we judge impartially between our standards and those of the Fiji Islanders? What warrant have we for saying that our code is a better one than theirs? Or how do we know that the whole thing is not superstition?

What is the nature of that intrinsic goodness upon which ultimately all valuations rest?

As a matter of fact, underneath the manifold disagreements as to good and bad, there is a deep stratum of absolute certainty. It is only in the more complex and delicate matters that doubt arises; all men share in those elementary perceptions of good and bad that make up the bulk of human valuation. To men everywhere it is an evil to be in severe physical pain or to be maimed in body, to be shut away from air, from food, from other people. It is a good to taste an appetizing dish, to exercise when well and rested, to hear harmonious music, to feel the sweet emotion of love. The fact that men agree upon judgments does not prove them true; but these are not judgments, they are perceptions. [Footnote: Or affections. Let no one quarrel about the psychological terms used; the only important matter is to note the fact, however it be phrased, that "good" and "bad" in their basic usage are DESCRIPTIVE terms. A toothache is bad just as indisputably as the sky is blue. The word "bad" has a definite meaning, just as the word "blue" has; and the toothache is, among other things, precisely what we mean by "bad," just as the look of the cloudless sky by daylight is what we mean by "blue."] To call love good is not to give an opinion, it is to describe a fact. It is a matter of direct first-hand feeling, whose reality consists in its being felt. To say that these experiences are good or bad is equivalent to saying that they FEEL good or bad; there can be no dispute about it. This is the bottom fact of ethics. Different experiences have different intrinsic worth as they pass. There is a chiaroscuro of consciousness, a light and shade of immediate goodness and badness over all our variegated moments. The good moments are their own excuse for being, a part of the brightness and worth of life. They need nothing ulterior to justify them. The bad moments feel bad, and that is the end of it; they are bad-feeling moments, and no sophistication can deny it. Conscious life looked at from this point of view, and abstracted from all its other aspects, is a flux of plus and minus values. Certain of its moments have a greater felt worth than others; some experiences are intrinsically undesirable, the shadows of life; others, intrinsically sweet, a part of its sunshine. In the last analysis, all differences in value, including all moral distinctions, rest upon this disparity in the immediate worth of conscious states. [Footnote: Cf. G. Santayana, The Sense of Beauty, p. 104: "All worth leads us back to actual feeling somewhere, or else evaporates into nothing-into a word and a superstition." I cannot but feel that contemporary definitions of value that omit reference to hedonic differences e.g. that of Professor Brown (Journal of Philosophy, Psychology, and Scientific Methods, vol. II, p. 32): "Value is degree of adequacy of a potentiality to the realization of the effect by virtue of which it is a potentiality"-miss the real meaning of "value." We do, indeed, speak occasionally of x as having value as a means to y, when y is not good or a means to a good. But that seems to me a misuse of the word.] We may say absolutely that if it were not for this fundamental difference in feeling there would be no such thing as morality. There might conceivably be a world in which consciousness should exist without any agreeable or disagreeable qualities; in such a world nothing would matter; all acts would be equally indifferent. Or there might be a world in which all experiences were equally pleasurable or painful; in such a case all acts would be equally good or equally sad; there would be no ground for choice. One might in any of these hypothetical worlds be driven by mechanical impulse or fitful whim to do this or that, but there would be no rational basis for preference. Such, however, is not the case. Comparative valuation is possible; all secondary goods and evils arise, all morality, all art and religion and science have their wellspring in this brute fact, this primordial parting of the ways between the more and the less desirable phases of possible conscious life. Morality of an elementary type would exist on this level even without the further complications of actual life. At least a very important art would arise; whether or not we should call it morality is a mere matter of definition. For a choice between alternatives immediately felt goods would arise, and the problem of how to get the better kinds of experience and avoid the worse would demand solution. Every bit of plus value added to experience would make the world so much the brighter, as would every bit of pain avoided. There are, to be sure, the mystical optimisms and pessimisms to be reckoned with, the sweeping assertions of certain schools and individuals that everything is equally good or equally bad. Such undiscriminating formulas are either the mere objectification of a mood, of some unusual period of ecstasy or sorrow, a blind outcry of thanksgiving or of bitterness, or they are the clumsy expression of some practical truth, as, the wisdom of acquiescence, and the futility of preoccupation with evil. But taken seriously and literally such statements are simply untrue to the facts and blur our fundamental perceptions. If actually accredited, either would lead to quiescence; if everything were equally good or evil all striving would be meaningless, one might as well jump from a housetop or walk into the fire. But as a matter of fact such mystical assertions are indulged in only in the inactive moments of life, and mean no more than a lyric poem or a burst of music. Every one in his practical moments acknowledges tacitly, at least, the difference between the intrinsic goodness and badness of experiences. A life of even delight or even wretchedness, or of colorless indifference, is not inconceivable, but it is not the lot of any actual human beings.

The larger quarrel between optimists and pessimists need not, for our purposes, be settled. Life may be a very good thing, on the whole, or a very bad thing. The only point we need to note is that it is at any rate a varying thing. Some experiences are more worth having than others. Moral theory needs no further admission to find its foothold. Nor do we need to discuss the problem of evil. It may be that all pain has its ultimate uses that nothing is "really" bad, if we take that to mean that all evil has a necessary existence as a means to a good otherwise unattainable and worth the cost. But however useful as a means evil may be, it is nonetheless evil and regrettable. It is not good qua pain. If the same amount of good could be obtained without the preliminary evil, it were better to skip it. In short, the existence of different values in immediate experience is indisputable; we may call them for convenience intrinsic goodness and badness.

What is extrinsic goodness?

But there is a radically different sense of the words "good" and "bad"; namely, that in which we say that a thing is good FOR this or that. This is the kind of goodness the THINGS about us have; they are good for the production of intrinsic goodness (as we are using that phrase), which is always (so far as we know) something produced in living organisms. [Footnote: We also occasionally speak of things as being "good for" something else when that something else is not a good or a means to a good (see preceding footnote); as, "sunshine is good for weeds." But as applied to evils, the phrase "good for" more often means "good to abolish"; as, "hellebore is good for weeds." These usages illustrate the ambiguity of all our common ethical terms. To consider them here would be, however, needlessly confusing. The two senses of the term "good" mentioned in the text are the only senses we need to bear in mind for the purposes of ethics.] To put the same truth in other terms, things are good or bad only with respect to their effect upon our conscious experience. [Footnote: I am fully aware of the widespread current distaste for the word "consciousness," with

- 49 -

its idealistic associations. The term seems to me too useful to discard; but I wish to point out that, as I use it, it involves no metaphysical viewpoint, but is equally consonant with idealism or realism of any sort.] Primitive man, indeed, imagines inanimate things as having intrinsic goodness or badness, i.e., as feeling happy or unhappy, benevolent or malignant. We still speak of a serene sky, an angry storm cloud, a caressing breeze, and in a hundred ways read our affective life into material objects. But we now recognize all these ascriptions as cases of the pathetic fallacy, poetically significant but literally untrue. Animism, which looms so large in primitive religion, consists in thus objectifying into things the emotions they arouse in us. In reality all of these affective qualities exist in us, not in the outer objects; so far as our epithets have an objective truth they describe not the content of the objects, but their function in our lives. When we speak of delicious food, beautiful pictures, ugly colors, we mean strictly that these objects are such as to arouse in us certain peculiar pleasant or unpleasant feelings. So that apart from the existence of consciousness there would be no goodness or badness at all. [Footnote: The neo-realists would prefer to say, perhaps, "apart from the existence of organisms,"] and this may be an exacter phrase; we from previous page [Footnote: pleasures and pains that remain out of connection with that interrelated stream of experience to which we usually limit the term "consciousness." On the other hand, MAY it not be that God, and angels, or other disembodied beings, have consciousness, and intrinsic goodness, without having organisms? Of course, for all we know, the world about us may be chock full of pleasures and pains. But for practical purposes, and so far as our morality is concerned, either the statement in the text or the suggested equivalent is true. The point is, that the foundation of morality is in US—whether you call US in the last analysis consciousnesses or organisms]

It is the existence of felt goodness, intrinsic goodness, and its opposite, that allows us to attribute to objects another kind of goodness or badness, according as they are calculated to produce in us the former kind. This kind of goodness and badness we may call extrinsic. It is only by thus attributing a sort of goodness and badness to senseless objects that we can aim for and avoid the good and bad phases of conscious life. In themselves these conscious moments are largely unnamable and inexpressible. There are, as it is, dumb objectless ecstasies that are of transcendent sweetness; but we do not usually know how to reproduce them, and for the most part we have to overlook these goods in our ideals and aim only for those that we can associate with recognized outer stimuli. For practical purposes we think rather in terms of outer objects than of our states of experience; nature has had need to make men but very slightly introspective. And so it is that this derived use of our eulogistic and disparaging terms plays a larger part than its primary application. But the essential point to note is that "goodness" and "badness" in the first instance refer to the fundamental cleavage between the affective qualities of experience, and only secondarily and by metonymy apply to objects in the physical world which affect our conscious states. The next point to note is that our conscious experiences and activities themselves have not only their intrinsic value, as they pass, but an extrinsic value, as means toward future intrinsic values. Each phase of experience has its own worth, while it lasts, and also has its results in determining future phases with their varying degrees of worth. Our reveries, our debauches, our sacrifices are good or bad in their effects as well as in themselves. Thus all experience has a double rating; acts are not only pleasant, agreeable, intrinsically desirable, but also wise, prudent, useful, virtuous, i.e., extrinsically desirable. These extrinsic values usually bulk much larger in the end than the first transitory intrinsic value; but our natural tendency is to forget them and guide our action by immediate values. Hence the need of a continual disparagement of the latter, and the many means men have adopted of emphasizing the importance of the former. Yet, after all, our concern for the extrinsic value of acts has to do only with means to ends; and unless acts tend to produce intrinsic goodness somewhere they are not extrinsically good. There is no sense in sacrificing an immediate good unless the alternative act will tend in its ultimate effects to produce a greater good, or unless the act sacrificed would have brought, after its present intrinsic good, some greater intrinsic evil. The sacrifice of a good for no greater good is asceticism or fanaticism. From this there is no ultimate salvation but by referring all acts to the final touchstone—asking which will produce in the end the greatest amount of intrinsic good and the least intrinsic evil. What sort of conduct, then, is good? And how shall we define virtue? We are brought thus to the conception of an art which shall not only teach us which of two immediate, intrinsic, goods is the better, but shall consider all the near and remote consequences of acts, and direct us to that conduct which will produce most good in the end. [Footnote: The impossibility of finding any other ultimate basis for our conception of moral "good" or "bad" is well expressed by Socrates in Plato's Protagoras (p. 354): "Then you think that pain is an evil and pleasure is a good, and even pleasure you deem an evil, when it robs you of greater pleasure than it gives, or causes pain greater than the pleasure. If, however, you call pleasure an evil in regard to some other end or standard, you will be able to show us that standard. BUT YOU HAVE NONE TO SHOW... And have you not a similar way of speaking about pain? You call pain a good when it takes away greater pains than those which it has, or gives pleasures greater than the pains." He then goes on to explain the need of morality,-to guide us, in the face of the foreshortening effects of our particular situation, to what will make for the greatest happiness in the long run (p. 356): "Do not the same magnitudes appear larger to your sight when near, and smaller when at a distance? Now suppose happiness to consist in doing or choosing the greater, and in not doing or avoiding the less, what would be the saving principle of human life? Would not the ACT OF MEASURING be the saving principle?"] is best which will in the long run bring into being the greatest possible amount of intrinsic goodness and the least intrinsic evil. For goodness of conduct we commonly use the term "virtue"; and for intrinsic good the most widely accepted name-though one which is misleading to many is "happiness." So we may say, in sum, that virtue is that manner of life that tends to happiness. Objection is occasionally made that happiness is too vague a term, too elusive a concept, to be set forth as the ultimate aim of conduct. "Alas!" says Bradley, "the one question which no one can answer is, what is happiness?" But this is a palpable confusion of thought. If we mean by the question, "Wherein is happiness to be found, by doing what can we attain it?" then the answer is, indeed, uncertain in its completeness; it is precisely to answer it that we study ethics. Or if we mean, "What is the psychology of happiness?" the answer is as yet dubious; but it is irrelevant. Whatever its psychological conditions and the means to attain it, we know happiness when we have it. The puzzle is not to recognize it, but to get it. By happiness we mean the steady presence of what we have called intrinsic goodness and the absence of intrinsic badness; it is as indefinable as any ultimate element of experience, but as well known to us as blackness and whiteness or light and dark. Take, as a typical moral situation, a case in which a thirsty man drinks polluted water. In the diagram the arrow represents the direction of the flow of time, and each of the ribbons below represents the stream of consciousness of an individual concerned-the uppermost being that of the thirsty man himself, the others those of his wife, children, or friends. The plus sign early in the drinker's stream of experience stands for the plus value which drinking the water effects-the gratifying taste of the water and the allaying of the discomfort of thirst-real values, whose worth cannot be gainsaid. Following, in his own stream of experience, are a row of minus signs, indicating the undesirable penalties in his own life which follow-disease, pain, deprivation of other goods. No good accrues to others, unless the slight pleasure of seeing his thirst allayed. But evils follow in their experience: worry, sympathetic pain at his suffering, expense of doctor's bills, perhaps (which means deprivation of other possible goods), etc. It is clear at a glance that the positive good attained is not worth the lingering and widespread evils; and the act of drinking the polluted water, though to a very thirsty man a keen temptation, is immoral. Morality is thus an acting upon a right perspective of life. Personal morality considers the goods and evils in the one stream of consciousness, social morality the goods and evils in other conscious lives concerned. Between them they sum up the law and the prophets.

The best life for humanity is that which is, on the whole, felt best; not necessarily that which is judged best by this man or that, for our judgments are narrow and misrepresent actual values,-but that which has had from beginning to end the greatest total of happiness. No other ultimate criterion for conduct can ever justify itself, and most theoretical statements reduce to this. To be virtuous is to be a virtuoso in life. All sorts of objections have been raised to this simple, and apparently pagan, way of stating the case; they will be considered in due time. The reader is asked to refrain from parting company with the writer, if his prejudices are aroused, until the consonance of this sketchy account of the basis of morality with Christianity and all idealism can be demonstrated.

H. Spencer, Data of Ethics, chap. III. S. E. Mezes, Ethics, chap IX. Leslie Stephen, Science of Ethics, chaps. II, IX. F. Thilly, Introduction to Ethics, chaps. IV, V. F. Paulsen, book II, chap. I. J. S. Mill, Utilitarianism. B. P. Bowne, Principles of Ethics, chap. II. The classic accounts of a rational foundation of ethics are to be found by the discerning reader in Plato's Protagoras, Gorgias, and Republic (esp. books. I, II, IV), and Aristotle's Ethics (esp. books. I and II). For refinements in the definition of right and wrong, see G. E. Moore, Ethics, chaps. I-V; B. Russell, Philosophical Essays, I, secs. II, III. International Journal of Ethics, vol. 24, p. 293. Definitions of value without reference to pleasure or pain will be found in Journal of Philosophy, Psychology, and Scientific Methods, vol. II, pp. 29, 113, 141. An elaborate and careful discussion will be found in G. H. Palmer's Nature of Goodness.

CHAPTER VIII
THE MEANING OF DUTY

Why are there conflicts between duty and inclination?

IF virtue is simply conduct that makes most truly for happiness, why are not all but fools virtuous? The answer is, in a word, because what will bring about the greatest good in the long run, and to the most people, is not always what the individual desires at the moment. The two great temptations are the lure of the selfish and the lure of the immediate. To purchase one's own happiness at the expense of others, and to purchase present satisfaction by an act which will bring less good in the end-these are the cardinal sins, and under these two heads every specific sin can be put. The root of the trouble is that, in spite of the superposition of conscience upon their primitive impulses, human organisms have not yet motor-mechanisms fully adjusted to their individual or combined needs. Some instincts are over-strong, others under-developed, none is delicately enough attuned to the changing possibilities of the situation. Our desires tug toward all sorts of acts which would prove disastrous either to ourselves or others. Many of our faults we commit "without realizing it"; we follow our impulses blindly, unconscious of their treachery. Other sins we commit knowingly, because in spite of warning voices we cannot resist the momentary desire. Readjustment of our impulses is always painful; it is easier and pleasanter to yield than to control.

Duty is the name we give virtue when she is opposed to inclination. She is the representative at the helm of our conduct of all absent or undeveloped impulses. The saints have no need of the concept; virtue to them is easy and agreeable; they have learned the beauty of holiness and have no unruly longings. Sometimes this happy adjustment of desire to need has been won by severe struggle; the dangerous impulses have been trained to come to heel through many a painful sacrifice. In other cases an approximation to this ideal state is the result of early training; by skillful guidance the growing boy or girl has had his safe impulses fostered and his perilous desires atrophied with disuse. The proverb, "Bring up a child in the way he should go, and when he is old he will not depart there from," has much truth in it. But no parent and no man himself can ever breathe quite safe; we can never tell when some submerged animal instinct will rise up in us, stun all our laboriously acquired morality into inactivity, and bring on consequences that in any cool headed moment we should have known enough to avoid. Thus duty, although she is the truest friend and servant of happiness, figures as her foe. And some moralists, realizing vividly the frequent need of opposing inclination, have generalized the situation by saying that happiness cannot be our end. "Foolish Word-monger and Motive grinder," shouts Carlyle, "who in thy Logic-mill hast an earthly mechanism for the Godlike itself, and wouldst fain grind me out Virtuefrom the husks of Pleasure, I tell thee, Nay! Is the heroic inspiration we name Virtue but some Passion, some bubble of the blood, bubbling in the direction others PROFIT by? I know not; only this I know, If what thou namest Happiness be our true aim, then are we all astray. 'Happy,' my brother? First of all, what difference is it whether thou art happy or not! 'Happiness our being's end and aim,' all that very paltry speculation is at bottom, if we will count well, not yet two centuries old in the world" [Footnote: Sartor Resartus: "The Everlasting No" Past and Present: "Happy" Leaving aside this last statement, which is an irrelevant untruth, we probably feel an instinctive sympathy with Carlyle, and a sort of shame that we should have thought of happiness as the goal of conduct. Carlyle goes so far in his tirades as to call our happiness-morality a "pig philosophy," which makes the universe out to be a huge "swine's trough" from which mankind is trying to get the maximum "pigs" wash. Again he calls it a "Mechanical Profit-and-Loss theory" In such picturesque language he embodies a point of view which in milder terms has been expressed by many.] But to say that we must often oppose inclination in the name of duty is by no means to say that we must do what in the end will make against happiness. The trouble with inclination and passion is precisely that they are often ruiners of happiness. The very real and frequent opposition of desire and duty is no support of the view that duty is irrelevant to happiness, but quite consistent with the rational account of morality-that dates at least back to the ancient Greeks-which shows it to be the means to man's most lasting and widespread happiness.

Must we deny that duty is the servant of happiness?

We may go on to point out various flaws in the doctrine, of which Carlyle is one of the extreme representatives, that the account of morality as a means to happiness is immoral and leads to shocking results.

(1) The plausibility of the doctrine rests largely on its confusion with the very different truth that we should not make happiness our conscious aim. It is one of the surest fruits of experience that happiness is best won by forgetting it; he that loses his life shall truly find it. To think much of happiness slides inevitably over into thinking too much of present happiness, and more of one's own than others' happiness; it leads to what Spencer properly dubs "the pursuit of happiness without regard to the conditions by fulfillment of which happiness is to be achieved." Carlyle is practically on the right track in bidding us think rather of duty, of work, of accomplishment. But that is far from denying that these aims have their

ultimate justification in the happiness they forward. In order that remote ends may be attained, it is often necessary to cease thinking of them and concentrate the mind upon immediate means. To acquire unconsciousness of manner, the last thing to do is to aim directly for it; to acquire happiness, the worst procedure is to make it one's conscious quest. Yet in the former case the attainment of the ease of manner sought, and in the latter case the attainment of the happiest life for one's self and those whom one's action affects is the touchstone which at bottom determines the method to be adopted. The proper method, we contend, is-morality. It is the method that Carlyle recommends. So that in practice we agree with him, while parting with him in theory.

(2) Carlyle evidently has in mind usually the thought that it is one's own happiness only that is put up as the end by the moralists he opposes. This was pure misunderstanding, however, or perversity. Other men's happiness has intrinsic worth (or IS intrinsic worth, for the word and the phrase are synonymous) as truly as mine; and morality is concerned quite as much with guiding the individual toward the general good as toward his own ultimate welfare. To this point we must return, merely mentioning here the fact that no reputable moralist now preaches the selfish theory.

(3) A part of Carlyle's ammunition consists in the slurring connotations which have grown up about the word "pleasure," and even the word "happiness." Because of the practical need of opposing immediate in the interests of remoter good, the various words that designate intrinsic and immediate value have come to have a less worthy sound in our ears than those words which indicate control for the sake of more widespread or lasting interests-such as "prudence," "duty," and "virtue." Moreover, the word "pleasures" commonly connotes the minor goods of life in contrast with the great joys, such as the accomplishment of some worthy task or the service of those we love. Again, it commonly connotes things passively enjoyed, rather than the active joys of life, which are practically more important. So that to condemn "pleasure" as an end arouses our instinctive sympathy. A "pleasure" is any bit of immediate good, however involved with pain, however transitory, and dangerous in its effects. "Happiness" generally refers to a more permanent state of satisfaction, including comparative freedom from pain; a stable and assured state of intrinsic worth, good to reflection as well as to sense. Pleasures are easy enough to get, but this safe state of happiness, full of rich positive worth, and immune from pain both in action and in moments of retrospect, is far from easy. Hence it is better to use the word "happiness" for our goal than the word "pleasure." Carlyle, however, takes "happiness" in the lower sense and rejects it in favor of what he calls "blessedness." This gives him the advantage of seeming to have a new and superior theory. But when we ask

what "blessedness" is, it is apparent that it can be nothing but what we call "happiness" or the living of life in such a way as to lead to happiness.

(4) There is another important practical insight underlying the protests of Carlyle and those of his ilk, namely, that it pays to disregard the minor ills and discomforts of life and keep our thoughts fixed on the big things. These minor ills do not matter much as they pass; they are transient, and usually leave little pain for reflection. It is the fear of them, the complaining about them, the shrinking from them, the attending to them, that constitutes the greater part of their badness. Carlyle has the same practical common sense that the Christian Scientists show; but, as in their case, he lets his practical wisdom confuse his theoretical insight.

Sympathize, then, as we all must with these anti-happiness preachers, we may point out that their intuitions are quite compatible with a sane view of the ultimate meaning of morality. If morality does not exist for human welfare, what is it good for? And what else can welfare ultimately be but happiness? Other proposed ends we shall presently consider. But the happiness-account of morality leads to no dangerous laxity. If any eudemonistic moralists have lived loosely, it was because they did not realize what really makes for happiness or had not strength of will to cleave to it, not because they saw happiness as the criterion. An immature perception of this as the criterion without a full recognition of its bearings may have misled some; it is possible to see a general truth clearly and yet evaluate wrongly in concrete situations. But the converse of the truth that morality makes for happiness is the truth that the way to attain happiness is morality. No lesson could be more salutary. Correct concrete evaluations are more important than correct abstract generalizations, and Carlyle is nearly always on the right side in the former. But his influence would have been still more wholesome if he had added to his sound sermonizing a sane and clearly analyzed theory.

Does the end justify the means?

Our account of morality may be called the eudemonistic account, from the Greek eudemonia, happiness, or the teleological account, from telos, an end. It asserts, that is, that morality is to be judged by the end it subserves; that end is happiness. We have seen the sort of protest that arises with respect to the word "happiness." We may now note a danger that arises from the use of the concept "end"; it finds expression in the familiar proverb, "The end justifies the means." Conduct is to be judged by the end it subserves; therefore, if the end is good any means may be used to attain it. This has been the defense of much wrongdoing. The Jesuits who lied, slandered, cheated, and murdered, to promote the interests of the Church, the McNamara brothers, who dynamited buildings and bridges as a means toward the final end of attaining for laborers a just share of the fruits of their labor, the suffragettes who have been burning private houses, sticking up mail-boxes, and breaking windows, have justified their crimes by reference to the great ends they expected thereby to attain. What shall we say to this plea?

(1) The motto means: Conduct in itself undesirable may be justified IF the end attained is important enough to warrant it. In every case, then, the question must arise: Is the end to be attained worth the cost? To justify means that are intrinsically bad, it must be shown that the end attained is so good as to overbalance this evil. WAS the advancement of the Church worth the cost in human suffering, estrangement, and bitterness that the Jesuits exacted? IS the advancement of labor interests worth the destruction of property and life, the fostering of class-enmity and of moral anarchism that the criminal wing of the I. W. W. stands for? ARE votes for women worth the similar evils which British suffragettes are drifting into? Sometimes a cause is so important that almost any act is justified in its advancement. But such cases are rare, at least in modern life. Always there must be a balancing of good and evil. And the trouble with the attitude of mind which we have illustrated is that the end sought is usually not so all-important as to warrant the grave evils which its seekers cause. When the Titanic was sinking, the boat's officers shot several men who tried to jump into the lifeboats ahead of the women and children. It was probably the only way to stop a mad panic stricken rush, which would have endangered the lives of all as well as broken the chivalrous code which is worth so much sacrifice. The evil of shooting down unarmed and frightened men was great; but it was undoubtedly justified by the end attained. Whether any of the other instances mentioned are cases where the evil done would be similarly justified by the end, if thereby attained, we shall not here discuss. But the principle is evident. The end justifies evil means only if it is so supremely good as to overbalance that evil.

(2) It is pertinent, however, to add two considerations. First, we must feel sure that no less harmful means are available. And secondly, we must feel sure that these evil means are really adapted to attain the purpose. Is there no other way of securing votes for women than by the hysterical and criminal pranks our British sisters have been playing? And will those irritating acts actually forward their cause, or tend to bring about a revulsion of feeling? Did the crimes of the Jesuits make the Church triumphant? Not in the long run. Immediate gains may often be won by unpleasant methods, as in the case of the Titanic. But when the struggle is bound to be a long one, as in the case of woman's suffrage and industrial justice, methods which (not to beg the question) would ordinarily be criminal are seldom in the end advantageous. The McNamara case hurt the I. W. W. sorely.

Suffrage legislation has possibly been retarded in Britain. And in both cases there are probably more efficacious, as well as less harmful, ways of attaining the desired end.

(3) It is strictly true that THE end, human welfare, justifies any means necessary to attain it. Whatever pain must be caused to bring about the greatest possible human happiness is thereby exempt from reprobation. Whatever conduct is necessary for that supreme end BECOMES morality, or virtue; for that is precisely what morality IS. For example, it is undoubtedly necessary at times to murder, to steal, and to lie for the sake of human welfare; in such cases these acts are universally approved. Only, we give the acts in such cases new names, that the words "murder," etc, may retain their air of reprobation. We call murder of which we approve "capital punishment" or "justifiable homicide" or "patriotic courage." If taking a man's property without his consent is stealing, then the State steals; but, approving the act, we call it "eminent domain."

(4) The motto has its chief danger, perhaps, in the tendency it encourages to ignore remoter consequences for the sake of immediate gain. This point we will consider under the following topic.

What is the justification of justice and chivalry?

If the greatest total of human happiness is the supreme end of conduct, was not Caiaphas right in deeming it expedient that one man should die for the people, even though he were innocent of all sin? Were not the French army officers sane in preferring to make Dreyfus their scapegoat rather than bring dishonor and shame upon their army? For that matter, does not the aggregate of enjoyment of a score of cannibals outweigh the suffering of the one man whom they have sacrificed to their appetite, or the delirious excitement with which a brutal crowd witnesses a lynching overbalance the pain of their solitary victim? Yet our souls revolt against such things. We cry, ruat caelum, fiat justitia! Justice is prior to all expediency! Is this irrational, or can it be shown to be teleologically justifiable?

Justice is undoubtedly justifiable; and the only reason that we ever hesitate to acknowledge it in any concrete case is that we tend to overlook indirect and remote results and see only the immediate effect of action. The harm done by injustice consists not merely in the pain inflicted upon the victim. There is the sympathetic pain caused in all those who are at all tender hearted. There is the sense of insecurity caused in each by the realization that he too might some day be a victim; when justice is not enforced no man is safe. There is the stimulation given to human passions by one indulgence which will breed a whole crop of pain. There is the danger that if injustice is allowed in one case where a great good seems to warrant it, it will be practiced in other cases where no such necessity exists. Men are not to be trusted to judge clearly of relative advantages where their passions are concerned; they must bind themselves by an inflexible code. The cases cited are comparatively clear. No one would seriously contend that cannibalism or lynching, the execution of Christ, or the banishment of Dreyfus, made in the direction of the greatest happiness of mankind. But it has been seriously urged that the insane and the feeble and the morally worthless should be killed off, as they were in some sterner ancient states. Why should we guarantee life and liberty to such as are a useless drag upon the community, spend upon them millions which might be spent for bringing joy and recreation to the rest of us? Or again, if medical men need a living human victim to experiment upon, in order to conquer some devastating disease, why not pounce upon some good-for-nothing member of the community and force him to undergo the pain? The considerations enumerated in the preceding paragraph, however, bid us halt. Imagine the anxiety and the anguish that would be caused if some commission were free to determine who were insane or feeble or worthless enough to be put out of the way! Or free to select a human victim for vivisection whenever experts deemed it wise! The widespread horror and uneasiness of such a regime, the callousness to suffering it would engender, the private revenges and crimes that might insidiously creep in under the guise of public good, are alone enough to render vicious such a procedure.

It is true that one person's suffering is less of an evil than the suffering of many. The State, by universal consent, inflicts undeserved suffering upon individuals when the social welfare seems to require it; as when it takes away a man's beloved acre to built a railroad or highway, or when it compels vaccination, or when it drafts soldiers for the national defense and sends them to their death. When a man volunteers to risk his life or to endure pain for his fellows we rightly applaud his act. In such a case the ill effects above-mentioned do not follow, and the gain is clear; in addition, the stimulating value of the voluntary self-sacrifice is great. The American soldiers, who risked their lives to rid Cuba and the world of yellow fever, by offering themselves for inoculation with the disease, stand among the world's heroes.

It is also true that "rights" are not primitive and transcendent; their existence rests upon purely utilitarian grounds. The right to liberty and life is limited by the community's welfare. So is the right to property. But in estimating advantage we must beware of a superficial calculation. The concept of justice, and the enthusiasm for it, have been of enormous value to man's happiness. It is of extreme importance, from a eudaemonistic standpoint, to cherish that ideal. Even if in some individual case a greater general happiness would result from infringing upon it, we cannot afford to do so; we should find ourselves lapsing into less advantageous habits and incurring unforeseen penalties.

Chivalry is in like case with justice. It might have seemed better for the world that the able and distinguished men should have been saved from the Titanic-some of them were men of considerable importance in various lines of work-rather than less-needed women. But the effect of the noble example in strengthening the will to sacrifice self for others, and in maintaining our beautiful devotion to woman, was worth the cost. Fox was right when he said, "Example avails ten times more than precept." Even if the loss had been greater than it was, it would have been better to incur it than to allow an exception to the code of chivalry. Such codes are formed with infinite pains and are very easily shattered; a little laxity here, a tolerated exception there, and the selfishness and passions of men rise to the surface and undo the work of years. AT ALL COSTS WE MUST MAINTAIN THE CODE. In the end it pays. The greatest genius must run the risk of drowning in the endeavor to save the life of some unknown person who may be a worthless scamp. He may die and the scamp live, a great loss to the world. But only so can the code of honor be maintained which in the long run adds so much positive joy to man and saves him from so much pain.

In most instances, though not in some of those cited, the reward of justice and chivalry is sufficient for the individual himself. As Socrates said to Theodoras, [Footnote: Plato, Theoetetus, 176.] "The penalty of injustice cannot be escaped. They do not see, in their infatuation, that they are growing like the one and unlike the other, by reason of their evil deeds; and the penalty is, that they lead a life answering to the pattern which they resemble." "On the other hand,"-to supplement Plato with Emerson, [Footnote: Essays, First Series: "Spiritual Laws." Cf. George Eliot, in Romola: "The contaminating effect of deeds often lies less in the commission than the hero the avowal of a just and brave act, it will go unwitnessed and unloved. One knows it himself and is pledged by it to sweetness of peace and to nobleness of aim, which will prove in the end a better proclamation of it than the relating of the incident." And, we may add, a greater joy.]

But even in view of the cases where no apparent compensation comes to the individual, the ideals of justice and chivalry, like the more general concept of duty, are among the most valuable possessions of man's fashioning. Cross our inclinations as they often do, cost dearly as they sometimes will, the habit of unquestioning allegiance to them is one of the greatest of all gains as means to the attainment by mankind of a stable and assured happiness.

A brief discussion of the conflict of duty and inclination will be found in Dewey and Tufts, Ethics, chap. XVII, first few pages. Carlyle's declamations against happiness are too scattered and unsystematic to make reference to specific chapters useful. The general point of view may be found, more temperately stated, in F. H. Bradley's Ethical Studies, the chapter entitled "Why Should I be Moral?" Contemporary accounts of the nature of obligation will be found in the International Journal of Ethics, vol. 22, p. 282; vol. 23, pp. 143, 323.

A discussion of the motto, "The end justifies the means" will be found in F. Paulsen's System of Ethics, book II, and chap. I, sec. 4. The justification of justice is treated in J. S. Mill's Utilitarianism, chap. V. [in the consequent adjustment of our desires, the enlistment of our self-interest on the side of falsity. The purifying influence of public confession springs from the fact that by it the hope in lies is forever swept away, and the soul recovers the noble attitude of simplicity.]

CHAPTER IX
THE JUDGMENT OF CHARACTER

Wherein consists goodness of character?

Character is the sum of a man's tendencies to conduct. Our estimate of a man's character is a sort of weather forecast of what he will do in various situations. Goodness of character consists, then, of such an organization of impulses as will lead to good acts-to acts productive ultimately of a preponderance of intrinsic good, or happiness. The blame and approval that attaches in our minds to certain acts becomes attached also to the disposition that is fruitful of such acts. A good man is he whose mind is so set and adjusted that it will turn away from evil deeds and espouse the right. We can say, then, with Dewey and Tufts, "Goodness consists in active interest in those things which really bring happiness." [Footnote: Ethics, p. 396.] Similarly, Paulsen writes, "Virtues may be defined as habits of the will and modes of conduct which tend to promote the welfare of individual and collective life." [Footnote: System of Ethics, Eng. p. 475.] And Santayana puts it more tersely in the statement, "Goodness is that disposition that is fruitful in happiness." [Footnote: Reason in Common Sense, p. 144.] It is easy, then, to understand the enthusiasm that men feel for goodness; it is the resultant of the passionate longing to be delivered from the domination of evil impulses, the instinctive joy in splendid and unselfish acts, the sense of relief and gratitude felt toward those from whom one has nothing to fear. Contrariwise, the shrinking from a bad man springs primarily from the dread of what he may do, from the disgust which the sight of his foolish and ruinous acts inspires and from various other reactions of the spectator which we need not enumerate. If character were a sort of merely inward possession, unconnected with conduct, we should not Jeel thus toward it. Merely to FEEL virtuous is pleasant, but it is not important. Imputed goodness must be judged by the kind of conduct it yields, and that conduct in turn by its consequences. "By their fruits ye shall know them." But this inward disposition, though important chiefly for its effects, is more important therefore than we are apt to realize. "As a man thinketh in his heart, so he is." The scientific study of psychology has emphasized the fact, which is open to everyday observation, that even secret thoughts and moods influence inevitably a man's outward acts. What we do depends upon what we have been thinking and imagining and feeling. The Great Teacher was right when he bade men refrain not merely from murder, but from angry thoughts; not merely from adultery, but from lustful glances; not merely from perjury, but from the desire to deceive. Epictetus puts it,

"What we ought not to do we should not even think of doing." And Marcus Aurelius writes, "We should accustom ourselves to think upon othing that we should hesitate to reveal to others if they asked to know it." This is sound advice. Without attempting to settle the problem of determinism or indeterminism, which falls properly within the sphere of natural rather than of moral philosophy, it is evident that our conduct is largely the result of that set of potentialities which we call character, that our happiness is in great degree shaped by our inward mental states.

Hence the large role of "motive" and "intent" in ethical theory. High motives and good intentions lead-sometimes to disastrous, acts we know what place is paved therewith. We need the wisdom of the serpent as well as the innocence of the dove. But other things being equal, pure desires tend to right conduct. A man whose mind dwells upon the good side of his neighbors, who loves and sympathizes, and enjoys their friendship, will be far less likely to give vent to acts of cruelty or malice than one who indulges in spiteful feelings, fault finding, and resentment. Our habitual thoughts and desires make us responsive to certain stimuli and indifferent to others. The words of our mouth and the meditations of our heart, as well as the trifling acts that we perform, in themselves however unimportant, have their subtle and accumulative influence in determining our momentous acts. The familiar case of the drinker who says, "This glass doesn't count" can be paralleled in every field of life. It pays to keep in moral training, to cultivate kindly and disciplined thoughts, to forbid ill natured and unworthy feelings, and self-indulgent dreams. Otherwise before we know it the barriers of resistance will crumble and we shall do what we had never supposed we should do, some act that is the fruit of our unregulated inner life. [Footnote: Cf. George Eliot in Romola: "Tito" (who, having posed as a rich and noble gentleman, being unexpectedly confronted with his plebeian father, on the spur of the moment disowned him with the merciless words, "Some madman, surely!") "Was experiencing that inexorable law of human souls, that we prepare ourselves for sudden deeds by the reiterated choice of good or evil that gradually determines character."] Can we say, with Kant, that the only good is the Good Will? It is not uncommon for instrumental goods to come to receive a homage greater than that which is paid to the ends they serve. It is notably and necessarily so with the various aspects of the concept of morality; virtue, conscience, goodness of character are actually more important for us to think about and aim for than the happiness to which they ultimately minister. But this apotheosis denial of its fundamentally instrumental value. As with the miser who rates his bank notes more highly than the goods he could purchase with them, an abstract moralist occasionally exalts the means at the expense of the end. We are told that only goodness counts; that its worth has nothing to do with its relation to happiness; that goodness would command our allegiance even if it brought nothing but misery in its train.

The best-known exponent of this blind worship of goodness is Kant. He writes, "A Good Will is good, not because of what it performs or effects, not by its aptness for the attainment of some proposed end, but simply by virtue of the volition; that is, it is good in itself Its fruitfulness or fruitlessness can neither add nor take away anything from this value ... Moral worth ... cannot lie anywhere but in the principle of the Will, without regard to the ends which can be attained by the action." [Footnote: The Metaphysic of Morality. To be found in Kant's Theory of Ethics, trans. by Abbott, pp. 10, 16.]

So far does Kant carry this worship of the idea of goodness that he separates it from the several virtues that make up goodness in the concrete and bows down before the resulting bare abstraction Good Will, the will to do good. This leads him to a curiously dehumanized position. Prudential acts, he declares, are obviously good in their consequences; they therefore deserve no praise; whatever one does calculatingly, with view to future results, has no moral worth. And on the other hand, whatever good acts one does instinctively, pushed on by animal impulses, including love and sympathy, deserve no praise and have no moral worth. It is only what one does from the single motive of desiring to do the right that awakens Kant's enthusiasm. "The preservation of one's own life, for instance, is a duty; but, as every one has a natural inclination to which most men usually devote to this object has no intrinsic value, nor the maxim from which they act any moral import." [Footnote: The Metaphysic of Morality, sec. I.] What shall we say to this?

(1) Kant's statements are a mere crystallization of an unanalyzed feeling; their plausibility rests upon our ingrained enthusiasm for goodness. But if that enthusiasm be challenged, how shall we justify it? How do we know that good will is good, unless we can see WHY it is good? Many other things appeal to our instincts as good; may not this particular judgment be mistaken, or may not all these other things be equally good with good will? Kant's Hebraic training is clearly revealed in his exaltation of good will; it reflects the practical Lebensweisheit we have learned from the Bible. To the Greek it would have been foolishness, fanaticism. We want not only good will, but wisdom, sympathy, skill, common sense. Also we want health, love, wives and children, friends, and congenial work. All of these things are part of the worth of life. What would it profit us if we lost all these and had only our good will! [Footnote: A reduction ad absurdum of the Kantian view may be found in Cardinal Newman's statement of the Catholic Christian view. "The Church holds that it were better for sun and moon to drop from heaven, for the earth to fall, and for all the many millions who

are upon it to die of starvation in extremist agony, so far as temporal affliction goes, than that one soul, I will not say should be lost, but should commit one single venial sin, should tell one willful untruth, though it harmed no one, or steal one poor farthing without excuse." (Anglican Difficulties, p. 190.)] The valuation that ignores all natural goods but one is unreal, inhuman, fanatical; it leads when unchecked to the emasculated life of the anaemic mediaeval saint or anchorite. Kant's eloquent eulogy of good will appeals to one of our noblest impulses; but that impulse is as much in need of justification to the reason as any other, and it is only one of a number of equally healthy and justifiable natural preferences. Good will, the desire to do right, is perhaps, on the whole, IN THE EMERGENCY, a safer guide to trust than warm-blooded impulse or reasoned calculation. Moreover, it has a thin, precarious existence in most of us at best, and needs all the encouragement it can get. Practically, we need Kant's kind of sermonizing; we need to exalt abstract goodness and resist the appeal of immediate and sensuous goods. So Kant has been popular with earnest men more interested in right living than in theory. But as a theorist he is hopelessly inadequate.

(2) It is true that we admire good will without consideration of the effects it produces, and even when it leads to disaster. But if good will USUALLY led to disaster we should never have come to admire it. Chance enters into this world's happenings and often upsets the normal tendencies of acts. But we have to act in ways that may normally be expected to produce good results. And we have to admire and cherish that sort of action, in spite of the margin of loss. The admiration that we have come to feel for goodness is partly the result of social tradition, buttressing the code that in the long run works out to best advantage; and partly, of course, the spontaneous emotion that rises in us at the sight of courage, heroism, self-sacrifice, and the other spectacular virtues. But however naive or sophisticated a reaction it may be, its psychogenesis is perfectly intelligible, U and its existence is no proof of the supernal nature of the goodness of "good will."

(3) Kant argues as follows: "Nothing can possibly be conceived, in the world or out of it, which can be called good WITHOUT QUALIFICATION, except a good will." [Footnote: Op. cit, sec. I.] He goes on to show that wit, courage, perseverance, etc, are all bad if the will that makes use of them is bad as in the case of a criminal; while health, riches, honor, etc, may inspire pride or presumption, and so not be unmitigated thing that can in every case be called good.

But is this so? May not a man have good will and yet do much mischief? If courage, wit, etc, need to be employed by good will, so does good will need to be joined with common sense, knowledge, tact, and many other helpers. Good will is good only if it is sanely and wisely directed; else it may go with all sorts of fanaticism. If one says, "It is still good qua good will," we may reply, "Yes, but so are all goods; courage is always good qua courage, knowledge qua knowledge," etc. All harmless joys are good without qualification, and all goods whatever are good except as they get in the way of some greater good or lead to trouble.

(4) Kant's formula "good will" is ambiguous. OF COURSE a GOOD act of will is good; that is a mere tautology, and gives us no guidance whatever. Which acts of will ARE good is our problem. Kant, however, worked out his empty formula into a concrete maxim, "Act as if the maxim of thy action were to become by thy will a universal law of nature." But how should we WISH others to act in the given situation? It would be quite possible for a lustful man to be willing that unrestrained lust should be the general rule; he would be much more comfortable and freer if it were. There is nothing in the law of consistency to direct him; men might be consistently bad as well as consistently good. We have still no criterion, only an appeal to coolness, to detachment from hot impulses and selfishness.

Practically, what the Kantian viewpoint amounts to is an exaltation of conscience-a much more concrete (and variable) thing than this abstract formula. Do your duty, at any cost! Our hearts respond to such preaching, but our intellects remain perplexed, if the practical apotheosis of goodness is not supplemented by an adequate theoretic justification thereof.

What evils may go with conscientiousness?

At this point it may repay us to note more carefully the inadequacy of that mere blind conscientiousness which is the practical burden of the Kantian teaching. One would think that the only source of our troubles lay in our lack of desire to do right! As a matter of fact, there is a vast amount of good will in the world which effects no good, or does serious harm, for want of wise direction. Much of the tragedy of life consists of the clashes between wills equally consecrated and pure. Conscientious cranks and blunderers are perhaps even more of a nuisance than out-and-out villains; they hurt every good cause they espouse and bring noble ideals into ridicule; they provoke discouragement and cynicism. There is hardly a folly or a crime that has not been committed prayerfully and with a clear conscience; the saint and the criminal are sometimes psychologically indistinguishable indeed, by which name we call a fanatic may depend upon which side we are on. We may discriminate among the types of perverted conscience:

(1) The fanatical conscience, the meddling conscience, that feels a mission to stir up trouble. Under this head come the parents who interfere needlessly with their children's ways when different from their own, the breakers-up of love-affairs, the fault-finders, the militantly religious, all that

great multitude of men who with prayer and tears have felt it their duty to override others' wills and impose their codes upon the world.

(2) The obstructive conscience, that has become set and will not suffer change. Here we can put all the earnest "stand-patters," who resist innovation of every sort. Slaves of the particular standards that they happen to have grown up in, unable to conceive that their individual brand of religion may not be the ultimate truth, horror-struck at the suggestion that we should forsake the ways of our fathers, their conscientious conservatism stands like a rock in the way of progress.

(3) The ascetic conscience, that overemphasizes the need of sacrifice, and deletes all the positive joy of life for the sake of freedom from possible pain. This particular misdirection of conscience is not prominent in contemporary life; but at certain periods, as among some of the mediaeval saints, or the early Puritans, this hypertrophy of conscience has been a serious blight.

(4) The anxious conscience, that magnifies trifles and gives us no rest with its incessant suggestions, lest we forget, lest we forget. This type of over conscientiousness is a form of unhealthy self consciousness, a bane to its possessor and a nuisance to every one within range.

These familiar evils that may go with the utmost good will show us that good will or conscientiousness is not enough. The conscientious man may not only leave undone important duties; his good will may lead him to push in exactly the wrong direction and do great harm. There are thus two ways of judging a man. First, did he do the best he knew? Did he live up to his conscience? Secondly, did he do what was really best? Was his conscience properly developed and directed? Our approval must often be divided; we may rate him high by the standard of conscientiousness, but low in his standard of morality. This is the familiar distinction between what is objectively right and what is subjectively right. An objectively right action is "one such that, if it be done, the total value of the universe will be at least as great as if any other possible alternative had been done by the agent"; whereas "it is subjectively right for the agent to do what he judges to be most probably objectively right on his information"-whether he judges correctly or not. [Footnote: C. D. Broad in International Journal of Ethics, vol. 24, pp. 316, 320.] It may then be right (in one sense) for a man to do an act which is wrong (in the other sense) [Footnote: Strictly speaking, there are four possible usages of the word "right": An act is right which (a) is actually going to have the best consequences; which (b) might be expected, on our best human knowledge, to have the best consequences; which (c) the actor, on his partial information, and with his partial powers of judgment, expects to have the best consequences; or which (d) his conscience approves, without reference to consequences.] What is the justification of praise and blame? Kant was expressing a familiar thought when he wrote that a man deserved no praise for either instinctive or calculating acts. Why should we praise a man for doing what he wants to do, what is the most natural and easy thing for him to do, or what he can foresee will bring about desirable consequences? Should we not praise only the man who fights his inclinations, does right when he does not want to, and without foresight of ultimate gain?

As a matter of fact, however, we do praise and admire and love the saints who do right easily and graciously. We do not refuse our admiration to Christ because it was his meat and drink, his deepest joy, to do his Father's work; nor do we imagine him as having to wrestle with inner devils of spitefulness and ill-temper. The type of character we rate highest is that from which all these lower impulses have been finally banished, the character that inevitably seeks the pure and the good. And on the other hand, as we have just seen, we often blame the man who, with the noblest intentions, and at great cost to himself, does what we consider wrong.

It is thus true that our reactions of praise and blame are complicated and inconsistent. We often praise a man and blame him at the same time; praise him for following his conscience, and blame him for having a narrow and distorted conscience to follow. Different people in a community will praise or blame him according as they consider this or that aspect of his conduct. What, then, is the rationale of these emotion-reactions?

Obviously, the same natural forces which have produced morality have, pari passu, produced these emotions; they are one of the great means by which men have been pushed into being moral. We praise people, ultimately, because it is socially useful to praise them; the approbation of one's fellows is one of the greatest possible incentives to right conduct. We blame people that they and others may be thereby deterred from wrongdoing. For ages these emotions have been arising in men's hearts, veering their fellows toward moral action. Neither blamer nor blamed has realized the purpose nature may be said to have had in view; the emotional reaction has been instinctive, like sneezing. But if it had not been for its eminent usefulness it would never have developed and become so deep-rooted in us. If blame did no good, if it did not tend to correct evildoing, it would be an unhappy and undesirable state of mind, to be weeded out, like malice or discouragement. Praise might be kept for its intrinsic worth, its agreeableness, like sweet odors and pleasant colors. But actually we need to conserve these reactions for their extrinsic value, as spurs and correctives.

The man who acts upon a calculated expectation of consequences is, indeed, to be praised, if the ends he has sought are good and his calculation correct. Prudence, foresight, thoughtfulness are among the most important virtues. On the other hand, the man who does right instinctively is to be most admired; for to reach that goal is the aim of much of our inner struggle. The approbation we heap upon him, if not needed to keep him up to his best, at least is beneficial to others, who thereby may be stimulated to imitate his goodness. Any sort of conduct that is in line with human welfare is to be praised and loved and sung, and kept before the minds of the young and plastic.

More deeply rooted, perhaps, than the disparagement of praise, is the compassionate revulsion from blame. "He meant well"; "His conscience is clear"; "How could he help sinning with such a bringing-up!" such pleas pull us up in the midst of our condemnation. And they must have their weight. Conscientiousness must be praised, while in the same breath we blame the folly or fanaticism it led to. And the visibly degrading effects of environment should make us tender toward the erring, even while, for their own sakes and the sake of others, we continue to blame the sin. Society cannot afford to overlook sin because it sees provocation for it. There is always provocation, there are always causes outside the sinner's heart. But there is also always a cause within the heart, an openness to temptation, and acquiescence in the evil impulse, which we must try to reach and influence by our blame and condemnation. No doubt in like circumstances we should do as badly, or worse. But to blame does not mean that we set ourselves up as of finer clay; it means only that we continue to use a weapon of great value for the advancement of human welfare. A man always "could have helped it" he could have if his inward aversion to the sin had been strong enough; and it is precisely because blame tends to make that aversion stronger in the sinner and in all who are aware of it, that we must employ it. Reward and punishment are the materialization of praise and blame and have the same uses. We reward and punish men not because in some unanalyzable sense they "deserve" it, but ultimately in order to foster noble and heroic acts and deter men from crime. The giving of rewards for good conduct has never been systematized (except for Carnegie medals, school prizes, and a few other cases), and the practical difficulties in the way are probably insuperable. Indeed, the natural outward rewards of fame, position, increased salary, etc, would be spur enough, if they could be made less capricious and more certain. But to restrain its members from injury to one another is so necessary to society, and so difficult, that elaborate systems of punishment have been used since prehistoric times. To a consideration of the contemporary problems concerning punishment we shall return at a later stage in our study.

What is responsibility?

There is one plea which exempts a person from blame- when we say he was not responsible. Responsibility means accountability, liability to blame and punishment. We do not hold accountable those classes whom it would do no good to blame or punish. Babies, the feeble minded, the insane, are not deterred by blame; hence we do not hold them responsible. Beyond these obvious exemptions there are all sorts of degrees of responsibility, carefully worked out in that branch of the law known as "torts." The principle upon which man has instinctively gone, and which the law now recognizes, in holding men accountable or, in other words, imputing responsibility-is the degree in which they might have been expected to foresee the consequences of their acts. The following set of cases will illustrate the principle:

(1) We do not hold a man responsible at all for unforeseeable results of his action. If because of turning his cows into pasture a passing dog gets excited and tramples a neighbor's flower-bed, the owner of the cows is not responsible for the damage; it would do no good to exact punishment for what was so indirectly and unexpectedly due to his action.

(2) But if his cows got over the wall and trampled the beds, he would be held responsible, in different degrees, according to the circumstances. If he had inspected the wall with eyes of experience and honestly thought it would keep the cows in, we deem him only slightly responsible. He could have done nothing more; yet he must learn more accurately to distinguish safe walls from unsafe. It is fairer for him to pay for the damage than for the owner of the flower- bed to suffer the loss; such risks must be assumed as a part of the business of keeping cows.

(3) If he was ignorant of the necessary height or strength of wall, we blame him more. He has no business-keeping cows until he knows all aspects of the business.

(4) If there was a gap in the wall which he would have noticed if he had taken ordinary care, we hold him still further to blame, and his punishment must be severer.

(5) If he remembered the gap in the wall and did not take the trouble to repair it, thereby consenting to the damage his cows might do, his case is still worse.

(6) Finally, if he deliberately turned the cows into his field with the hope that they would go through the gap and damage his neighbor's flower-beds, he is the most dangerous type of criminal, of "malice aforethought," and his punishment must be severest of all.

In such ways do we distinguish between traits of character more and more dangerous to society, and adjust our blame and punishment to their different degrees of danger, and the differing degrees of efficacy that the blame and punishment may have. But throughout these are purely utilitarian, an unhappy necessity for the preservation of human welfare.

On goodness of character: Dewey and Tufts, Ethics, chap. XII. F. Paulsen, System of Ethics, book II, chap, I, secs. 3, 5. Leslie Stephen, Science of Ethics, chap. VII.

The Kantian theory: Kant's Metaphysic of Morality. A good edition in English is Abbott's Kant's Theory of Ethics. There are many discussions of his theory. An interesting recent one is Felix Adler's, in Essays Philosophical and Psychological in Honor of William James; see also the chapter of Dewey and Tufts, Ethics, above mentioned; Paulsen, System of Ethics, book II, chap. V, secs. 3, 4; American Journal of Psychology, vol. 8, p. 528. On responsibility: Mezes, op. cit, pp. 29-35. Sutherland, op. cit, vol. II, chap. XVIII. Alexander, Moral Order and Progress, book III, chap, III, sec.

CHAPTER X
THE SOLUTION OF PERSONAL PROBLEMS

PERSONAL morality is the way to live the most desirable, the most intrinsically valuable, life-in the long run, and in view of the inescapable needs and conditions of human welfare; the way to avoid the snares and pitfalls of impulse and attain those sweetest goods that come only through effort and sacrifice of lesser goods. That is what morality is, with reference to the single individual alone, and that is ample justification for it. A recent writer phrases it as follows: "I would define goodness as doing what one would wish one had done in twenty years-twenty years, twenty days, twenty minutes, twenty seconds, according to the time the action takes to get ripe Perhaps when we stop teasing people and take goodness seriously. and calmly, and see that goodness is essentially imagination that it is brains, that it is thinking down through to what one really wants goodness will begin to be more coveted. Except among people with almost no brains or imagination at all, it will be popular." [Footnote: Gerald Stanley Lee. Cf. also G. Lowes Dickinson, The Meaning of Good, p. 141. Of morality he says: "Its specific quality consists in the refusal to seize some immediate and inferior good with a view to the attainment of one that is remoter but higher".] The difference between the moral and the immoral man is not that the latter allows himself to enjoy pleasant and exciting phases of experience which the former denies himself for the sake of some good lying outside of experience, but that the latter indulges himself in any agreeable sensation that he chances to desire, while the former conflict with greater, being content not with any goods that may come to hand, but only with the attainable best. [Footnote: Cf. G. Santayana, Reason in Science, pp. 252-53: "Happiness is hidden from a free and casual will; it belongs rather to one chastened by a long education and unfolded in an atmosphere of sacred and perfected institutions. It is discipline that renders men rational and capable of happiness, by suppressing without hatred what needs to be suppressed to attain a beautiful naturalness."] What are the inadequacies of instinct and impulse that necessitate morality? It would seem as if the best way to live should be obvious and irresistible in its appeal. But in truth we are commonly very blind and foolish about this business of living; we lack wisdom, and we lack motive-power at the right place. Instinct is altogether too clumsy and impulse too uncertain. We need a more delicate adjustment; for this, intelligence and conscience have been developed. Morality is the way of life that intelligence and conscience oppose to instinct and impulse. Not to be guided by their wisdom is to forfeit our birthright, like Esau, for a mere mess of pottage. Some of the main types of difficulty that necessitate their overruling guidance we may now note.

(1) Our impulses are often deceptive. What promises keen pleasure turns flat in the tasting; what threatens pain may prove our greatest joy. Most men are led astray at one time or other by some delusory good, some ignis fatuus-whoring, money-making, fame are among the commonest which has fascinated them, from the thought of which they cannot tear themselves away, but which brings no proportionate pleasure in realization, or an evanescent pleasure followed by lasting regret. "Pleasures are like poppies spread, You seize the flow'r, its bloom is shed".

All sorts of insidious consequences follow secretly in the train of innocent-seeming acts; the value of following a given impulse is complicated in many ways of which the impulse itself does not inform us. We are the frequent victims of a sort of inward mirage, and have to learn to discount our hopes and fears. Morality is the corrector of these false valuatiens; it discriminates for us between real and counterfeit goods, teaches us to discount the pictures of our imagination and see the gnawed bones on the beach where the sirens sing.

(2) Our impulses often clash. And since, as we have just said, the relative worth to us of the acts is not always accurately represented by the impulses, we need to stand off and compare them impartially. No single passion must be allowed to run amuck; the opposing voices, however feeble, must be heard. When desires are at loggerheads, when a deadlock of interests arises-an almost daily occurrence when life' is kept at a white heat-there must be some moderator, some governing power. Morality is the principle of coordination, the harmonizer, the arbitrator of conflicting claims.

(3) We often lack impulses which would add much to the worth of our lives; we are blind to all sorts of opportunities for rich and joyous living. We need to develop our latent needs, to expand our natures to their full potentiality, to learn to love many things we have not cared for. In general we ignore the joys that we have not ourselves experienced or imagined, and those which belong to a different realm from that of our temporary enthusiasms. A lovesick swain, an opium fiend, are utterly unable to respond to the lure of outdoor sport or the joy of the well-doing of work; these joys, though perhaps acknowledged as real possibilities for them, fail to attract their wills, touch no chord in them, have no influence on their choices. Morality is the great eye-opener and insistent reminder of ignored goods.

(4) We often have perverted impulses. We inherit disharmonies from other conditions of life, like the vermiform appendix and the many other vestigial organs which have come down to us only for harm. In general we inherit

bodies and brains fairly well organized for our welfare; but there are still atavisms to be ruthlessly stamped out. The craving for stimulants or drugs, sexual perversions, kleptomania, pyromania, and the other manias, bad temper, jealousy- there is a good deal of the old Adam in us which is just wholly bad and to be utterly done away with; rebellious impulses that are hopelessly at war with our own good and must go the way of cannibalism and polygamy. Morality is the stern exterminator of all such enemies of human welfare.

What factors are to be considered in estimating the worth of personal moral ideals?

This summary consideration of the obstacles that block the path to happiness through the heedless following of impulse, shows the necessity of moral ideals; that is to say, of directive codes which shall steer the will through the tumultuous seas of haphazard desire into the harbor of its true welfare. How, then, can we decide between conflicting ideals and estimate their relative value? It can only be by judging through experience the degree of happiness which they severally effect in the situations to which they are to be applied. But there are many factors which contribute to or detract from that happiness in its totality; and a proper estimation of ideals must note the degree in which they provide for each possible element of satisfaction.

(1) In the first place, the mere fact of yielding to an impulse, of whatever sort, brings a relief from craving, and a momentary satisfaction. Just to do what we wish to do is, negatively at least, a good; and in so far every act desired is really desirable. An ideal which crosses inclination must have this initial price debited against it. At times the restlessness of pent-up longing is so great that it pays to gratify it even at some cost of pain or loss. But in general, desire can be modified to fit need; and rational ideals rather than silly wishes must guide us. It is dangerous to lay much stress on the urgency of desire, and almost always possible with a little firmness to hush the blind yearning and replace it with more ultimately satisfying desires.

(2) Normally, however, our desires represent real goods, which must bulk much larger in our calculation than the mere relief of yielding to the impulse. Not only is it ipso facto good to have what we want, but what we want is usually something that can directly or indirectly give us pleasure. The pleasure, then, to be attained through following this or that impulse is to be estimated, both in its intensity and its duration. The certainty or uncertainty of its attainment may also legitimately be considered. And this pleasure, though it is but one phase of the total situation, must be taken seriously into account in our appraisal of ideals which permit or forbid it.

(3) A further question is as to the purity of this pleasure, i.e, its freedom from mixture with pain. Most selfish and sensual pleasures, however keen, are so interwoven with restlessness, shame, or dissatisfaction, or so inevitably accompanied by a revulsion of feeling, disgust or loathing, that they must be sharply discounted in our calculus. Whereas intellectual, aesthetic, religious pleasures are generally free from such intermixture of pain, and so, though milder, on the whole preferable even in their immediacy and apart from ultimate consequences.

(4) But the most imperious need of life lies in the tracing-out and paying heed to these extrinsic values, these after effects of conduct. The drinking of alcoholic liquors, for example, not only stills a craving that arises in a man's mind, not only brings pleasure of taste and comfort of oblivion, not only brings the quick revulsion of emotional staleness and headache, but has its gradual and inevitable effects in undermining the constitution, lessening the power of resistance to disease, and decreasing the vitality of offspring. Quite commonly these ultimate consequences are the most important, and so the determining, factors in deciding our ideals. Among them may be included the influence of single acts in increasing or decreasing the power to resist future temptations, and the gradual paralysis of the will through unchecked self-indulgence.

(5) Another important aspect of any moral situation lies in the rejection which every choice involves. Not only must we ask what a given impulse has to offer us, in immediate and remote satisfaction; we must consider what alternative goods its adoption precludes. What might we have been doing with our time and strength or money? Is this act not only a good one, is it the best one for that moment of our lives? An important function of ideals is to point us to realms of happiness into which our preexisting impulses might never have led us, and whose existence we might scarcely have suspected.

(6) Finally, we may ask of every proposed line of conduct, what will be its worth to us in memory? Not only in our leisure hours, but in a current of subconscious reflection that accompanies our active life, we constantly live in the presence of our past. And the nature of memory is such that it cannot well retain the traces of certain of our keenest pleasures, but can continually feed us upon other joys of our past. It is imperative, then, for a happy life, so to live that the years are pleasant to look back upon. Vicious self-indulgence and selfishness are rarely satisfying in retrospection, whereas all courage and heroism and tenderness are a source of unending comfort. For better or worse, we are, and cannot shirk being, judges of our own conduct. We may be prejudiced, and may properly try to correct our prejudices; we may discount our own disapprovals, and seek to escape from our own self- condemnation. But after all, we must live with ourselves; and

it pays to aim to please not only the evanescent impulses whose disapproval will soon be forgotten, but that more deeply rooted and insistent judgment that cannot wholly be stilled. Regret and remorse are among the greatest poisoners of happiness, and prospective ideals must bear that truth in mind. "No matter what other elements in any moment of consciousness may tend to give it agreeable tone, if there is not the element of approval, there is not yet any deep, wide, and lasting pleasantness for consciousness. A flash of light here, a casual word there, and it is gone. "Just when we are safest, there's a sunset- touch; A fancy from a flower-bell, some one's death, A chorus ending from Euripides, And that's enough" to bring the shock of disapproval, and with it disagreeable feeling- tone continues till disapproval is removed or approval is won. If there be won this approval, other elements of disagreeableness, however great, can be endured. The massive movement of the complex unified consciousness of a Socrates drinking hemlock, of a Jesus dying on the cross, whatever strong eddies of pain there be in it, is still toned agreeably, as it makes head conqueringly toward that end which each has ideally constructed as fit." [Footnote: H. G. Lord, in Essays Philosophical and Psychological in Honor of William James, p. 388-89.] No reference has been made, in this summary of the factors which determine our estimate of the worth of personal ideals, to the bearing of these ideals upon other people's lives. Actually, of course, the social values of even primarily personal ideals are impossible to overlook, and often bulk larger than the merely personal values. This whole side of the matter will be left for convenience, however, to the following chapter.

Epicureanism vs. Puritanism.

Personal ideals have swung historically between two magnets, richness and purity, self-expression and self-repression, indulgence and asceticism. The crux of the individual's problem is the question how much repression is necessary; and man's answer has wavered somewhere between these extremes, which we may designate by the names of their best-known exemplars, Epicureanism and Puritanism. Many differences in degree or detail there have been, of course, in the various historic embodiments of these ideals; but for the sake of making clear the fundamental contrast we may neglect these individual divergences and group together those on the one hand who have called men to a fuller, completer life and those who have summoned them to an austerer and purer life, free from taint of sin and regret. We shall then put in the first group such well-known seers and poets as Epicurus, Lucretius, Horace, Goethe, Shelley, Byron, Walter Pater, Walt Whitman; we shall think of the Greek gods, of the Renaissance artists, the English cavaliers. We shall think of the motto, "Carpe diem," and "Gather ye rosebuds while ye may"; and perhaps of Stevenson's

"The world is so full of a number of things, I'm sure we should all be as happy as kings." [Footnote: An excellent brief plea for this ideal of the life that shall be rich in experience can be found in Walter Pater's Renaissance, the "Conclusion."] In contrast to these followers are afraid of impulse, those who warn and rebuke and seek to save life from its pitfalls. We shall think of Buddha, the Stoics, the Hebrew prophets, the mediaeval saints, Dante and Savonarola, the English and American Puritans, or, in modern times, of Tolstoy. The ideal of such men is expressed not by the wholesomely happy and carefree Greek gods, but by haloed saint, by the calm-eyed Buddha of Eastern lands, by the figure of Christ on the cross. The answer to the Epicurean's heedlessness is expressed in such lines as "What is this world's delight? Lightning that mocks the night, Brief even as bright."

It is condensed in the familiar "Respice finem"; the peace of its self- denial shines out in Christ's "Not my will but thine," and in Dante's "In His will is our peace." Meager and cold and repellent as this ideal in its extreme expressions often seems, it appeals to us as the softer and irresponsible ideal of the Epicureans cannot. But obviously our way lies between the extremes. And after all that has now been said, our summary of the dangers inherent in each ideal may be very brief.

What are the evils in undue self-indulgence?

Apart from the selfishness of self-indulgence, which is obvious upon the surface, but with which we are not now concerned,

(1) Self-indulgence, if unbridled, leads almost inevitably to pain, disease, and premature death. For in the majority of men there are certain instincts so strong and so dangerous -as, the sex-instinct, the craving for stimulants and excitement-that where no repressive principle exists they tend to override the grumblings of prudence and drag their possessor to disaster. It is impossible for most men, if they give themselves over to the pursuit of personal pleasure, to keep to the quiet, refined, healthful pleasures which Epicurus advocated. Their feet go down to death.

(2) But even if the worst penalties are escaped, indulgence brings at least satiety, the "heart high cloyed," a blunted capacity for enjoyment, ennui, restlessness, and depression of spirit. Keen as its zest may be at the outset, it is short-lived at best; and with the ensuing emotional fatigue, pleasures pall, life seems empty, robbed of its meaning and glory.

(3) Moreover, pleasure-seeking is cursed with the specter of aimlessness; it entirely misses the deepest and most satisfying joys of life, the joy of healthy, unspent forces and desires, the joy of purpose and achievement, the joy of the pure, disciplined, loyal life. It renders these joys unattainable;

we cannot serve God and sense, ideals and lusts of the flesh. The parting of the ways lies before every man; and it is the perennial tragedy of life that so many, misled by impulse and blinded by desire, fail to see the beauty of holiness and choose the lesser good.

(4) Especially as we grow older does it matter less and less what evanescent enjoyments we have had, and more and more what we have accomplished. Our happiness lies increasingly with the years in the memory, subconscious most of the time but constantly potent in its influence, of our past. To have gratified the senses, to have tasted the superficial delights of life, to have yielded to the tug of desire, leaves little in the way of satisfaction behind; but to have done something worthy, to have lived nobly, even to have fought and failed, is a lasting honor and joy.

What are the evils in undue self-repression?

Asceticism, like self-indulgence, is selfish. It asks, "What shall I do to be saved?" rather than "What shall I do to serve?" Endlessly preoccupied with the endeavor not to do wrong, the ascetics have failed to do the positive good they ought. The grime that comes through loving service is better than the stainlessness of inactivity; as the poet Spenser puts it, "Entire affection hateth nicer hands." And the emphasis upon freedom from taint of sin tends to produce a scorn of others who do not thus deny themselves, a self-righteousness and Pharisaism, a callousness to others, which distorts the judgment as well as dries up the sympathies.

But apart from these dangers, and from a purely personal point of view, asceticism has its evil side.

(1) An overemphasis upon self-denial sacrifices unnecessarily the sweetness and richness of life, stunts it, distorts it, robs it of its natural fruition. The denial of any satisfaction is cruel except as it is necessary. Purity, carried to a needless extreme, became celibacy; the virtue of frugality became the vice of a starvation diet, producing the emaciated and weakened saints; the unworldliness which can be in the world but not of it was transformed into the morbidly lonely and futile isolation of the hermits. These are abnormal and undesirable perversions of human nature.

(2) A reaction from needless repression is almost inevitable. The attempt radically to alter and repress human nature is nearly always disastrous. Most of the ascetics had to pass their days in constant struggles against their temptations, and many of them recurrently lapsed into wild orgies of sin, the result of pent-up impulses denied their natural channels. Morality should be rather directive than repressive, using all of our energies for wise and noble ends, and overcoming evil with good. A merely negative morality implies the continual dwelling of attention upon sin and the continual

rebellion of desire. It keeps the soul in a state of unstable equilibrium, and defeats its own ends.

R. B. Perry, Moral Economy, chap, II, secs, II, III; chap, III, secs, II, III, IV. F. Paulsen, System of Ethics, book III, chap. II. S. E. Mezes, Ethics, chap, X, XI, Dewey and Tufts, Ethics, chap, XVIII, secs. 1, 2, 4; chap, XIX, sees. 1, 2, 4. Matthew Arnold, Culture and Anarchy, chap. IV. H. C. King, Rational Living, pp. 93-102. W. dew. Hyde, The Five Great Philosophies of Life, chaps, I-IV. H. Bashdall, Theory of Good and Evil, book II, chap. III.

CHAPTER XI
THE SOLUTION OP SOCIAL PROBLEMS

DUTY, like charity, begins at home; and we need to take the motes out of our own eyes before we can see clearly how to help our fellows. To keep physically well, pure, and prudent, following worthy purposes and smothering unruly desires, is our first business; and there would be much less to do for one another if every one did his duty by himself.

But even with our best endeavors we need a helping hand now and then, and, indeed, are continuously dependent upon the work and kindness of others for all that makes life tolerable, or even possible. And the other side to this truth is that we are never free from the obligation of doing our duty squarely by those whose welfare is in some degree dependent upon us. No man can, if he would, live to himself alone; life is necessarily and essentially social. Personal and social duties are so inextricably interwoven that it is impossible except by an artificial abstraction to separate them. The cultivation of one's own health, for example, is a boon to the community; and to care for the community's health is to safeguard one's own. Every advance in personal purity, culture, or self-control increases the individual's value and diminishes his menace to his fellows; while every step in social amelioration makes life freer and more comfortable for him. So close- knit is society today that an indifference to sanitation in Asia or a religious persecution in Russia may produce disastrous results to some innocent and utterly indifferent individual in Massachusetts or California. On the other hand, there is no vice so solitary and so can widespread social results. [Footnote: Cf. George Eliot in Adam Bede: "There is no sort of wrong deed of which a man can bear the punishment alone. Men's lives are as thoroughly blended as the air they breathe; evil spreads as necessarily as disease."] Society has a vital interest in the personal life of its members, and every member, however self- contained he may be, has a vital interest in the general standards of morality. For purposes of analysis, however, it is convenient to make the distinction between the two aspects of morality, the governance of intra-human and of inter-human relations; the ordering of the single life and the ordering of the community life. Of the two the latter is even more imperative than the former, the arbitration of clashes between individuals even more difficult than the governing of the impulses within a single heart. We turn, therefore, to consider the problems involved in the general conception of social morality, which we may define as the direction of the action of each toward the greatest attainable welfare of all. Why should we be altruistic? That altruism (action directed toward others' welfare) is best for the community as a whole is obvious. In order to maintain his life in the face of the many obstacles that thwart and dangers that threaten him, man must present a solid front to the universe. All clashes of interest, friction, and civil strife, all withholding of help, means a weakening of his united forces, an invitation to disaster. And even where life becomes relatively secure and individualism possible, the greatest good for the greatest number is attainable only by continual cooperation and mutual sacrifice. So vital is it to each member of the community that selfishness and cruelty in others be repressed, that society cannot afford to leave at least the grosser forms of egoism unpunished. Men must enforce upon one another that mutual regard which individuals are constantly tempted to ignore, but without which no man's life can find its adequate fulfillment or security. No man, then, can be called moral, can be said to have found a comprehensive solution of life, however self-controlled and pure he may be, if he is cruel, or even lacking in consideration for others. This is the most glaring defect in both Epicureanism and asceticism; both are fundamentally selfish. For the proper adjustment of life to its needs we must turn rather to Christianity, or to Buddhism, with their ideals of service; to the patriotic ideals of the noblest Greeks; to Kant, with his "So act as to treat humanity, whether in their own person or in that of any other, as an end, never as a means only"; or to the British utilitarians with their "Every one to count for one, and only one." The question, however, persistently recurs, Why should the INDIVIDUAL be altruistic? What does HE get out of it? To this we may reply:

(1) The life of service is, in normal cases, a happier life in itself than the life that is preoccupied with self. It is richer, fuller in potentialities of joy; it is freer from regrets and the eventual emptiness of the self-centered life. [Footnote: Cf. Mill, Utilitarianism, chap. 2: "When people who are tolerably fortunate in their outward lot do not find in life sufficient enjoyment to make it valuable to them, the cause generally is, caring for nobody but themselves."] It is saner, less likely to be veered off on some tangent of morbid and ultimately disastrous indulgence

(2) The altruistic life earns the gratitude and love of others, while the selfish life remains isolated, unloved, without their stimulus and help. Ingratitude there is, of course, and the returning of evil for good; on the other hand, the selfish man may hope for undeserved forgiveness and even love from his fellows. But in the long run it pays to be good to others; bread cast upon the waters does return after many days; normally unkindness provokes dislike, contempt, open hostility, retaliation, while kindness finds a natural and proper reward in return favors, esteem, and affection. No man can tell when he will be in need of sympathy or of aid; it is folly so to live as to forfeit our fellows' good will. And finally, selfishness carried

beyond a certain point brings the penalty not only of the unfavorable opinion and private retaliations of others, but of the publicly enforced law. "In normal cases," we have said. And we must add that there are cases though they are less common than we are apt to suppose in which the good of the individual is hopelessly at variance with that of the community. If our fellows could be counted on for a fair reciprocity of self-denial and service, we should not begrudge these necessary sacrifices. The sting lies not so much in the loss of personal pleasures as in the lack of appreciation and return; to do our part when others are not doing theirs takes, indeed, a touch of saintliness. Socrates drinking the hemlock, Jesus dying in agony on the cross, Regulus returning to be tortured at Carthage, were deliberately sacrificing their personal welfare for the good of other men. And in numberless ways a host of heroic men and women have practiced and are daily practicing unrewarded self-denial in the name of love and service, self-denial which by no means always brings a joy commensurate with the pain. These are the abnormal cases; but the abnormal is, after all, not so very uncommon. And for these men and women we must grieve, while we honor and admire them and hold them up for imitation. Society must insist on just such sacrifices when they are necessary for the good of the whole, and must so train its youth that they will be willing to make them when needful.

What is the exact meaning of selfishness and unselfishness?

Selfishness is the pursuance of one's own good at the expense of others. A mistaken idea, which it is necessary to guard against, is that selfishness must be conscious, deliberate. It is not uncommon for a person accused of selfishness to say, or think, "This is an unjust accusation; I have not had a selfish thought!" But unconscious selfishness is by far the commoner sort; millions of essentially good- hearted people are guilty of selfish acts through thoughtlessness and stagnant sympathy. Conscious cruelty is rare compared with moral insensibility. It cannot be too often repeated that selfishness is not a way of feeling about people, it is a way of acting toward them. To be wholly free from selfish conduct necessitates insight into the needs and feelings of others as well as a vague good will them. The girl who allows her mother to drudge that she may have immaculate clothes, the mother who keeps her son at home when he ought to be given the opportunity of a wider life, is conscious only of love; but she is really putting her own happiness before that of the loved one. The owner of the vilest tenement houses is sometimes a generous and benevolent-minded man, the luxuriously rich are often honest and glad to confer favors, the political boss is full of the milk of human kindness; but the superficial or adventitious altruism of such men should not blind us to their fundamental, though often entirely unrealized, selfishness. A complementary fallacy is that which denies the epithet "unselfish" to a man who enjoys helping others. Who has not heard the cynical remark, "There's nothing unselfish about So-and-So's benevolence that is his enjoyment in life!" Such a comment ignores the fact that the goal of moral progress lies precisely at the point where we shall all enjoy doing what it is our duty to do. Altruistic impulses are our own impulses, as well as egoistic ones; the distinction between them lies not in the pleasure they may give to their possessor, or the sacrifice they may demand, but in the objective results they tend to attain. Happy is the man whose DELIGHT is in the law of the Lord! Unselfish action is, in the broader sense, all action that is not selfish; in the narrower and positive sense, it is all action that tends to the welfare of others at the expense of the narrower interests of the individual.

Are altruistic impulses always right?

It would be an easy solution for our problems if we could say, "In every case follow the altruistic impulse." But this simplification is impossible; the ideal of service is not such an Open Sesame to our duty. And this for several reasons:

(1) There are frequently clashes between altruistic impulses. In fact, almost all moral errors have some unselfish impulse on their side which helps to justify them in the eyes of the sinner and his friends. The politician who gets the best jobs for his supporters, the legislator who puts through a special statute to favor his constituents, the jingo who helps push his country into war for its "honor" or "glory"-these and a host of other wrongdoers are conscious of a genuine altruistic glow. They ignore the fact that they are doing, on the whole, more harm than good to others, because the smaller group that is apparently benefited looms larger to the eye than the more widely distributed and less directly affected sufferers.

All of our most vexing moral problems are those in which benefit to some must be weighed against benefit to others. Shall a man who is needed by his family risk his life to save a ne'er-do-well? Shall we insist that people unhappily married shall endure their wretchedness and forego the possibility of a happier union in order that heedlessness and license may not be encouraged in the lives of others? Life is full of such two- sided problems; it is not enough that an act may bring good to some, it must be the act that brings most good to most.

(2) An apparently altruistic act, dictated by sympathy, and productive of happiness, may not be for the ultimate good of the very person made happy. To give everything they want to children is inevitably to "spoil" them, as we rightly say; to spoil their own happiness in the long run as well as their usefulness to others. To condone another's sin and save him the unpleasantness of rebuke or the inflicting of a penalty is often the worst

thing that could be done to him. To give alms to a beggar may mean to assist his moral degeneration and in the long run increase his misery.

(3) Even when an act superficially egoistic conflicts with one that seems altruistic, the greatest good of the community often dictates the former. There is, as Trumbull used to put it, a "duty of refusing to do good." A man who can best serve the common good by concentrating his strength on that work where his particular ability or training makes him most effective, may be justified in refusing other calls upon his energies, however intrinsically worthy. An Edison would be doing wrong to spend his afternoons in social service, a Burbank has no right to diminish his resources by giving a public library. Emerson deserves our commendation for refusing to be inveigled into the various causes that would have drafted his time and strength. Even to the anti-slavery agitation he refused his services, saying, "I have quite other slaves to free than those Negroes, to wit, imprisoned thoughts far back in the brain of man, which have no watchman or lover or defender but me." This brings us to the question how far a man may legitimately live a self- contained life. Certainly there is a measure of truth in Goethe's saying, "No man can he isolates himself"; in Ibsen's "The most powerful man is he who is most alone"; and in Matthew Arnold's

"Alone the sun rises, and alone Spring the great streams."

A multiplicity of interests distracts the soul and often confuses our ideals. By keeping free from social burdens some men, like Kant, have accomplished tasks of unusual magnitude.

On the other hand, we can match Goethe's assertion with another of his own: "A talent forms itself in solitude, a character in the stream of the world." Isolation tends almost inevitably to narrowness, to an abnormal and cramped outlook, to willfulness or Pharisaism, and usually to loneliness and depression. The only pervasively happy life for man is the life of cooperation and loyalty. We may well "withdraw into the silence," take our daily communion with God in our closets, or our forty days in the wilderness, to win clearer vision and steadier purpose. But solitude should, in normal cases, be only an interlude of rest, or a quiet maturing for service. The ideal is perhaps expressed in Wordsworth's sonnet on Milton:

"Thy soul was like a star and dwelt apart. …. And yet thy heart The lowliest duties on herself did lay."

The organization of life implies a criticism of and control over altruistic as well as egoistic impulses. There is nothing inherent in the fact of a good being OTHERS' good to make it necessarily the greatest good in a given situation. The ultimate criterion must always be the greatest good of the greatest number; but an altruistic as well as an egoistic impulse may stand in the way of that end. Our altruistic inclinations are often perverted, non-representative, a matter of instinctive and irrational sympathy or shortsighted impulse. And so, while one of the great tasks of moral education is to make men unselfish, that alone is not enough; unselfishness must be directed by reason and tact, rendered far-sighted and intelligent.

What mental and moral obstacles hinder altruistic action?

Although an altruistic impulse is not necessarily a right impulse to follow, there are a great many altruistic duties which are clear and summoning; and it is a never ending disappointment to the man of social conscience to behold the apathy wherewith obvious social duties are regarded. It will be worthwhile to pause and note the chief mental and moral obstacles that prevent a more general devotion to social betterment.

(1) The most formidable obstacle, perhaps, is the selfishness of those who are themselves .well enough off. Our cities, and even, to some extent, our small towns, grow up in "quarters"; the rich living in one district and the poor in another. This permits the suffering of the latter to go unknown or only half-realized by the former. The well-to- do have many interests and many pleasant uses for their money; the call of the unfortunate-"Come over and help us!"- rings faint and far away in their ears. Or they may excuse their callousness by the assertion that the poor are used to their evil living conditions, do not mind them, and are as contented, on the whole, as the rich; complacently ignoring the fact that being used to conditions is not the same as enjoying or profiting by them, and that contentment by no means implies a useful or desirable life. It is true that the needy are often but dimly conscious of their needs; in that very fact lies a reason why the favored classes should rouse them out of their dullness, save them from the physical and moral degeneration into which they so unconsciously and helplessly drift. The indifference of the fortunate comes not so often from a deliberate hardening of the heart as from a lack of contact with the needy or imagination to picture their destitution. But blame must rest upon all comfortable citizens who do not bestir themselves to help in social betterment because it is too much trouble or requires a sacrifice they are not willing to make.

(2) Another serious obstacle lies in the distrust with which many people regard any duty which they have not been accustomed to regard as a duty. This may take the form of an overdeveloped loyalty, that bows before the sacredness of existing institutions and labels any reform as "unconstitutional," a departure from the ways that were good enough for our fathers. It may wear the guise of a lazy piety that would leave everything with God, accepting social ills as manifestations of his will, and interference as a sort of arrogant presumption! It may be a mere mental apathy, an

inertia of habit, that sees no call for a better water supply or bothersome laws about the purity of milk. Or it may defend itself by pointing out the uncertainties that attend untried ways and warning against the danger of experimentation. To these warnings we may reply that our altruistic zeal must, indeed, be coupled with accurate thinking; unless we have based our proposals on wide observation and cautious inference we may find unexpected and baneful results in the place of our sanguine expectations. But we may point out that it is "nothing venture nothing have"; we cannot work out our social salvation without experimenting; and, after all, ways that do not work well can readily be discontinued. What is vital is to keep alive an intolerance of apathy and contentment, to realize that we are hardly more than on the threshold of a rational civilization, to recognize evils, cherish ideals, and maintain our determination in some way to actualize them.

(3) A further steady damper upon our altruistic zeal is the dread of raising the taxes. Humanitarian movements are well enough, but they cost so much! What is needful is to point out that poverty, unemployment, disease, and the other social ills are also costly; indeed, they cost the public in the long run far more than the expenditure necessary for their abolition or alleviation. It pays in dollars and cents, within a generation or two at least, to make and keep the social organism sound. A wise altruism is not merely a matter of philanthropy; it is also a matter of economy; a means of saving individuals from suffering, but at the same time a means of safeguarding the public treasury. If the community does not pay for the curing of these evils it will have to pay for their results. "It seems to me essentially fallacious to look upon such expenditures as indulgences to be allowed rather sparingly to such communities as are rich enough to afford them. They are literally a husbanding of resources, a safeguard against later unprofitable but compulsory expenditure, a repair in the social organism which, like the repair of a leaky roof, may avert disaster." [Footnote: E. T. Devine, Misery and its Causes, p. 272.] The public must be educated to see the wisdom of investing heavily in long-neglected social repairs and reconstruction, which in the end will far more than pay for itself in the lowering of expenses for police, courts, prisons, hospitals, asylums, and almshouses, in the lowered death-rate, immunity from costly disease, and increased working capacity of the people.

(4) Finally, a hopelessness of accomplishing anything often paralyzes our zeal. This sometimes takes the form of a more or less honest conviction that poverty, unemployment, and other maladjustments are simply the result of moral degeneration-of the laziness, extravagance, drinking, or other wrongdoing of the poor; their suffering is their own fault, and they must be left to endure it. Of course such factors often-though by no means

always-enter in. One may well say, "Who are we of the upper classes to throw the first stone?" Under like conditions most of us would have become as discouraged or demoralized, yielded to the consolation of some vice, or balked at the monotonous grind of factory labor. But however that may be, in so far as social evils are due to these faults, the faults must be attacked, not accepted as inevitable and incurable. The pressure that pushes men into them must be eased, the ignorance and foolishness that foster them must be dissipated by education and moral training. And for all the social maladjustments that are NOT due to vice and sin, other remedies must be found. The road to social salvation is long and beset with many difficulties, but the goal is not hopeless of attainment; and every step toward the goal is so much gain. Because we cannot now see how to remedy all evils must not be a pretext for refusing to lend a hand to movements that are of proved value.

How can we reconcile egoism and altruism?

Although altruism is usually wise from the individual's own standpoint, it does not always seem so. The commonest moral clash is between the individual's apparent good and that of others; the cases in which one man's position, wealth, success precludes another's are everyday occurrences. Must this conflict be eternal? Is there any way of reconciling these opposing interests except by an unhappy and regrettable sacrifice? Must life be a perpetual compromise, a "social contract," a treaty to make reciprocal concessions, with every one's real interests at war with every one else's? Certainly the altruistic summons cannot be ignored; we cannot all follow our egoistic impulses; in the common disaster we should be individually involved. And, indeed, the altruistic impulses have become so deeply rooted in our natures that, turn away from them as we might, they would yet persist in the form of an undercurrent of dissatisfaction and remorse. The only possible solution of the deadlock lies in the killing-off of the selfish impulses.

This is not a fantastic dream. We see in the ideal mother, father, husband, wife, in the ardent patriot and religious devotee, this sloughing-off of the egoistic nature already accomplished. Love, and joy in service, are not alien to us; they are as instinctive as self- seeking; the hope of ultimate peace lies in the strengthening of these impulses till they so dominate us that we no longer care for the selfish and narrow aims. We must cultivate the masculine aspect of unselfishness, the loyalty of the Greeks, the impulse to stand by and fight for others; and we must cultivate its more feminine side, the caritas of I Corinthians XIII, the love that suffereth long and is kind, the sympathy and tenderness infused into a rough and rugged world by Christianity. In this highest developed life there will then be no dualism of motive; at the top of the ladder of moral progress individual and social goods coincide. It is joy to the righteous to do righteousness; it is the keenest delight in life for the lover of men to serve.

The unselfish impulse has thus a double value; it blesseth him that gives and him that takes. It is more blessed to give than to receive, when the giver has reached the moral level where giving is his greatest joy. The development of sympathy and the spirit of service in modern times gives great hope that the time will come when men will universally find a rich and satisfying life in ways which bring no harm but only good to others.

H. Spencer, Data of Ethics, chaps, XI-XIV. R. B. Perry, Moral Economy, chap, II, secs, IV, V.; chap, III, secs, V, VI. F. Paulsen, System of Ethics, book II, chap. I, sec. 6; chap, VI; book III, chap, X, sec. 1. Dewey and Tufts, Ethics, chap, XVIII, sec. e. W. K. Clifford, Right and Wrong, On the Scientific Basis of Morals, in Lectures and Essays, vol. II. R. M. McConnell, Duty of Altruism. B. Russell, Philosophical Essays, chap. I, sec. V. J. Royce, Problem of Christianity, vol. I, chap. III.

CHAPTER XII
OBJECTIONS AND MISUNDERSTANDINGS

HAVING now outlined the eudfemonistic account of morality, we may note certain objections that are commonly raised to it, and certain is understandings that constantly recur.

Do men always act for pleasure or to avoid pain?

Many of the earlier theorists, not content with showing that the good consists ultimately in a quality of conscious states, asserted that all of men's actions are actually DIRECTED TOWARD the attainment of agreeable states of experience or avoidance of disagreeable states. There is no act but is aimed for pleasure of some sort or away from pain; men differ, then, only in their wisdom in selecting the more important pleasures and their skill in attaining what they aim for. This assertion, easily refuted, has seemed to some opponents of the eudemonistic account of morality so bound up with it as to involve its downfall.

The classic statement of this erroneous psychology, which has been the source of much satisfaction to anti-eudemonistic philosophers, is to be found in the fourth chapter of Mill's Utilitarianism. "There is in reality nothing desired except happiness. Whatever is desired otherwise than as a means to some end beyond itself, and ultimately to happiness, is desired as itself a part of happiness, and is not desired for itself until it has become so. Human nature is so constituted as to desire nothing which is not either a part of happiness or a means to happiness" A careful reading of Mill shows that he did not mean these statements without qualification. But since they, and similar sweeping assertions, [Footnote: Cf. Leslie Stephen, Science of Ethics, p. 44: "The love of happiness must express the sole possible motive of Judas Iscariot and of his Master; it must explain the conduct of Stylites on his pillar or Tiberius at Caprae or A Kempis in his cell or of Nelson in the cockpit of the Victory."] have been a stumbling-block to many, we must pause to note their inaccuracy, while insisting that they are no part of a sound utilitarian, or eudemonistic, theory. Far from the desire for happiness being the universal motive, it is one of the less common springs of conduct. Habit, inertia, instinct, ideals drive us this way and that; we do a thousand things daily without any thought of happiness, because our minds are so made that they naturally run off into such action. We desire concrete THINGS, without reference to their bearing on our happiness. We even go directly and consciously counter to our happiness at times, deliberately sacrifice it, perhaps for some foolish fancy. The idealist in politics expects to get no pleasure out of what his associates deem his pigheadedness; but he has seen a vision and he keeps true to it. Regulus did not go back to Carthage to be tortured to death for the pleasure of it, or to avoid the greater pain of an uneasy conscience; he went in spite of foreseen pain and the allurement of possible pleasure. When a man endures privations for the sake of posthumous fame, it is not that he expects to enjoy that fame when it comes, or expects others to enjoy it; he is simply so made that he cannot resist the sway of that ambition which will bring him no good. The pursuit of pleasure is a sophisticated impulse which appears in marked degree only in a few self-conscious and idle individuals. William James gave the deathblow to this pleasure-seeking psychology. "Important as is the influence of pleasures and pains upon our movements, they are far from being our only stimuli. With the manifestations of instinct and emotional expression, for example, they have absolutely nothing to do. Who smiles for the pleasure of smiling, or frowns for the pleasure of the frown? Who blushes to escape the discomfort of not blushing? Or who in anger, grief, or fear is actuated to the movements which he makes by the pleasures which they yield? In all these cases the movements are discharged fatally by the vis a tergo which the stimulus exerts upon a nervous system framed to respond in just that way. The IMPULSIVE QUALITY of mental states is an attribute behind which we cannot go." [Footnote: W. James, Psychology, vol. II, p. 550.] It is not true, then, that love of pleasure and fear of pain are the universal motives. It is not true that we inevitably act along the line of least hedonic resistance, that pain necessarily veers us off and pleasure irresistibly attracts. By force of will, by "suggestion" or training, we can go directly counter to the pull of pleasure. It is true that we should not have the instincts and habits and impulses that we do were they not in general useful for our existence or happiness. But the evolutionary process has been clumsy; we are not properly adjusted; we become the victims of ideas fixes; ideas and activities obsess us quite without relation to their hedonic value. So pleasure and pain are not usually the impelling force or conscious motive behind conduct. What they are is-the touchstone, the criterion, the justification.

We do not act in ways that bring the greatest happiness, but we ought to. We do not consciously seek happiness, and we ought not to. We ought to continue to care for THINGS and for IDEALS; but the things and ideals we care and work for ought to be such that through them man's welfare is advanced.

Are pleasures and pains incommensurable?

An objection commonly raised is that pleasures and pains of various sorts are incommensurable; that therefore no calculation of relative advantage is possible; and that the eudaemonistie criterion for action is thereby made impracticable and useless.

(1) To this we may reply that the estimation of the relative worth of different kinds of experience is, indeed, often very difficult. But on any theory the decision as to the right is equally complicated and puzzling. The fact that the criterion is difficult to use is no evidence that it is not the right criterion. Which set of consequences will be of most intrinsic worth, it is sometimes impossible to know. But one set is, nevertheless, of more intrinsic worth, and the act that secures them is the best act, even though we do not recognize it as such. There will continue to be, many differences of judgment as to which of alternative possible experiences is the more desirable. But that uncertainty does not alter the fundamental fact that some experiences ARE intrinsically more desirable than others and more deserving of pursuit.

"A debtor who cannot pay me offers to compound for his debt by making over one of sundry things he possesses- a diamond ornament, a silver vase, a picture, a carriage. Other questions being set aside, I assert it to be my pecuniary interest to choose the most valuable of these, but I cannot say which is the most valuable. Does the proposition that it is my pecuniary interest to choose the most valuable, therefore, become doubtful? Must I not choose as well as I can, and if I choose wrongly, must I give up my ground of choice? Must I infer that in matters of business I may not act on the principle that, other things equal, the more profitable transaction is to be preferred, because, in many cases, I cannot say which is the more profitable and have often chosen the less profitable? Because I believe that of many dangerous courses I ought to take the least dangerous, do I make 'the fundamental assumption' that courses can be arranged according to a scale of dangerousness, and must I abandon my belief if I cannot so arrange them?" [Footnote: H. Spencer, Data of Ethics, chap. IX.]

(2) If it is practically impossible to calculate the relative worth of consequences in many cases, it is yet easy enough to do so in the great majority of moral situations. In most cases the preponderance of value is clear. That selfishness and self-indulgence are not worth while; that abstinence from pleasure-giving drugs and intoxicating liquors is worth the sacrifice; that truth and honesty, the law-abiding spirit, the spirit of service, friendliness and courtesy, sanitary measures, incorruptible courts, and a thousand other things are worth the effort and cost of acquiring them, is indisputable. It is only in some peculiarly balanced situations that we find practical difficulty in deciding. If morality were limited to the cases where we can be sure on which side the greater good or lesser evil lies, we should not be shorn of much of our present code.

(3) It would, of course, be impracticable to stop and calculate at the moment when action is needed. But such continual recalculation is unnecessary. Our ancestors, after many experiments, have found solutions for all the familiar types of situation; the results of their thought are crystallized for us in the ideals that press upon us from without and the voice of conscience that calls to us within. Forces beyond the individual human mind have taken care of these things and slowly steered man, with all his passions and caprices, toward his own better welfare. It is only in moments when we long to understand and justify our ideals, or when some unusually baffling problem arises, that we need to calculate and weigh relative advantage and disadvantage. And that is what, in such situations, most people do.

Are some pleasures worthier than others?

Undiscriminating critics have often condemned the eudsemonistic criterion on the ground that any sort of pleasure is rated equally high on its scale so long as it is pleasure. "Pushpin as good as poetry!" seems to some the height of sarcasm. Socrates says in the Philebus, "Do we not say that the intemperate has pleasure, and that the temperate has pleasure in his very temperance, and that the fool is pleased when he is full of foolish fancies and hopes, and that the wise man has pleasure in his wisdom? And may not he be justly deemed a fool who says that these pairs of pleasures are respectively alike?"

Why, however, do we rate the pleasures of temperance and wisdom above those of intemperance and folly? Simply because of their respective EFFECTS. INTRINSICALLY they may be equally desirable, or the latter may even be keener pleasures? that depends upon the individual circumstances; but there is no question about their relative EXTRINSIC value. There is always "the devil to pay" for intemperance and folly; while temperance and wisdom lead to health, love, honor, achievement, and many another good. As to push- pin-or let us say baseball-VERSUS poetry, it is only prejudice that makes us say we rate the latter higher. Outdoor games are not only productive of a keener delight to most people, they are extrinsically good as well, conducing to health, quickness of wit, self-control, and other goods. They ARE, in their time and place, as good as poetry. The reason for the greater reverence we feel, or feel we ought to feel, for poetry lies in the fact that it takes much more mental cultivation to acquire the taste for it; the love of poetry is a sort of patrician distinction. It is also true that poetry opens up to its lover a much wider range of enjoyments; it opens his eyes to the beauty and significance and pathos in the world; it is immensely educative, and inspiring to the spiritual life. The love of broadening and inspiring things requires cultivation in most of us; so that we praise and honor such things and urge people toward them.

Pushpin, or baseball, NEEDS no apotheosis. But if we ever develop into a race of anaemic bookworms, we shall have to glorify sport and learn to shrug our shoulders at the soft and easy enjoyments of poetry. Nothing is more obvious than the utilitarian nature of such habitual judgments and attitudes.

One of the Platonic illustrations, often brought up, is that of the happy oyster. [Footnote: Philebus, 22. "Is such a life eligible?" asks Socrates. Later (40), he agrees that "a man must be admitted to have real pleasure who is pleased with anything or anyhow," but asks if it is not true that some pleasures are "false." Protarchus hits the nail on the head by replying, "No one would call pleasures bad because they are 'false,' but BY RASON OF SOME OTHER GREAT EVIL TO WHICH THEY ARE LIABLE," i.e, because of their after-effects.] Who would wish, however miserable, to exchange places with it! Are there not other things to be considered besides happiness? "It is better to be a Socrates dissatisfied than a fool satisfied." And why? In the first place, we suspect that the oyster's, or even the fool's, range of happiness is very limited. We should hesitate to forego such joys as we do have, even if sorrow attends them, at so great a sacrifice. In the second place, each of us has a deep-rooted love of his own personal memories and expectations; and except in cases of unusual depression of spirits few of us would wish to lose our identity and become some other person or thing even if we knew that other being to be happier. In the third place, a man knows HE could NOT be happier as an oyster; an oyster's joys (whatever they may be) would not satisfy him; he has other needs and desires. He must find happiness, if at all, in the satisfaction of his human cravings. The oyster's life, however satisfactory to the oyster, would leave him restless and bored. If you are a Socrates, you realize similarly that you could not FIND satisfaction in the fool's life. You know that although you have sorrows the fool wots not of, you also have a whole range of joys beyond his ken; and those joys are particularly precious to you. In the fourth place, the very words "oyster" and "fool" beg the question. "Fool" means by very definition a sort of person one would NOT choose to be; and the very visualization of an oyster is repellent. Were one to offer as the alternative a happy lion or eagle; or a happy, free- hearted savage such as Chateaubriand and Rousseau painted, one suspects that not a few suffering men and women would jump at the chance.

It is not really important to decide, however, what any one would choose. Our choices are biased and often foolish. The actual question is, Is the happiness of a fool, or of an oyster (if happiness it has) as worthy, as objectively desirable, as that of a wise man? And here again we have to say, not EXTRINSICALLY so desirable. The wise man is he who finds his happiness in activities that conduce to his ultimate welfare and that of others. The happiness of fool or oyster is transitory, blind, and fraught with unseen dangers; it is of no value to the community in which they live. But INTRINSICALLY, just qua happiness, it is-if it is-as good. What makes one form of happiness more worthy than another is simply, in the first place, its greater keenness or extent or freedom from pain, and in the second place its potentialities of future happiness or pain for self and others. When Mill wrote, therefore, in his classic treatise, that "some KINDS of pleasure are more desirable and valuable than others," he showed a-for him unusual-failure to analyze. Some kinds of PLEASURES are more desirable, for the reasons summarized above. But PLEASURE, in the abstract, pleasantness, agreeableness, intrinsic worth, whatever you choose to call it, is itself a quality; there can be more or less of it in a concrete experience, that is all. To speak of KINDS of pleasure is to mean KINDS OF EXPERIENCE which have the common attribute of pleasantness. In themselves all kinds of experience that are equally pleasant are equally worthy; there is no meaning to that adjective as applied to intrinsic immediate good. "Worthy" and "unworthy" apply to experience only when we begin to consider their consequences.

Is morality merely subjective and relative?

Different people find happiness in different ways; if morality is simply the means to happiness, is it not relative to their varying desires; is it not a purely subjective matter and without a fixed objective nature?

We must discriminate. Morality is not relative to our inclinations and desires, because those often do not rightly represent our own true welfare, still less the general welfare. Happiness is desirable whether our impulses are adjusted so as to aim for it or not. Nor is morality relative to our opinions; an act may be wrong though the whole world proclaim it right. It is a matter not of opinion but of fact whether an act is going to bring the greatest attainable welfare or not. However biased and shortsighted we may. be, the consequences of acts will be what they will be. In a very real sense, then, morality is objective; it is valid whether we recognize its validity and want it or not. It represents our needs more truly than our own wills, and thus has a greater authority, just as the rules of dietetics are not a matter of appetite or whim, but have a rational authority over our caprices. Morality is not, like imagination, something we can shape at will; it is imposed upon us from without, like sensation. Its development is predetermined by the structure of human nature and its environment; we do not invent it, we accept it. [Footnote: Cf. Cudworth (ca. 1688), Treatise, chap, n, sec. 3: "It is so far from being true that all moral good and evil, just and unjust, are mere arbitrary and factitious things, that are created wholly by will, that (if we would speak properly) we must needs say that nothing is morally good or evil, just or unjust, by mere will without nature, because everything is what it is by nature, and not by will." A good recent discussion bearing upon the question of the relativity of morality will be found in Santayana's Winds of Doctrine, pp. 138-154.] But although imposed upon our restive impulses, it is not imposed by any alien and arbitrary will. It is imposed by the same cosmos that set our consciousness into relation with a given kind of body in a given world. Submission to it is simply submission to the laws of our own natures. Lasting happiness can be found only in certain ways; we must make the best of it, but it is for our own good that we obey. Morality is relative to our organic needs and particular environment. It is a function of human nature, varying with its variations. A different race of beings on another planet might have to have a very radically different code. Ours is a distinctively human code, bearing the earmarks of our humanity and stamped with the particular nature of our earth-life.

To say this is to admit that morality varies with different temperaments and different needs. What is best for one person is not necessarily best for another; what is right for an early stage of civilization is not always right for a later. The patriarchal family was a source of strength in primitive society; today it would be a needless tyranny. Life in a tropical isle frees man from the necessity of many virtues which a more rigorous climate entails. The poet needs to live in a different way from the coal-heaver. Just so far as our individual and racial needs vary-our real needs, not our supposed needs and pathological desires (and always bearing in mind the needs of others)-just so far is what is right for one different from what is right for another. This is no condemnation of eudsemonistic morality. On the contrary, a clear recognition of this truth would happily relax the sometimes over-rigid conventions of society, its cut-and- dried- made-on-one-pattern code, and make it more elastic and suitable to individual needs.

However, we are not so different from one another as we are apt to think. The extenuation of sin on the plea that the "artistic temperament" demands this, or a "sensitive nature" needs that, is much overdone. Differences in temperament are superficial compared with the miles of underlying strata of plain human nature. "A man's a man for a' that," and must submit to the rules for human life. The man of "artistic temperament" does not know himself well enough. He feels superficial and transient cravings; he ignores his underlying needs, and the fundamental duties which, in common with all other men, he owes to his fellows.

The standard of morality is absolute and objective, then, for each individual, and approximately the same for all human beings. He is wise who seeks not to mould his life according to his longings, but who accepts the rules of the game and follows the paths blazed by the seers and doers before him. Only those individuals and those nations have achieved success that have been willing to learn and follow the ideals which life itself imposes, the eternal laws which religious men call the will of God.

For criticisms of the account of morality here defended: F. Paulsen, System of Ethics, book II, chap. II. J. Martineau, Types of Ethical Theory, book II, chaps, I, II. T. H. Green, Prolegomena to Ethics, book in, chap. I, first half, book IV, chap. III. Dewey and Tufts, Ethics, chap. XIV. J. S. Mackenzie, Manual of Ethics, 2d ed, chap. vi. H. Rashdall, Theory of Good and Evil, book I, chap, III; book II, chaps, I, II. W. Fite, Introductory Study of Ethics, part I. G. E. Moore, Ethics, chap. VII. In rebuttal of some of these arguments: J. S. Mill, Utilitarianism, chaps, II and IV. H. Spencer, Data of Ethics, chaps, IX, X. Leslie Stephen, Science of Ethics, chap. X.

CHAPTER XIII
ALTERNATIVE THEORIES

AFTER this summary answer to the commoner objections to our account of morality, we should notice a few of the more persistently recurrent formulas that seem inconsistent with this explanation of its fundamental nature.

Is morality "categorical," beyond need of justification?

To Kant and his followers, as well as to many less philosophical minds, the justification of morality by its utility has seemed unworthy. Morality is much more ultimate and imperious. The pursuit of happiness is not binding; morality is. The way to attain happiness is dubious and variable; the commandments of morality are clear-cut and certain. Different people find happiness in different activities; the laws of morality are universal and changeless. Morality, therefore, is prior to the pursuit of happiness; its dictates are known by an independent faculty. There is in us all an unanalyzable and unavoidable "ought"; ours not to reason why; ours but to do-and die, if need be. Morality is not a means to employ IF we wish happiness; in that case its precepts would be but hypothetical, if you wish happiness, do so and so. No, its commands are categorical. The inescapable fact of "oughtness" is the bottom fact upon which our ethics must be built. To the truth in this manner of speech we must all respond. As we have seen, morality is not purely subjective and relative; it carries the authority not of opinion but of fact. The right, the best way, IS unconditionally best, whether we are wise enough to desire it or no. The greatest good IS the greatest good, however narrow or short- sighted our impulses. Kant expresses eloquently the absolute and inescapable nature of duty in its perennial opposition to our transitory and nickering desires.

(1) But Kant is unfair in his picturesque contrast between the perplexities attending the pursuit of happiness and the certainty attachable to morality. As a matter of observation, moral codes have varied quite as much as man's different ways of finding happiness. Cases of moral perplexity are as common as cases of uncertainty with regard to the road to happiness; there is no such universality and changelessness about morality as he assumes. If a certain code seems fixed and indubitable to us, it is in large degree because we have become accustomed to it and given it our allegiance; a wider acquaintance with other codes, contemporary or past, would shake our confidence. Some fundamental rules are unquestionable-rules against

murder, rape, etc.; but just as unquestionable is the fact that these acts make against human happiness.

(2) Only a man with an Hebraic training and rigoristic temper could think of morality in this awestruck and unquestioning way. More Bohemian people feel no such "categorical ought" in their breasts. And if a man feels no such "categorical imperative," how can you prove to him it is there? Kant's theory is at bottom mere assertion; if because of your training and temperament you respond to it, and if you are content not to analyze and explain the existence of this imperious pressure upon your will, you are tremendously impressed. Otherwise the whole elaborate Kantian system probably seems to you an unreal brain-spun structure.

Kant, though a man of extraordinary mental powers, had but a narrow range of experience to base his theories upon, and lived too early to catch the genetic viewpoint. Hence there is a certain pedantic naivete in his constructions. No man with any modern psychological or historical training ought to be content to leave this extraordinary "categorical imperative" unexplained. It is quite possible to trace its origin and understand its function; there is nothing unique or mysterious about it. Why should we bow down to a command shot at us out of the air, a command irrelevant to our actual interests? Children have to do so, and the majority of the human race are still children, who may properly acquiesce in the rules of morality without clearly realizing why. But the reflective man should not be content to yield himself to the yoke unless he can see its necessity and value. The "ought," the knowledge of what is right, antedates the individual's experience of what is best, and so seems mysterious and a priori to him; but it does not antedate the racial experience; it is rather its fruit. The teleology of conscience is very simple, and its genesis and development purely natural.

(3) The "ought" seems more objective than "conscience," more impersonal. Just so does "beauty" seem more impersonal and objective than our pleasure in contemplating nature and art. It is a constant tendency of the mind to project its values out of itself; to create "universes of discourse" that seem more stable and real than its own fleeting states. All that exists psychologically is a sense of pleasure at looking at certain combinations of outer objects; but that pleasure is constantly evoked by that peculiar combination, both in our own mind and in others'. So we objectify that pleasure and call it the "beauty" of the object. Similarly, all that exists psychologically is a certain felt pressure, certain emotions and ideas and pushes whose teleology is not realized. But we objectify that constantly and pretty universally felt pressure and think of an impersonal, objective "ought." All the arts are expressible in "oughts"; and if there is a more authoritative and categorical nature to moral laws than there is, for example,

to the aesthetic laws that art-study reveals, it is because aesthetics deals with only one aspect of human good and ethics with its totality. Indeed, every impulse is, in its initial push, categorical, offering no reasons, simply pressing upon us with its requirements. Hunger and thirst and sex-desire do not say to us, "If you desire to be happy, eat, drink, and gratify your passion"; they call to us with an imperious and immediate demand. The demand of the moral law is more insistent and more authoritative simply because it represents a far more widespread and lasting need.

(4) Kant's "categorical imperative" is purely formal and empty. We OUGHT, we OUGHT-but what? It leads, if to anything, to a mere emotional reinforcement of our preexisting moral conceptions, to that canonization of good will as the one and only good, which is Kant's own position, but which we have found inadequate and misleading. When we come to new situations it has no clue to offer. How do we actually decide in such cases? By imagining the consequences of acts and seeing their relative productiveness of happiness and pain. Or else by finding some already decided case under which we can put the new instance. We are tempted to an act that promises profit, but something checks us. Ought we to do this? Gradually it comes over us that this would be stealing; and stealing we have already decided, or the race has decided for us, is wrong.

We have to decide things in terms of our welfare, or of those already stereotyped decisions which represent the half-conscious strivings of past generations for human welfare. There is no other way; the conception of an imperious impersonal "ought" bearing ruthlessly down upon us gives no help whatsoever.

A later and English expression of the feeling that morality needs no justification may be found in Bradley's ETHICAL STUDIES. [Footnote: Pages 56-57.] "To take virtue as a mere means to an ulterior end is in direct antagonism to the voice of moral consciousness. That consciousness, when unwarped by selfishness and not blinded by sophistry, is convinced that to ask for the Why is simple immorality; to do good for its own sake is virtue, to do it for some ulterior end or object...is never virtue...Virtue not only does seem to be, but is, an end in itself. Against the base mechanical which meets us on all sides, with its 'What is the use' of goodness, or beauty, or truth, there is but one fitting answer from the friends of science, or art, or religion and virtue, 'We do not know and we do not care.'"

(1) But morality would then be a mere arbitrary tyranny; if it were of no use, the sacrifices it demands would be sheer cruelty. A moral law irrelevant to human interests would have no possible authority over us; it would not be a moral, i.e,. a right, law for us.

(2) And what criterion should we have to judge what is virtuous? "Virtue for virtue's sake" is equivalent to "the best way because it is the best way." But what makes it the best way? And how shall we decide what is the best way?

(3) We must be blind not to see the use of morality, even if we feel that usefulness degrades it. All moralists agree that virtue does actually lead to happiness. But is that connection a mere accident? Is it not likely that the usefulness of virtue has something to do with its origin and existence?

(4) A real practical value of the motto "Virtue for virtue's sake" lies in the implied rejection of virtue for INDIVIDUAL profit merely. The moralist rightly feels that such proverbs as "Honesty is the best policy," "Ill-gotten gains do not prosper," do not strike deep enough. Even if ill-gotten gain should prosper, it would be wrong. But it would be wrong simply because of the damage to others' welfare, not for any transcendental reason. The opponent of the eudaemonistic account of morality nearly always identifies it with a selfish pursuit, by each individual, of his own personal happiness. But that is, of course, a very narrow and unjustifiable interpretation of it.

(5) Another practical value of the motto lies in the implied contrast of virtue with expediency. Questions of expediency are questions of the best means to a given end; questions of virtue ask which ends are to be sought. Expediency asks, "How shall I do this?" Virtue asks, "Shall I do this or that?" The counsels of expediency are thus always relative to the value of the end, in itself unquestioned; "this is the thing to do IF such and such an end is right to seek." The counsels of virtue are absolute-"This is the best thing to do." It is rightly felt that in matters of right and wrong there is no "if" about it; you act not with relation to an end which may be chosen or rejected, on ulterior grounds. The only end to which virtue is the means is-the living of the best life. Virtue is the ultimate expediency. But it is well contrasted with all those secondary matters of debate for which we reserve the name "expediency."

(6) Finally, the motto is practically useful in advising us not to rely upon calculation in the concrete emergency, but to fall back upon an already adopted code, to love virtue as one does the flag, and follow it unquestioningly, as the soldier does his general. We must be willing to accept guidance and leadership. But every one knows that the flag is but a symbol; that the general's word is authoritative because it serves the best interests of the country. And our impulsive allegiance to virtue, and love of it, would be a mere silly daydream and empty sacrifice were it not for its loyal safeguarding of human interests.

Should we live "according to nature," and adjust ourselves to the evolutionary process?

According to the Stoic philosophy, the criterion for conduct was to live "according to nature." "What is meant by 'rationally'?" asks Epictetus, and answers, "Conformably to nature." "Convince me that you acted naturally, and I will convince you that everything which takes place according to nature takes place rightly." [Footnote: Book III, chap, I; book I, chap. XI.] And Marcus Aurelius writes, "Do not think any word or action beneath you which is in accordance with nature; and never be misled by the apprehension of censure or reproach. I will march on in the path of nature till my legs sink under me. Philosophy will put you upon nothing but what your nature wishes and calls for." [Footnote: Book V.] Of this preaching Bishop Butler says that it is "a manner of speaking, not loose and indeterminate, but clear and distinct, strictly just and true." [Footnote: Preface to Sermons.] In modern times this doctrine has taken the form of exhortation to take our place in the evolutionary process. It is thought by some that to grasp the trend of existing natural forces is to know the direction of duty. We have only to keep in the current, to espouse heartily the "struggle for existence" and rejoice in the "survival of the fittest," because it is nature's way. In a recent book by a Harvard professor we read, "Whatever the order of the universe is, that is the moral order…The laws of natural selection are merely God's regular methods of expressing his choice and approval. The naturally selected are the chosen of God…The whole life of [moral] people will consist in an intelligent effort to adjust themselves to the will thus expressed." [Footnote: T. N. Carver, The Religion Worth Having, pp. 84-89.] It is easy enough to point out, however, that nature man to follow. "In sober truth, nearly all the things which men are hanged or imprisoned for doing to one another, are nature's everyday performances. Nature impales men, breaks them as if on the wheel, casts them to be devoured by wild beasts, crushes them with stones like the first Christian martyr, starves them with hunger, freezes them with cold, poisons them by the quick or slow venom of her exhalations." [Footnote: J. S. Mill, Three Essays on Religion: "Nature," p. 28.] The evolutionary process is cruel and merciless; multitudes perish for every one that survives, and the survivor is not the most deserving, but the strongest or swiftest or cleverest. Why should we imitate such ruthless ways? Nature is to be not followed but improved upon. Not only morality, but most of man's activity, consists in making nature over to suit his needs. "If nature and man are both the works of a Being of perfect goodness, that Being intended nature as a scheme to be amended, not imitated, by man." [Footnote: Ibid, p. 41.]

(2) Not only is there no reason WHY we should "follow nature," but the result of so doing would be any thing but what we agree is moral. Hardly a sin is committed but was "natural" to the sinner. It is "natural" to lose our tempers; to be vain, selfish, greedy, lustful. Nothing could be practically more pernicious than the idea that an impulse is right because it is natural;

that is, because it is common to most men. "Following nature" naturally means following our inclinations; nothing is more disastrous. Virtue necessitates self denial, effort, living by ideals, which are late and artificial products. It is actually true, in its metaphorical way, that we need to be born again, to be turned about, converted, saved from ourselves. The "natural" man is the "carnal" man; the "spiritual" man, while potential in us all, needs to be fostered and stimulated by every possible means if life is to be serene and full and beautiful. The difference between the "natural" man and the moral man is the difference between the untrained child, capricious, the victim of a thousand whims and longings, and the man of formed character whom we respect and trust. Morality is, of course, in a sense, natural too-everything that exists is natural; but in the sense in which the word has a specific meaning, it is flatly opposed to that making-over, that readjustment of our impulses, which is the very differentia of morality. There is, indeed, a eulogistic sense of the word "natural"; to Rousseau the "return to nature" meant the abandonment of needless artificiality and silly convention. But except in this sense, what is "natural" has no particular merit. The great achievements of man have consisted not in following natural, primitive instincts, but in controlling and disciplining those instincts.

If we were to imitate nature in making the survival of the fittest our aim, we should return to the barbaric ruthlessness of ancient Sparta or Rome, exposing infants, killing the feeble and insane, and becoming just such cold-blooded pursuers of efficiency as Nietzsche admires. That such pitiless competition is moral, or desirable, no one but a few cranks would on examination maintain. "Let us understand once for all," says Huxley," that the ethical progress of society depends not on imitating the cosmic process, still less in running away from it, but in combating it." [Footnote: Evolution and Ethics, title essay.]

(3) This cosmic defiance of Huxley's commands our approval; if morality interferes with the evolutionary process, let it interfere; the sooner an immoral process is stopped the better. But, after all, Huxley unnecessarily limits the meaning of the phrase "the cosmic process," applying it only to that stage which antedates the development of morality. That development, however, is itself natural selection, which in its earlier stages selects merely the strong and swift and clever, in its later stages selects also the moral races and individuals. So that to follow out the evolutionary process is, for man, after all, to follow morality as well as to cultivate speed and strength and wit.

There is, indeed, a danger to the race from the development of the tenderer side of morality, in the care for the feeble and degenerate which permits them to live and produce offspring, instead of being ruthlessly exterminated, as in ruder days. But this danger can, and will, be met by measures which, while permitting life and, so far as possible, happiness, to these unfortunates, will prevent them from having children. Except for this removable danger, the development of sympathy and tenderness by no means involves a lessening of virility, but is rather its necessary complement and check.

Is self-development or self-realization the ultimate end?

It is no justification of morality to say that it is "in harmony with nature." Is it an adequate justification to say that morality is what makes for self-development or self-realization? A number of classic and contemporary moralists, fighting shy of the acknowledgment of happiness as the ultimate end, have rested content with such expressions. Darwin wrote, "The term 'general good' may be defined as the rearing of the greatest number of individuals in full vigor and health, with all their faculties perfect, under the conditions to which they are subjected." [Footnote: Descent of Man, chap, iv.] Paulsen writes, "The value of virtue consists in its favorable effects upon the development of life…The value of life consists in the normal performance of all functions, or in the exercise of capacities and virtues…A perfect human life is an end in itself. The standard is what has been called the normal type, or the idea, of human life." [Footnote: System of Ethics, book II, chap. II.]

(1) Such a point of view gives opportunity for stimulating words. But it gives no guidance. Observation can teach us, slowly, what conduct makes for happiness; but what conduct makes for "self-development"? The fact is, the cultivation of any impulse will develop us in its direction and preclude our development in other directions; along which path shall we let ourselves develop? Every choice involves rejection; infinite possibilities diverge before us; which among the myriad impulses that call upon us shall we follow? While still young and plastic, we may develop ourselves into poets or philosophers or lawyers or businessmen. In which of these ways shall we "realize" ourselves? [Footnote: Cf. William James, Psychology, vol. I, p. 309: "I am often confronted by the necessity of standing by one of my empirical selves and relinquishing the rest. Not that I would not, if I could, be both handsome and fat and well dressed, and a great athlete, and make a million a year, be a wit, a bon-vivant, and a lady-killer, as well as a philosopher; a philanthropist, statesman, warrior, and African explorer, as well as a 'tone-poet' and saint. But the thing is simply impossible. The millionaire's work would run counter to the saint's; the bon vivant and the philanthropist would trip each other up; the philosopher and the lady-killer could not well keep house in the same tenement of clay. Such different characters may conceivably at the outset of life be alike possible to a man. But to make any one of them actual, the rest must more or less be suppressed."] It is evident that we need some deeper ground of choice. May

it not even be better drastically to choke our natures, better to get a new nature than to realize the old? Surely there are perverted natures, which ought not to be developed. In the name of happiness we can decide on development or non-development, as the need may be. But the ideal of "self development" gives us no criterion. It is too sweeping, too indiscriminate.

(2) Again, we may ask WHY we should develop ourselves. This ideal is in need of justification to the has a eulogistic connotation in our ears; but to rely upon that is to beg the question. Strictly, it means only the actualizing of potentiality, which may be potentiality for evil as well as for good. Concretely, if developing our natures led to pain and sorrow we should do well to resist such development. The plausibility of the formula lies in the fact that the development of one's self along any line is normally pleasant and normally conduces to ultimate happiness. The idea of it attracts us, and it is well that it should; it is intrinsically and extrinsically good. But it is the fact of possessing that intrinsic and extrinsic goodness that makes it a legitimate ideal. In sum, it is good to develop one's powers only because and in so far as such development makes for happiness or is itself an aspect of happiness. For happiness is the only sort of thing that is in itself intrinsically and obviously desirable, without need of proof.

(3) Practically, this ideal-tends to selfishness; it does not point to the fact that the best development of self lies in service. The ideal is capable of this interpretation, but its emphasis is in the wrong direction. It is essentially a pagan conception, and practically inferior to the Christian ideal of service. Service cannot be the ultimate ideal, any more than the Chinese in the story could support themselves by taking in one another's washing; and it needs to be justified, like self-development, by the happiness it brings. But for a working conception it is far better. Self-realization has never been the aim of the saints and heroes. Imagine a patriot dying for his country's freedom, or a mother giving years of sacrificing toil for her child, on the ground of self-development! The patriot may feel that through his sacrifice and that of his comrades his countrymen will be freer or more united or rid of some curse i.e., ultimately, happier. The mother thinks consciously of the happiness of the child she serves. But except for the young man or properly be for the time self-centered, self-development makes but a sorry ideal. We may admire a Goethe who cares primarily for the development and perfection of his own powers-if he is handsome and clever and of a winning personality. But the men we really love and reverence are those who forget themselves and prefer to go, if necessary, with their artistic sense undeveloped or their scientific sense untrained, so they may bring help and peace to their fellows. [Footnote: Cf. a recent story writer, Nalbro Hartley, in Ainslee's (a mountain-white is speaking): "I reckon the best way

to get on in this world is to learn just enough to make you all always want to know more but to be so busy usin' what you-all has learned that there ain't no time to learn the rest!"] Goethe, with all his genius, encyclopedic knowledge, and universality of experience, his wit and energy and power of expression, stands on a lower moral level than Buddha, St. Francis, Christ.

(4) Finally, the theory, if taken strictly, is immoral. To set up self- realization as the criterion is to say that the self-realizing act is to be chosen EVEN IF IT SHOULD PRODUCE LESS THAN THE GREATEST ATTAINABLE TOTAL GOOD. That such cases do not occur, no one can prove; in fact, observation tends to the belief that they do. This criterion is, then, not only practically but theoretically selfish. Perfection of character should be our aim, yes. But perfection of character is not to be found in a mere indiscriminate cultivation of whatever faculties we may have. It means the superposition of a severe discipline upon our faculties, a purification of the will, directed by more ultimate considerations. Is the source of duty the will of God? "Obedience to the will of God" describes the highest morality, as does the phrase "perfection of character." But is it, any more than that, the ULTIMATE JUSTIFICATION of morality? Is the will of God the SOURCE of morality? An adequate discussion of this question would involve a philosophy of religion, but a few considerations may be useful, and it is hoped, not misleading.

(1) How can we know what is the will of God except by considering what makes for human welfare? Our Bible is but one of a number of holy books which are held to be a revelation of God's will. Even if we grant the superior authority of the Hebrew- Christian Bible, can we rely on its teachings implicitly? How do we know that it is a revelation of God except by our experience of the beneficence of its teachings? As a matter of fact, there is wide disagreement, among those who accept the Bible as authoritative, over its real teachings. A text is available for every variety of belief. Christians usually emphasize those texts that make for what they hold true, and slur over others. "Look not on the wine when it is red" is preached in every Sunday School, while "Take a little wine for thy stomach's sake" is seldom quoted save by brewers. The Bible, the work of a hundred hands during a span of a thousand years, represents a great variety of views. It is certainly an inspired book if there ever was one; so much inspiration could not have come from it if none had gone into it. But to extract a satisfactory ethical code from it is possible only by a process of judicious selection and ingenious inference. The Mosaic code is held by Christians to be now abrogated; the recorded teachings of Christ are fragmentary and touch only a few fundamental matters. How, for example, shall we ascertain from the Bible the will of God with respect to the trust problem, or currency reform, or penal legislation? Times have changed, our

problems are no longer those of the ancient Jews; a hundred delicate questions arise to which no answers can be will of God to be clearly and unquestionably known, why should we obey it? Because he is stronger, and can reward or punish? If that is the reason, the freehearted man would defy Him. Might does not make right. If God were to command us to sin, it would not be right to obey Him. On the contrary, we should sympathize with Mill in his outburst: "Whatever power such a being may have over me, there is one thing which he shall not do: he shall not compel me to worship him. I will call no being good, who is not what I mean when I apply that epithet to my fellow creatures; and if such a being can sentence me to hell for not so calling him, to hell I will go." [Footnote: An Examination of Sir William Hamilton's Philosophy, chap. VI.] It is clear that God is to be obeyed only because He is good and his will right. Not the existence of a will, but its goodness makes it authoritative. But how do we know that it is good unless we have some deeper criterion to judge it by? How do we know that God is not an arbitrary tyrant? The answer must be that we judge the Christian teachings to be a revelation of God because we know on other grounds what we mean by "right" and "good," and see that these teachings fit that conception. If the teachings were coarse and low, no prodigies or miracles would suffice to attest them as God-given; it would be superstition to obey them. Experience alone can be judge; the experience of the beneficence of the Christian ideal. The Way of Life that Christ taught verifies itself when tried; that it is the supreme ideal for man is proved by the transfiguration of life it effects. Christ and the Bible deserve our allegiance because they are worthy of it; from them we can learn the secrets of man's true welfare. Morality is, indeed, older than religion. It develops to a certain point, and in some cases very highly, without the concept of God. It has an and needs no supernatural prop. Religion is not the root of morality, but its flower and consummation. The finest ideals, the loftiest heights of morality, merge into religion; but even these spiritual ideals have their ultimate root in the common soil of human welfare, and are rational ideals because they minister to human need.

For the "categorical" theory of morality, see Kant's Theory of Ethics, trans. Abbott; F. H. Bradley, Ethical Studies; F. Paulsen, System of Ethics, book II, chap, V, secs. 3 and 4; Dewey and Tufts, Ethics, chap, XVI, sec. 2; H. Spencer, Data of Ethics, chap, III, sees. 12, 13. W. Fite, Introductory Study of Ethics, chap. X. H. Rashdall, Theory of Good and Evil, book I, chap. V. For the "according to nature" theory, see Epictetus and Marcus Aurelius, passim; Rousseau, Discourse on Science and Art, etc.; J. S. Mill, "Nature" in Three Essays on Religion; T.H. Huxley, Evolution and Ethics. T. N. Carver, The Religion Worth Having. For the "self-realization" theory, see T. H. Green, Prolegomena to Ethics; F. Paulsen, op. cit, esp. book II, chap, II, secs. 5-8; H. W. Wright, Self-Realization; J. S. Mackenzie, Manual of

Ethics, 2d ed, chaps, VI and VII. W. Fite, op. cit, chap. XI. For theological ethics, see any of the older theological books. A brief comment may be found in H. Spencer's Data of Ethics, chap, IV, sec. 18.

CHAPTER XIV
THE WORTH OF MORALITY

BEFORE proceeding to a more concrete unfolding of the difficulties and problems of morality, it will be well to formulate our theory in terms of modern biology, and then, finally, to answer those modern critics who reject not merely the rational explanation of morality but morality itself.

Morality as the organization of human interests.

The worth of morality is most commonly defended today, in biological terms, by describing it as a synthesis of human interests; it is valuable because it is what we really want and need. It does, indeed, forbid the carrying-out of any impulse which renders impossible greater goods; it flatly opposes that unrestrained satisfying of a part of our natures which we call self-indulgence, or of one nature at the expense of others which we call selfishness. But it stifles desire only for a greater ultimate good; it rejects that needless repression of a part of the self which we call asceticism, and an undue subordination of self to others. It is, then the organizing or harmonizing principle, subordinating the interests of each aspect of the self, and of the many conflicting selves, to the total welfare of the individual and of the community. As Plato pointed out, [Footnote: Republic, books. I-IV; e.g. (444): "Is not the creation of righteousness the creation of a natural order and government of one another in the parts of the soul, and the creation of unrighteousness the opposite?" and (352): "Is not unrighteousness equally suicidal when existing in an individual [as it is when it exists in the State], rendering him incapable of action because he is not at unity with himself, making him an enemy to himself?" and (443): "The righteous man does not permit the several elements within him to meddle with one another, or any of them to do the work of others; but he sets in order his own inner life, and is his own master, and at peace with himself; and when ... he is no longer many, but has become one entirely temperate and perfectly adjusted nature, then he will think and call right and good action that which preserves and cooperates with this condition." (In quoting Plato I have used Jowett's translation, with an occasional substitution; as, above, in the use of "righteousness" and "right" instead of "justice" and "just.")] representative of all other interests, the consensus of interest. Such a definition, we must admit, happily describes morality, showing us that if we would find its leading we must know ourselves; we must examine our actual existing needs and consider how best to attain them. The direction of morality is that of a carefully pruned and weeded human nature. But there are certain dangers inherent in this form of definition which we must note:

(1) We must not be satisfied with the synthesis of consciously felt desires. Many of our deepest needs fail to come to the surface and embody themselves in impulses; we do not know or seek what is really best for ourselves. There are possibilities of harmony and peace upon low levels. We must be pricked into desire for new forms of life and not allowed to stagnate in a condition which, however well organized and contented, is lacking in the richness and joy we might attain. We must include in the "interests" to be organized all our dumb and unrealized needs, all potential and latent impulses, as well as our articulate desires.

(2) On the other hand, there are perverse and pathological impulses which are deserving of no regard and must be simply cast aside in the organizing process, because they lead only to unhappiness. There is a difference between the desirable and the desired; morality is not merely an organizing but a corrective force, bringing sometimes not peace but a sword. A truer figure would be to represent it as a flowers and ruthlessly pruning or weeding out others, that the garden may be the most beautiful place.

(3) Moreover, this definition, while an excellent DESCRIPTIONTION of what morality in general is, is not a JUSTIFICATION of morality, does not point to its ultimate raison d'etre. To all this organizing activity we might say, Cui bono, for what good? WHY should we organize our interests; why not deny them like the ascetics? The mere existence of pushes, in this direction and that, affords no material for moral judgment; a harmonizing of them would make a mathematical resultant, but it would be of no superior WORTH. If there were no pleasure and pain in life, it would not MATTER in the least whether the various life forces were organized or not. In such a colorless world a unison of human impulses would be as morally indifferent as the convergence of tributary rivers or the formation of an organized solar system. It is only, as we long ago pointed out, [Footnote: Cf. ante, p. 74] when consciousness differentiates into its plus and minus values, pleasure and pain, that a reason arises why any forces in the cosmos should be thwarted or allowed free play. With the emergence of those values, however, everything that affects them becomes significant. If the complete transformation of our interests would make human life brighter, fuller of plus values, such a radical alteration, rather than a harmonization, would be our ideal. As it is, desire points normally toward the really desirable; the direction of human welfare lies, in general, along the line of our organic needs, of the avoidance of clashes, of the mutual subordination and cooperation of natural impulses. The principle of reason, of intelligence, is necessary in morality to find this way of cooperation, this ultimate drift of need; but without the potentiality of happiness chaos

would be as good as order, both within the individual soul and within the social group. [Footnote: Plato realized this, and in the Philebus points out that we cannot completely describe morality either in terms of pleasure-pain or in terms of reason (or wisdom), the organizing principle. Both aspects of morality are important. Cf, along this line, H. G. Lord, The Abuse of Abstraction in Ethics, in the James memorial volume.] Do moral acts always bring happiness somewhere? The ultimate justification of morality the value of synthesizing our interests, lies in the happiness men thereby attain. But there is one fundamental doubt that ever and anon recurs the doubt whether, after all, actions that we agree in calling virtuous always BRING happiness. If not, either our definition of morality, or our universal judgment as to what is moral, would seem to be in error. Perhaps morality is, after all, off the track, and to be discarded.

(1) We must first lay aside cases of perverted conscience, acts which are "subjectively moral," or conscientious, but not objectively best. These cases we have already glanced at; they need be no stumbling block.

(2) We must remember that the types of conduct which we have glorified by the concepts "virtue," "duty," etc, are those which TEND to produce happiness. We have to frame our judgments and pigeonhole acts according to their normal results. But it happens not infrequently that accidents upset these natural tendencies. For these unforeseeable eventualities the actor is not responsible; if his act was the best that could have been planned, in consideration of all known factors, it remains the ideal for future cases, it still retains the halo of "virtue" which must attract others to it. Good acts may lead, by unexpected chance, to evil consequences; bad acts may result, by some accident, in good. But to the interfering factor belongs the credit or blame; the act that would normally have led to good or to evil remains right or wrong. To rescue a drowning man is right, for such action normally tends to human welfare; if the rescued man turns out a great criminal, or escapes this death to suffer a worse, the act of rescuing the drowning remains a desirable and therefore moral act. On the other hand, if one man slanders another, with the result that the latter, refuting the slander, thereby attains prominence and position, the act of slander, normally harmful, remains an immoral act.

It is a failure to recognize this necessarily general character of our moral judgments that raises the problem of Job. The ancient Israelites saw clearly that righteousness was the road to happiness; [Footnote: Cf. for example, "Righteousness tendeth to life; he that pursueth evil pursueth it to his own death." "Blessed is every one that feareth the Lord, that walketh in his ways. Happy shalt thou be, and it shall be well with thee."] and when a righteous man like Job fell into misfortune, they accused him of secret sin. Job is conscious of his innocence, of having done his part aright, and cannot understand how he has come to such an evil pass. It would have brought him no material alleviation, but it might have saved him some mental chafing, to recognize that morality is simply doing our part. When we have done our best we are still at the mercy of fortune. Happiness, as Aristotle pointed out, is the result of two cooperating factors, morality and good fortune. [Footnote: Nichomachean Ethics, book I, several places: e.g, in chap. VII, "To constitute happiness there must be, as we have said, complete virtue and fit external conditions."] If either is lacking, evil will ensue. If all men were perfectly virtuous, we should still be at the mercy of flood and lightning, poisonous snakes, icebergs and fog at sea, a thousand forms of accident and disease, old age and death. The millennium will not bring pure happiness to man; he is too feeble a creature in the presence of forces with which he cannot cope. Morality is just-the best man can do; and it is not to be blamed for the twists of fate that make futile its efforts. (3) Are there not, however, cases where conduct which we agree is right is not even likely to bring the greatest happiness attainable; where not only immediate but lasting happiness is to be deliberately sacrificed in the name of morality? Suppose, for example, a politician who becomes convinced of the evils of the liquor trade ruins his career in a hopeless fight against the saloons. He loses his office, his income, his honor in the sight of his associates; he brings suffering upon his innocent wife and children; and all for no good, since his fight is futile and ineffective. Surely any one could foresee that such action would make only for unhappiness, or for no happiness commensurable with the sacrifice. Yet if we agree with his premise, that the liquor trade is a curse to humanity, we deem his conduct not only conscientious but objectively noble and right. How can we justify that judgment?

In the first place, we cannot be sure, beforehand, that such a fight will not be successful. Forlorn hopes sometimes win. We must encourage men to venture, to take chances; only so can the great evils that ride mankind be banished. If there is a fighting chance of accomplishing a great good it is contemptible not to try; society must maintain a code that leads at times to quixotic acts.

In the second place, the fight, even if in itself hopeless, is sure to have valuable indirect results. It arouses others to the need; it stimulates in others the willingness to sacrifice self-interest and work for the general good. Every such honorable defeat has its share in the final victory. The subtle benefits that result from such moral gallantry are not evident on the surface, but they are there. No push for the right is wholly wasted. It pays mankind to let its heroes lavish their lives in apparently ineffective struggles; through their example the apathetic masses are stirred and moved a little farther toward their goal.

In general, we may say that the belief that virtue is not the right road to happiness betrays inexperience and immaturity of judgment. A moderate degree of morality saves man from many pitfalls into which his unrestrained impulses would lead him. The highest levels of morality bring a degree of happiness unknown to the "natural man." Who are the happiest people in the world? The saints; those who are inwardly at peace, who play their part with absolute loyalty. Even the irremediable misfortunes of life do not affect them as they do the worldly man; they have "learned the luxury of doing good." Of morality a recent writer says, "Its distribution of felicity is ideally just. To him who is most unselfish, who sinks most thoroughly his own interests in those of the race of which he is a unit, it awards the most complete beatitude." [Footnote: J. H. Levy, of London, in a funeral oration.] To him who complains that he is moral but not happy, the answer is, Be more moral! A high enough morality, a complete enough consecration, will lead, in all but very abnormal cases, to happiness in the individual life, as well as make its due contribution to the happiness of others.

Is there anything better than morality?

It is this lack of vision, this immature skepticism as to the service of morality to human welfare, that has fired a flame of revolt in certain minds, a revolt not merely against incidental defects and outworn conceptions of morality, but against morality uberhaupt. The declamations of these Promethean rebels make it clear, however, that their protest is but the old fault of condemning a necessary institution altogether for its imperfections or its abuses. Morality has been blended with superstition and tyranny, has been often blind, perverted, narrow, checking noble impulses and choking the rich and happy development of life. But it is one thing to arraign these accidents and corruptions of morality; it is quite another to discard the whole system of guidance of which they are but the excrescences and mistakes. This usurping is, of course, also in large part a thirst for novelty, a love of paradox, of practicing ingenuity in making the better appear the worse; it is in part a volcanic eruption of suppressed longings and a protest against the inadequacy of our present code to provide opportunity and happiness for the masses. The motives vary with the individual rebels.

It must suffice, however, from among the many leaders of this revolt, to quote that clever but unbalanced German iconoclast, Nietzsche. Typical of his doctrine is the following: [Footnote: Genealogy of Morals (ed. Alex. Tille), Foreword, p. 9.] "Never until now was there the least doubt or hesitation to set down the 'good' man as of higher value than the 'evil' man- of higher value in the sense of furtherance, utility, prosperity, as regards MAN in general (the future of man included). What if the reverse were true? What if in, the 'good' one also a symptom of decline were contained, and a danger, a seduction, a poison, a narcotic by which the present might live AT THE EXPENSE OF THE FUTURE? Perhaps more comfortably, less dangerously, but also in humbler style- more meanly? So that just morality were to blame, if a HIGHEST MIGHTINESS AND SPLENDOR of type of man-possible in itself were never attained? And that, therefore, morality itself would be the danger of dangers?"

The point of this tirade is that morality puts a wet blanket over human powers; it is a bourgeois ideal, saving men, indeed, from pain, but also robbing life of its picturesqueness and glory. Many people frankly prefer "interesting" to "good" people; Nietzsche generalizes this feeling. Morality is to him uninteresting, dull, a code for slaves, for the clash of combat, the tang of cruelty and lust, the tingle of unrestrained power. Every man for himself then, and the Devil take the hindmost. Shocked as we are by this brutal platform, there is something in it that appeals to the red blood and adventurous spirit in us; after all, we are not far removed from the savage, and the thought of a psalm-singing, tea-drinking, tamely good world is abhorrent to the marrow of us. Stevenson, with his delightfully irresponsible audacity, sighs for an occasional "furlough from the moral law"; and there are times for most of us when it seems as if we should choke and smother under the everlasting "Thou shalt not!" But the daring rebel, the defiant Titan, comes creeping back to the shelter of morality with a headache or something worse, and discovers that his Promethean boldness was but childish petulance; that it is futile and foolish to try to escape the inexorable laws of human life. There are, in fact, two adequate answers that can be made to the despiser of morality:

(1) Dull or not, repressive or not, morality is absolutely necessary. It is better than the pain, the insecurity, the relapse into barbarism, that immorality implies. Our whole civilization, everything that makes human life better than that of the beasts of prey, would collapse without its foundation of moral obedience. The regime of slashing individualism would kill off many of the weaker who are precious to humanity-a Homer (if he was blind), a Keats, a Stevenson; nay, if carried to extreme, it would put an end to the race. For who are the weakest, the "hindmost," but the babies! Sympathy and love and self sacrifice, at least in parents, are necessary if the race is to endure a generation. But even for the individual, the penalties of immorality are too obvious to need recapitulation. If morality is repression, it is the minimal repression consistent with the maintenance of successful and happy life. Its real aim is to bring life, and life more abundantly.

(2) But if we are looking for something great, for adventure and excitement and battle against odds, we can find it much better than in brutally slashing at our fellows, or running amuck at the beck of our impulses, by putting our valor at the service of some really great human endeavor. If we want to

get into the big game, the great adventure, we must pit ourselves, with the leaders of mankind, against the hostile universe. The men and women who set our blood tingling and our hearts beating fastest are-Darwin, discoverer by patient labor of a great cosmic law; Pasteur, conqueror at last over a terrible human disease; Peary, first to plant foot upon the axis of the world; Goethals, builder of a canal that links the oceans. The steady march of a moralized civilization, presenting united front to the cosmos, is infinitely more glorious than the futile, aimless, and petty struggles of an anarchic immorality. Our half-disciplined life is already far richer and more romantic than the life of Nietzsche's "supermen" could be; and we are only a little way along the road of moral progress. The real superman will be a BETTER man, a man of tenderness and chivalry, of loyalty and self-control, a man of disciplined heart and purified will; to attain to such a supermanliness is, indeed, a heroic and splendid achievement, worthy of our utmost endeavor, and calling into play all our noblest powers.

Some there are, accustomed to the vision of tables of stone engraved by the hand of God and set up for man's obedience amid Sinaitic thunders, for whom the discovery of the humble human and prehuman origin, and the stumbling hit-or-miss evolution, of morality dulls its sanctity. But any one who is tempted for this reason to deride morality may console himself with the reflection that everything else of supreme importance in human life is of plebeian ancestry. Reason, art, government, religion, had their crude and superstition-ridden beginnings. Man himself was once hardly different from a monkey. Yet there is a spark of the divine in him and in all these arts and institutions which he with the aid of the cosmic forces has evolved. Surely a juster judgment may find a sublimity in this age-long march from the clod toward the millennium that could never belong to the spectacular but very provincial myths of the Semites. The emotions ever lag behind the intellect; and our hearts may still yearn for the neighborly and passionate battle-god of the Pentateuch. Moreover, we shall continue to recognize a vast fund of truth and insight in those early folk tales and primitive codes. But there comes a deeper breath to the man who realizes that morality and religion long antedate the Jewish revelation, and comes to see God in the tens and hundreds of thousands of years of slow but splendid human progress. Historical codes of morals are, indeed, seamed with superstition and are progressively displaced; but morality persists. At no time has man wholly solved the problem of life, but he must ever live by the best solution he has found. The innumerable codes are so many experiments, their very differences bearing witness to the need of some set of guiding principles for conduct.

It is sometimes said that morality, being a merely human invention, may be discarded when we choose. To this we may reply that morality bears, indeed, the indisputable marks of human instinct, will, and reason; but it is not an invention; it is a lesson, slowly learned. In its humanness lies its value. It is not an alien code, irrelevant to human nature; it is a natural function; it is the greatest of human institutions unless that be religion, which is its flower and consummation. Morality is made for man, for his use and guidance; what could possibly have greater sanctity or authority for him? Rebel as he may, and chafe under its restraints, he always comes back to morality; perhaps to a revised code, but to essentially the same control; for he cannot do without it. Our morality has its defects, but it is on the right track. A clearer insight into its teleological necessity, the purpose it exists to serve, will direct us in our efforts to revise it, so to fashion it as to make it productive of still greater good in the time to come. But if we discard it altogether, we are "like the base Indian" who "threw a pearl away, Richer than all his tribe."

What we need is not to abandon but to steadily improve our code; and whereas any one can pick flaws, only the man of trained mind and controlled desire can discover feasible lines of advance. "When all is said, there is nothing as yet to be changed in our old Aryan ideal of justice, conscientiousness, courage, kindness, and honor. We have only to draw nearer to it, to clasp it more closely, to realize it more effectively; and, before going beyond it, we have still a long and noble road to travel beneath the stars." [Footnote: Maeterlinck, "Our Anxious Morality," in The Measure of the Hours.] The conception of morality as the organization of interests will be found in Plato's Republic and Aristotle's Ethics, and in many recent ethical books and papers. Among them are R. B. Perry's Moral Economy, G. Santayana's Reason in Science (chap. IX); William James, "The Moral Philosopher and the Moral Life" (in the Will to Believe and Other Essays).

A discussion of whether morality really makes for happiness will be found in Leslie Stephen, System of Ethics, chap. X; W. L. Sheldon, An Ethical Movement, chap. VIII. For Nietzsche's theory, see his Beyond Good and Evil. There are many excellent replies; a brief but adequate one will be found in Perry, op. cit, chap. I.

PART III
PERSONAL MORALITY

CHAPTER XV
HEALTH AND EFFICIENCY

With the general nature and justification of morality in our minds, we may now seek to apply our criteria of conduct to the concrete problems that confront us, first taking up those problems which, however important their social bearings, are primarily problems of private life, problems for the individual to settle, and then turning to those wider problems which the community as a whole must grapple with and solve by public action.

Bodily health is the foundation of personal morality; to act at all there must be physical energy available; and, other things equal, the man with the greatest store of vitality will live the happiest and most useful life. Christianity has too often forgotten this fundamental truth, which needs emphasis at the very outset of our concrete studies in morality.

What is the moral importance of health?

(1) Health is in itself a great contribution to the intrinsic worth of life. To awake in the morning with red blood stirring in the veins, to come to the table with hearty appetite, to go about the day's work with the springing step of abounding energy, and to reach the close of day with that healthy fatigue that quiets restless desire and betokens the blessed boon of sound and dreamless sleep-this is to be a long way on the road to contentment. Health cannot in itself guarantee happiness if other evils obtrude; but it removes many of the commonest impediments thereto, and normally produces an increase in all other values. Heightened vitality means an increased sense of power, a keener zest in everything; troubles slide off the healthy man that would stick to the less vigorous. Bodily depression almost always involves mental depression; our "blues" usually have an organic basis. It was not a superstition that evolved our word "melancholy" from the Greek "black (i.e., disordered) liver" nor is it a mere pun or paradox to say that whether life is worth living depends upon the liver.

More than this, health is opportunity. The man of abundant energy can taste more of the joys of life, can enlarge the bounds of his experience, can use precious hours of our brief span which the weakling must devote to rest, can learn more, can range farther, can venture all sorts of undertakings from which the other is precluded by his lack of strength. All these experiences, if they are guided by prudence and self-control, bring their meed of insight and skill and character. It is only through living that we grow, and health means the potentiality of life.

(2) Health means efficiency, more work done, greater usefulness to society. Sooner or later every man who is worth his salt finds some task the doing of which arouses his ambition and becomes his particular contribution to the world. How bitterly will he then regret the heritage denied him or foolishly squandered, the handicap of quivering nerves, muscular flabbiness, wandering mind, that impedes its accomplishment! Determination and persistence may, indeed, use a frail physique for splendid service; such names as Darwin, Spencer, Prescott, remind us of the strength of human will that can override physical obstacles and by long effort produce a great achievement. But for one victor in this struggle of will against body there are a hundred vanquished; and even these men of genius and grit could have accomplished far more if they had had normally serviceable bodies.

(3) Health makes morality easier and likelier. The pernicious influence of bodily frailty and abnormality upon mind and morals has always been recognized (cf. the mens sana in corpore sano of the ancients), but was never so clearly seen as today. The lack of proper nutrition or circulation, the state of depressed vitality resulting from want of fresh air, exercise, or sleep, are important factors in the production of insanity and crime. Over fatigue means a weakening of the power of attention, and hence of will, a paralyzing of the highest brain centers, a lowered resistance to the more primitive instincts and passions. Chronic irritability, moroseness, pathological impulses of all sorts, generally betokens eyestrain, dyspepsia, constipation, or some other bodily derangement. With the regaining of normal health the unruly impulses usually become quieter, sympathy flows more freely, the man becomes kinder, more tolerant, and morally sane. Professor Chittenden of Yale is quoted as saying that "lack of proper physical condition is responsible for more moral ... ills than any other factor." Certain temptations, at least, bear more hardly upon the man of weak and unstrung nerves; in Rousseau's well known words, "The weaker the body, the more it commands." And in general, abnormal organic conditions involve a warping of the judgment, a twisted or unbalanced view of life (e.g. Wordsworth's "Spontaneous reason breathed by health"), which leads away from the path of virtue. All honor, then, to the men who have kept clean and true and cheerful through years of bodily depression; such conquest over evil conditions is one of the finest things in life. But nobility of character is hard enough to attain without adding the obstacle of a reluctant body; and although some virtues are easier to the invalid, and some temptations removed from his circumscribed field of activity, it remains true in general that health is the great first aid to morality.

Can we attain to greater health and efficiency? If health is, then, so important to the individual and society, its pursuit is not a selfish or a trivial matter; it is rather a serious and unavoidable duty. The gospel of health is sorely needed in our modern world. Young men and women use up their apparently limitless capital with heedless waste; those who start with a lesser inheritance neglect the means at their command for increasing their stock of strength and winning the power and exuberance of life that might be theirs. There are, of course, many cases of undeserved ill health; we ill understand as yet the causes and enemies of bodily vigor, and many a gallant fight for health has gone unrewarded. But in the great majority of cases a wise conduct of life would retain robust strength for the threescore or more years of our allotted course, increase it for those who start poorly equipped, and regain it for those who by mischance, blunder, or imprudence have lost their heritage. Yet half the world hardly knows what real health is. Our hospitals and sanitariums are crowded, our streets are full of half-sick people-hollow chests, sallow faces, dark-rimmed eyes, nervous, run-down, worn-out, brain-fagged, dragging on their existence, or dying before their time, robbed by stupidity and ignorance of their birthright of full-breathed rosy-cheeked health, and robbing the society that has reared them of the full quota of their service. Health is not merely freedom from disease; we have a right to what Emerson called "plus health." And among the men who rightly awaken our enthusiasm are those who out of a frail childhood have built up for themselves by perseverance and will a manhood of physical power, endurance, and efficiency.

The principles of health for the normal man are few and simple, the reward great; what stands in the way is partly our apathy and indifference, partly our incontinent appetites, partly the unwholesome and deadening social influences in which we find ourselves enmeshed. For those who care enough, almost unlimited vistas open up; as Spinoza has it, "No one has yet found the limits of what the body can do." William James was convinced [Footnote: See his essay, "The Energies of Man," in Memories and Studies.] that the potentialities of human energy and efficiency are but half realized by the best of us. We must learn better to run the human machine. Our prevalent disregard of the conditions of bodily vigor, our persistent carelessness in the elementary matters of hygiene and health, is nothing short of criminal.

"We would have health, and yet still use our bodies ill; Bafflers of our own prayers from youth to life's last scenes."

Happiness that impairs health seldom pays. Where it is a question of useful work done at the expense of our fatigue, there may be more question; normally such sacrifices are undesirable; but what seems over fatigue may not really be so, and the earnest man will err on this side rather than run risk of pusillanimous shirking. Moreover, some work practically requires an over effort for its accomplishment; and no man of mettle will begrudge his very life-blood when necessary. Overwork is "the last infirmity of noble minds." Yet when not really necessary, it must be ranked as a sin, and not too generously condoned. The intense competition of modern industry, the complexity of our economic machinery, the colossal accumulation of facts which must be mastered for success, bring heavy pressure to bear upon those who have their way to make in the world. The pace is fast, and many there are that die or break from overstrain when at the height of their usefulness. Such, overpressure does not pay; it means that less work will in the end get done. When we consider also the moral dangers it involves, the glumness or irritability of taut nerves, the unhealthy tension that demands strong excitements and does not know how to rest or enjoy quiet and restorative pleasures; when we consider the broken men and women that have to be taken care of, the widows and children of the workers who have died before their time, the children perhaps weakened for life because of the tired condition of their parents at birth; when we consider the number of defective children born to such overworked parents, we realize that it is not primarily a question of enjoying life more or less, it is a matter of grave economic and moral import. [Footnote: Cf. M. G. Schlapp, in the Outlook, vol. 100, p. 782.] Whether we actually work harder, on the whole, than our forebears, and whether there is actually a decrease in the health and endurance of the younger generation today owing to the overstrain of their parents, is open to dispute. Certainly when one compares a portrait of Reynolds, Gainsborough, or Stuart with one by Sargent, Thayer, or Alexander, there is a noticeable difference of type, indicative of a different ideal of life in the upper stratum of society, an ideal of effort and efficiency, which is far better than a patrician dilettantism, but has in turn its dangers.We need to recall the line of AEschylus, "All the gods' work is effortless and calm." Or Matthew Arnold's sonnet on Quiet Work:

"One lesson, Nature, let me learn of thee, A lesson that on every wind is borne, A lesson of two duties kept at one Though the loud world proclaim their enmity: Of toil unsevered from tranquility, Of labor that in lasting fruit outgrows Far noisier schemes, accomplished in repose, Too great for haste, too high for rivalry..."

Most of us would find our powers adequate to our duties if we learned to rest when we are not working, and spend no energy in worry and fretfulness. [Footnote: Cf. W. James's essay on "The Gospel of Relaxation," in Talks to Teachers and Students, or Annie Payson Call's books, of which the best known is Power Through Repose.] This nervous leakage is a notoriously American ailment; we knit our brows, we work our fingers, we fidget, we rock in our chairs, we talk explosively, we live in a quiver of excitement and hurry, in a chronic state of tension. We need to follow St. Paul's exhortation to "Study to be quiet"; to learn what Carlyle called "the great art of sitting still." We must not lower our American ideal of efficiency, of the "strenuous life"; but it is precisely through that self-control that is willing to live within necessary limitations, and able to cut off the waste of fruitless activity of mind and body, that our national efficiency can be maintained at its highest.

Is continued idleness ever justifiable?

We do not need Stevenson's charming Apology for Idlers, to know that rest and recreation are as wholesome and necessary as work. But idleness is only profitable and really enjoyable when it comes as an interlude in the midst of activity. There is much to be done, and no one is free to shirk his share of the world's work; we may enjoy our vacations only as we have earned the right to them. Except for invalids and idiots, continued idleness never justifiable. Clothes we must have, and food, and shelter, and much else; if a man does not produce these things for himself, or some equivalent which he can fairly exchange for them, he is a parasite upon other men's labor. "Six days shalt thou labor" is the universal commandment, and "In the sweat of thy brow shalt thou eat bread." An old Chinese proverb runs, "If there is one idle man, there is another who is starving." Certainly a state in which the masses will have their drudgery lightened for them and opportunity for a well rounded human life given, will be attained only in a society where there are no drones; and no man or woman worthy of the name will be content to live idly on the labor of others. "Others have labored, and we have entered into their labors"; it is not fair to accept so much without giving what we can in return.

For most men and women there is, of course; no alterative; they must work or live a wretched, comfortless life, with the actual risk of starvation. A few may prefer the precarious existence of the tramp, or pauper; but they must pay the price in homelessness and hazard. Except for abnormal social conditions, the vile housing of the poor, the hopeless monotony and overlong hours of most forms of unskilled labor, the lure of drink, and the deprivation of the natural joys of life, there would be few of these voluntary idlers among the poor. The aversion to work, when it is decently agreeable, in decent surroundings, and not carried to the point of fatigue, is abnormal; and it is by the improvement of the conditions and remuneration of labor that we must seek to cure that unwillingness to work, in the poor, which Tolstoy came to believe was their greatest curse. [Footnote: See his What Shall We Do Then? (or What to Do?)]

Much more difficult to cure is the curse of idleness among the rich. The absence of the need of working, and the possibilities of pleasure seeking which money affords, are a constant temptation to them to live a life of ease. The spectacle is not unfamiliar of rich young men traveling about the world, living at their clubs, spending their energies in gayeties and sports, with hardly a sense of the responsibilities which their privileges entail. Fortunately, however, there is, in America at least, a pretty widespread sense of shame among men about such shirking, and the idler has to face a certain amount of mild contempt. Upon women the pressure of public opinion has not yet become nothing upper-class ladies who spend their time at cards, at teas, at the theater, who think of little but dress and gossip, or of the latest novels and music, who evade their natural duties of motherhood or give over care of home and children to hired servants, that they may be freer to live the butterfly life, are still too little rebuked by their hard-working sisters and by men. We must impress it upon all that the inheritance of money does not excuse laziness; if the pressure to earn a living is removed, there are numberless ways in which the rich can serve, privileged ways, happy ways, which there is far less pretext for avoiding than the poor have for hating their grim toil. In Carlyle's words, "If the poor and humble toil that we have food, must not the high and glorious toil for him in return, that he may have light, have guidance, freedom, immortality?" The rich commonly point the finger of scorn at the poor who turn away from honest work; we may well wonder if they would work themselves at such dirty and dangerous occupations. Many a charity visitor who preaches the gospel of toil is herself, except for some fitful and ineffective "social work," a useless ornament to society who hardly knows the meaning of "toil." If idleness is a mote in the eyes of the poor, it is a beam in the eyes of the rich. Neither blood nor rank nor sex excuses from the universal duty. "We must all toil or steal (howsoever we name our stealing), which is worse." [Footnote: Carlyle's writings are full of such wholesome declarations. And cf. W. Dew. Hyde: "An able-bodied man who does not contribute to the world at least as much as he takes out of it is a beggar and a thief; whether he shirks the duty of work under the pretext of poverty or riches." Cf. also Tolstoy, in What to Do? For example (from chap. XXVI), "How can a man who considers himself to be, we will not say a Christian, or an educated and humane man, but simply a man not entirely devoid of reason and of conscience, how can he, I say, live in such a way that, not taking part in the struggle of all mankind for life, he only swallows up the labor of others, struggling for existence, and by his own claims increases the labor of those who struggle, and the number of those who perish in struggle?"] relieved from the necessity of earning a living" (unless one intends to use that freedom for unpaid service), an ideal dangerous to social welfare, and shortsighted for the individual. Work makes up a large part of the worth of life. Drudgery it may be at the time, a weary round, with no compensation apparent; but it is of just such stuff that real life is made. What ennobles it, what gives it meaning, is the courageous attack, the putting of heart into work, the facing of monotony, the finding of the zest of accomplishment. There is no such thing as "menial" work; the washing of dishes and the carting away of garbage are just as necessary and important as the running of a railway or the making of laws. The real horror is the dead weight of ennui, the aimlessness and fruitlessness of a life that has done nothing and has nothing to do. If the thought of the day's work depresses, it is probably because of ill health, over fatigue, unpleasant surroundings or companions, because of worry, or because the particular work is not congenial. The finding of the right work for the right man and woman is one of the great problems which we have hardly begun to solve. But all of these sources of the distaste for work can normally, or eventually, be reached and the evil remedied. In spite of the burden and the strain, if we could have our way with the order of things, one of the most foolish things we could do would be to take away the necessity of work. Here, as usual, personal and social needs coincide; in the working life alone can be found a lasting satisfaction for the soul and the hope of salvation for society. Are competitive athletics desirable? As samples of the concrete problems involved in the ideal of health and efficiency, we may briefly discuss two questions that confront particularly the young man. And first, that concerning athletic sports are of marked value:

(1) They are to any normal man or woman, and especially to the young who have not yet become immersed in the more serious game of life, one of the greatest and most tonic joys. The stretching and tension of healthy muscles, the deep draughts of out-of-door air, the excitement of rivalry, the comradeship of cooperative endeavor, the ABANDON of effort, the glow of achievement, contribute much in immediate and retrospective pleasure to the worth of living.

(2) When not carried too far, the physical gain is clear. Regular exercise is necessary for abundant health; and of all forms of exercise the happiest is, other things equal, the best.

(3) In many ways there are potentialities of moral gain in athletics which do not result from ordinary exercise. There is the stimulus to intense effort, the awakening of strenuousness which may carry over into other fields of activity. Here, at least, indolence is impossible, alertness is demanded, and the willingness to strive against obstacles. To put one's whole soul into anything is wholesome, even if it be but a game; and the man who bucks the line hard on the gridiron has begun a habit which may serve him well when he meets more dangerous obstacles and more doughty opponents on a larger field.

(4) The lesson of cooperation taught by teamwork of any sort is a valuable schooling. One of the prime needs of our day is the development of the spirit of loyalty, the willingness to subordinate individual welfare to that of a

group, and to look upon one's own work as part of a larger endeavor. The man who has learned to take pride in making sacrifice hits is ripe to respond to the growing sense of the dishonorableness of making personal profit the aim of business or of politics.

(5) Athletic games, where properly supervised, inculcate the spirit of sportsmanship. To keep to the rules of longing, to restrain temper and accept the decisions of the umpire without complaint, to take no unfair advantage and indulge in no foul play, to give a square deal to opponents and ask no more for one's own side, to endure defeat with a smile and without discouragement- surely this is just the spirit we need in everything. It is vitally important that unsportsmanlike conduct should be ruthlessly stamped out in all competitive sports, and that every team should prefer to lose honorably than to win unfairly. [Footnote: There has been a good deal of criticism of American intercollegiate athletics on the ground of their fostering unsportsmanlike conduct. A recent paper in the Atlantic Monthly (by C. A. Stewart, vol. 113, p. 153) concludes with this recommendation: "A forceful presentation of the facts of the situation, with an appeal to the innate sense of honor of the undergraduates; such a revision of the rules as will retain only those based upon essential fairness; and a strict supervision by the faculty;-upon the success of these three measures rests the hope that college athletics may be purged of trickery and the spirit of 'get away with it.' ... A few men expelled for lying about eligibility, and a few teams disbanded because of unfair play, would arouse undergraduates with a wholesome jolt."]

(6) Wherever they are taken seriously athletic contests require a preliminary period of "training," which includes abstinence from sex incontinence, from alcohol, smoking, overeating, and late hours. The discipline which this involves is an object lesson in the requirements for efficiency in any undertaking, and excellent practice in their fulfillment. How far athletes learn this lesson and apply it to wider spheres of activity, it would be interesting to discover. In any case, they have proved in themselves the ability to repress inclination and find satisfaction in what makes for health and efficiency; and all who know the implications of "training" have received a subconscious "suggestion" in the right direction. The other side of the problem is this:

(1) Competitive athletics, if taken seriously contests,inevitably take more time and energy than their importance .warrants. A member of a college football or baseball team can do little else during the season. Studies are neglected, intellectual interests are subordinated, college figures essentially as a group of men endeavoring to beat another college on the field. If a man is bright he may "keep up with" his studies, but his intellectual profit is meager; his energies are being absorbed elsewhere. This phenomenon has

given rise to much satire and to much perplexity on the part of college administrations. A few have gone so far as to banish intercollegiate contests, asserting thatthe purpose of coming to college is primarily to learn to use the brain, not the muscles.

(2) The strain of intense rivalry is too severe on the body. It is now known that the intercollegiate athlete is very probably sacrificing some of his life when he throws his utmost effort into the game or the race. The length of life of the big athletes averages considerably shorter than that of the more moderate exercisers. From the physical point of view, interclass or interfraternity contests, not taken too earnestly, are. far better than the intercollegiate struggles. They also have the advantage that far more can participate. The problem before our college authorities and leaders of student sentiment is how to check the fierceness of the big contests-shortening them, perhaps, possibly forbidding entirely the more strenuous and how to provide sports for all members of the college; so that, instead of a few overstrained athletes and a lot of fellows who under exercise, we shall see every man out on the field daily, and no one overdoing. This ideal necessitates far larger athletic grounds than most of our colleges have reserved. It may necessitate the abolition of some of the big contests that have been the excitement of many thousands. But it must not be forgotten prelude and preparation for life; they must not be allowed to usurp the chief place in a man's thoughts or to unfit him for his greatest after-usefulness. [Footnote: Cf. Atlantic Monthly, vol. 90, p. 534; Outlook, vol. 98, p. 597.] Is it wrong to smoke? Statistics taken with care at many American colleges show with apparent conclusiveness that the use of tobacco is physically and mentally deleterious to young men. [Footnote: See, e.g., in the Popular Science Monthly for October, 1912, a summary by Dr. F. J. Pack of an investigation covering fourteen colleges. Similar investigations have been made by several others, with generally similar results.] It seems that smokers lose in lung capacity, are stunted slightly in their growth, are lessened in their endurance, develop far more than their proportion of eye and nerve troubles, furnish far less than their proportion of the athletes who win positions on college teams, furnish far less than their proportion of scholarship men, and far more than their proportion of conditions and failures. It is perhaps too early to be quite sure of these results; but in all probability further experiment will confirm them, and make it certain that tobacco is physically harmful as has long been recognized by trainers for athletic contests. The harm to adults seems to be less marked; perhaps to some it is inappreciable. And if there is appreciable harm, whether it is great enough to counterbalance the satisfaction which a confirmed smoker takes in his cigar or pipe, or any worse than the restlessness which the sacrifice of it might engender, is one of those delicate personal problems that one can hardly solve for another. But certainly

where the habit is not formed, the loss of tobacco involves no important deprivation; its use is chiefly a social custom which can be discontinued without ill effects. Effort should be made to keep the young from forming the habit; college "smokers," where free cigarettes and cigars are furnished, should be superseded by "rallies," where the same amount of money could provide some light and harmless refreshment. This is not one of the important problems. But, after all, everything is important; and men must, and ultimately will, learn to find their happiness in things that forward, instead of thwarting, their great interests; what makes at all against health and efficiency-when it is so needless and artificial a habit as smoking, so mildly pleasant and so purely selfish-must be rooted out of desire. The great amount of money wasted on tobacco could be far more wisely and fruitfully expended. We shall not brand smoking as a sin, hardly as a vice; but the man who wishes to make the most of his life will avoid it himself, and the man who wishes to work for the general welfare will put his influence and example against it.

H. S. King, Rational Living, chap. VI, secs. I, II. J. Payot, The Education of the Will, book III, sec. IV. J. MacCunn, The Making of Character, part II, chap. II. W. Hutchinson, Handbook of Health. L. H. Gulick, The Efficient Life. F. Paulsen, System of Ethics, book III, chap. III. T. Roosevelt, The Strenuous Life. P. G. Hamerton, The Intellectual Life, part I.

CHAPTER XVI
THE ALCOHOL PROBLEM

OF all the problems relating to health and efficiency there is none graver than that of the narcotic-stimulants. With the exception of tobacco, which is probably, for adults, but mildly deleterious, their use is fraught with danger, both physical and moral; beyond the narrowest limits it is certainly baneful, while it is as yet an open question whether even a very slight use is not distinctly harmful. The exact physiological effects of the several narcotic-stimulants are different, but they are alike in stimulating certain activities and depressing others; and their attraction for men is similar. Opium, morphine, and cocaine are more powerful drugs, and more inherently dangerous; but alcohol is much the most widely used and so most productive of evil. The hypodermically used narcotics need not be here discussed; for although they can give a far keener pleasure than alcohol, the penalty they inflict is more evident. Moreover, since their sale is not pushed by such powerful interests as continually stimulate the use of alcohol, they can, by the vigilant enforcement of existing laws, be readily removed from any general use. We turn, then, to the consideration of the one which has got a universal hold on the imagination and social habits of men, the only one that constitutes at present a serious and complicated problem.

What are the causes of the use of alcoholic drinks?

(1) We may dismiss at once the suggestion that alcoholic liquors are drunk for the pleasantness of their taste or for their food value. To some slight extent these factors enter in; but neither is important. The taste for them is for most men an acquired taste; and with so many other delicious drinks to be had, especially in recent years, drinks that are far less expensive and without their poisonous effects, it is safe to say that the mere taste of them would not go far toward explaining the lure they have for men. As to their food value, there are those who justify themselves on the score of the nutrition they are getting from their wine or beer. But careful experiments have shown that the food value of alcohol is slight; and certainly, for nutrition received, these are among the most expensive foods, to be ranked with caviar and pate de foie gras. Beer is the most nutritious of the alcoholic drinks; but the same amount of money spent on bread would give about thirty times the nutrition, and a more all-round nutrition at that. Alcoholic liquors as food are, as has been said, like gunpowder as fuel very costly and very dangerous. [Footnote: See H. S. Williams, Alcohol, p. 133;

H. S. Warner, Social Welfare and the Liquor Problem, p. 80, and bibliography, p. 95.]

(2) A much commoner plea for drinking rests upon its sociability. But this is a matter of convention which can readily enough be altered. There is nothing inherently more sociable in the drinking of wine than in the drinking of grape-juice, or coffee, or chocolate, or tea. Indeed, one may well ask why the chief social bond between men should consist in drinking liquids side by side! Games and sports, in which wit is pitted against wit, or which bring men together in happy cooperation, together with the great resource of conversation, are more socially binding than any drinks. There will, indeed, be a temporary social hardship for many abstainers until the custom is generally broken up; one runs the risk of being thought by the heedless a prig and a Puritan. But that is a small price to pay for one's health and one's influence on others.

(3) More important than any of these causes is the craving for a stimulant. The monotony of work, the fatigue toward the end of the day, the severity of our Northern climate, the longing for intenser living, lead men to seek to apply the whip to their flagging energies. This stimulus to the body is, however, largely if not wholly, illusory. The mental-emotional effects, noted in the following paragraph, give the drinker the impression that he is physically fortified; but objective tests show that, after a very brief period, the dominant effect upon the organism is depressant. The apparent increase in bodily warmth, so often experienced, is a subjective illusion; in reality alcohol lowers the temperature and diminishes resistance to cold. Arctic explorers have to discard it entirely. The old idea of helping to cure snake bite, hydrophobia, etc, by whiskey was sheer mistake; the patient has actually much less of a chance if so drugged. Only for an immediate and transitory need, such as faintness or shock, is the quickly passing stimulating power of alcohol useful; and even for such purposes other stimulants are more valuable. Reputable physicians have almost wholly ceased to use it. [Footnote: See H. S. Williams, op. cit, p. 4, 124-127; H. S. Warner, op. cit, pp. 87]

(4) The one real value of alcohol to man has been the boon of stimulating his emotional and impulsive life, bringing him an elevation of spirits, drowning his sorrows, helping him to forget, helping to free his mind from the burden of care, anxiety, and regret. As William James, with his unerring discernment, wrote twenty-five years ago: "The reason for craving alcohol is that it is an unaesthetic, even in moderate quantities. It obliterates a part of the field of consciousness and abolishes collateral trains of thought." [Footnote: Tolstoy also hit the nail on the head in his little essay, Why do Men Stupefy Themselves?] This use, in relieving brain-tension, in bringing a transient cheer and comfort to poor, overworked, worried, remorseful men,

is not to be despised. Dull lives are vivified by it, a fleeting anesthesia of unhappy memories and longings is effected, and for the moment life seems worth living.

Without considering yet the physical penalty that must be paid for this evanescent freedom, we may make the obvious remark that it is a morally dangerous freedom. As the Odyssey has it, "Wine leads to folly, making even the wise to love immoderately, to dance, and to utter what had better have been kept silent." Alcohol slackens the higher, more complicated, mental functions-our conscience, our scruples, our reason- and leaves freer from inhibition our lower passions and instincts. We cannot afford thus to submerge our better natures, and leave the field to our lower selves; it is a dangerous short cut to happiness. A far safer and more permanently useful procedure for the individual would be so to live by his reason and his conscience that he would not need to stupefy them, to forget his life as he is shaping it from day today. And the lesson to the community is so to brighten the lives of the poor with normal, wholesome pleasures and recreations, so to lift from them the burdens of poverty and social injustice, that they will not so much need to plunge into the grateful oblivion of the wine-cup.

(5) The most tenacious hold of the alcohol trade lies, however, in two things not yet enumerated. The one is, that much use of alcohol creates a pathological craving for it; the man who is accustomed to his beer or whiskey is restless and depressed if he cannot get it, and will sacrifice much to still for the nonce that insatiable longing. The other and even more important fact is, that the sale of liquor is immensely profitable to the manufacturers and sellers. The fighters for prohibition have to encounter the desperate opposition of those who have become slaves to the drug-many of whom may never get intoxicated, and would resent the term "slaves," but who have formed the abnormal habit and cannot without discomfort get rid of it. They have to meet the still fiercer hostility of those who are making money from the sale of liquor and do not intend to let go their opportunity. What are the evils that result from alcoholic liquors?

The one real value of alcohol, we have said, lies in its temporary mental effects. It raises the hedonic tone of consciousness; it brings about, when taken in proper amounts, the well-known happy-go-lucky, scruple-free, expansive state of mind. What now is the price that must be paid for its use?

(1) The physical harmfulness of even light drinking is considerable.

(a) Alcohol, even in slight doses, as in a glass of wine or beer, has poisonous effects upon some of the bodily functions, which are clearly revealed by scientific experiment. [Footnote: See, for one testimony out of very many in medical literature, an article by Dr. Herbert McIntosh in the Journal of Advanced Therapeutics for April, 1912, p. 167: "Alcohol and ether are the two great enemies of the electrochemical properties of the salts necessary to organic life." He speaks of "paralysis of the vaso-constrictor nerves," "inhibition of the cortical centers," etc.] Hence the temporary cheer must be paid for with usury by a much longer depression, resulting from the poisonous effects of alcohol upon the body. A jolly evening is followed by the familiar symptoms of the morning after. The extent of the physical and mental depression caused is not always realized, because it is spread out over a considerable period of time and may not be acute; a healthy person can stand a good deal without being conscious of the ill effects. But they are there. In bodily vigor, and so in mental buoyancy, the abstainer is IN THE END better off than if he drank even a little, or seldom.

(b) Careful and repeated experiments seem to show that even a very little drinking-a glass of beer or wine a day- decreases the capacity for both muscular and mental work. This loss of ability is not usually perceptible to the drinker; he often feels an illusory glow of power; but he cannot do as much. A bottle of beer a day means an appreciable loss in working efficiency. [Footnote: Accounts of the experiments will be found in H. S. Williams, op. cit, pp. 5-23, 128, 137; H. S. Warner, op. cit, p. 116. They had some realization of this truth even in the days of the Iliad. Hector says, "Bring me luscious wines, lest they unnerve my limbs and make me lose my wonted powers and strength."]

(c) Even a moderate use of alcohol increases liability to disease and shortens the chances of life. In any case of exposure to or contraction of disease, the total abstainer has a proved advantage over even the light drinker. The British life insurance companies reckon that at the age of twenty a total abstainer has an average prospect of life of forty-four years, a temperate regular drinker a prospect of thirty-one years, and a heavy drinker of fifteen years. Many other factors enter into the individual situation, of course; we know many cases where inveterate drinkers have lived to a ripe old age; it takes a great deal to break the iron constitutions of some men. But averages tell the story. An authority on tuberculosis states that "if for no other reason than the prevention of tuberculosis, state prohibition would be justified" The use of alcohol predisposes the body to many kinds of disease; and according to conservative figures, approximately seventy thousand deaths yearly in the United States are caused by alcoholism and diseases that owe their grip to the use of alcohol. Besides this, a great deal of insanity and chronic invalidism, and a large proportion of deaths after operations, are due to this cause. [Footnote: See H. S.

Williams, op. cit, pp. 25- 43, 149, 150; H. S. Warner, op. cit, chap. IV, and bibliography at end.]

(d) The chances of losing children at chances of begetting feeble-minded or degenerate children, are markedly greater for even moderate drinkers than for abstainers. Children of total abstainers have a great advantage, on the average, in size, stature, bodily vigor, intellectual power; they stand, on the average, between a year and two years ahead in class of the children of moderate drinkers, they have less than half as many eye, ear, and other physical defects. This proved influence of even light drinking upon the vitality and normality transmitted to children should be the most serious of indictments against self-indulgence. Truly the sins of the fathers are visited upon the second and third generation. [Footnote: See Journal of Philosophy, Psychology, and Scientific Methods, vol. IX, p. 234; H. S. Williams, op. cit, pp. 44-47.]

(2) The economic waste is enormous:

(a) Nearly, if not quite, two billion dollars a year are spent by the people of the United States for intoxicating beverages. Between fifty and seventy-five million bushels of grain are consumed annually in their production, besides the grapes used for wines. Nor does the money spent for liquors go in any appreciable degree into the pockets of the farmers who raise the grains; less than a thirtieth part finds its way to them, the brewers, distillers, and retailers getting about two thirds. The money invested in the beer industry alone was in 1909 over $550,000,000. [Footnote: See Independent, vol. 67, p. 1326; Year-Books of the Anti-Saloon League. For this whole subject of the cost of the liquor trade, see chap. V, in H. S. Warner, op. cit, and the bibliography appended.] The importance of the national liquor bill can be realized by a simple computation; it would suffice to pay two million men three dollars a day, six days in the week, year in and year out; it would suffice to build four or five Panama Canals (at $400,000,000) a year. When we reckon up the total liquor bill of the world, a sum many times this, we can see what a frightful waste of man's resources is going on; for not only is there no a tremendous additional drain of wealth caused indirectly thereby.

(b) Among the factors in this additional drain of wealth, which must be added to the figures given above in estimating the total financial loss to the community, are: the loss in efficiency of workers through the- usually unrealized- toxic effects of alcohol; the loss of the lives of adult workers due to alcoholic poisoning-an annual loss greater than that of the whole Civil War; the support by the State of paupers, two fifths of whom, it is estimated, owe their status to alcoholism; [Footnote: See H. S. Williams, op. cit, p. 85] the support by the State of the insane, from a quarter to a half of whom owe their insanity directly or indirectly to alcohol; [Footnote: Ibid, p.

63] the support of destitute and deserted children; [Footnote: Ibid, p. 89] the maintenance of prisons, of courts, and police - the Massachusetts Bureau of Labor Statistics has shown that eighty-four per cent of all criminals under conviction in the correctional institutions of that State committed their crimes under the influence of alcohol. [Footnote: Ibid, p. 72] When we add to this the still greater numbers of incapables supported by their families and friends, we realize that the national drink bill is really very much greater than the mere sums spent for liquor. Comparative statistics show graphically how strikingly pauperism, crime, and destitution are diminished by prohibition. It is variously estimated that a fourth or a third or more of all acute poverty is due directly or indirectly to alcohol. Our municipalities are always poor; all sorts of needed improvements are blocked for lack of funds. If this leakage of the national wealth can be stopped we shall be able with the money saved to create a radically different and higher civilization.

(3) The moral harm of alcohol is comparable to its physical and economic harm.

(a) As we noted when considering the value of alcohol, the higher nature is stupefied, leaving the emotions less controlled. The silliness, the irritability, the glumness, the violence, the lust of men are given freer rein. The effect of alcohol is coarsening, brutalizing; we are not our best selves under its influence. The judgment is dulled, the spirit of recklessness is stimulated-an impatience of restraint and a craving for further excitement. Even after the palpable effects of a potation have disappeared, a permanent alteration in the brain remains, which makes it likely that the drinker will "go farther" next time or the time after. The accumulation of such effects leads finally to the complete demoralization of character, to the point where a man's higher nature can no longer keep control over his conduct. This is what is meant by saying that alcohol undermines the will power. [Footnote: See H. S. Williams, op. cit, p. 56] In particular, most sexual sins are committed after drinking; and the gravity of the sex problem is so great that this fact alone would justify the banishment of alcohol, the greatest of sexual stimulants. [Footnote: Cf. Jane Addams, A New Conscience and an Ancient Evil, p. 189: "Even a slight exhilaration from alcohol relaxes the moral sense and throws a sentimental or adventurous glamour over an aspect of life from which a decent young man would ordinarily recoil; and its continued use stimulates the senses at the very moment when the intellectual and moral inhibitions are lessened."]

(b) A very large proportion of the crimes committed are committed under the influence of alcohol. In Massachusetts, for example (in 1895), only five per cent of convictions for crime were of abstainers. In general, statistics show that from a half to three quarters of the total amount of crime has drinking for a direct contributing cause. When we add to this the crime-inducing influence of the poverty, ill health, and immoral social conditions caused by drink; we can form some idea of the moral indictment against alcohol. [Footnote: H. S. Warner, op. cit, p. 261.]

(c) The liquor trade is the most powerful of all "interests" in the corruption of politics, one of the most demoralizing phases of our American life. [Footnote: H. S. Warner, op. cit, chap. XI.] The saloon power is in politics with a grim determination to keep its business from extermination. It is able to throw the votes of a large body of men as it wills. It maintains a powerful lobby at Washington and at the state capitals. In many places it has had a strangle hold on legislation. The trade naturally tends to ally itself with the other vicious interests that live by exploiting human weakness-the gamblers, the fosterers of prostitution, the keepers of vile "shows"; it has a vast revenue for the purchasing of votes, and, in the saloon, the easiest of channels for reaching the bribable voter. Corrupt political machines have been glad to use its support, and have derived a large measure of their strength there from. Were the liquor trade destroyed, the greatest obstacle in the way of political reform would be removed. In sum, we can say that the evils caused by alcohol, instead of having been exaggerated, have never until very recently been sufficiently realized. The half hath not been told.

What should be the attitude of the individual toward alcoholic liquors?

In the light of our present knowledge, the attitude toward liquor demanded by morality of the individual admits of no debate. He may love dearly his wines or his beer, but his enjoyment is won at too dear a cost to himself and others; his support of the liquor trade is very selfish. He has no right to poison himself, to impair his health and efficiency, as even a little drinking will do. He has no right to run the risk of becoming the slave of alcohol, as so many of the most promising men have become; the effect of the drug is insidious, and no man can be sure that he will be able to resist it. He has no right to spend in harmful self-indulgence money that might be spent for useful ends. He has no right to incur the, however immeasurable, moral and intellectual impairment which is effected by even rather moderate drinking. He has no right to bequeath to his children a weakened heritage of vitality. He has no right, by his example, to encourage others, who may be far more deeply harmed than he, in the use of the drug; "let no man put a stumbling-block or an occasion to fall in his brother's way." The influence of every man who is amenable to altruistic motives is needed against liquor, to counteract its lure; we must create a strong public sentiment and make it unfashionable and disreputable to drink. Happily the tide of liquor-drinking, which has been rising rapidly in the last half- century, owing to the increase in prosperity, the great influx of immigrants from liquor-drinking countries, and the stimulation of the trade by the highly organized liquor industry, has at last, by the earnest efforts of enlightened workers, been turned. Men of influence are standing out publicly against it. Grape-juice has been substituted for wine in the White House; Kaiser Wilhelm has become an abstainer, with a declaration that in the present era of fierce competition the nations that triumph will be those that have least to do with liquor. So conservative and cautious a thinker as ex-President Eliot of Harvard has recently become an abstainer, saying, "The recent progress of science has satisfied me that the moderate use of alcohol is objectionable." The yearly per capita consumption of alcoholic liquors, which rose from 8.79 gallons in 1880 to 17.76 in 1900 and 22.79 in 1911, fell in 1912 to 21.98. It is to be devoutly hoped that the tide will ebb as rapidly as it rose. What should be our attitude toward the use of alcoholic liquors by others? The consideration of this question falls properly under the head of "Public Morality." But it will be more convenient to treat it here, following the presentation of the facts concerning alcohol. The right of the community to interfere with the conduct of its members will be discussed in chapter xxviii, and we must assume here the result therein reached, that whatever is deemed necessary for the greatest welfare of the community as a whole may legitimately be required of its individual members, however it may cross their desires or however they may consider the matter their private concern. The argument against prohibition on the ground that it interferes with individual rights would apply also to child-labor legislation, to legislation against street soliciting by prostitutes or the sale of indecent pictures, and, more obviously still, against anti-opium and anti-cocaine legislation. As a matter of fact, the older individualistic point of view has been generally abandoned now, and we are free to discuss what is desirable for the general welfare. We may at once say that whatever method will most quickly and thoroughly root out the evil should be adopted. Different methods may be more or less efficacious in different places; it is a matter for legitimate opportunism. But the goal to be kept in sight can only be absolute prohibition of the manufacture, sale, and importation of all alcoholic liquors for beverages. Education on the matter, and exhortation to personal abstinence, must be continued. But education and exhortation are not alone sufficient; self-restraint cannot be counted on, constraint must be employed.

"High License" and "Regulation" have been thoroughly tried and have not checked the evil; moreover, it has been a serious blunder to make the State or municipality dependent upon the liquor trade for revenue, and therefore eager to retain it. The "State Monopoly" system has not proved a success in this country in lessening the evil; it made the liquor power a more sinister influence than ever in politics. If liquor must be sold, the "Company," or Scandinavian system, which eliminates the factor of private profits, without fostering political corruption, is probably the least harmful method of selling. But no method of selling liquor can be more than a temporary expedient. We must work inch by inch to extend the boundaries of absolutely "dry" territory. "Local Option" has been of very great value in this movement, and may still in some States be the best attainable status. Option by counties, with a prohibition of the shipment of liquor from "wet" to "dry" counties, is the preferable form. Statewide prohibition, for a while in disrepute because of open violation of the law, is again gaining ground, ten of the forty-eight States being entirely "dry" at time of writing. The ultimate solution can only be the adoption of an amendment to the National Constitution enforcing nation-wide prohibition; the agitation for such an amendment is already acute, and the promise of its passage within a generation bright. The arguments against prohibition are not strong. That the law is poorly enforced in localities where public sentiment is against it is natural; but no law is universally obeyed, and that a law is broken is a poor reason for removing it from the statute books. No one would suggest repealing the laws against burglary or seduction because they are daily disobeyed. This pseudo-concern for the dignity of the law is simply a specious argument advanced by those who have an interest in the trade, and accepted by those who suppose liquor drinking to be wrong only in excess and harmless in moderation. The reply is to show that alcohol, practice that is always harmful must be fought by the law as well as by moral suasion. Public sentiment must be educated up to the law; and the existence of the law is itself of educative value. Moreover, the old observations of non-enforcement must now be modified; recent experience shows that the prohibition States are on the whole increasingly successful in enforcing their laws. The new national law prohibiting importations from "wet" to "dry" States helps immensely; and with the forbidding of importations from abroad and of the manufacture of liquor anywhere in the country, the problem of enforcement will settle itself. Except for the precarious existence of "moon-shiners," and for what individuals may make for themselves, the stuff will not be obtainable. [Footnote: For the arguments for prohibition, see H. S. Warner, op. cit, chaps. IX, XII. Artman, The Legalized Outlaw. Fehlandt, A Century of Drink Reform. Wheeler, Prohibition.] That prohibition involves the ruin of a great industry is true; these millions of workers will be free to give their strength to productive labor, these millions of dollars can be invested in some industry useful to mankind. Confiscation will work hardship to the brewers and distillers; so it does to the opium-growers, the makers of indecent pictures, and counterfeit money. A trade so inimical to the general interest deserves no mercy. The States that have unwisely used the "tainted money" drawn from the industry by license will have a far richer community to tax in other ways; for every dollar got in liquor-license fees, many dollars have been lost to the State. As Gladstone said, "Give me a sober population, not wasting their earnings in strong drink, and I shall know where to obtain the revenue." Pending the enactment of legal prohibition, what is called industrial prohibition is proving widely efficacious. Growing numbers of manufacturers, railway managers, and storekeepers are refusing to employ men who drink at all. The United States Commissioner of Labor reports that ninety per cent of the railways, eighty-eight per cent of the trades, and seventy-nine per cent of the manufacturers of the country discriminate already against drinkers. The only other point to be noted is that the saloon-the "public house," the "poor man's salon"-must be replaced by other social centers, that give opportunities for recreation, cheer, and social intercourse. The question of substitutes for the saloon will be alluded to again, in chapter xxx. [Footnote: See Raymond Calkins, Substitutes for the Saloon. H. S. Warner, op. cit, chap. VIII. Forum, vol. 21, p. 595.] The nation-wide campaign against alcohol is on, the area of its legalized sale is steadily diminishing. We who now discuss it may live to see it swept off the face of the earth; if not we, our children or children's children. And we must see to it that no other drug opium, morphine, or the like gets a similar grip on humanity. Our descendants will look with as great horror upon the alcohol indulgence of our times as most of us now do upon opium smoking. "O God, that men should put an enemy into their mouths to steal away their brains! that we should, with joy, pleasance, revel, and applause, transform ourselves into beasts!"

The best book for practical use is H. S. Warner's Social Welfare and the Liquor Problem (revised edition, 1913), where extensive references to the authorities will be found. Two other excellent popular books are H. S. Williams, Alcohol (1909), and Horsley and Sturge, Alcohol and the Human Body (1911). See also Rosanoff, in McClure's Magazine, vol. 32, p. 557; Rountree and Sherwell, The Temperance Problem and Social Reform; T. N. Kelynack, The Drink Problem: Scientific Conclusions concerning the Alcohol Problem (Senate Document 48, 61st Congress, 1909); and the five volumes of conclusions of the Committee of Fifty, published by Houghton, Mifflin Co, under the general title, Aspects of the Liquor Problem; a summary of these conclusions is published with the title The Liquor Problem, ed. F. J. Peabody. Barker, The Saloon Problem and Social Reform. Fanshawe, Liquor Legislation in the United States and Canada. C. B. Henderson, The Social Spirit in America, chap. XVI. The best available data, to date, on the physiological questions underlying the moral questions may be found in G. Rosenfeld, Der Einfluss des Alkohols auf den Organismus (1901) A.B.Cushney, The Action of Alcohol (1907)-paper read before the British Association; Meyer and Gottlieb, Pharmacology (1914).

CHAPTER XVII
CHASTITY AND MARRIAGE TEMPERANCE

In the indulgence of the appetites is a manifest necessity for health and efficiency-temperance in work and play, in eating and drinking, in novel reading and theater going, in whatever activity desire may suggest. But two appetites stand on a different footing from the others, and demand more than temperance. The love of alcohol and the other narcotics, being, as we have seen, a pathological and highly dangerous appetite, productive of scarcely any real good, must be completely rooted out of human nature, as it readily can be, to the great advantage of mankind. The other great appetite, that of sex, cannot be treated so cavalierly; to eradicate it or deny its fulfillment would be to put a speedy end to the human race. The solution of the problems of sex is therefore not so simple, the remedying of the evils of which sexual passion is the source not so feasible. On the one hand, we have to recognize the sex instinct as normal and necessary, the source of the keenest, and, indirectly, of some of the most lasting, pleasures of life; the denial of its enticements to the extent which our Christian ideal demands provokes perennial resentment and rebellion. On the other hand, we are confronted by the incalculable evils which unrestrained lust produces, and forced to admit the imperious necessity of some strictly repressive code. To many, the gravest dangers in life lie here; the sex instinct is the great rebel, promising a glorious liberty, a melting of the barriers between human bodies and souls, an ecstasy of mutual happiness that nothing else can offer. Yet beyond these transient excitements lie the saddest tragedies-disease and suffering, unwished childbirth, heartbreak and death. Desire sings a siren music in our ears; but the bones of those who have surrendered to the song lie bleaching on the rocks. These sweet anticipations presage sorrow and ruin; there is no heavier sight than to see happy, heedless youth caught by the lure of this strange, mysterious thrill and drifting to their destruction-"As a bird hasteth to the snare, And know not that it is for his life." So much is at stake here that we must be more than ordinarily sure that we are not biased, that we are not binding ourselves by needless restrictions. But after whatever doubts and wanderings, the man of mature experience comes back to the monogamous ideal with the conviction that in it lies not only our salvation but our truest happiness. A thousand pities that so many learn the lesson too late! Nothing in the whole field of ethics is more important than for each generation, as it stands on the threshold of temptation and opportunity, to see clearly the basic reasons for our hard-won and barely maintained code of chastity. A reverence for authority, a deep- implanted sentiment, a recurrent emotional appeal, and a barrier of scruples and pledges may keep many within the lines of safety. But the morality of sentiment and authority must always be based on a morality of reason and experience. We must therefore begin by recapitulating the fundamental reasons for our monogamous ideal.

What are the reasons for chastity before and fidelity after marriage?

(1) The most glaring danger for a man in unchastity is disease. The venereal diseases are among the most terrible known to man; they are highly contagious-one contact, and that not necessarily actual intercourse, sufficing for infection-and at present only very partially curable. Practically all prostitutes become infected before long; the youngest and prettiest are usually diseased; the chance of indulging in promiscuous intimacies without catching some form of infection is slight. The only sure way of escape from this imminent danger is by the exclusive love of one man and one woman. Moreover, these diseases are, in their effects, transmissible from husband to wife and from wife to children. Many women's diseases, a large part of their sterility, of miscarriages and infant deaths, a large proportion of the paralysis, insanity, and blindness in the world, are due to the sins of a husband or parent. Thus the penalty for a single misstep may be very grim; and the worst of it is that it must often be shared by the innocent. [Footnote: See Prince Morrow, Social Diseases and Marriage. W. L. Howard, Plain Facts on Sex Hygiene.]

(2) For a girl the danger of disease is not all. There is the additional danger of pregnancy, which means, and must mean, for her not only pain and risk of life, but lasting shame and disgrace. Even paid prostitutes, who are willing to employ dangerous methods to prevent conception, and soon become nearly sterile through disease or overindulgence, often have to resort to illegal operations, at the risk of their lives, and not infrequently come to childbirth. The virgin who gives herself to her lover under the spell of his ardent wooing is very much more likely to conceive. It cannot be too bluntly stated that the barest contact may suffice for conception; for a momentary intimacy two lives, or three, have often been ruined.

(3) The reason why society cannot afford to be lenient with illegitimacy is that there is no proper provision for rearing children born out of wedlock. The woman and the child usually need the financial support of the man; they always need his love and care. If the man marries the girl he has wronged, there is not only the disgrace still attaching to her (and rightly to him, still more), but the fact of a hasty and unintended and probably more or less unhappy marriage. Certainly in every such case the girl has a right to demand that the man shall marry her; whether or no she will wish him to, or will prefer to bear her burden and disgrace alone, is for her to determine.

But this is sure that any man who takes the chance of ruining a foolish and ignorant or oversusceptible girl "and all for a bit of pleasure, as, if he had a man's heart in him, he 'd ha' cut his hand off sooner than he'd ha' taken it" [Footnote: George Eliot's Adam Bede, from which these words are taken, ought to be read by every boy and girl.]- ought to be despised and socially ostracized by his fellows. Except for the penalty of disease, women have always borne the brunt of sexual follies, though men have been the more to blame. It is high time that this injustice were remedied to such extent as law and public opinion can do it.

(4) The employment of paid prostitutes for man's gratification keeps in existence the unhappiest and most degraded class in the world. Brutalized and worn by their abnormal life, treated with coarse indignities which they cannot resent, deprived of their birthright of genuine love, of wifehood and motherhood, stricken with disease and doomed to an early death, thousands of the prettiest, reddest-blooded, most promising young girls of our land, the girls who ought to be bearing healthy children and rearing the future citizens of the State, now walk the streets painted and gaudily bedecked, seeking their miserable livelihood, and snaring the heedless and restless youth of the cities, the "young men void of understanding," to their common degradation. This human wastage is worse upon the race than war; and all the more pathetic because it consists of girls scarcely past the threshold of their maidenhood. When we consider further the indescribably horrible cruelty of the "white-slave trade," which the insatiable lust of men has brought into being, we may begin to realize to what the absence of restraint upon this appetite has led.

It is quite conceivable that within the near future the venereal diseases will be rendered entirely curable by the progress of medicine. It is possible that some certain and harmless method of preventing conception will be found and become so universally known that the danger of unintentional childbirth will become practically nonexistent. Such a situation would remove the most obvious reasons for chastity, and would insure a rapid growth of free-love sentiment. It would be pointed out that free love would do away with the shameful existence of the paid prostitutes, and that thus all four of the basic reasons above given for chastity would no longer exist. To discuss such possibilities may seem premature. But as a matter of fact, even now every one who indulges in "free" love hopes to escape disease and conception. And there is an increasing propaganda insisting on the removal of the old conventions and the permission of promiscuous love. The spirit of adventure is in the air; and with even a good chance of escaping the penalties, there are many who will seize their opportunities for enjoyment, preferring a present pleasure with its spice of risk to a dull negation of desire. We must then go on with the argument and point out that even where these terrible results are escaped, the way of free love is not the happiest way.

(5) Freedom from restraint in inter-sex relations inevitably leads, in the majority of men and women, to an overindulgence which seriously impairs health and efficiency. The one salient motive for the opposition of ancient codes to sex license was the necessity of preserving the virility of the young men for war. Today athletes are enjoined to chastity. But, indeed, if a man would succeed in anything, he must check this so easily overdeveloped impulse. Promiscuity means a continually renewed stimulus; the passion, which quickly becomes normal and intermittent when it spends itself upon one object, is apt to become an abnormal and almost continuous craving when it is solicited by a succession of novel and piquant attractions. The advocates of free love assert that it is unnatural repression that creates an undue and morbid longing; that freedom to satisfy the instinct would tend to keep it in its properly subordinate place. But the contrary is, in reality, true. More usually, as Rabelais has it, "the appetite comes during the eating." The absence of temptation will leave an instinct dormant which free opportunity to indulge will develop into a dominant appetite. And nothing more quickly drafts strength or ambition than absorption in sex pleasures; we need to put our energies into something that instead of being inimical is forwarding to the rest of our interests.

(6) Sexual intemperance coarsens, blunts delight in the less violent and more delicate emotions. The pleasures of sex, though of the keenest, are not lasting, like those of the intellect, of religion, art, and manly achievement. But if recklessly indulged in, they inevitably sap our interest in these other ideals. Except where they spring from and reinforce true affection, they are an opiate, taking us into a dream world that makes actual life stale and tasteless. "Hold off from sensuality," says Cicero; "for if you give yourself up to it, you will be unable to think of anything else." There is so much else that is worthwhile, life has so many possible values, that for our own final happiness, we cannot afford to let this instinct usurp too great a place. The vision of God is worth many hours of transient and shallow excitement; and that vision comes only to the pure in heart.

(7) But even for the greatest pleasure in sex itself, incontinence is a blunder. The one telling argument for free love is the sweetness of the delights that the chaste must miss; the bodily intimacy that soothes the lonely heart, the adventurous excitement of breaking down barriers, of dominance and surrender, with its quickened breathing and heightened sense of living. But the plea comes usually from the inexperienced; it is the yearning of youth toward the lure of the untried ways, of the untasted joys. Actually, where passion is unbridled, the halo and the vision quickly vanish; the sated impulse becomes a restless craving for more violent stimulation, a thirst

that no mere physical intimacy can ever assuage; or it leaves the heart cloyed and despondent and resourceless. This is the natural history of undisciplined passion; it cheapens love, it robs it quickly of its exquisiteness and charm. The faithful lover, on the other hand, by checking premature intimacies, and keeping true to the one woman who calls or will some day call out all his love, knows a steady joy that bulks in the end far greater than the flaring and fitful and quickly disillusioned passions of unearned love. Where the veil of mystery is not too rudely drawn aside, the ability to respond to the charm of girlhood and of ripe womanhood may be long retained; the pleasures of sex that count for most in the end are not the moments of passion, but the daily enjoyment of companionship with the opposite sex, the assurance and comfort of mutual fidelity, the love that feeds on daily caresses, endearing words, and acts of tender service. And these lasting joys do not accrue to the man or woman who is not willing to wait, or who squanders his potentialities of love in reckless and fundamentally unsatisfying debauchery. This is the paradox of love; whoso would find its best gifts must be willing to deny himself its gaudiest. The old love of twos, the loyalty of man and wife that bring to each other pure hearts and bodies, is best.

(8) There are, besides, certain practical consequences of which experience warns. Free love would mean that the pretty and well- developed girls, the handsomer and physically stronger men, would be besieged with solicitations and almost inevitably debauched by excess of temptation, while the less attractive would starve for love. It would mean jealousies, deserted lovers, and broken hearts. Free love is especially hard on a woman; she readily becomes attached, and craves loyalty. Inconstancy, though it is so natural to man as often to need the pressure of law and convention for its repression, is not only the worst enemy of his own happiness, but the inevitable source of friction and clash between men and between women. If freedom to break the troth that love instinctively plights is allowed, the chances are numerous that one or the other will some day discover another "affinity" that, at least for the time, seems closer and better suited to him; unless a stern loyalty prevents, one or two or three hearts may be broken. Our monogamous code-whose iological value is clearly indicated by its adoption by most of the higher animals (not counting the domesticated animals, whose morals have been hopelessly ruined)-stands among the wisest of our ideals.

What safeguards against unchastity are necessary?

Overwhelming as is the argument for monogamy, it runs counter to such violent impulses that it needs every prop and sanction that can be given it. It must shelter itself under the law, keep on its side the conscience of men, and be hallowed by alliance with religion. All this is partially attained by the social-religious institution of marriage. The wedding ceremony itself, adding as it does dignity and symbolism, the memory of a beautiful occasion, and the witness of friends to the plighting of mutual vows, is of appreciable value. We must now consider the practical question how, in the face of almost inevitable temptation, the young man and woman may keep chaste during the years prior to marriage. If pre-marital chastity is maintained, there is comparatively little danger of infidelity when chosen love and loyalty to vows come to reinforce the earlier motives.

(1) Certain abstinences, that might not seem in themselves important, are necessary. Little familiarities, kisses and caresses, must be avoided; they are a playing with fire; and the youth never knows when the electric thrill will vibrate through his being, awakened by a touch, that will summon him to a new world wherein he must not yet enter. The finest men do not take these liberties, nor do well-bred girls permit them or respect those who seek them. Vulgar jokes and stories must be despised, as well as all allusions to vice as a natural or amusing thing. Alcohol, gambling, and all unhealthy excitements must be shunned. Above all, the imagination must be controlled; nothing is more dangerous than the indulgence in voluptuous dreams. Longings so fostered, so pent up without outlet, are too apt to break out, in despite of scruples and resolves, if a favorable and alluring opportunity occurs. The battle against sin is won more in private than in the actual moments of temptation.

(2) But in this matter, as always, we must not merely avoid evil, we must overcome evil with good; we can best hope to escape the sirens not as Ulysses did, by having himself bound to the mast, but as Orpheus did, by playing a sweeter music still than they. The best antidote to impurity is a pure love, the next best the dedication to a love yet to be found. The passionate youth must speak in the vein of the Knight in Santayana's poem:

"As the gaudy shadows Stalked by me which men take for beauteous things, I laughed to scorn each feeble counterfeit, And cried to the sweet image in my soul, How much more bright thou wast and beautiful."

Normal friendships with pure girls are vitally necessary for a man, and comradeship with men important for women. Normal interests of all sorts are necessary; the man or woman who has a full, all-round life, who cultivates wholesome intellectual, aesthetic, religious activities, is in far less danger of an unregulated passion. Human energy must find some happy outlets, or it will tend to run amuck; what we become depends largely on what we get interested in. In particular, the abundant physical activity of robust health makes it much easier to banish immoderate desires.

(3) There are certain safeguards that the community should erect. (a) Among these are the conventions that control intimacy between the sexes.

On the one hand, the wholesome comradeship of boys and girls, above desiderated, must be encouraged, not only for the removal of that loneliness and morbid curiosity which are among the greatest of sex irritants, but in order that husband and wife may be wisely chosen. On the other hand, the attractiveness of the other sex may easily draw too much attention from the studies and sports that ought to make up the bulk of the activity of youth; and too great freedom of companionship leads to an unnecessary amount of temptation. The fearless, heart- free friendship of chaste youths and maidens is a priceless boon. But close lines must be drawn, and a certain amount of wise chaperonage is necessary. Too free a physical intimacy between the sexes leads almost irresistibly on, with many, to actual intercourse; the instinct is too imperious to be withstood when opportunity is too easy, if there are not many barriers to be broken first.

(b) Another duty of the community lies in the fight against the public sources of sensual appeal not merely the houses of prostitution and street solicitation, but the vile shows, indecent pictures and books, and other means by which the greed of money panders to the sex instinct. The questions concerning the drama, the ballet, and the nude in art will recur when we come to discuss the general relations of art and morality. Closely parallel are the problems concerning the costume of women; these are phases of the eternal conflict between beauty and morality. What is pretty is tempting. How can we have enjoyment without being wrecked by it; how can we make life rich and yet keep it pure? Some line must be drawn; just where, we have not space to discuss.

(c) Education on matters of sex must probably be attended to in the public schools. It were better done by parents, perhaps; but parents cannot be depended upon to do it. The dangers that await indulgence, the cruelty and brutality of prostitution, should be universally but cautiously taught; too many boys and girls wreck their lives for l ack of such knowledge. It is indeed a delicate task to instruct adolescents in these matters; there is, as Professor Munsterberg has well pointed out, a grave danger of stimulating, by calling attention to it, the very impulse which it is desired to curb, of dissipating the fear of the unknown which may be greater than that of clearly understood, and thereby, perhaps, avoidable dangers, and of breaking down barriers of shyness and reticence, which form one of the most effective of safeguards. Personal attention to the individual needs of boys and girls of widely differing temperaments and mental condition is imperative. But in general, it is to be remembered that almost every boy and girl learns, somehow, long before marriage, the main facts concerning sex-relations. And it is far better that that knowledge should be imparted reverently, accurately, unemotionally, and with due emphasis upon perils and penalties, than that it should be gained in coarse and exciting ways, or remain half understood and with a glamour of mystery about it.

What are the factors in an ideal marriage?

Celibacy is neither natural nor desirable; a happy marriage should be the goal of every healthy man's and woman's thought. The economic situation that prevents so many from marrying till nearly or quite thirty is thoroughly unwholesome and must in some way be remedied. Marriage in the early twenties is not only an important safeguard against unchastity; it is physiologically better for the woman and her offspring. The danger and pain in childbirth to a woman of twenty or twenty-five are less than in later life, and the children have a better chance of health. Moreover, young people are mentally and morally more plastic; they have not yet become so "set" in their ways as they will later become, and are more likely to grow together and make easily those little compromises and adjustments which the fusing of two lives necessitates. And it is always a pity that the two who are to be life comrades should fail to have these years, in some ways the best of their lives, together.

Yet this sacred and exacting relationship must not be hastily entered, for nothing more surely than marriage makes or mars character and happiness. Too early marriage is apt to be impulsive and thoughtless. It is true that many confirmed bachelors and maiden ladies lose through an excess of timidity the great experiences and joys which a little boldness, a little willingness to take a risk and put up with the imperfect would have brought them. No man or woman is perfect; no one can expect to find a wholly ideal mate; it is foolish to be too exacting, and it is conceited, implying that one is flawless one's self. Nevertheless, the counsel of caution is more commonly needed. Happily we have pretty generally got away from mariages de convenance, marriages for money, or title, or other extraneous advantages. And we have recognized the right of the two who are primarily concerned to make their own choice without interference, other than friendly counsel and warning, from others. But we still have many marriages from which the basic desiderata are in too great degree absent.

(1) There should be genuine sex attraction; not necessarily a violent passion, or love at first sight, but some measure of that instinctive organic attraction, that unpredictable and irrational emotional satisfaction in physical proximity, which differentiates sex love from the love of men or women for one another. Not that "platonic" relations between husband and wife are not possible or permissible; but if a young couple are not linked by this sweetest of bonds, they not only miss much of the charm and mutual drawing- together of marriage, but they stand in gravest danger of an eventual arousing of the instinct by another-and that means either a bitter

fight for loyalty or actual tragedy. It is never to be forgotten that husband and wife have to spend a great part of their life in the same house, in the same room. No degree of similarity of interests can take the place of that mere instinctive liking, that pervasive content at each other's presence, that enjoyment in seeing each other about, and in the daily caresses and endearing words that rightly mated couples know.

(2) But this underlying physical attraction, however keen at first is not of guaranteed permanence; it must be buttressed by common tastes and sympathies. To like the same people, to enjoy doing the same things, to judge problems from the same angle, to cleave to similar moral, aesthetic, religious canons is of great importance. A certain amount of contrast in ideas and ideals is, indeed, piquant and stimulating; and where marriage is early there is likelihood of an adequate convergence in Weltanschauung. But too radically different an outlook upon life may lead to continual friction, to loneliness, and mutual antagonism. The two who are to be comrades in the great experiment of life must be able to help each other, strengthen each other's weaknesses, and admire each other's aims and achievements. In particular, religious fanaticism is an intractable enemy of marital happiness. As Stevenson puts it, "There are differences which no habit nor affection can reconcile, and the Bohemian must not ntermarry with the Pharisee. The best of men and the best of women may sometimes live together all their lives, and, for want of some consent on fundamental questions, hold each other lost spirits to the end."

(3) It scarcely needs to be added that there must be on both sides a high standard of morality. Truthfulness, sincerity, self-control, the willingness to work, to sacrifice personal desires and pull together for the common welfare of the house, are essential, as well as fidelity to marriage vows and abstinence from all intemperance and lawbreaking. Common tastes can be formed after marriage; even the organic attraction is pretty sure to be awakened in some degree if the pair are not actually repulsive to each other; but low moral ideals at the age of marriage are seldom radically transformed afterward and render any happiness in home-making insecure.

(4) Perhaps some day it may become incumbent upon the suitor to weigh the matter of the heredity back of the lady of his choice, and consider whether she is best adapted, by mating with him, to give birth to normal and healthy children; or for the maiden sought to regard with equal care the antecedents of the suitor. But-fortunately for lovers' consciences-we know too little at present about heredity and the breeding of human beings to give much useful advice or make any demands of the prospective couple, except to insist that those who are tainted with hereditary disease or feeble-mindedness shall refrain from marriage. To this subject we shall recur in chapter XXX.

Is divorce morally justifiable?

If marriage were always undertaken with adequate caution, there would seldom be need of annulling it. But since mistakes are bound to be made and unhappy unions result; since, further, matters arising after marriage often tend to push couples apart and engender a state of friction or absolute antagonism, a necessary postscript to the questions concerning marriage must be that concerning divorce. It is matter of common knowledge that there is a marked tendency in recent years toward a loosening of the marriage bond; the ease with which divorces are granted in some States has become a national scandal. Among the causes for this are the lessening of allegiance to religious authority, the loss of the older fears and restraints, the growing spirit of adventure and iconoclasm. With the breaking-up of traditions, the lure of freedom has been strong, especially upon the so-long- dominated and docile sex. Women are becoming better educated and asserting their rights everywhere; they are now able to earn their living in many independent ways, and are in a position to break loose; the era of the subjection of women is over, and it is natural that many, particularly of the idle and frivolous, should turn this new-won liberty into license.

But, indeed, human nature being as it is, there would inevitably arise, and have always arisen, many cases of strain and friction in marriage relations. As Chesterton says, a man and a woman are, in the nature of the case, incompatible; and that underlying incommensurability of viewpoint easily results in clash where a deep-rooted affection and a habit of self-control are absent. Innumerable couples have suffered and hated each other and made the best of it; nowadays they are deeming it better frankly to admit and end the discord. And the problem, Which solutionis better? is by no means an easy one. We can but make here a few general suggestions.

(1) Divorce must certainly not be so easy as to encourage hasty and unconsidered marriage, or to turn this most sacred of relationships into a mere experimental and provisional alliance. "Trial marriage" is a palpably reprehensible scheme, involving an unwarrantable stimulus to the sex appetite; many men would enjoy taking one woman after another, until their passion in each case had exhausted its force with the lapse of novelty; women, who are not so naturally promiscuous, would suffer most. What would become of the children is a question whose very posing condemns the proposal. But a lax divorce law provides practically for trial marriage; one or the other party may enter into the contract and pronounce the solemn vows without any intention of keeping them when it shall cease to be for his or her pleasure. Not in this way is to be got the real worth of marriage; the conscious and earnest effort, at least, must be to keep to it for life. An easy short cut to freedom would tempt too many from the harder

but nobler way of compromise, conciliation, and self-subordination. If one is weak and erring, or petulant and unkind, the other must patiently and lovingly seek to help, to educate, to uplift; seventy times seven times is not too often for forgiveness; and many a marriage that seemed hopelessly wrecked has been saved by magnanimity and tactful affection. There is a fine disciplinary value in these forbearances, and much opportunity for spiritual growth in the persevering endeavor toward harmony and mutual understanding. Many a man and woman who might have been lost if divorced, has been saved for a better life by the unwillingness of wife or husband to desert under grievous provocation. There comes an ebb to most conjugal disputes; men and women grow wiser, and often gentler, with age; while there is any hope for readjustment and revival of love it is wrong to break marital vows. Many a divorce has been as hasty and ill considered as the marriage it ended, and has left the couple in the end less happy and useful members of the community. Particularly when there are children should the parents sacrifice much for the sake of giving them a real home, with both mother- and father-love.

(2) Yet there are cases where love is hopelessly killed and harmony is impossible; cases where much suffering, and even moral degeneration, would result from continuance of the married life. Where a man transfers his love to another or indulges in infidelity to his vows; where he crazes himself with liquor or some other narcotic, and will not give it up; where he treats his wife with cruelty or contempt, or through selfishness or laziness deserts or refuses to support her; where she refuses to perform her wifely duties, gives herself to other men, makes home intolerable for him—in short, in any case where mutual loyalty and cooperation are hopeless of attainment, it is surely best that there should be separation. It does not make for the welfare of the children, or for the sanctity of marriage, that such wretched travesties of it should continue. Moreover, for eugenic reasons, we must urge the freeing of wives from husbands who have transmissible diseases, inheritable defects, or chronic alcoholism. Nor should the fact of one mistake preclude the injured party from another opportunity for happiness and usefulness. Whether the guilty man or woman, the one wholly or chiefly to blame for the failure, should be permitted to remarry is another matter; but probably, on the whole, it is better than the alternative encouragement of immorality and illegitimacy.

(3) The community should exert its influence toward the remedying of the present anomalies and uncertainties by making both marriage laws and divorce laws more stringent, and uniform throughout the country. Statutes that will render impulsive marriage impossible, by requiring an interval to elapse after statement of intention to marry, and making a clean bill of health necessary; divorce laws that shall refuse to pander to caprice and

willfulness, but shall make it easy, without scandal or needless publicity, to deliver a woman or a man from an intolerable and irremediable situation, and that shall not be appreciably more lenient in one State than in another, will go far toward curing contemporary evils. It may yet be that the Constitution will be so amended as to permit the National Government to control these matters and thus replace our present chaos with order.

Dewey and Tufts, Ethics, chap. XXVI. Scharlieb and Silby, Youth and Sex. C. Read, Natural and Social Morals, chap. VII. Anon, Life, Love, and Light (Macmillan), pp. 84-96. R. C. Cabot, What Men Live By, chaps. XXIV-XXIX. W. L. Sheldon, An Ethical Movement, chaps. XI, XII. C. F. Dole, Ethics of Progress, part VII, chap. III. Felix Adler, Marriage and Divorce, The Spiritual Meaning of Marriage. N. Smyth, Christian Ethics, pp. 405-15. B. P. Bowne, Principles of Ethics, part III, chaps. VIII, IX. W. E. H. Lecky, The Map of Life, chap. XIV. Stevenson, Virginibus Puerisque. G. E. C. Gray, Husband and Wife. J. Rus, The Peril and Preservation of the Home. Thompson and Geddes, Problems of Sex. H. Munsterberg, "Sex-Education" (in Psychology and Social Sanity). H. G. Wells, "Divorce" (in Social Forces in England and America). C. J. Hawkins, Will the Home Survive? Biblical World, vol. 43, p. 33. International Journal of Ethics, vol. 17, p. 181. For the data: United States Department of Commerce and Labor, Reports on Marriage and Divorce. Publications of the National League for the Protection of the Family (Secretary S. W. Dike, Auburndale, Massachusetts) and of the Society of Sanitary and Moral Prophylaxis (105 West 40th Street, New York). Howard, MATRIMONIAL INSTITUTIONS. Sutherland,
ORIGIN AND GROWTH OF THE MORAL INSTINCT of the Moral Instinct,
chaps. vii, ix. Lestourneaux, EVOLUTION OF MARRIAGE.

CHAPTER XVIII
FELLOWSHIP, LOYALTY, AND LUXURY

EVERY man has to solve the problem of how far he will live for his smaller, personal self, and how far for that larger self that includes the interests of others. The general principles involved we have discussed in chapter XI; we may now proceed to consider their application to the concrete situations in which we find ourselves. What social relationships impose claims upon us?

(1) The relations of husband and wife and of parenthood are most sacred and exacting, because they are voluntarily assumed, and because the need and possibilities of help are here greatest. A man or woman may without odium remain free from these obligations; but once they have made the vows that initiate the dual life, once they have brought a helpless child into the world, neither may evade the consequent responsibilities. If undertaken at all, these duties must be conscientiously fulfilled; and whatever sacrifices are necessary must, as a matter of course, and ungrudgingly, be made.

(2) Next in inviolability to these claims are those of father and mother, brother and sister, and other near relatives. Involuntary as these relations are, the natural piety that accepts the burdens they entail must not be allowed to grow dim. Those nearest of kin are the natural supports and helpers of the weak and dependent; and though patience and resources be severely taxed, it is better to let blood ties continue to involve obligation than to permit the selfish irresponsibility of a freer and more individualistic society. Much provocation can be borne by remembering "She is my mother"; "He is my brother"; after all, their interests are ours, and our lives are impoverished, as well as theirs, if we ignore them.

(3) The voluntary bonds of friendship entail somewhat vaguer obligations, since the closeness of the tie is not clearly fixed, as it is in the case of blood relationship. But "once a friend always a friend" is the truehearted man's motto. "Assure thee," says one of Shakespeare's heroines, "if I do vow a friendship, I'll perform it to the last article." No one who has won another's friendship, and, however tacitly, pledged his own, is thenceforth free to ignore the bond. Here are for most men the happiest opportunities for fellowship, for inward growth, and for service; for if the love of wife surpasses that of friends, it is not only on account of the fascination of sex, but because marriage may be the supreme friendship. Emerson declared that "every man passes his life in the search after friendship"; and the greatest of Stevenson's three desiderata for happiness was - "Ach, Du lieber

Gott, friends!" Human beings, even when brought up in a similar environment, are so infinitely divergent in temperament and ideal, that the near of kin seldom meet a man's deepest needs, and he must wait and watch to find one here and there with whom he can clasp hands in real mutual comprehension and accord. Want of this spontaneous comradeship sadly limits a life; nothing pays more in joy than the circle of friends that a man can draw about him. Nothing, likewise, is more morally stimulating. "What a friend thinks me to be, that must I be." This linking of our lives to others draws us out of ourselves, corrects our cramped and distorted vision, and reinforces our wavering aspirations. Hence those who are so critical and fastidious as to make few friends ill serve their own interests. A certain heartiness and fearlessness of trust is necessary; reproaches and suspicions, accusations and demands for explanations, must not be indulged in, even if wrong is actually done. A presumption of good intentions must always be maintained, even if appearances are black. It is more shameful, as La Rochefoucauld said, to distrust a friend than to be deceived by him. Indeed, these deceptions and disillusions are oftenest the result of our own mistaken idealization; we must expect neither perfection nor those particular virtues in which we ourselves are especially punctilious, and undertake to love and cleave to a mortal, not an angel. Friendship requires not only that we lend a hand when help is needed; it implies patience and tact and the endeavor to understand. Through common experiences, repeated interchange of thought and observation, mutual enjoyment of beauty and fun, particularly in expressing common ideals and working together for common causes, there grows to maturity this wonderful relationship "the slowest fruit in the whole garden of God, which many summers and many winters must ripen."

(4) Beyond the boundaries of blood and friendship lie a whole hierarchy of lesser relationships-to neighbors, to employees, to fellow townsmen, to human beings the world over. Mere proximity constitutes a claim that is not commonly acknowledged when distance interposes; most men would be mortally ashamed to let a next-door neighbor starve, although they may feel no call to lessen their luxuries when thousands, whom they could as easily succor, are perishing in the antipodes. And there is a measure of necessity in this; to burden our minds with the thought of the suffering in India, in Russia, in Japan, leads to a paralyzing sense of impotence. If we confine our thought to the dwellers on our street or in our town, it may not seem utterly hopeless to try to remedy their distress; to improve the situation of the laborers in one's own shop or factory lies within the limits of practicability. But the Christian doctrine of the universal brotherhood of man is becoming a working principle at last; and millions of dollars and thousands of our ablest young men and women are crossing the oceans to uplift and civilize the more backward nations, in deference to the

admonition that we are our brothers' keepers. At home this recognition of the basic human relationship of living together on this little sphere, that is plunging with us all through the great deeps of space, should help to obliterate class lines and snobbishness and bring about a real democracy of fellowship.

(5) Finally, we have a duty to those dumb brothers of ours, the animal species that share with us the earth. For they, too, feel pain and pleasure, and are much at our mercy. We must learn "Never to blend our pleasure or our pride With sorrow of the meanest thing that feels."

All needless hurting of sentient creatures is cruelty, whether of the boy who tortures frogs and flies, or of the grown man who takes his pleasure in hunting to death a frightened deer. Beasts of prey must, indeed, be ruthlessly put to death, just as we execute murderers; among them are to be counted flies, mosquitoes, rats, and the other pests so deadly to the human race and to other animals. But death should be inflicted as painlessly as possible; no humane man will prolong the suffering of the humblest creature for the sake of "sport" or take pleasure in the killing. We must say with Cowper "I would not enter on my list of friends, (Though graced with polished manners and fine sense, Yet wanting sensibility) the man Who needlessly sets foot upon a worm."

This does not necessarily imply that we may not rear and kill animals for food. When properly slaughtered, they suffer inappreciably-no more, and probably less, than they would otherwise suffer before death; the fear of the hunted animal is not present, and there is no danger of leaving mate and offspring to suffer. Indeed, the animals that are bred for food would not have their chance to live at all but for serving that end; and their existence is ordinarily, without doubt, of some positive balance of worth to them. Certainly the rearing of cattle and sheep and chickens adds appreciably to the picturesqueness and richness of human life; and if dieticians are to be believed, their food value could hardly be replaced by substitutes.

The question of vivisection is not a difficult one. Certainly experimentation on living animals should be sharply controlled, anesthetics should be used whenever possible, and the needless repetition of operations for illustrative purposes should be forbidden. But it is far better for the general good that necessary experimentation should be performed upon animals than upon human beings; not at all as a partisan judgment, to shift suffering from ourselves to others, which would be unjustifiable, but because animals are less sensitive to pain, and unable to foresee and fear it as human beings would. The human lives saved have been of far greater worth not only to themselves but objectively than the animal lives sacrificed. Moreover, except for a few glaring instances, vivisection has involved little cruelty; and the crusade against it, though actuated by a noble impulse, has rested upon misrepresentation of facts and exaggeration of evils.

What general duties do we owe our fellows?

(1) The abstract duty to refrain from hurting our fellows, and to give positive help, to whomever we can, will find constant application in connection with each specific problem we are to study. But a few general remarks may be pertinently made here. In the first place, we need to be reminded that to help requires insight and tact and ingenuity; it is not enough to respond to obvious needs or actual requests; we must learn to understand our fellows' wants, remember their tastes, seek out ways to add to their happiness or lighten their burdens. For another must realize the importance of manners, cultivate kindliness of voice and phrase, courtesy, cheerfulness, and good humor. Surliness and ill temper, glumness, touchiness, are inexcusable; nor may we needlessly burden others with our troubles and disappointments - the motto, "Burn your own smoke," voices an important duty. Again, we must remember that people generally are lonely and in need of love; we must be generous in our affection. It is sometimes said that love given as a duty is a mockery; and doubtless spontaneous and irresistible love is best. But it is possible to cultivate love. If we think of others not as rivals or enemies, but as fellows whose interests we ourselves have at heart, if we try to put ourselves in their place, see through their eyes, and enjoy their pleasures and successes, we shall find ourselves coming to want happiness for them and then feeling some measure of affection. Men and women do not have to be perfect to be loved; all or nearly all are love worthy, if we have it in us to love. (2) The question how far we should tolerate what we believe to be wrong in others, and how far we should work to reform them, is of the most difficult. Certainly moral evil must be fought; the counsel to "resist not evil" cannot be taken too sweepingly. No one can sit still while a big boy is bullying a smaller, while vice caterers are plying their trades, while cruelty and injustice of any sort are being perpetrated. In lesser matters, too, we must not be inactive, but use our influence and persuasion to call our fellows to better things. They may well at some later day reproach us if we shirk our duty to help them see and correct their faults; still more may we be reproached by others who have been harmed by faults that we might have done something toward curing. Often a single gentle and tactful admonition has turned the whole current of a man's life. The truest friendship is not too easy- going; it stimulates and checks as well as comforts. Emerson happily phrases this aspect of the matter: "I hate, when I looked for a manly furtherance, or at least a manly resistance, to find a mush of concession. Better be a nettle in the side of your friend than his echo."

This is, however, only half the truth. What Stevenson calls the "passion of interference with others" is one of the wretchedest poisoners of human happiness. People are, after all, hopelessly at variance in ideals, and we must be content to let others live in their own way and according to their own inner light, as we live by ours. Probably neither is the light of perfect day. Parents are particularly at fault in this respect; rare is the father or mother who is willing that son and daughter should leave the parental paths and follow their own ideals. Incalculable is the amount of needless suffering caused by the conscientious attempt to make others over into our own image. As Carlyle wrote, "The friendliest voice must speak from without; and a man's ultimate monition comes only from within." We need not only a shrugging "tolerance," but a willingness to admit that those who differ from us may after all be in the right of it. It often happens that as we live our standards change, and we come to see that those whom we were anxious to reform were less in need of reformation than we; and very likely while we were blaming others, they in their hearts were blaming us. The older we grow the less we feel ourselves qualified for the office of censor.

Certain practical counsels may perhaps be not too impertinent: Be sure you can take advice yourself without offense or irritation before you proffer it to others; there may be beams in your own eyes as well as motes in your neighbors'. Be sure you see through the other's eyes, and get his point of view; only so can you feel reasonably confident that you are right in your advice or reproof.[Footnote: Cf. W. E. H. Lecky, The Map of Life, p. 68: "Few men have enough imagination to realize types of excellence altogether differing from their own. It is this, much more than vanity, that leads them to esteem the types of excellence to which they themselves approximate as the best, and tastes and habits that are altogether incongruous with their own as futile and contemptible."] Be sure that you are saying what you are saying for the other's good, and not to give vent to your own irritability or selfishness or sense of superiority; say what must be said sweetly or gravely, never patronizingly or sharply, with resentfulness or petulance. Be sure you choose your occasion tactfully, and above all things do not nag; it is better to have it out once and for all than to be forever hinting and complaining and reproving. Praise when you can, temper advice with compliments, make it apparent that your spirit is friendly and your mood good-tempered. Talk and think as little as possible of others' faults; he who is above doing a low act is above talking about another's failings. The only right gossip is that which dwells upon the pleasant side of our neighbors' doings. Avoid all impatience, contempt, and anger; they poison no one so much as him who feels them. Cultivate kindliness and sympathy; love opens blind eyes, helps us to understand our neighbor, and to help him in the best way. Are the rich justified in living in luxury? Of all the problems that loyalty to our fellows involves, none is acuter, to the conscientious man, than that concerning the degree of luxury he may allow himself. It is strictly things in the world is limited; the more I have, the less others have. How can a good man be content to spend unnecessary sums upon himself and his own family, when within arm's reach men and women and children are being stunted mentally and morally, are living in dirt and squalor, are succumbing to disease, are actually dying, for lack of the comfort and opportunity that his superfluous wealth could give? "Wherever we may live, if we draw a circle around us of a hundred thousand [sic], or a thousand, or even of ten miles' circumference, and look at the lives of those men and women who are inside our circle, we shall find half- starved children, old people, pregnant women, sick and weak persons, all working beyond their strength, with neither food nor rest enough to support them, and so dying before their time."[Footnote: Tolstoy, What Shall We Do Then? chap. xxvi.] It is only a lack of imagination and sympathy, or an actual ignorance of conditions, that can permit so many really kind-hearted people to spend so much money upon clothes, amusements, elaborate dinners, and a lot of other superfluities, in a world so full of desperate need. It would be well if every citizen could be compelled to do a little charity-visiting, or something of the sort, that he might see with his own eyes the cramping and demoralizing conditions under which, for sheer lack of money, so many worthy poor, under the present crude social organization, must live. It is the segregation of the well to do in their separate quarters that fosters their shameless callousness, and leads, in the rich, "to that flagrant exhibition of great wealth which almost frightens those who know the destitution of the poor."

There is, however, a growing uneasiness among those who have, an increasing sense of responsibility toward those who have not; there are hopeful signs of a return to the sane ideal of the Greeks, who deemed it vulgar and barbaric to spend money lavishly on self. The compunctions of the rich are indicated, on the one hand, by generous donations made to all sorts of causes, and on the other hand, by the arguments which are now thought necessary to justify the selfish use of money. These arguments we may cursorily discuss.

(1) A clever writer in a recent magazine [Footnote: Katherine Fullerton Gerould, in the Atlantic Monthly, vol. 109, p. 135.] speaks of "factitious altruism"; with this "altruism of the Procrusteans" who would reduce every one to the simple life-she has "little patience." "Thousands of people seem to be infected with the idea that by doing more themselves they bestow leisure on others; that by wearing shabby clothes they somehow make it possible for others to dress better- though they thus admit tacitly that leisure and elegance are not evil things. Or perhaps-though Heaven forbid they should be right!-they merely think that by refusing nightingales'

tongues they make every one more content with porridge. Let us be gallant about the porridge that we must eat; but let us never forget that there are better things to eat than porridge."

This philosophy, less gracefully expressed, is not uncommon. Luxury is, other things equal, better than simplicity. But other things are not equal when our neighbors are cold and sick and hungry. What self- respecting man can eat "caviar on principle" when another has not even bread? By wearing plainer clothes we can make it possible for others to dress better, by denying ourselves nightingales' tongues we can buy porridge for the poor. It surely betokens a low moral stage of civilization that so many, nevertheless, choose the Paquin gowns and the six-course dinners. Luxury is better than simplicity if it can be the luxury of all. If not, it means selfishness, callousness, and broken bonds of brotherhood. Moreover, it has personal dangers; it tends to breed softness and laziness, an inability to endure hardship, what Agnes Repplier calls "loss of nerve." It tends to choke the soul, to crush it by the weight of worldly things, as Tarpeia was crushed by the Sabine shields. "Hardly can a rich man enter the kingdom of heaven." Simple living, with occasional luxuries, far more appreciated for their rarity, is healthier and safer, and in the end perhaps as happy. Certainly the luxury of the upper classes has usually portended the downfall of nations. "It is luxury which upholds states?" asks Laveleye; "yes, just as the executioner upholds the hanged man." "Ill fares the land, to hastening ills a prey, Where wealth accumulates and men decay."

(2) There is a patrician illusion prevalent among the rich, to the effect that they are more sensitive than the poor, have higher natures which demand more to satisfy them; that the lower classes do not need and would not appreciate the luxuries which are necessary to their existence. To this the reply is, "Go and get acquainted with them; you will find that they are just the same sort of people that you and your friends are"-not so educated, very likely, nor so refined of speech and manner, but with the same longings and capacities for enjoyment. Of course, they become used to discomfort and deprivation, seared by suffering; so would you in their place. Human nature has a fortunate ability to adjust itself to its environment. But even if the poor do not realize what they are missing, that is scant excuse for not bringing to them, as we can, new comforts and opportunities.

(3) The commonest fallacy lies in the argument that by lavish consumption the rich provide employment for the poor. They provide employment, yes, in serving them. They create needless work, where there is so much work crying to be done. If that money is put into the bank, instead, or into stocks and bonds, it will employ men and women in really useful tasks. If it is given to some of the worthy "causes" which are always handicapped for

lack of funds, it will employ men in caring for the sick, in educating the ignorant, in feeding the hungry, or in bringing recreation and relief to the worn. Every man or woman whose time and strength we buy for our personal service-valet, maid, gardener, dressmaker, chef, or what not-is taken away from the other work of the world.

(4) A certain hopelessness of effecting any good often paralyzes good will. The help a little money can give seems like a drop in the bucket; its assistance is but for a day, and the need remains as great as ever. It may even be worse than wasted; it may encourage shiftlessness, it may pauperize. There is no doubt that indiscriminate and thoughtless charity is dangerous; the crude largesse of a few rich Romans of the Empire bred vast corruption and pauperism. But there is much that can safely be done; there are many wise and cautious agencies at work for aid and uplift; and every little, if given to one of them, is of real help.

(5) It is sometimes said that if society discountenances luxury, the motive for hard and efficient work will be too much reduced; we need this extra spur to exertion. But the earning of what may permissibly be spent on self is spur enough; there is no need of inordinate luxury to foster faithfulness and exertion. The praise of superiors and equals, a moderate rise in scale of living, the shame of shirking, the instinctive glory in achievement, and the joy of helping others, are stimuli enough.

(6) Finally, the last argument of the selfish man is that "he has earned his money; it is his; he has a right to do with it as he pleases" This we cannot admit. Legally he is as yet free so backward is our social order-to accumulate and spend upon himself vast sums. But it is not best for society that he should, and so he is not morally justified therein. We must agree with Carnegie that "whatever surplus wealth comes to him (beyond his needs and those of his family) is to be regarded as a social trust, which he is bound to administer for the good of his fellows"; and with Professor Sager, that "the general interest requires acceptance of the maxim: the consumption of luxuries should be deferred until all are provided with necessaries." This does not mean that we need live like peasants, as Tolstoy advised, make our own shoes, and till our own plot of ground; nor that we must come down to the level of the lowest. By doing that we should lose the great advantages of our material progress, which rests upon the high specialization of labor and reciprocal service. We should lose the charm and picturesqueness of highly differentiated lives, and sink into the dull, monotonous democracy which Matthew Arnold so dreaded. We must work where we can best serve; we must try to make our lives and their surroundings beautiful, so far as beauty does not require too great cost. We must save up for a rainy day, for insurance against illness and old age, for wife and children. We may properly invest money, where it will be used to

good ends - so that we beware of spendthrift or lazy heirs. We must keep up a reasonably comfortable and beautiful standard of living, such a standard as the majority could hope to attain to by hard work and abstinence and thrift. But all the money one can earn beyond this ought to be used for service. The extravagance and ostentation and waste of many even moderately well to do are a blot upon our civilization. The insane ideal of lavish adornment, of fashionable clothes and costly furnishings, of mere vain display and wanton luxury, infects rich and poor alike, isolating the former from the great universal current of life, and provoking in the latter bitterness and anarchism. Let us ask in every case, Does this expenditure bring use, health, joy commensurate with the labor it represents? A great deal of current expense in dressing, in entertaining, in eating, could be saved by a sensible economy, with no appreciable loss in enjoyment. We must not forget that everything we consume has been produced by the labor and time of others. What fortune, or our own cleverness, has put into our hands that we do not need for making fair and free our own lives, and the lives of those dependent upon us, we should pass on to those whose need is greater than ours. Is it wrong to gamble, bet, or speculate? A corollary to our discussion of the duties appertaining to the use of money must be a condemnation of gambling. Its most obvious evil is the danger of loss of needed money; most gamblers cannot rightly afford to throw away what ought to be used for their real needs and those of their families. Notably is this the case with college students, supported by their parents, who heedlessly waste the money that others have worked hard to save. But even if a man be rich, he should steward his wealth for purposes useful to society. And he must remember that if he can afford to lose, perhaps his opponent cannot. Moreover, if many cannot afford to lose, no one can afford to win. Insidiously this getting of unearned money promotes laziness, and the desire to acquire more money without work. It makes against loving relations with others, since one always gains at another's expense. It quickly becomes a morbid passion, an unhealthy excitement, which absorbs too much energy and kills more natural enjoyments. The gambling mania, like any other reckless dissipation, easily leads to other dissipations, such as drinking and sex indulgence. These disastrous consequences are, of course, by no means always incurred. But in order that the weaker may be saved from them, it behooves the stronger to abstain. All betting, all playing games for money, all gambling in stocks is wrong in principle, liable to bring needless unhappiness. The honorable man will hate to take money which has not been fairly earned; he will wish to help protect those who are prone to run useless risks against themselves. The safest place to draw the line is on the near side of all gambling, however trivial.[Footnote: See H. Jeffs, Concerning Conscience, Appendix. R. E. Speer, A Young Man's Questions, chap. xi B. S. Rowntree, Betting and

Gambling. International Journal of Ethics, vol. 18, p. 76.] General relations to others: F. Paulsen, System of Ethics, book III, chap. IX, sec. 6; chap. X, secs. 3, 4, 5. G. Santayana, Reason in Society. J. S. Mackenzie, Manual of Ethics, 2d ed, chap. IX. Emerson, Society and Solitude title essay. P. G. Hamerton, The Intellectual Life, part IX. Friendship: Aristotle, Ethics, books. VIII, IX. Emerson, "Friendship" (in Essays, vol. I). H. C. Trumbull, Friendship the Master Passion. Randolph Bourne, in Atlantic Monthly, vol. 110, p. 795. Luxury: E. de Laveleye, Luxury. E. J. Urwick, Luxury and Waste of Life. Tolstoy, What Shall We Do Then? (or, What To Do?) Maeterlinck, "Our Social Duty" (in Measure of the Hours). F. Paulsen, System of Ethics, book III, chap. IV, secs. 3, 4. T. W. Higginson, in Atlantic Monthly, vol. 107, p. 301. H. Sidgwick, Practical Ethics, chap. VII. Hibbert Journal, vol. II, p. 39. H. R. Seager, Introduction to Economics, chap. IV, secs. 43-45.

CHAPTER XIX
TRUTHFULNESS AND ITS PROBLEMS

Sins of untruthfulness are not so seductive or, usually, so serious as those we have been considering; but for that reason they are perhaps more pervasive - we are less on our guard against them. What are the reasons for the obligation of truthfulness? Truthfulness means trustworthiness. The organization of society could not be maintained without mutual confidence. This general need and the specific harm done to the individual lied to, if he is thereby misled, are sufficiently plain. [Footnote: I will content myself with quoting one sentence from Mill (Utilitarianism, chap. II), warning the reader to take a deep breath before he plunges in: "Inasmuch as the cultivation in ourselves of a sensitive feeling on the subject of veracity is one of the most useful, and the enfeeblement of that feeling one of the most hurtful, things to which our conduct can be instrumental; and inasmuch as any, even unintentional, deviation from truth does that much towards weakening the trustworthiness of human assertion, which is not only the principal support of all present social well-being, but the insufficiency of which does more than any one [other] thing that can be named to keep back civilization, virtue, everything on which human happiness on the largest scale depends, - we feel that the violation, for a present advantage, of a rule of such transcendent expediency, is not expedient, and that he who, for the sake of a convenience to himself or to some other individual, does what depends on him to deprive mankind of the good, and inflict upon them the evil, involved in the greater or less reliance which they can place in each others' words, acts the part of one of their worst enemies."] The evil resulting to the man who lies is less generally recognized. We may summarize it under three heads:

(1) It is much simpler and less worrisome, usually, to tell the truth. A lie is apt to be scantly on our guard; and one lie is very likely to need propping by others. We are led easily into deep waters, and discover "what a tangled web we weave When first we practice to deceive." But when we tell the truth, we have no need to remember what we said; there is a carefree heartiness about the life that is open and aboveboard that the liar, unless he has given up trying to maintain a reputation, never knows.

(2) Lying is usually a SYMPTOM - of selfishness, vanity, greed, slovenliness, or some other vicious tendency which a man cannot afford to tolerate. Refusing to give vent in speech to these undesirable states of mind helps to atrophy them, while every expression of them insures them a deeper hold. Untruthfulness is the great ally of all forms of dishonesty; and

strict scruples against lying make it much easier to clear them from the soul. This is the best vantage point from which to attack the half-conscious egotism which seeks to create a false impression of one's virtues or powers, the insidiously growing avarice that instinctively overvalues goods for sale and disparages what is offered. It is a good vantage point from which to attack carelessness, inaccuracy, and negligence; the man who has trained himself to precision of speech, who is painstakingly honest in his statements, who qualifies and discriminates, and hits the bull's eye in his descriptions of fact, can be pretty safely depended upon to do things rightly as well. The selfish lie is never justifiable, because selfishness is never justifiable; the cowardly lie - "lying out of" unpleasant consequences - is wrong, because cowardice is wrong. To banish the symptoms may not wholly banish the underlying causes, but it is one good way to go about it. At least, the lies are danger signals.

(3) The habit of lying is very easily acquired; and the habitual liar is sure, sooner or later, to be caught and to be despised. He has forfeited the confidence of men and will find it almost impossible to regain it or to win a position of trust. If one must lie, then, it pays to lie boldly, as a definite and authorized exception to one's general rule; in this way one may keep from sliding unawares into the habit. All equivocations and dissimulations, all literal truths that are really deceptions, all attempts to salve one's own conscience by making one's statements true "in a sense," and yet gain the advantage of an out-and- out lie, are miserable make-shifts and utterly demoralizing. There is "not much in a truthfulness which is only phrase-deep." Whether we deceive others or no, we cannot afford to deceive ourselves; we should never deviate a hair's breadth from the truth without acknowledging the deviation to ourselves as a necessary but unfortunate evil. A man may say nothing but what is true, and yet intentionally give a wrong impression; "truth in spirit, not truth to the letter, is the true veracity." "A lie may be told by a truth, or a truth conveyed by a lie." "A man may have sat in a room for hours and not opened his teeth, and yet come out of that room a disloyal friend or a vile calumniator."[Footnote: Stevenson, Virginibus Puerisque, chap. IV.] If a man lies deliberately and regretfully, for an end that seems to him to require it, he may be making a mistake; but he is escaping the worst danger of lying. He is not corrupting his soul, blurring his vision of the line between sincerity and insincerity, and numbing his conscience so that presently he will lie as a matter of course - and be universally distrusted. All of this is very clear, and sufficiently explains our ideal of veracity. But it is not enough for moralists to dwell upon the general necessity of truthfulness; the problems connected therewith arise when one asks, Are there not legitimate or even obligatory exceptions to the rule? Except for a few theorists who are more attracted by unity and simplicity than by the concrete complexities of life, practically

all agree that there are occasions when lying is necessary, occasions when the confidence of men would not be destroyed by a lie because of the clearly exceptional nature of the case. Can we lay down any useful rules in the matter, indicating what types of cases require untruthfulness? What exceptions are allowable to the duty of truthfulness? Love undoubtedly sometimes requires, and oftener still excuses, a lie.

(1) There are the trite cases where by misinformation a prospective murderer is misled and his potential victim saved;[Footnote: Cf. the somewhat similar situation in Victor Hugo's Les Miserables (Fantine, last chapter) where Soeur Simplice lies to Javert about Jean Valjean. Hugo applauds the lie perhaps too extravagantly ("O sainte fille! que ce mensonge vous soit compte dans le paradis!"); but few probably would condemn it. Another interesting case is that of a French girl in the days of the Commune. On her way to execution her fiance tried to interfere; but she, realizing that if he were known to be her lover he would likewise be executed, looked coldly upon him and said, "Sir, I never knew you!"] where a sick man, who would have less chance of recovery if he realized his dangerous condition, is cheered and carried over the critical point by loving deception; where a theater catches fire and a disastrous panic is averted by a statement to the audience that one of the actors has fallen ill, and the performance must be ended. In such cases it is foolish to talk of the possibility of evasion; it is direct misstatement that is necessary to prevent the great evil that knowledge, or even suspicion of the truth, might entail. Truthfulness under such circumstances, or even the taking of a chance by attempting to effect deception without literal untruth, would be brutal and inexcusable. As Saleeby puts it, "When the choice is between being a liar or a brute, only brutal people can tell the truth or hesitate to lie - and that right roundly.[Footnote: Ethics, p. 103.] In such cases the public, including the very people deceived (except the murderer, who deserves no consideration), applaud the lie; no lack of confidence is engendered. Other cases, less commonly discussed, are equally clear. A mother has just lost a son whom she has idealized and believed to be pure; his classmates know him to have been a rake. If she asks them about his character, will not all feel called upon to deceive her, and leave her in her bereavement at least free from that worst sting? When a timid woman or a sensitive child is alarmed, say, for example, at sea in a fog, will not a considerate companion reiterate assurance that there is little or no danger, even when he himself believes the risk may be great? When a man is asked about some matter which he has promised to keep secret, if the attempt to evade the question in the nature of the case is practically a letting-out of the secret, there seems sometimes to be hardly an alternative to lying. Mrs. Gerould puts it thus: "A question put by some one who has no right to the information demanded, deserves no truth. If a casual gossip should ask me whether my unmarried great-aunt

lived beyond her means, I should feel justified in saying that she did not although it might be the private family scandal that she did. There are inquiries which are a sort of moral burglary" [Footnote: In the Atlantic essay referred to at the end of this chapter. The unassigned quotations following are from that paper, which I am particularly glad to commend after rather curtly criticizing that other essay of hers in the preceding chapter.]

(2) In regard to the little lies which form a part of the conventions of polite society, there may be difference of opinion. Their aim is to obviate hurting people's feelings, to oil the wheels of social misled by them. When asked by one's hostess if one likes what is apparently the only dish provided, or if one has had enough when one is really still hungry, the average courteous man will murmur a gallant falsehood. What harm can be done thereby, and why cause her useless embarrassment? "We simply have to be polite as our race and clime understand politeness, and no one except a naive is really going to take this sort of thing seriously." To thank a stupid hostess for the pleasure she has not given, is loving one's neighbor as one's self. "I know only one person whom I could count on not to indulge herself in these conventional falsehoods, and she has never been able, so far as I know, to keep a friend. The habit of literal truth-telling, frankly, is self-indulgence of the worst." In some circles, at least, the phrase "not at home" is generally understood as a politer form of "not seeing visitors." It must be admitted, however, that there is danger in these courteous untruths. If the visitor does not understand the "not at home" in the conventional sense, she may be deeply hurt and lose her trust in her friend, if she by chance discovers her to have been in the house at the time. Nor is it always wise to truckle to sensibilities that may be foolish; blunt truthfulness, even if unpalatable, is often in the end the best service. There are cases where untruthfulness is shirking one's duty, just as there are cases where truthfulness is mean or brutal.

To tell what we honestly think of a person, or his work, may mean to discourage him and invite demoralization or failure; to attribute virtues or powers to him which he actually does not possess may be to foster those virtues or powers in him. Or the reverse may be the case; his individual need may be of frank criticism or rebuke. The concrete decision can only be reached by following the guidance of the law of kindness, the Apostle's counsel of "speaking truth in love."

(3) In this connection it may be well to go further and emphasize the fact that there are many cases, not necessitating a lie, where the truth is not to be thrust at people. "Friend, though thy soul should burn thee, yet be still. Thoughts were not meant for strife, nor tongues for swords, He that sees clear is gentlest of his words, And that's not truth that hath the heart to

kill." There are usually pleasant enough things that one CAN say - though one may be hard put to it; and if the truth must be told, it may often be sugarcoated. President Hadley, when a young man, was receiving instructions for a delicate negotiation. "If the issue is forced upon us," he interrupted, "there is, I think, nothing to do but to tell the truth." "Even then," replied his chief, "not butt end foremost." Cases of religious disbelief will occur to every one. While all hypocrisy and truckling to the majority opinion is ignoble, the blunt announcement of disbelief may do much more harm than good. Truth is not the only ideal; men live by their beliefs, and one who cannot accept a doctrine which is precious and inspiring to others should think twice before helping to destroy it. Not only may he, after all, be in the wrong, or but half right; even if he is wholly right, it may not be wise to thrust his truth upon those whom it may discourage or morally paralyze. [Footnote: On the ethics of outspokenness in religious matters, see H. Sidgwick, Practical Ethics, chap. VI; J. S. Mill, Inaugural Address at St. Andrews; Matthew Arnold, Prefaces to Literature and Dogma and God and the Bible F. Paulsen, System of Ethics, book III, Chap. XI, sec. 10.] In what directions are our standards of truthfulness low? Truthfulness in private affairs averages fairly high in our times. Many people will, indeed, lie about the age of a child for the sake of paying the half- fare rate, use the return half of a round-trip ticket sold only for the original purchaser's use, or look unconcernedly out of the window if they think the conductor will pass them by without collecting fare. Certain forms of such oral or tacit lying are so common that people of looser standards adopt them with the excuse that "every one does it," or that "the company can afford to lose it." But in more public matters the prevalence of untruthfulness is much more shocking. Standards are low or unformulated, and it is often extremely difficult for the honorable man to know what to do; strict truthfulness would deprive him of his position. We may barely hint at some of these situations.

(1) In business, misstatement is generally expected of a salesman. Advertisements of bargains, for example, have to be discounted by the wary shopper. "$10 value, reduced to $3.98," may mean something worth really $3. "Finest quality" may mean average quality; goods passed off as first-class may be shoddy or adulterated. Labels on foodstuffs and drugs are, happily, controlled to some degree by the national government; there ought to be a similar control over all advertising. Much is being done by the better magazines in investigating goods and refusing untruthful advertising; and many houses have built up a deserved reputation for reliability. But still the economical householder has to spend much time in comparing prices and studying values, that he may be sure he is not being cheated.

(2) In politics, frank truth telling is almost rare. It is deemed necessary to suppress what sounds unfavorable to a candidate's chances, to make unfair insinuations against opponents, to juggle statistics, emphasize half-truths, and work generally for the party by fair means or foul. Too great candor in admitting the truth in opponents' arguments or the worth of their candidates would be sharply reprimanded by party leaders. Especially in international diplomacy is truthfulness far to seek. Secretary Hay, indeed, stated in the following words: "The principles which have guided us have been of limpid simplicity. We have set no traps; we have wasted no time in evading the imaginary traps of others. There might be worse reputations for a country to acquire than that of always speaking the truth, and always expecting it from others. In bargaining we have tried not to get the worst of the deal, alway remembering, however, that the best bargains are those that satisfy both sides. Let us hope we may never be big enough to outgrow our conscience." Other American diplomats have followed the same ideal. But American diplomacy has been labeled abroad as "crude," and is perpetually in danger of lapsing from this moral level.

(3) The profession of the lawyer presents peculiarly difficult problems. May he so manipulate the facts in his plea as to convince a jury of what he is himself not convinced? May he by use of the argumentum ad populum, by his eloquence and skill, win a case which he does not believe in at heart? In some ancient codes lawyers had to swear not to defend causes which they believed unjust. But this is hardly fair to a client, since, even though appearances are against him, he may be innocent; whatever can be said for him should be discovered and presented to the tribunal. Dr. Johnson said: "You are not to deceive your client with false representations of your opinion, you are not to tell lies to the judge, but you need have no scruple about taking up a case which you believe to be bad, or affecting a warmth which you do not feel. You do not know your cause to be bad till the judge determines it. An argument which does not convince you may convince the judge, and, if it does convince him, you are wrong and he is right." [Footnote: Quoted by W. E. H. Lecky, The Map of Life, p. 110. The chapter which contains this quotation gives an interesting discussion of the ethics of the lawyer and some further references on the subject.] This dilemma of the lawyer could be matched by equally doubtful situations that confront the physician, [Footnote: See, for a discussion of the ethics of the medical profession, G. Bernard Shaw, Preface to The Doctor's Dilemma, and B. J. Hendrick, "The New Medical Ethics," in McClure's Magazine, vol. 42, p. 117.] and members of the other professions. There is need of acknowledged professional codes, drawn up by representative members, and enforced by public opinion within the profession and perhaps by the danger of expulsion from membership in the professional associations. It is largely the variation in practice between equally conscientious members that

causes the distrust and disorder of our present situation. Truthfulness must be standardized for the professions. [Footnote: On professional codes, see H. Jeffs, Concerning Conscience, chap. VIII.]

(4) The author, whether of books or essays or reviews, has to face particularly powerful temptations. It is so easy to overstate his case, to omit facts that make against his conclusions, to use colored words, to beg the question adroitly, to create prejudice by unfair epithets, to evade difficult questions, to take the popular side of a debated matter at the cost of loyalty to truth. Controversy almost inevitably breeds inaccuracy; there are few writers who fight fair. Quotations, torn from their context, mislead; carefully chosen figures give a wrong impression; the reviewer is tempted to pick out passages that support only his contention, whether eulogistic or depreciatory. Leslie Stephen speaks of "the ease with which a man endowed with a gift of popular rhetoric, and a facility for catching at the current phrases, can set up as teacher, however palpable to the initiated may be his ignorance." A larger proportion of the great mass of books yearly published are mere trash, appealing to untrained readers, and only confirming them in unwarranted beliefs and opinions. Few there are who are really fit to teach the public; and of those there are fewer still who love truth more than the triumph of their opinion, who are candid, scrupulous, and exact in their statements. There is doubtless little conscious deception; but there is a great deal of misstatement which is inexcusable, and due either to slovenliness, lack of proper training, or partisanship.

This brings us to the similar and even graver evils in our modern newspapers, which we must pause to study in somewhat greater detail. For nowhere is untruthfulness so rampant and so shameless as in contemporary journalism. The ethics of journalism.

(1) The gravest evil, perhaps, in journalistic practice is the suppression or distortion of news in the interest of political parties and "big business." It is impossible to rely on the political information given in most of our newspapers; they are dominated by a party, subservient to "the interests," afraid to publish anything that will offend them. They misrepresent facts, give prejudiced accounts of events, gloss over occurrences unfavorable to their ends, circulate unfounded rumors to create opinion, pounce upon every flaw in the records of opponents,- going often to the point of shameless libel,- while eulogizing indiscriminately the politicians of their own party. Many of them cannot be counted on to attack corruption or politically protected vice. They are organs neither of an impartial truth seeking nor of public service. However conscientious the reporters and editors might wish to be, they are bound, by the fear of dismissal, to follow the policy of the owners.

(2) No less reprehensible, though somewhat less important, is the toadying of the newspapers to their advertisers. The average paper could not exist were it not for this source of income, and it cannot afford to refuse the big advertisements even when they are pernicious to the morals or health of the community. So we are confronted daily by the premedicine fakirs, who injure the health and drain the pocketbooks of the guileless. So we are exposed to the plausible suggestions of the swindlers, feasted with glowing prospectuses of mines that will never yield a dividend, or eulogistic descriptions of house lots to be sacrificed at a price that is really double their worth. In a recent postal raid the financial frauds exposed had fleeced the public of nearly eighty million dollars, about a third of which had been spent in advertising.

Not only do the newspapers accept such advertisements, and those of the brewers, the cigarette-makers, and the proprietors of vile theaters, but they do not dare in their columns to denounce these frauds or undesirable trades. They are muzzled because they cannot afford to tell the truth when it will offend those who supply their revenue.

(3) Less harmful, but more superficially conspicuous, is the tendency toward the fabrication of imaginary news, to attract attention and sell the paper. Huge headlines announce some exciting event, which below is inconspicuously acknowledged to be but a rumor. It will be denied the next day in an obscure corner, while the front page is devoted to some new sensation. This "yellow journalism" is very irritating to one who cares more for facts than for thrills; and the more reputable newspapers have stood out against this disgraceful habit of their less scrupulous rivals. Mr. Pulitzer, the son of the famous editor of the New York "World," in an address at the opening of the Columbia University School of Journalism, spoke vehemently against this evil: "The newspaper which sells the public deliberate fakes instead of facts is selling adulterated goods just as surely as does the rascal who puts salicylic acid in canned meats or arsenical coloring in preserves; and it ought to be subject to the same penalties for adulteration as are these other adulterators. The fakir is a liar if he is guilty of a fake that injures people, he is not only a vicious liar but often a moral assassin as well; but in either event he is a liar, and it is only by treating him uncompromisingly as such that he may be corrected if he is not yet a confirmed fakir, or rooted out if he is an inveterate fakir." There is surely enough, for those who have eyes to see, that is dramatic and exciting in actual life without depending upon fictitious news. Chesterton berates the contemporary press for failing to give us the thrill of reality. It "offends as being not sensational or violent enough; . . . does not merely fail to exaggerate life-it positively underrates it. With the whole world full of big and dubious institutions, with the whole wickedness of civilization staring

them in the face, their idea of being bold and bright is to attack the War Office. . . . Something which is an old joke in fourth-rate comic papers." [Footnote: "The Mildness of the Yellow Press," chap. VIII of Heretics.]

(4) Another danger of our irresponsible journalism lies in pandering to prejudices and antipathies, in stirring up class hatred or national jingoism. Evil motives are attributed to foreign powers; the German Emperor has designs upon South America; the Japanese are preparing to invade our Pacific Coast. Insignificant words of individuals are headlined and treated as portentous; foreign peoples are caricatured; our national "honor" is held to be in danger daily. Or the capitalists are pictured as universally fat and greedy and unscrupulous; anarchism is encouraged-as in the case of the murderer of McKinley, who was directly incited to his deed by the violent diatribes of a contemporary newspaper. Such demagoguery might flourish even with strict regard for truthfulness; but it becomes far worse when, as usual, in its appeal to popular prejudices, it exaggerates and invents and suppresses facts.

(5) The notorious emphasis upon crime and summary of journalistic evils. Every unpleasant fact that ought, from kindness to those concerned and from regard to the morals of the readers, to be ignored or passed lightly over, is instead dragged out into the light. The delight in besmirching supposedly respectable citizens, the brutal intrusion into private unhappiness, the detailed description of domestic tragedy, is nothing short of outrageous. Pictures of adulterers and murderers, of the instruments and scenes of crimes, precise instructions to the uninitiated for their commission, explanations of the success of burglary or train-wreckers, help marvelously to sell a paper, but do not help the morals of the younger generation. No one can estimate the amount of sexual stimulation, of suggestion to sin and vice, for which our newspapers are responsible.

(6) In conclusion, we may mention a trivial matter which, however, brings our newspapers into deserved disrepute-their self-laudation ad boasting. How many "greatest American newspapers" are there? There are even, in this country alone, more than one "World's greatest newspaper!" From this principle of conceit there are all gradations down to the humblest village paper that lies about its circulation and extols itself as the necessary adjunct of every home. These overstatements are pernicious in their influence upon public standards of accuracy and honesty.

The newspaper is potentially an instrument of incalculable good. No other influence upon the minds and morals of the people is so continuous and universal. Through the newspapers knowledge is disseminated, judgment and outlook upon life are crystallized, political and social beliefs are shaped. They might be the means of great social and moral reforms. But so long as they are subject to the struggle for existence which, necessitates their truckling to parties, to advertisers, and to public prejudices and passions, so long their influence will be largely unwholesome. If public opinion cannot force them to a higher moral level in their present status as sources of private profit, they must be published by the State or by trustees of an endowment fund. Municipally owned papers are liable to partisanship and corruption, in their way, and endowed papers to an undue regard for the interests of the class to which the majority of the trustees may belong. But the dangers would probably be far less than are inherent in our present system, where morals have to defer to pocketbooks; and when municipal government in this country is finally ordered in a sensible way, so that corruption is much more difficult and easily detected, the municipal newspaper, run after the "city manager" plan, will probably become universal.

F. Paulsen, System of Ethics, book III, chap. XI. L. Stephen, Science of Ethics, chap, V, sec. IV. C. F. Dole, Ethics of Progress, part VII, chaps, I, II. E. L. Cabot, Everyday Ethics, chaps. XIX, XX. T. K. Abbott, Kant's Theory of Ethics, Appendix I. Stevenson, Virginibus Puerisque, chap. IV. E. Westermarck, Origin and Development of Moral Ideas, chap. XXXI. K. F. Gerould, in Atlantic Monthly, vol. 112, p. 454. Ethics of Journalism: H. Holt, Commercialism and Journalism. H. George, Jr, The Menace of Privilege, book VII, chap. I. W. E. Weyl, The New Democracy, chap. IX. Educational Review, vol. 36, p. 121. Atlantic Monthly, vol. 102, p. 441; vol. 105, p. 303; vol. 106, p. 40; vol. 113, p. 289. Forum, vol. 51, p. 565. E. A. Ross, Changing America, chap. VII. North American Review, vol. 190, p. 587.

CHAPTER XX

CULTURE AND ART

THE function of the newspaper, which we have been discussing, is, to a considerable extent, to widen our horizon, to give us new ideas and sympathies, to enrich and brighten our lives; in greater degree, that is the role of the fine arts, and of that wide conversance with beauty and truth that we call culture. Man is not a mere worker, and efficiency is not the only test of value; the pursuit of truth and beauty for its own sake is a legitimate human ideal. But beauty, as we have seen, brings temptations; and even the search for truth may lure a man away from his duty. We must consider, then, how far culture, and its outward expression in art, may rightly claim the time and energies of man.

What is the value of culture and art?

(1) Culture, according to Matthew Arnold, [Footnote: Culture and Anarchy, Preface, and chap. I.] is "the disinterested endeavor after man's perfection . . . . It is in endless additions to itself, in the endless expansion of its powers, in endless growth in wisdom and beauty that the spirit of the human race finds its ideal." This wisdom, this beauty that culture offers us, does not need extrinsic justification; it is, as Emerson so happily said, its own excuse for being; it is a fragment of the ideal; and it means that life has in so far been solved, its goal attained. It is in itself a great addition to the worth, the richness and joy, of life, and it is a pledge to the heart of the possibility of the ideal, a realization of that perfection for which we long and strive.

It means a multiplication of interests, a participation by proxy in the throbbing life of mankind, which lifts us above the disappointments of our personal fortunes, helps us to identify ourselves with the larger currents of life, and to live as citizens of the world. A limitless resource against ennui, it refreshes, rests, and recreates, relieves the tension of our working hours, makes for health and sanity. "If a man find himself with bread in both hands," said Mohammed, "he should exchange one loaf for some flowers of the narcissus, since the loaf feeds the body, indeed, but the flowers feed the soul."

There is in certain quarters a tendency to disparage culture as not practical-" a spirit of cultivated inaction" -unworthy of the attention of serious men. The word connotes, perhaps, to these critics certain superficial polite accomplishments, mere frills and decorations, which fritter away our time and dissipate our ambitions. But in its proper sense, culture is far more than that; it is the comprehension of the meaning of life and the appreciation of its beauty. And grim as is the age-long struggle with evil, insistent as is the duty to toil and suffer and achieve, it were a harsh taskmaster who should refuse to poor driven men and women the right to snatch such innocent joys as they can by the way, to try to understand the whirl of existence in which they are caught; in short, to really live, as well as to earn a living. It would be a sorry outcome if when we reached the age of complete mechanical efficiency, with all the machinery of a complex industrial life well oiled and perfected, we should find ourselves imaginatively sterile, hopelessly utilitarian, earthbound in our vision.

(2) But the moralist need not rest with this apology for culture. By helping us to understand the life about us, culture shows us the better how to solve our own problems, and saves us from the tragedy of putting our energies into fiction, poetry, and the drama give us an insight into the longings, the temptations, the ideals of others, and so indirectly into our own hearts. Thus a normal perspective of values is fostered; we come to learn what is base and what is excellent, and have our eyes opened to the inferior nature of that with which we had before been content. There is a pathos in the ignorance of the uncultivated man as to what is good. Give him money to spend and he will buy tawdry furniture and imitation jewelry, he will go to vulgar shows and read cheap and silly trash. He is unaware of what the best things are, and unable to spend his money in such a way as really to improve his mind, his health, or his happiness. Even in his vocation he could be helped by a background of culture; the college graduate outstrips the uneducated man who has had several years the start of him. And no one can tell how many an undeveloped genius there may be, now working at some humble and routine task, who might have contributed much to the world if his mental horizon had been widened and his latent powers unfolded. Knowledge is power; we never know what bit of apparently useless insight may find application in our own lives and help us to solve our personal problems.

(3) Moreover, culture is not only informative, it is inspirational. History and biography fire the youth with a noble spirit of emulation; poetry, fiction, and the drama, and to some extent music, painting, and sculpture, arouse the emotions and direct them-if the art is good-into proper channels. Meunier's sculptured figures, Millet's Angelus or Man with the Hoe, the oratorio of the Messiah or a national song like the Marseillaise, have a stirring and ennobling effect upon the soul; while such a poem as Moody's Ode in Time of Hesitation, a story like Dickens's Christmas Carol, or a play like The Servant in efficacious than many a sermon. The study of any art has a refining influence, teaching exactness and restraint, proportion, measure, discipline. And in any case, if no more could be said, art and culture substitute innocent joys and excitements for dangerous ones, satisfy the craving for sense-enjoyment by providing natural outlets and developing normal powers, thus tending to check its crude and

unwholesome manifestations. In these ways they are valuable moral forces, whose usefulness we ought not to neglect.

(4) Culture socializes. It adds to our competitive life, to our personal ambitions and self-seeking, an unselfish pleasure, a pleasure which we can share with all, and which needs to be shared to be best enjoyed. Nothing binds men together more joyously and with less likelihood of friction than their common love of the beautiful. All classes and all peoples, men of whatever trade or interests, may learn to love the same scarlet of dawn, the same stir and heave of the sea, that Homer loved and fixed in winged words for all men of all time. From whatever land we come we may thrill to the words of English Shakespeare or Florentine Dante, to the chords of German Wagner and Italian Verdi, to the colors of Raphael and Murillo, to the noble thoughts of Athenian Plato, Roman Marcus Aurelius, and Russian Tolstoy. Our opinions differ, our interests diverge, our aims often cross; but in the presence of high truth and beauty, fitly expressed, our differences are forgotten and we are conscious of our essential unity. Prejudices and provincialisms crumble, personal eccentricities fade, barriers are broken, all sorts of fanaticisms and frictions are choked off, under the influence of a widespread cultural education. What is most important in cultural education? Wisdom and beauty are vague words; and to make our discussion practical we must indicate what in the ideal curriculum. It is a matter of relative values, since nearly every study is of some worth; and the detailed decision as to subjects and methods must be left to the expert on pedagogy. But to present the general needs that education must meet falls within our province. In addition, then, to the particular vocational education which is to fit each man for his specific task, in addition to that physical development which must always go hand in hand with intellectual growth, in addition to that moral-religious training and that preparation for parenthood, of which we shall later speak, we may mention three important ideals to be grouped under our general conception of culture.

(1) First, we must have KNOWLEDGE of the world we live in -not so much masses of facts as a comprehension of principles, insight into relations and tendencies. A man should be at home upon the earth; he should be able to call the stars by name, to realize something of the immensities by which this spinning planet is surrounded, and to see in every landscape a portion of the wrinkled, water-eroded surface of the globe. He should see this apparently solid sphere as a whirl of atoms, and come face to face with the old puzzles of matter and mind. He should be able to trace in imagination the growth of stellar systems; the history of our own earth; the evolution of plant and animal life, from the first protoplasmic nuclei to the mammoth and mastodon; the emergence of man from brute hood into self-consciousness, his triumph over nature and the other animals, and his

achievement of civilization. He should watch primitive man wrestling with problems as yet partly unsolved, see him gradually establishing law and order, inventing and discovering, mastering his fate. He should follow the floods and ebbs of progress, the rise and fall of nations, know the great names of history and have for friends humanity's saints and heroes. He should be at home in ancient Israel, in classic Greece, in Rome of the Republic, in Italy of the Renaissance, especially in the early days of our own land, learning to comprehend and sympathize with the struggles and ideals that have made our nation what it is. He should understand the clash of creeds and codes, follow the thoughts of Plato, of Bacon, of Emerson, and grasp the essence of the problems that now confront us. What dangers lie before us, what the great statesmen and reformers are aiming at, what are the meaning and use of our institutions, our government, our laws, our morals, our religion - here is a hint of the knowledge that every man who comes into the world should amass. To know less than this is to be only half alive, and unable to fulfill properly the duties of citizenship. Widespread ignorance of the larger social, moral, political, religious problems of the day, is ominous to the Republic; and it is impossible to understand aright without a background of history and theory. The aim of the schools should be to give not only some detailed information but a structural sense of life as a whole, a sane perspective; and to inspire an enthusiasm for intellectual things which shall outlast the early years of schooling. The few facts imparted should suggest the vast fields beyond, and stir youth to that passion for truth which shall lead to ever-new vistas and farther horizons.

(2) But the most encyclopedic acquaintance with facts, or even with principles, is not enough; TRAINING TO THINK ACCURATELY, to reason logically, so as to arrive at valid conclusions and be able to discriminate sound from unsound arguments in others, is vitally necessary. With new and intricate problems continually confronting us, we need the temper that observes with exactness, and without prejudice or passion, that judges truly, that thinks clearly, and forms independent convictions. There has been in our educational system an overemphasis on the acquirement of facts, a natural result of our modern dependence upon books; too much is accepted on authority, too little thought out at first hand. We must "banish the idolatry of knowledge," as Ruskin exhorted, and "realize that calling out thought and strengthening the mind are an entirely different and higher process from the putting in of knowledge and the heaping up of facts." We have many well-informed scholars to one clear and reliable thinker; the world is full of books, widely read and applauded, in which the trained mind detects false premises, fallacious reasoning, unwarranted conclusions. When the public is really educated, these superficially plausible arguments will not be heeded, these appeals to the prejudices and emotions of the

reader will not be tolerated; a stricter standard of logic will be demanded, and we shall be by so much the nearer a solution of our perplexing problems.[Footnote: This mental training can be given not merely by a specific course in logic, but by an insistence on exactness and the critical spirit in every study. It is particularly easy to cultivate this temper in scientific study. So Karl Pearson, for example, pleads for more science in our schools: "It is the want of impersonal judgment, of scientific method, and of accurate insight into facts, a want largely due to a non-scientific training, which renders clear thinking so rare, and random and irresponsible judgments so common in the mass of our citizens today." (Grammar of Science, Introductory.) Cf. Emerson, "Education," in Lectures and Biographies: "It is better to teach the child arithmetic and Latin grammar than rhetoric or moral philosophy, because they require exactitude of performance; it is made certain that the lesson is mastered, and that power of performance is worth more than the knowledge." There is in our modern get-knowledge-easy methods a grave danger of letting the child absorb wisdom so comfortably, so almost unconsciously, that its wits shall not be sharpened to grapple with fallacies, to refute specious arguments, and to find their way through a chaos of facts to a correct conclusion. By way of contrast with these pleas for science, the student should read Arnold's argument for the superiority of literature, in the address on "Literature and Science" included in Discourses in America.] We may include under our ideal of clear thought, the ability to use clearly and efficiently the language by which the steps and conclusions of thought are formulated and expressed. Thought proceeds, where it is precise and logical, by words; unless a man's vocabulary is wide, unless his understanding of the language is exact, his thoughts must inevitably be vague and muddled. Moreover, he will be unable to transmit his thoughts clearly and readily to others. The most important tool for the carrying on of life is- language; the slovenliness and inadequacy of the average man's speech is a sad commentary on our boasted educational system.

(3) Wide information and a trained mind must be supplemented by a SOUND TASTE. To love excellence everywhere, to appreciate the good and the beautiful in every phase of life, should be the third, and possibly most important, aim of cultural education. It is, at least, the prime function of art. Art informs us of life, its pursuit trains in precision and judgment; but above all, it opens our eyes to beauty. The man who is versed in the work of the masters can never after be content with the ugliness and squalor that our industrial civilization continually tends to increase. He has caught the vision of beauty, and must strive to shape his environment toward that high ideal. The artist sees what we had not learned to see; by isolating and perfecting this bit of the ideal, he directs our attention to it and teaches us to love it. No one can feel the spell of a landscape by Corot

or Innes without delighting more deeply in such scenes in the outdoor world; no one can live long in the atmosphere of Greek art without longing for such a body and such a poise of spirit. We are not accustomed to look at nature, or at man, with observing eyes, to see the richness of color in sun-kissed meadows or humming city streets, the infinite variations of light and shade, the depth of distance, the charm of line and composition. The picturesque is everywhere about us, undiscerned and unloved. So us the marvelous varieties in human character and circumstance, the humor and dignity and pathos of life. Literature and art, by revealing to us unsuspected possibilities of beauty, breed a healthy discontent with ugliness and urge us on to its banishment. The ultimate aim of art should be to make life beautiful in every nook and corner, to elevate the humdrum working days of common men by fair and sunny surroundings, to make manners gentle and gracious, speech melodious and refined, homes, pleasant and restful.

But art has a further function. However beautiful and harmonious our lives, they are at best confined within narrow boundaries; and the lover of beauty will always rejoice in the glimpses which art affords into an ideal realm beyond his daily horizon. He will gaze eagerly at the masterpieces of color and form that he cannot have forever about him, he will enrich his imagination with the great scenes of drama, he will solace his soul with the cadenced lines of poetry and the melody of music, he will live with the heroes of fiction for a day, and return to his work ennobled and sweetened by the contact with these forms of excellence which lie beyond the bounds of his own outward life. In two ways the fine arts add to the preexisting beauty in a man's life: by representing to him beautiful scenes and objects which he cannot enjoy in themselves, because he cannot go where they are, and by creating from the artist's imagination a new universe of emotions and satisfactions, congenial to the human spirit and full of a refined and pure joy.

What dangers are there in culture and art for life?

We must now glance at the other side of the picture. Enormous as are the potentialities for good in culture and art, they also have their perils.

(1) Culture and art must not take time, energy, or money that is needed for work. Achievement necessitates concentration and sacrifice; beauty must not beguile men away from service. [Footnote: Cf. what Pater says of Winckelmann (The Renaissance, p. 195): "The development of his force was the single interest of Winckelmann, unembarrassed by anything else in him. Other interests, practical or intellectual, those slighter motives and talents not supreme, which in most men are the waste part of nature, and drain away their vitality, he plucked out and cast from him."] The boys and girls who squander health in their eagerness to explore the new worlds

opening before them, the older folk who give a disproportionate share of their time and money to music or the theater, the voracious readers who pore over every new novel and magazine without really assimilating and using what they read, are turning what ought to be recreation or inspiration into dissipation, and thereby seriously impairing their efficiency. It is so much easier to read something new than to meditate fruitfully upon what one has read, to pass from picture to picture in a gallery and win no genuine insight from any. A single great book thoroughly mastered-the Bible, Homer, Shakespeare-were better for a man than the superficial skimming of many, one beautiful picture well loved than a hundred idly glanced at and labeled with some trite comment. Too many of the upper class, for whom limitless cultural opportunities are open, dabble in everything, know names and schools, repeat glibly the current phrases of criticism, but miss the lesson, the clarification of insight, the vision of the author or artist. Such superficial culture is a futile expenditure of time and money. [Footnote: For an arraignment of the money thrown away on modern decadent art, see Tolstoy's What is Art? chapter I.]

In this connection we must mention the waste of time over what Arnold called "instrument knowledge." Years are spent by most upper-class boys and girls in half-learning several languages which they will never use, in acquiring the technique of the piano, or of some other art which they will never learn to practice with proficiency. There is, to be sure, a certain mental training in all this, but no more than can be found in more useful studies. A foreign language is essentially a tool for carrying on conversation with its users, or for utilizing the literature written therein; the technique of an art is a tool for producing or copying beautiful forms of that art. And except as these tools are actually so utilized, the time spent on learning to handle them might better be otherwise occupied.

(2) More than this, cultural interests may fritter away in passive and useless thrills the emotions and energies that ought to stimulate moral and practical activity. It is so easy, where there is money enough to live on, to let one's faculties become absorbed in the fascinations of study, without applying it to practice; to enjoy the relatively complete attainment possible in the fine arts, and keep out of the dust and chaos and ugliness of real life. Or, when the student or art-lover does return to realities, after his absorption in some dream-world, there is danger that he carry over into actual moral situations his habit of passive contemplation, that he be content to remain a spectator instead of plunging in and taking sides. He has learned to enjoy the spectacle-sin, suffering, and all-and lost the primitive reaction of protest against evils, of practical response to needs, and the impulse to realize ideals in conduct. Thus culture and art may relax human energy or scatter it in trivial accomplishments; the dilettante spends his days in dreaming rather

than in doing. [Footnote: Cf. William James, Psychology, vol. I, pp. 125-26: "Every time a fine glow of feeling evaporates without bearing practical fruit is worse than a chance lost; it works so as positively to hinder future emotions from taking the normal path of discharge. There is no more contemptible type of human] Footnote continued from Page 269 [character than that of the nerveless sentimentalist and dreamer, who spends his life in a weltering sea of sensibility and emotion, but who never does a manly concrete deed. . . . The habit of excessive novel reading and theater going will produce true monsters in this line. The weeping of a Russian lady over the fictitious personages in the play, while her coachman is freezing to death on his seat outside, is the sort of thing that everywhere happens on a less glaring scale. Even the habit of excessive indulgence in music, for those who are neither performers themselves nor musically gifted enough to take it in a purely intellectual way, has probably a relaxing effect upon the character. One becomes filled with emotions which habitually pass without prompting to any deed, and so the inertly sentimental condition is kept up. The remedy would be, never to suffer one's self to have an emotion at a concert, without expressing it afterward in some active way. Let the expression be the least thing in the world-speaking genially to one's aunt, or giving up one's seat in a horse-car, if nothing more heroic offers-but let it not fail to take place." Professor James also refers in this connection to an interesting paper by Vida Scudder in the Andover Review for January, 1887, on "Musical Devotees and Morals."]

(3) Graver still, however, is the risk of the overstimulation of certain dangerous emotions. The "artistic temperament" is notoriously prone to reckless self- indulgence; the continual seeking of the immediately satisfying tends to weaken the powers of restraint. Artists and poets, and those who immerse themselves constantly in the pleasures of sense, tend to chafe under the dull repressions of morality and crave ever-new forms of excitement. Art is an emotional stimulant; and unless the emotions aroused are harnessed in the service of morality, they are apt to run amuck. Artists and authors often take to drink, and almost always have to meet exceptional sexual temptations. The most beautiful forms of art are those which have the element of sex interest, and the general emotional susceptibility of the creator or lover of beauty makes the sex emotion particularly inflammable. Other emotions also may be unwisely stimulated by art. In times of international friction, war-songs, "patriotic" speeches, or martial processions may arouse an unreasoning jingo spirit. The love of deviltry is fostered in boys by many of the penny novels, by sensational "movies" and newspaper "stories"; a famous detective has said that seventy per cent of the crimes committed by boys under twenty are traceable to "suggestions" received from these sources. Should art be censored in the interests of morality? Art, then, with its vast potentialities of both good and harm,

needs supervision in the interests of human welfare. The motto, "Art for art's sake," should not be taken to mean that what is detrimental to human life must be tolerated, just because it is art. There is, indeed, this truth in the adage, that art does not need to have a moral or practical use to justify its existence. It may be merely pleasant, serving no end beyond the enjoyment of the moment. But it must not be harmful. It is but one of the many interests in life, and must be judged, like any other interest, in the light of the greatest total good. We cannot say, "Work for work's sake," "Education for education's sake"; not even, "Morality for morality's sake"; it is work, education, morality, for the sake of the ultimately happiest human life. The moralist must not despise forms of art which have no ulterior, utilitarian value; but he must insist that no enjoyment of art is really, in the long run, good for man which influences his life in the unwholesome ways we have indicated. Since morality is that way of life that gives it its greatest worth, indulgence in art at the expense of morality is seizing an immediate but lesser good at the expense of an ultimately greater good. Practically, however, the censorship of art is the most delicate of matters, because the influence of the same work of art on one person may be widely different from its effect upon another. A play or a picture that pleases or even inspires one spectator may be disastrous to his neighbor. And it is always difficult to decide between the claims of an immediate good and the warnings of dangers that may lurk therein. But we universally acknowledge the duty of some censorship, by prohibiting the most openly tempting pictures, plays, and literature. And there can be no doubt that this supervision should be carried further than it now is.

The most pressing contemporary problem is that concerning the stage. [Footnote: See J. Addams, The Spirit of Youth and the City Streets, chap. IV. P. MacKaye, The Civic Theatre in Relation to the Redemption of Leisure. H. Munsterberg, Psychology and Social Sanity, pp. 27-43. J. H. Coffin, The Socialized Conscience, pp. 130-41. Outlook, vol. 92, p. 110; vol. 101, p. 492; vol. 107, p. 412. Atlantic Monthly, vol. 89, p. 497; vol. 107, p. 350.] Any number of boys and girls owe their undoing to the influences of the theater. No other form of art now tolerated so frequently overstimulates the sex instinct. The scant costumes permitted, with their conscious endeavor to reveal the feminine form as alluringly as possible, the voluptuous dances and ballets, the jokes, stories, and suggestive gestures, and often the low moral tone of the play, making light of sacred matters and encouraging lax ideas on sex relations, are powerful excitants. Many theaters frankly pander to the desire for such stimulation; and they are crowded. For while human nature remains as it is, the young will flock whither they can find sex excitement. Scarcely less dangerous are the magazines and books that by their pictures and their stories play up to this eternal instinct. Even painters in oils often use this drawing card; the Paris salons have always a considerable sprinkling of nudes, in all sorts of voluptuous attitudes, making a frank appeal to desire. French literature abounds in books, some of great literary merit, that exploit this aspect of human nature; but in every tongue there are the Boccaccios and the Byrons.

Plato found this problem in planning his ideal republic, and decreed that all voluptuous and tempting art must be banished. We are rightly unwilling to sacrifice beauty and enjoyment to so great an extent; such Puritanism inevitably provokes reaction, besides sadly impoverishing life. The feminine form, at its best, is exquisitely lovely; and a perfect nude is one of the most beautiful things in the world. [Footnote: On the moral problem of the nude in art, see Atlantic Monthly, vol. 88, pp. 286, 858.] How we shall retain this beauty to enrich our lives while avoiding the overstimulation of an already dangerously dominant instinct, is a problem whose gravity we can but indicate without presuming to offer a satisfactory solution.

What can emphatically be said is that artists must subordinate themselves to the welfare of life as a whole. And this is not so great a loss, for only that art is of the deepest beauty which expresses noble and wholesome feelings. The trouble with the artist is apt to be that he becomes so absorbed in the solution of the practical difficulties attendant upon his art that he cares primarily for triumphs of technique, irrespective of the worth of the feelings which that technique is to express. Indeed, there is actually a sort of scorn of beauty in certain studies and studios; the "literary" or "artistic" point of view is taken to mean a regard only for skill of execution, rather than for that beauty of whose realization the skill should be but the means. There is, indeed, a beauty of words and rhythms, of brushwork, of modeling; but if the poet does not love beautiful thoughts and acts, no verbal power can make his product great; and if the artist paints trivial or vulgar subjects he wastes his genius. Too much poetry that is sensual, flippant, drearily pessimistic, morbid, or obscure, is included in anthologies because cleverly wrought, with a sense for form and cadence. Too many stories, too many pictures, are applauded by critics, though in subject and tone they are contemptible. As proofs of human skill these works may excite such admiration as we give to a juggler's feats; as practice in handling a stubborn medium they may be valuable. But the artist who does not have a sane and high sense of what is really noble and beautiful in life prostitutes the talents by which he ought to serve the world. Often one feels as Emerson felt when he wrote of another, "I say to him, if I could write as well as you, I would write a good deal better." The bald truth is that artists are seldom competent to be final judges of art; they are too much behind the scenes, concerned too constantly with problems of method. The final judgment as to beauty can come only from one who combines a delicate appreciation of technique with a wide insight into life and a sane perspective of its values. For lack of such a criticism of art, the average man wanders distracted through our art-museums, with their hodge-podge of beautiful and ugly pictures, wades through the ingeniously clever stories and sensationally original but often meaningless or trivial verses in the magazines, goes to a concert and joins others in applauding some brilliant display of vocal gymnastics, some instrumental pyrotechnics, while his heart is thirsting for high and noble feelings, for something to elevate and inspire his life. The great poets, the great painters, the great dramatists and novelists, have been high-souled men as well as artists, lovers of the really beautiful in life as well as masters of their medium. Their art has no conflict with morality; it is rather its greatest stimulus and stay. To the lesser brood with the gift of melody, of rhythm, with an eye for color or form, but without a true perspective of human values, we must repeat sadly, or even sternly, the poet's reproof: "Can'st thou from heaven, O child Of light, but this to declare?"

On culture: Matthew Arnold, Culture and Anarchy; "Literature and Science" (in Discourses in America). F. Paulsen, System of Ethics, book III, chap. V. H. Spencer, Education. H. Sidgwick, Practical Ethics, chap. VIII. Atlantic Monthly, vol. 90, p. 589; vol. 97, p. 433; vol. 109, p. 111. International Journal of Ethics, vol. 23, p. 1. On the moral censorship of art: Plato, Republic, books. I, III, X. Aristotle, Poetics. Ruskin, Lectures on Art. Tolstoy, What is Art? G. Santayana, Reason in Art, chaps. IX, XI. R. B. Perry, Moral Economy, chap. V. H. R. Haweis, Music and Morals. Mackenzie, Manual of Ethics, chap. XVI. C. Read, Natural and Social Morals, chap. X. Forum, vol. 50, p. 588. Outlook, vol. 107, p. 412.

CHAPTER XXI

THE MECHANISM OF SELF-CONTROL

To discuss, as we have been doing, the various duties which are the unavoidable pre-conditions of a lasting and widespread welfare for men, would be futile, if we had not the ability to fulfill them. The power of self-control is the sine qua non of a secure morality, and therefore of a secure happiness. But this power seems often bafflingly absent. Hard as it is to know what is right to do, it is harder yet for many of us to make ourselves do what we know is right. Life for the average conscientious man is a perpetual battle between two opposing tendencies, that which his better self endorses, and that which is easiest or most alluring at the moment of action. The latter course too often seduces his will; and for the earnest and aspiring this continual moral failure constitutes one of the most tragic aspects of life. [Footnote: Cf. Ovid's Video meliora proboque, deteriora sequor. And St. Paul's "To will is present with me, but how to perform that which is good I find not. For the good that I would I do not, but the evil which I would not, that I do." From pagan and Christian pen alike there comes testimony to this universal and disheartening experience.] There is no greater need for most men than that of some wiser and more effective method whereby those who have ideals beyond their practice may regularly and consistently realize them.

What are our potentialities of greater self-control?

The encouraging side of the matter is that there have been many, of very various codes and creeds, who have attained to a nearly perfect self-control, who easily and almost inevitably govern their conduct by their ideals. Puritans with their personal Devil, Christian Scientists who believe that there is no evil at all-Christians, Buddhists, atheists-there have been saints in all the folds. The fact seems to be that the particular form which our moral ideas take matters much less than the completeness with which they possess the mind. Almost any of the many motives to right conduct will reform a character if it be so stamped into the mind as to become the dominant idea. What is necessary is some vivid and dominating anti-sinning idea rammed deep into the brain. The religions have been the chief means of effecting this; and the Church, that draws men together, and into the presence of God, for the reinforcing of their better selves, is the most efficacious of instruments for the control of sin. But the existence of a vast, and by most men hardly tapped, reservoir of power for righteousness (whether or not it is thought of as God) is recognized today by science as well as by religion; and we must here discuss the matter in a purely secular way. We can control our conduct if we care enough to set about using the forces at our disposal. The various religions have found and used them;

modern psychology, analyzing their success, shows us clearly and exactly how to succeed, even if we stand aloof from religion altogether.

Psychologically considered, this whole affair of saintliness or sinfulness is a matter of the preponderant idea. To have merely resolved is not enough; our moral forces must be drilled and made ready before the battle. This fortifying process we nowadays call "suggestion." By it we can so "set" our minds, so deepen the channels that flow toward the right actions, that when the time of conflict comes our minds will work along those grooves. Habit, to be sure, means a deep-cut channel in the mind; it may require much effort to dig a deeper one to take its place. Unless the work is persistently carried through, the mental currents, diverted temporarily into the new course, will soak through the barriers and find their old bed again. Moreover, different minds differ greatly in their plasticity, their susceptibility to suggestion. But the great fact remains that habits can be made over, temptations rendered harmless, and character formed, by this simple means.

It may be worthwhile to remind ourselves of the remarkable power of suggestion. It is most strikingly seen at work in the phenomena of hypnotism, because a person who is hypnotized is in a peculiarly susceptible state; he is asleep to everything but the words of the hypnotist, which thus have full influence over him, except as checked and balanced by the preexisting bias of his mind. Hypnotism is simply the perfect case of suggestion, isolated from disturbing factors. The hypnotizing process itself, the putting to sleep, is only preliminary to the suggestion; and to patients who are difficult to hypnotize, "waking suggestion" is given, with the patient in as relaxed and empty a state of mind as possible. The popular notion that healing through hypnotism is uncanny and dangerous is, of course, entirely erroneous. To be sure, every great power has its dangers from misuse, and hypnotism is not to be used except for proper ends; but there is nothing occult about it. It simply uses the psychological truth that the mind acts on the predominating idea, by lulling to sleep all ideas but the one wanted and impressing that upon the mind. Immediate and lasting moral changes are daily being effected through suggestion by professional hypnotists.

But though the power of suggestion is most obvious when employed by the scientifically trained physician of today, it has been successfully, though often unconsciously, used in all times. Prophets and saints of old, the touch of a king's hand, the sight of relics or images, have wrought striking moral and physical cures through this same mental law. Christian Scientists and mental healers of various sorts are curing people daily through them. Cases of religious conversion, where a man's whole inner life is turned about through a powerful emotional appeal, show best of all the possibilities of suggestion in the moral field. These are the extreme cases. But, indeed, all our moral education is, in psychological language, but so much "suggestion." The imperious necessity for man of preaching, of ritual and liturgy, of prayer and praise, is to drive home the high and noble thoughts which in his sanest moments he recognizes to be what he needs. The aim of the preacher is to bring to his hearers ideals of right living and to make them as appealing and vivid as possible. Yet even the best preaching comes only on Sundays, and there are six days between of other sorts of suggestion, which are often counter- suggestions, so that it is no wonder we lag so far behind our Sabbath- day ideals. In subtle and unrealized ways all the factors of our environment are so many sources of suggestion, constantly working upon our minds. Could we always command powerful and inspiring moral influences, and keep out of range of evil ones, our morals would perhaps take care of themselves. But while seeking so far as possible these external props, and if necessary having recourse to the still more effective help of the professional hypnotists, there remains a vast deal that we must do for ourselves if we are to resist successfully the downward pull of evil influences, solve our own individual problems, conquer our own peculiar temptations, and attain our ideals. We must practice autosuggestion. It is noteworthy that the loftiest spirits have always practiced it, in their habit of daily prayer. For whatever else prayer accomplishes, it certainly brings the mind back to its ideals, concentrates it earnestly engaged in, is the best possible form of suggestion. The lapse of this habit helps to explain why unbelievers so often degenerate morally. Comte, that positive disbeliever in supernatural dogmas, clearly recognized this danger, and enjoined upon his followers a consecration prayer three times a day. In recent years the writers who call their doctrine by the name of The New Thought - and other kindred thinkers have called attention to the possibilities of self- help, directing us to "retire into the silence," there to concentrate our minds upon those beliefs that are comforting and inspiring to us; and have helped many thereby to attain peace and self-possession. But still the conscious use of autosuggestion for the attainment of personal ideals has been very little discussed, and in the employment of this great power we are astonishingly backward.

A practicable mechanism of self-control.

Let us, then, outline briefly the chief points necessary to note in using this force for our own benefit. A necessary preliminary is to study our problems, analyze our difficulties, make sure exactly what we want to do and wherein we fail; and thereby to pin our aspirations down to definite resolves to act in certain ways rather than in certain other ways. Our ideals are apt to be vague and even conflicting, or else so abstract and general as to fail to direct us with precision to any concrete act. We realize dumbly that we are not what we should be, and we grope for better things; but just wherein the difference consists, just where is the point where we go off the track, is uncertain in our minds. As in physical achievement, half the success lies in applying the effort at just the right place. The men who have accomplished much are those who have known exactly what they wanted to do and have concentrated their energies upon that. If we have so much self-reformation to accomplish as to dissipate our attention, it may be wise to decide which changes are most immediately important and to limit our endeavors at first to those.

Included in this preliminary task is the fixation in our minds of the reasons for the lines of conduct we intend to follow, all the motives that draw us toward them. This will show us whether we, i.e., our better selves, really wish to acquire these new habits, are really convinced that they are right, or whether we are merely putting before ourselves some one else's ideal which we vaguely feel we ought or are expected to follow. One can often convince one's self quite thoroughly of ideas one did not really believe in by this method of suggestion; but if we are to control our own morals we wish to control them not by some one else's ideals but by our own. If a thing is really right to do there must be definite and legitimate reasons for the doing which can appeal to our intelligence and our emotions; these we should bring into the foreground of our thought and express as clearly and forcibly as possible.

We have now the material for our work. We must so hammer these resolutions and the motives to them into our heads that they will be vividly conscious to us when they are needed. In this process there are three main points to be remembered - Concentration, Iteration, and Assertion.

(1) Concentration. The more completely the mind can be concentrated upon the resolution and its motives the deeper will they penetrate into it, to lie there ready for use at the moment of action. A definite time should be set apart when the mind can be withdrawn from other thoughts and compelled to give all its attention to this matter. On first waking, or just before going to sleep. If one is not too tired-one can usually best get away from the distracting details of life. The resolutions should be written down, with the most important words or phrases underlined, to serve as catchwords and mottoes. They should be read aloud and repeated from memory, as well as thought over silently, thus adding visual and auditory images to the mental concepts. In meditating upon them one's thoughts should not be allowed to wander too far, but must be constantly referred to the definite numbered resolutions. The use of symbols, of colors, etc, will readily occur to any one who goes into this matter with lively interest. Always repeat the resolutions with the greatest possible emphasis and enthusiasm, so as to carry them away ringing in the mind. Remember that

the astonishing results of hypnotism and mental healing are due simply to the complete possession of the mind by the new idea.

(2) ITERATION. The oftener the mind is fixed upon the resolution and its motives, the more deeply will they become engraved in it. Sometimes one determined concentration will carry the day; but if this quick assault does not win the victory a long-continued siege can do it. By hammering away continually at the same spot the requisite impression will finally be made. A momentary rehearsal of the resolutions may be made a hundred times a day, in passing; and immediately before the time for execution, if it can be foreseen, forces should be rallied, even if only by an instantaneous flash of determination. Above all, one should not be discouraged and stop trying; for every renewed effort, even if showing no reward in success, produces its exact and unfailing effect. Keeping everlastingly at it is as necessary for success in morals as in everything else.

(3) ASSERTION. The more vigorously we assert our power to keep our resolutions the more likely we are to do so. It is largely lack of confidence in ourselves that paralyzes us. The religions have realized the need of inspiring hope and confidence in their converts by preaching the necessity of faith.

The faith we need is not necessarily faith in any supernatural help, but only in the demonstrated fact of the possibility of controlling our own minds and morals by going at it in the right way. But we must not passively wait for faith to possess us, we must grasp it, cleave to it, assert it. We must repeat our resolutions always with the conviction that we are really going to carry them out. We must picture ourselves at the time of temptation, with the triumphant thought of how splendidly we are going to worst the Devil, and never for a moment think or talk of ourselves as likely to forget or yield. Such persistent assertion, even if there is a background of distrust that we cannot wholly banish from our minds, will greatly help. Whatever we may think about the ethics of belief as applied to supernatural things, the "will to believe" in our own power is certainly legitimate and important. [Footnote: The important problem of the ethics of belief, as applied to religious matters, has not been discussed in this volume. The present writer hopes to discuss it fully in a later volume, to be called Problems of Religion.] Various accessoriesand safeguards. The dogged and hearty practice of auto-suggestion, whether in the secular form above outlined, or in the warmer and more satisfying form of prayer, is sufficient to keep a man master of himself and above the reach of whatever temptations he recognizes and chooses to resist. But there are various other furtherances to self- control that may be briefly suggested.

(1) The method of "turning over a new leaf" is of the utmost value to minds of a certain type. To declare a definite break with the old life, a fresh beginning, unstained and full of hope, often gives just the extra impetus that was needed. We are weighted by the memory of our failures, we live in the shadow of the past, and easily slide into a hopelessness and sense of impotence which a mere dogged persistence cannot overcome. New Year's Day, a birthday, any change in place or manner of life, may well be made the occasion for a bout of "moral house-cleaning," which will give a new enthusiasm and vitality to our better natures. The essential thing in such cases is to look out for the first tests, and not allow a single exception to the new resolutions. A slight lapse, that seems inconsequential, may serve to check the new momentum; as La Rochefoucauld says, "It is far easier to extinguish a first desire than to satisfy all those that follow in its train."

There is, however, a real danger in this method, of a discouragement and demoralization resulting from the collapse of enthusiastic hopes. And there is the further danger that a man will excuse indulgence in such hours of discouragement, on the ground that he is going to turn over another new leaf to-morrow and might as well have a good fling to- day. It is well to remember the truth that Martineau expressed by his apt phrase, "the tides of the spirit." "But, alas," Stevenson puts it, "by planting a stake at the top of the flood, you can neither prevent nor delay the inevitable ebb." After all, in most of our moral warfare, "it's dogged as does it." "He that stumbles and picks himself up is as if he had never fallen."

"We cannot kindle when we will The fire which in the heart resides; The spirit bloweth and is still, In mystery our soul abides. But tasks in hours of insight will'd Can be through hours of gloom fulfill'd."

If we do try the abrupt break, it is of the utmost importance to utilize every opportunity for the carrying out of the new program, to hunt up occasions while the will is strong and the courage high. One actual fulfillment of a resolution is worth many mental rehearsals. And when the enemy is repulsed by this charge with the bayonet, vigilance must not be relaxed, lest he return to take us unawares. [Footnote: I cannot forbear including, in this connection, the admirable remarks of William James (Psychology, vol. I, pp. 123-24): "The first [maxim] is that in the acquisition of a new habit, or the leaving off of an old one, we must take care to LAUNCH OURSELVES WITH AS STRONG AND DECIDED AN INITIATIVE AS POSSIBLE. Accumulate all the possible circumstances which shall reinforce the right motives; put yourself assiduously in conditions that encourage the new way; make engagements incompatible with the old; take a public pledge, if the case allows; in short, envelop your resolution with every aid you know. This will give your new beginning such a momentum that the temptation to break down will not occur as soon as it otherwise might; and every day during which a breakdown is postponed adds to the chances of its not occurring at all. "The second maxim is: NEVER SUFFER AN EXCEPTION TO OCCUR TILL THE NEW HABIT IS SECURELY ROOTED IN YOUR LIFE. Each lapse is like the letting fall of a ball of string which one is carefully winding up; a single slip undoes more than a great many turns will wind again. The need of securing success at the OUTSET is imperative. Failure at first is apt to dampen the energy of all future attempts, whereas past experience of success nerves one to future vigor. It is surprising how soon a desire will die of inanition if it be NEVER fed. "A third maxim may be added to the preceding pair: SEIZE THE VERY FIRST POSSIBLE OPPORTUNITY TO ACT ON EVERY RESOLUTION YOU MAKE, AND ON EVERY EMOTIONAL PROMPTING YOU MAY EXPERIENCE IN THE DIRECTION OF THE HABITS YOU ASPIRE TO GAIN. It is not in the moment of their forming, but in the moment of their producing MOTOR EFFECTS that resolves and aspirations communicate the new 'set' to the brain."]

(2) It is an excellent thing to do a little gratuitous spiritual exercise every day, just to keep in training, to get the habit of conquering impulse, of doing disagreeable things. Nothing is more useful to a man than that power. We must not let our lives get too easy and our wills too soft. To jump out of bed when the whistle blows, instead of dawdling just for a minute more in indolent comfort, to make one's self take the cold bath that is abhorrent to the flesh, to deny one's self the cigar or the candy that may not be in itself particularly harmful-by some means or other to keep one's self in the saddle and riding one's desires, may enable one when some crisis comes to thrust aside a man too fatally accustomed to doing things in the easiest way.

(3) Discretion is sometimes the better part of valor. Besides strengthening our own wills, it is wise to seek in every way to remove temptation from our path, and, if need be, to run away from it. We must keep away from situations that experience warns are dangerous for us, however innocent they may be to others. If a man find that dancing, or the theater, arouses his passionate nature, it may be better to avoid it entirely till his hypersensitive state is normalized. Always alcoholic liquors are to be avoided; they cloud the reason and the will, and let impulse loose. Always overexcitement and overfatigue are to be avoided. "The power to overcome temptation," Jane Addams writes, "reaches its limit almost automatically with that of physical resistance."

(4) We must follow Bossuet's advice not to combat passions directly so much as to turn them aside by applying them to other objects. Our emotional nature is a gift of the gods; the sinner might have been a saint if his emotions had only been enlisted under the right banner. Something

good to love, to work for, and think about, something that can arouse our whole nature and relieve it from suppression, is the best antidote to morbid desire. It is sometimes alleged that it is better to satisfy a passion than to keep it pent up within the organism. But satisfying a wrong passion not only brings its inevitable unhappy consequences, to one's self and to others, it makes it far harder to resist the passion again, when it recurs. The only safe outlet is one that leads into right conduct; under skilful guidance all passions can be transmuted into valuable driving forces and allies of morality.

(5) Even if one seems to be playing a losing game, one can still keep up the fight. One can spoil one's enjoyment in self-indulgence or selfishness; one can refuse to give in all over. This minority representation of the better impulse will suffice to keep it alive in us; and when the revulsion from sin comes we shall be in better shape to make the fight next time. A hundred failures need not discourage; some of the greatest men have gained the final ascendancy over their weaknesses only after a long and often losing struggle. The case is hopeless only for the man who stops fighting.

Self-control is the measure of manhood. It is the most important thing in the personal life. And it is within the reach of any man who can be brought to understand the mechanism where through it can be attained. It remains true that it is best attained through religion, which utilizes the power of prayer, of faith, the enthusiasm of a great cause and motive, and the comradeship and help of others engaged in the same eternal war with sin. But religion, to be efficacious, must be not passively accepted, but USED. Its help comes not to him who saith "Lord, Lord!" but to him who earnestly seeks to do the will of the Father. J. Payot, Education of the Will. H. C. King, Rational Living, chap. VI, sec. III; chap. X. W. James, Psychology, vol. I, pp. 122-27; vol. II, pp. 561-79. W. E. H. Lecky, Map of Life, chap. XII. A. Bain, The Emotions and the Will, part II, chap. IX. L. H. Gulick, in World's Work, vol. 15, p. 9797. Bossuet, Connaissance de Dieu et de Soi meme, chap. III, sec. 19. St. Augustine, Confessions, book VIII, chap. V. Janet, Elements de Morale, chap. X, sec. 3. W. L. Sheldon, An Ethical Movement, chap. X. A. Bennett, The Human Machine, chaps. I-V. O. S. Marden, Every Man a King.

CHAPTER XXII
THE ATTAINABILITY OF HAPPINESS

WE have now discussed the more recurrent problems of the individual, and pointed out the salient duties that private life entails. But there remains something to be added before we shall have clearly pointed the way to personal happiness. "Mere morality," even when coupled with good fortune, is not enough; a sinless man, scrupulous to fulfill the least command of the law, may yet be anxious, restless, depressed, unsatisfied. We need more than morality, as the word is commonly used; we need religion - or something of the sort. There is no doubt that for the attainment of a pervasive and stable happiness there is nothing so good as the best sort of religion; but, as in discussing self- control, we must here steer clear of religious controversy and phrase what we have to say in the colder terms of "mere morality." And though there will be a great loss in feeling, in persuasiveness and unction thereby, there will be gain in clearness. It is possible to express in the drab tones of morality the profound insights which have made religion the great guide to happiness; and even the man who deems himself irreligious may, if he takes to heart these more prosaic counsels, find something of the peace that has been the boon of true believers.

The threefold key to happiness:

I. HEARTY ALLEGIANCE TO DUTY.

The one thing above all others that makes life worth living is the utter devotion of the heart and will to the commands of morality. To throw one's self whole-heartedly into the game, to play one's part for all it is worth, transforms what were else a grim and unhappy necessity into a glorious opportunity. The happy man is the loyal man, the man who has taken sides, who has enrolled himself definitely on the side of right and tastes the zest of battle. He has something to live for, and something lasting. He has put his heart into a cause that the limitations and accidents of life cannot take from him, he has laid up his treasure in heaven, where moth and rust doth not corrupt or thieves break through and steal.

Any cause, any ambition, any great endeavor that can stir the blood, and give a life direction, purpose, and continuity of achievement, has the power to rescue life from ennui, from emptiness, and give it positive worth. But most ambitions pall in time, and many a cause that has taken a man's best energies has come to seem mistaken or futile with the years. There is only one great campaign which is so eternal, so surely necessary, so clear in its summons to all men, that the heart can rest in it as in something great enough to ennoble a whole life. That is the age-long war against evil, the unending summons to duty, the service of God. Once a man learns this deepest of joys, nothing can take it from him; whatever his limitations, however narrow his sphere, there will not fail to be a right way, a brave way, a beautiful way to live. There is comradeship in it; in this common service of God - or of good, if we must avoid religious terms - we stand shoulder to shoulder with the saints and heroes of all races and times, with all, of whatever land or tongue, who are striving to push forward the line, to make the right prevail and banish evil. Every effort, every sacrifice, has its inextinguishable effect; in his moral conquests a man is no longer an individual, he is a part of the great tide that is resistlessly making toward the better world of the future, the Kingdom of God. The great Power in the world that makes for righteousness is back of him, and in him; in no loyal moment is he alone. . . . Inevitably the tongue slips into religious language in dealing with these high truths; but nonetheless are they scientific truths, matters of plain every day observation.

The essential point is, that it is not enough to obey the Law; we must ESPOUSE the Law, clasp it to our bosoms, love it, and give ourselves to it utterly. We must - to use the pregnant words of James "base our lives on doing and being, not on having"; base our lives solidly upon it, so that everything else is secondary. The pleasures of life are well enough in their time, but they must not usurp the chief place in a man's thought.[Footnote: Cf. J. S. Mill, Autobiography, p. 142: "The enjoyments of life are sufficient to make it a pleasant thing, when they are taken en passant, without being made a principal object. The only chance is to treat, not happiness, but some end external to it, as the purpose of life."] His first concern must be to keep true, to play the game; he must seek first the Kingdom of God and His righteousness, if he would have these other things added unto him. He must lose his life his worldly interests, his dependence upon ease and luxury, and even love if he would truly find it. In a hundred such phrases from the Great Teacher's lips one finds the secret. More baldly expressed, it comes to this, that only through putting the main emphasis upon doing the right, obeying the call of duty, only through the courageous attack and the giving of our utmost allegiance, can we keep a positive zest in living, exorcise the specter of aimlessness and depression, and lift ordinary commonplace life to the level of heroism. Blessed is the man whose DELIGHT is in the law of the Lord.

II. HEARTY ACQUIESCENCE IN OUR LOT.

The fighter, for whatever cause, can bear the blows that come as a part of the battle; if a man has put his heart into living by his ideal, he is immune from the disappointments and irritations that beset man upon a lower level.

But it is well to take thought also for this side of the matter, to cultivate deliberately the spirit of acquiescence in the inevitable pain and losses of life. Many of the sweetest pleasures are by their nature uncertain or transient; these we must hold so loosely that, while not refusing to enjoy their sweetness, we are]ot dependent upon them and can let them go without losing sight of the steady gleam that we follow. However dear to us are the people we love, and the material things we own, we must keep the underlying assurance that if they be taken from us life will still bring us in other ways renewed opportunities for that loyalty to duty, that faithful living, which is after all the end for which we live. We must count whatever comes to us, whether sweet or bitter, as the conditions under which we serve, the material with which we have to work, the stuff which we have to "try the soul's strength on." For there is no way to be armor-proof against unhappiness but by seeing to it that our hearts are not set on anything but doing or being; nothing else is reliably permanent amid the fitful sunshine and shadow of human life. "Make hy claim of wages a zero; then hast thou the world at thy feet." [Footnote: In Maeterlinck's Measure of the Hours, he speaks of a sundial found near Venice by Hazlitt with the inscription, Horas non numero nisi serenas and quotes Hazlitt's remarks thereon: "What a fine lesson is conveyed to the mind to take no note of time but by its benefits, to watch only for the smiles and neglect the frowns of fate, to compose our lives of bright and gentle moments, turning always to the sunny side of things and letting the rest slip from our imaginations, unheeded or forgotten."] This necessity of detaching the heart from dependence upon uncertainties found extreme expression in the various historic forms of asceticism and monasticism. Such a running away from the world does not satisfy our age, with its eagerness for life and life more abundantly; if it escapes the poignant sorrows it cannot happiness, or make life better for others. But we may well take to heart the half-truth taught by the hermits and monks of the past. We may be "in the world," indeed, but not "of it"; we, too, may make no claims upon life, while putting our hearts into playing our own part in it well. The writings of Epictetus and Marcus Aurelius are full of passages that express the gist of the matter, such as the following: "It is thy duty to order thy life well in every single act; and if every act does its duty as far as is possible, be content; no one is able to hinder thee so that each act shall not do its duty. But something external will stand in the way? Nothing will stand in the way of thy acting justly and soberly and considerately. But perhaps some of thy active powers will be hindered? Well, by acquiescing in the hindrance, and being content to transfer thy efforts to that which is allowed, another opportunity of action is immediately put before thee in place of that which was hindered." What is this but saying in other words that not in having lies our life, but in doing and being. Not even in succeeding, we must remember; and this is perhaps the hardest part of our lesson. It is one thing to bear with serenity those blows of fortune against which we are obviously defenseless; it is another thing, when there seems a chance for averting the disaster, when our whole heart and soul are thrown into that effort, to await the outcome with tranquility, to bear failure without complaint. The "might have been's" and the "perhaps may yet be's" are the greatest disturbers of our peace. To use our keenest wits for attaining what seems best, to use our utmost persuasion for protecting ourselves from the selfishness and stupidity of others, and then if we fail, if the fair hope slips from our grasp, if the thoughtlessness or cruelty of men prevails against us, to smile and attack the next problem with undaunted cheerfulness, requires, indeed, to attain to that level may well be called "the last infirmity of noble minds." For the very concentration of life upon doing and being carries with it the danger of staking happiness upon the success of the doing, the attainment of the ideals. We must count even the stupidity and impulsiveness of our own mental make-up as among the materials we have to work with, and not allow remorse for our own part in past failures to interfere with the joyful earnestness with which we attack the problems of the eternal present. We may, indeed, often succeed, and that may be a very great and pure joy to us; but we are not to count upon success; or, to put it another way, we are to think of the real success as lying in the dauntless renewal of the effort rather than in the show of outward result. "To have often resisted the diabolic, and at the end to be still resisting it, is for the poor human soldier to have done right well. To ask to see some fruit of our endeavor is but a transcendental way of serving for reward." This is not pessimism, it is the first step toward a sound and invulnerable optimism. We must recognize once for all that this world is not the world of our dreams, and cease to be so pathetically surprised and hurt when it falls short of them. Were we to be rebellious at life for not being built after the pattern of our ideals there would be no limit to our faultfinding. We may, indeed, long in our idle hours with Omar "To grasp this sorry scheme of things entire, shatter it to bits-and then Remould it nearer to the heart's desire!" But in our daily life a braver and saner attitude befits us; for it is not in such an ideal world but in the actual world that we have to live. Evils there are in it and will yet be- why we cannot tell and need not know; the only alternative we have is to take them cheerfully or gloomily, to rebel or to accept the situation. Our duty then is clear. To face the events of life as they come to us, without discouragement or dismay, to laugh at them a little and learn to carry on our lives through them with steadfast heart and smiling face- surely that is the part of wisdom and of true manliness. The ugly things in life seem much less formidable when thus boldly faced than when we try to shut our eyes to them, with the consequent disillusion at their continual reappearance. Confess frankly the faults of life and it becomes tolerable, is even in a fair way to become lovable. For after all, when its obvious imperfections do not blind us to its good points, it is a dear old world we live in, and the healthy minded man loves it, as he loves his friends in spite of their faults loves it, and finds it a world gloriously worth living in.

III. HEARTY APPRECIATION OF THE WONDER AND BEAUTY IN LIFE.

Finally, when we have our great purpose in life, and have overcome the fear of pain and loss, we must learn to see and appreciate the beauty of the world we live in. The man who refuses to be downed by trouble is in a condition to enjoy each bit of good fortune that comes to him, to welcome each as a pure gift or addition to life, and to know that gifts of some sort or other will always come. Holding all things with that looser grasp that is ready to let them go if go they must, he can relish the good things of life the more freely for not having counted on them, as he can the more freely admire the virtues of his friends for not having expected them to be perfect. He can feel the beauty of the world without being dependent upon it, not looking for mortal things to be immortal or human things to be ideal, but whole-heartedly enjoying today what he has today and tomorrow what he shall have to-morrow. The things he cannot have at all, instead of spoiling his happiness in what he has, will rather add to it by forming another dimension of the actual, full of beautiful visions and glorious possibilities. And meantime the real world, of events that actually occur, will not fail, in spite of its flaws and rebuffs, to bring him ever-fresh delights. Let no one minimize these delights. There is more beauty, more interest here in this mundane existence of ours, more inspiration, more inexhaustible possibility of enjoyment than the keenest of us has dreamed of. We need some sort of shaking up to rouse us to the beauty of common things- the freshness of the air we breathe, the warmth of sunshine, the green of trees and fields and the blue of the sky, the joy in exercise of brain and muscle, in reading and talking and sharing in the life of the world; and in such daily things as eating at the family table when we are hungry, or a good night's sleep when we are tired. We need some teacher like Whitman to open our eyes to the beauty not only of flowers but of leaves of grass, to the picturesqueness and significance of so dull a thing as a ferryboat; or like Wordsworth, with his picturing of homely country scenes and events, with his emotion at the sight of the sleeping city- "a sight so touching in its majesty." This sense of the meaning of common things floods most of us at one time or another, and we see what in our blindness we have been overlooking. Go without your comfortable bed for a while, your well-cooked food, your home, friends, neighbors, and you will discover how rich you have been. Your mother's face hinted by some stranger in a foreign land will some day overcome you with the realization of the comfort of her love; and unless you are a crabbed egotist the life of your fellows can furnish you with endless pleasures. It is not necessary to own things to enjoy them; our interests and enjoyments may well overlap and include those of our friends and neighbors, and even those of strangers. The smile of a happy child, a friend's good fortune a sunrise or moonlit cloud-strewn sky, should bring a pure gladness to any one who has eyes to see and heart to feel. We must "Learn to love the morn, Love the lovely working light, Love the miracle of sight, Love the thousand things to do." [Footnote: These lines are Richard Le Gallienne's. Cf. also Matthew Arnold's lines: "Is it so small a thing To have enjoyed the sun, To have lived light in the spring, To have loved, to have thought, to have done, To have advanced true friends and beat down baffling foes? The sports of the country people, A flute note from the woods, Sunset over the sea; Seed-time and harvest, The reapers in the corn, The vinedresser in his vineyard, The village girl at her wheel. . ."] The true lover of beauty will not need to seek forever-new scenes and objects to admire. He will find that which can feed his heart in the clouds of morning, the blue of noon, or the stars of night. One graceful vase with a flower-stalk bending over to display its drooping blossoms, will fill him with a quiet happiness; the merry laughter of a child, the tender smile of a lover, the rugged features of a weather beaten laborer, will stir his soul to response; a few lines of poetry remembered in the midst of work, a simple song sung in the twilight, a print of some old master hanging by his bedside, a bird-call heard at sunset or the scent of evening air after rain, may so speak to his spirit that he will say, "It is enough!" It is not the number of beautiful things that we have that matters, but the degree in which we are open to their influence, the atmosphere into which we let them lead us. Our hearts must be free from self-seeking, from regret, from anger, from restlessness. The vision comes not always to the connoisseur, comes to him whose life is simple, earnest, open-eyed and openhearted. In the pauses of his faithful work he will refresh his soul with some bit of beauty that tells of attainment, of peace, of perfection. That is a proof to him of the beauty in the midst of which he lives, inexhaustible, hardly discerned; it carries him beyond itself into the ideal world of which it is a sample and illustration; unconsciously during the duties of the day he lives in the light of that vision, and everything is sweetened and blessed thereby.

Can we maintain a steady under glow of happiness?

Happiness—happiness sufficient to make life well worth living is, for most men at least, at most times, a real possibility. To be won it has but to be sought vigorously enough. It is to be sought, however, not primarily by changing one's environment but by changing one's self; not by acquiring new things, but by acquiring a new attitude toward things; not by getting what could make one happy, but by learning to be happy with what one can get. THE KINGDOM OF HEAVEN IS WITHIN YOU! This is not merely a moralist's theory, or an empirical observation; it is a scientific fact. We may restate the matter in psychological language by saying that happiness and unhappiness are responses of the organism to its environment, reactions upon a stimulus, our attitude of welcome or dissatisfaction toward the various matters of our experience. True, we often think of the quality of pleasantness as inhering in the things we enjoy, and speak of troubles and sorrows as objective. But this is only a shorthand way of describing experience. In reality the pleasure we feel in eating when we are hungry or in seeing a friend we love is something added to and different from the taste sensations, or the complex visual perceptions and memory images the friend arouses in us. So a cutting or burning sensation, the thought of a friend's death, or of our failure, on the one hand, and our unhappiness thereat on the other hand, are two distinct things, closely bound together in our minds but separable.

The separation is, indeed, difficult to bring about, because the age long struggle for existence has made unhappiness at physical pain and pleasure at the healthy exercise of our organs or satisfying of our appetite instinctive and immediate, that we may avoid what is harmful to life and pursue what is useful. All our cravings and longings and regrets have this biological value; they are the machinery by which nature spurs us on to better adjustment to the conditions of life. And in learning to do without the spur we must learn not to need it. Discontent is better than laziness, remorse better than callous selfishness, suffering under extreme cold better than recklessly exposing the body till it is weakened. But as soon as we have reached that stage of rationality where we can choose the better way and stick to it without the stinging goad of pain, the pain is no longer necessary and we may safely learn to weed it out.

A few blessed souls we know who have learned the secret, who go about with perpetually radiant face and take smilingly the very mishaps that worry and sadden the rest of us. To some extent this may be merely a matter of better nerves, of less sensitive temperament, of more abounding vitality; but there are many of the weakest and most sensitive among those who have learned that better way; they can turn everything into happiness as Midas turned everything into gold. It is surprising, looking through such a one's eyes, to see how full life is of delight. Yet in the same situations there may be room for endless complaint if "every grief is entertained that's offered." It all depends on the attitude taken. In trouble one man will fall to fretting, while another does what can be done and then turns his thoughts to something else; in discomfort one will lower the corners of his mouth and feel wretched, while the other finds it all vastly amusing; one will have his day quite spoiled by some disappointment which the other takes as a mere incident; one will find the same environment dull and stupid which the other finds full of interest and opportunity; and so out of like conditions one will make an unhappy, the other a happy life. [Footnote: Cf. "In journeying often, in perils of waters, in perils of robbers, in perils by mine own countrymen, in perils by the heathen, in perils in the city, in perils in the wilderness, in perils in the sea, in perils among false brethren, in weariness and painfulness, in watching often, in hunger and thirst, in fasting often, in cold and nakedness . . . yet always rejoicing!" "Rejoicing in tribulation" even, because to the brave man every obstacle and failure is so much further opportunity for courage and contrivance, for matching himself against things. "Human joy," writes the author of the Simple Life, "has celebrated its finest triumphs under the greatest tests of endurance." The Apostle Paul is but one of many who have welcomed each rebuff, and proved that if rightly taken life almost at its worst can be transmuted by courage into happiness.] This, then, is the philosophy of happiness in a nutshell: PUT YOUR HEART INTO DOING YOUR DUTY; DEMAND NOTHING ELSE OF LIFE THAN THE OPPORTUNITY TO DO YOUR DUTY; ENJOY FREELY AND WITHOUT FEAR EVERYTHING GOOD AND BEAUTIFUL THAT COMES IN YOUR WAY.

To acquire and keep this attitude of mind requires of course resolution and persistence. We must rouse ourselves and take sides. We must definitely pledge ourselves once and for all to happiness; and if we] cannot at a leap attain to it, we must still remember that we have committed ourselves to that side. We must pretend to be happy, throw aside all complaining and sighs and long faces; whatever comes, we must remember that we are on trial to preserve our buoyancy, our power not to be downcast. We shall not be able] to disuse our habit of unhappiness at once. But if we stick to our colors and refuse to add to whatever depression masters us by brooding upon it and giving it right of way; if we remember the conditions of happiness stated above, and thrust resolutely from us all thoughts and words incompatible with living according to them, the unhappiness will be gone before we know it. It is a well-known psychological law that if we choke the expression of an emotion, we shall presently find that we have smothered the emotion itself. It may seem like hollow pretense at first, but it will pay to pretend hard; when we have pretended long enough, we shall find we no longer need to pretend. There will always be those, no doubt, who will declare it impossible, and they will continue to be unhappy; there will be many others who will concede the possibility of it, but will not have the determination and persistence to effect it; but there will always be some who will say, "Happiness is possible!" who will set out to get it, and who will get it, as they will deserve to. Some men are born happy, some seem to have happiness thrust upon them, but some achieve happiness. It will not be the same kind of happiness that we had as children, before the shocks of life awoke us. It will be a happiness that meets and rises above pain. Life will always have its tragedies, sickness and separation, pain and sudden death. They are the common inheritance of mankind. But it is not these things in themselves that make life unendurable, it is the way we take them, our fear of them, our worry over them, our longings and rebelliousness, our magnifying and brooding over and shrinking from them; when we resolve to lift our heads and assert our power, we shall find life tragic, yes, but endurable, and full of a deep joy. The little worries and disappointments will cease to trouble us. And the same attitude that enables us to rise above them will, when more staunchly held, lift us over the great sorrows also, and keep alive in us an under glow of joy. An under glow of joy-that is what can be found in life in any but its highly abnormal phases, by conforming to its conditions and taking it for what it is, stuff which, we have to shape into service to the ideal. It should be recognized as the final word of personal morality that a man must train himself to a happiness that is independent of circumstances. We need no mystical painting out of the shadows, no blindness to facts, only a will to serve the right, a readiness to accept the imperfect, and eyes to see the beauty that surrounds us. "If I have faltered more or less In my great task of happiness, If I have moved among my race And shown no glorious morning face, If beams from happy human eyes Have moved me not; if morning skies, Books" and my food, and summer rain, Knocked on my sullen heart in vain. If, in short, we have not disciplined ourselves to happiness, it may well be maintained that we have left undone our highest duty to our neighbor and ourselves. And he may with good reason declare that he has solved the greatest problem of life who can proclaim with Tolstoy, "I rejoice in having taught myself not to be sad!" or with the Apostle Paul, "I have learned in whatsoever state I am therein to be content." Much of the secret of happiness is to be found in Epictetus and Marcus Aurelius and, of course, in the Gospels. Of modern writers, among the most useful are Stevenson and Chesterton. See, for example, Stevenson's Christmas Sermon, and J. F. Genung's Stevenson's Attitude toward Life. Chesterton's counsels are too sattered to make reference practicable.

See also C. W. Eliot, The Happy Life. C. Hilty, Happiness. P. G. Hamerton, The Quest of Happiness. P. Paulsen, System of Ethics, book m, chap, n, sees. 3, 6; chap, iv, sees. 1, 2. H. C. King, Rational Living, chap, x, sec. iv. J. Payot, Education of the Will, book iv, chap. iv. A. Bennett, The Human Machine, chaps, VI; Mental Efficiency, chap. ix. In Royce's Philosophy of Loyalty, Roosevelt's Strenuous Life, and Gannett's Blessed be Drudgery, we get valuable notes; and Carlyle has many, especially ID the latter chapters of Sartor Resartm.

PART IV
PUBLIC MORALITY

CHAPTER XXIII
PATRIOTISM AND WORLD-PEACE

THE goal of personal morality is reached with the adoption of that mode of life that leads to the stable and lasting happiness of the individual. Such a happiness necessarily presupposes relations of kindness and cooperation with those other persons that form the immediate environment. But it is quite compatible with a neglect of those wider aspects of duty that we call public morality. The Stoics, the anchorites, some communities of monks, and many a well-to-do recluse today, are examples of those who have found a selfish happiness for themselves without taking any hand in forwarding the general welfare. Yet the greatest total good is not to be attained in any such way; if man is to win in his inexorable war with a hostile and grudging environment, men must march EN MASSE, must work for ends that lie far beyond their personal satisfactions, for the welfare of the State and posterity. It is these larger, public duties that we must now consider. And it is here that our greatest stress must be laid; for these obligations are too easily overlooked, and toward them the contemporary conscience needs most sharply to be aroused. The first great public problem, historically, is that of war. And theoretically it may well come first, since the attainment of peace is the prerequisite of all other social advance. While a nation's energies are absorbed in war, nothing, or nearly nothing else can be done. So we turn to a consideration of war; and first, of that emotion, patriotism, whose training and redirection must underlie the movement toward universal peace.

What is the meaning and value of patriotism?

Matthew Arnold began his famous American address on Numbers by quoting Dr. Johnson's saying, "Patriotism is the last refuge of a scoundrel." We must admit that to certain forms of it the gibe is pertinent. But in its essence, patriotism is that most useful of human possessions, an emotion that turns a duty into a joy. It is necessary for men, however burdensome they may find the obligation, to be loyal to the interests of the State of which they are members. But the patriot feels it noburden; he loves his country, and serves her willingly, as his privilege and glad desire. To be conscious of belonging to a social group, whose interests are regarded as one's own, to mourn its disasters and rejoice in its successes, and give one's hands and brains without reluctance, when needed, to its service- that is patriotism. For the individual, its value is that it widens his sympathies, gives him new interests, stimulates his ambition, warms his heart with a sense of brotherhood in common hopes and fears; the "man without a country" is, as Dr. Bale's story graphically depicted, like a man without a home; the "citizens of the world," who voluntarily expatriate themselves, miss much of the tang of life that is tasted by him who keeps his local attachments and national loyalty. For the State, its value is that it welds men together, softens their civil strife, lifts them above petty jealousies, rouses them to maintain the common weal against all dangers, external and internal. Especially in view of our hybrid population is it necessary to stimulate patriotism, by the celebration of national anniversaries, the salutation of the flag in the public schools, and whatever other means help to enlist the emotions on the side of civic consciousness. But while seeking to foster patriotism, for its great potentialities of good, we must guard diligently against its lapse into forms that are really harmful to the community which it avowedly serves. Like every other great emotion, it needs to be controlled, developed along the lines of greatest usefulness, directed into proper channels. How should patriotism be directed and qualified?

(1) Patriotism must be rationalized, so as to be an enthusiasm for the really great and admirable phases of the national life. Instead of a pride in the prowess of army and navy, of yachts or athletes, it should become a pride in national efficiency and health, in the national art, literature, statesmanship, and educational system, in the beauty of public buildings and the standards of public manners and morals. It should think not so much of defending by force the national "honor," as of maintaining standards of honor that shall be worth defending. There may, indeed, still be occasions when we can learn the truth of the old Roman verse, Dulce et decorum est pro patria mori; but the newer patriotism consists not so much in willingness to die as in willingness to live, for one's country-to take the trouble to study conditions, to vote, and to work for the improvement of conditions and the invigorating of the national life. The real anti-patriots are not the peace-men, but the selfish and unscrupulous money-makers, the idle rich, the dissolute, the ill-mannered, all those who put private interest or passion above the public weal, help to weaken national strength and solidarity, and bring our country's name into disrepute.

(2) Patriotism must not merge into conceit and blind self-satisfaction. The superior, patronizing air of many Americans, their insufferable boasting and dogmatism, does more, perhaps, to prejudice foreigners against us than any other thing. We must teach international good manners, a becoming modesty, a generosity toward the prejudices of others, and a recognition of our own shortcomings. The blind patriotism that will not confess to any fault, that shouts, "Our country, right or wrong," leads in the direction of arrogance, wrongdoing, and dishonor. We must be free to criticize our own government; we must have no false notions about national "honor" such as were once held concerning personal "honor" in the days of dueling. We

shall doubtless be in the wrong sometimes; we must welcome enlightenment and try to learn the better way. Apologizing is sometimes nobler than bluster; and he is no true lover of his country who seeks to condone, and so perpetuate, her errors.

(3) Patriotism must not imply a hatred of, or desire to hurt, other countries. The sight of one great civilization seeking to injure another is the shame of humanity. For in the end our interests are the same; we should not profit by Germany's loss any more than Connecticut would gain by injury to Vermont. Jingoism, contempt of other peoples, and purely selfish diplomacy, are sinful outgrowths of patriotism. We must learn to be fair and good-tempered, to appreciate the admirable in other nations, to thrill to their ideals, and banish all suspicious, sneering, or hypercritical attitudes toward them. It is a pity that the mass of our people get their conceptions of foreign peoples and rulers so largely through newspaper cartoons and caricatures, which emphasize and exaggerate their points of difference and inferiority instead of revealing their power and excellence. It is a stupid provinciality that conceives a distaste for foreigners because of their alien manners and to us uncouth language, their different dress and habits. As a matter of fact, they feel as superior to us as we to them, and on the whole, perhaps, with as good a right. No one of the nations but has some noble ideals and achievements to its credit; if we do not appreciate them, we are thereby proved to be in need of what they have to give. And underneath these usually superficial differences, we are all just men and women, with the same loves and hatreds, the same needs, the same weaknesses and repentances and aspirations. If we realized our common humanity, we should try to treat them as we should wish to be treated by them; the Golden Rule, the Christian spirit, the method of reason and kindness, is as applicable to international as to inter-personal relations. We should not be too sensitive to the trivial breaches of manners, the intemperate words and selfish acts of neighbor-nations, but make allowances and preserve our good-fellowship, as we do in our personal life. We should beware of letting our own patriotism lead us into like misconduct. Above all, we must refuse to let it lead us into the lust of conquest; we must respect the rights and liberties of other peoples, keep strictly to our treaty obligations, honor less the patriots who have inflamed national hatreds and led us to battle against other peoples than those who have wrought for their country's righteousness and true honor, and let it be our pride to stand for international comity and good will. A question that may properly be discussed here is whether it is permissible to shift patriotism from one country to another. Such a change of loyalty is, in times of war, called treason, and naturally evokes the resentment of the deserted side. Even as impartial judges, we are properly suspicious of such action, as denoting a vacillating nature, devoid of the true spirit of loyalty, or as indicative of a

selfishness that follows its own personal advantage. And so far as that suspicion is well founded, we must condemn the traitor. But certainly, if a man experiences a sincere change of conviction, he should not be required to continue to serve the side that he now feels to be in the wrong; every man must be free to follow his conscience, even if it leads him to disavow his own earlier allegiance. Suppose Benedict Arnold to have developed a sincere conviction that the American revolutionists were in the wrong, and that the true welfare of both America and Britain lay in their continued union. In such a case he must, as a conscientious man, have transferred his allegiance to the Tory side. So a man who has been a worker for the saloon interests, who should become convinced of the anti-social influence of the liquor trade, would do right to come over to the anti- saloon side and work against his former associates. The really difficult question lies rather here: may such a man use for the advantage of the cause he now serves the knowledge he gained, the secrets entrusted to him, the power he won, as a worker for the opposite cause? If Benedict Arnold was a sincere convert to the British cause, did he do right in trying to deliver West Point into their hands? Or are we right in execrating him for his attempted breach of trust? May the former saloon-worker use his inside knowledge of the saloon men's plans, and his familiarity with the business, to help the cause to which he has transferred his allegiance? The two cases may be closely parallel; but each will probably be decided by most people according to the side upon which they stand. An impartial judgment will, perhaps, condemn all breaches of faith, all use of delegated power for ends contrary to those for which the power was delegated, including secrets deliberately entrusted, but will not condemn the use for the new cause of knowledge gained by the individual's own observation, or influence won through the power of his own personality.

What have been the benefits of war?

War has not been an unmitigated evil. In fairness we must note the following points:

(1) In spite of its danger, and its pain, war has been a great excitement and joy to men. Tennyson is doubtless true to life in making Ulysses exclaim "All times I have enjoyed Greatly, have suffered greatly. . . And drunk delight of battle with my peers, Far on the ringing plains of windy Troy. How dull it is to pause, to make an end, As though to breathe were life!"

In the Iliad, indeed, we read: "With everything man is satiated, sleep, sweet singing, and the joyous dance; of all these man gets sooner tired than of war." In primitive times, and even, though decreasingly, in modern times, the cause of war has lain not merely in the ends to be attained thereby, but in the sheer love of war for its own sake-the quickened heartbeats, the sense of power and daring and achievement, the joy in martial music and uniforms, in the rhythmic footsteps of marching men, in the awakened thrill of patriotism, the love of effort and sacrifice for a cherished cause.

To some extent this primitive lure of war still persists. But, fortunately, the glory and excitement of hand-to-hand conflict, the picturesque valor and visible achievement of earlier battles, are now gone. The soldier is but a cog in a machine, usually at a considerable distance from his enemy. He does not know whether his shot has hit or not; if he is wounded it is by an invisible hand. All the strain and fatigue and pain of war remain, but little of its glory and delight. Moreover, whatever normal satisfaction has been found in war can be had, as we shall presently note, in other ways- in all sorts of generous rivalries and useful as well as exciting endeavors that are open to the modern man.

(2) War has necessitated discipline, organization, courage, self- sacrifice, and has thus been a great stimulus to virtues which to some extent have carried over into other fields. It has kept men from sinking into inertia or mere pleasure seeking, fostered energy and hardihood, quieted civil strife, taught the necessity of union and justice at home. The patriotism awakened by struggle against a common enemy has often persisted when the conflict was over, given birth to art and history, and many an act of devotion to the State. But national solidarity and a regime of justice within the State are now our stable possession, while the hardier and heroic virtues can be awakened in other and less disastrous ways. War has ceased to have its former usefulness as a spur to personal and social morality.

(3) Wars of self-defense have often been necessary, to preserve goods that would have been lost by conquest; as when the Greeks at Marathon repelled the barbaric hordes of Asia, or when Charles Martel and the Franks checked the advance of the Saracens at Tours. Offensive wars, even, may have been necessary to wipe out evils, such as slavery or the oppression of neighboring peoples. But in modern times the moral justification of war on such grounds has usually been a flimsy pretext; and certainly the occasion for legitimate warfare is becoming steadily rarer. Nearly always the good aimed at could have been attained without the evils of war. If the American colonies had had a little more patience, they could have won the liberty they craved without war and separation from the mother country-as Canada and Australia have done. If the United States had had a little more patience and tact and diplomacy, it is probable that Cuba could have been saved from the intolerable oppression of Spain without war. Now that the moral pressure of the world's opinion is becoming so strong, and the Hague tribunal stands ready to adjust difficulties, there is seldom excuse for recourse to brute strength. The real cause of war lies far less often in the moral demand that prefers righteousness to peace than in the touchiness,

selfishness, and resentments of nations, or their desire for glory and conquest.

(4) War has, directly or indirectly, been the means of spreading the blessings of civilization. Alexander's campaigns brought Greek culture to the Eastern world, the Roman conquests civilized the West, the famous Corniche Road was built by Napoleon to get his troops into Italy, the trans-Siberian railway, the subsidized steamship lines of modern nations, the Panama Canal, owe their existence primarily to the fear of war. But today all lands are open to peaceful penetration; missionaries and traders do more to civilize than armies. And if the building of certain roads and railways and canals might have been somewhat postponed in an era of stable peace, many more material improvements, actually more imperative if less spectacular, would certainly have been carried out with the vast sums of money saved from war expenditures. Whatever good ends, then, war may have served in the past, it is now superfluous, a mere survival of savagery, a relic of our barbaric past, a clear injury to man, in ways which we shall next consider.

What are the evils of war?

(1) We need not dwell on the physical and mental suffering caused by war; General Sherman's famous declaration, "War is hell!" sums the matter up. Agonizing wounds, pitiless disease, the permanent crippling, enfeeblement, or death of vigorous men in the prime of life, the anguish of wives and sweethearts, the loneliness of widows, the lack of care for orphans-it is impossible for those who have not lived through a great war to realize the horror of it, the cruel pain suffered by those on the field, the torturing suspense of those left behind. It is, indeed, a sad commentary on man's wisdom that, with all the distress that inevitably inheres in human life, he should have voluntarily brought upon himself still greater suffering and premature death.

(2) But the moral harm of war is no less conspicuous than the physical. It fosters cruelty, callousness, contempt of life; it kills sympathy and the gentler virtues; it coarsens and leads almost inevitably to sensuality. After a war there is always a marked increase in crime and sexual vice; ex-soldiers are restless, and find it hard to settle down to a normal life. There is a permanent coarsening of fiber. Even the maintenance of armies in time of peace is a great moral danger. The unnatural barrack-life, the requisite postponement of marriage, the opportunity for physical and moral contagion, make military posts commonly sources of moral contamination. Prostitution flourishes and illegitimacy increases where soldiers are quartered; the army is a bad school of morals.

Add to this indictment the stimulus to national hatreds caused by war, the inflaming of resentments and checking of international good will. Frenchmen still nourish a bitter animosity against the Germans for the possession of Alsace and the occupation of Paris. The instinctive racial antipathies of the Balkan peoples have been immeasurably deepened by the recent wars on the peninsula. The eventual brotherhood of man is indefinitely postponed by every war and by every rumor of war.

The interest in war also takes attention and effort away from the remedying of social and moral evils; it is useless to attempt any moral campaign while a war is on. Jane Addams tells us, in Twenty Years at Hull House, that when she visited England in 1896 she found it full of social enthusiasm, scientific research, scholarship, and public spirit; while on a second visit, in 1900, all enthusiasm and energy seemed to be absorbed by the Boer War, leaving little for humanitarian undertakings.

(3) A less obvious, but even more lasting, evil is that caused by the loss of the best blood of a nation. In general, the strongest and best men go to the field; the weaklings and cowards are left to produce the next generation. The inevitable result is racial degeneration. The decline of the Greek and Roman civilizations was doubtless in large part due to the continual killing off of the best stocks, until the earlier and nobler breed of men almost ceased to exist. The effect of modern war is the exact opposite of that of primitive war, where all the men had to fight, and the strongest or bravest or swiftest survived; strength and valor and speed avail nothing against modern projectiles, and it is the stay-at-homes who are selected for survival, in general the weakest and least worthy. War is the greatest of dysgenic forces, and undoes the effect of a hundred eugenic laws.

(4) The vast and increasing expense of war is a very serious matter for the moralist, because it means a drain of the resources that might otherwise be utilized for the advance of civilization. The cost of a modern war goes at least into the hundreds of millions of dollars, and any great war would cost billions. Every shot from a modern sixteen inch gun costs approximately a thousand dollars! Add to this direct cost the indirect costs of war, not reckoned in the usual figures-the loss of the time and work of the hundreds of thousands of able-bodied men, the economic loss of their illness and death, the destruction of buildings, bridges, railways, etc, the obstruction of commerce, the paralysis of industry and agriculture, the ravages and looting of armies, the maintenance of hospitals and nurses, and then, finally, the money given in pensions.[Footnote: The recent Balkan war is reckoned to have cost nearly half a million men killed or permanently disabled, a billion and a half dollars of direct] Add further the cost of the expenditure, besides many billions of indirect expense. The colossal European war just beginning as these pages go to press bids fair to cost immeasurably more

aintenance of armies upon a peace-footing-the feeding and clothing of the men, the building and maintenance of barracks and forts, of battleships and torpedo boats, of guns and ammunition, automobiles, aeroplanes, and the increasing list of expensive modern military appurtenances. Europe spends nearly two billion dollars a year in times of peace on its armies and navies-money enough to build four or five Panama canals annually. The entire merchant marine of the world is worth but three billion dollars. More than this, over four million strong young men are kept under arms in Europe, a million more workers are engaged in making ships, weapons, gunpowder, military stores. Over a million horses are kept for army use. This money and these men, if used in the true interests of humanity, could quickly provide adequate and comfortable housing for every European, adequate schooling, clothing, and food for every one. Here is the great criminal waste of our times. In America our waste is less flagrant, but it is steadily increasing. We throw away money enough in these fratricidal preparations to cover the country with excellent roads in short order, or give every child a high school education.

In a way, however, the rapidly growing cost of war and preparation for war is to be welcomed. For it is this that is creating, more than all our moral propaganda, a rising sentiment against war, and will presently make it impossible. When the German militarists became excited over the Morocco incident in 1911, a financial panic ensued, credit was withdrawn, pockets were touched, and a great protest arose which did much to quench the jingo spirit. Japan was induced to sign her treaty of peace with Russia because her money was giving out. Turkey was unable, in the winter of 1913-14, to renew war with Greece for the Aegean Islands, because she could not raise a loan till she promised peace. The growing international financial network, and the revolt of the taxpayers against the incessant draining of their pocketbooks, promise a change for the better in European militarism before very long.

What can we do to hasten world-peace?

There are powerful forces, which without our conscious effort are making for the abolition of war: its growing cost; the extension of mutual knowledge, through the newspapers and magazines, through travel, through exchange professorships and Rhodes scholarships and all international associations; the growing sensitiveness to suffering; the spread of eugenic ideals; and the increasing interest in worldwide social, moral, and material problems. But the epoch of final peace for man can be greatly accelerated by means which we may now note.

(1) We may stimulate counter-enthusiasms to take the place of the passion for war. After all, the great war of mankind is the war against pain, disease,

poverty, and sin; the real heroes are not those who squander human strength and courage in fighting one another, but those who fight for man against his eternal foes. The war of man against man is dissension in the ranks. We must make it seem more glorious to men to enlist in these humanitarian campaigns than in the miserable civil wars that impede our common triumphs. [Footnote: Cf. Perry, Moral Economy, p. 32; "War between man and man is an obsolescent form of heroism. . . . The general battle of life, the first and last battle, is still on; and it has that in it of danger and resistance, of comradeship and of triumph, that can stir the blood." And cf. President Eliot's fine eulogy of Dr. Lazear, who died of yellow fever after voluntarily undergoing inoculation by a mosquito, in the attempt to learn how to stay the disease: " With more than the courage and] Further, we should awaken interest in innocent devotion of the soldier, he risked and lost his life to show how a fearful pestilence is communicated and how its ravages may be prevented."] excitements and rivalries-in sports, in industrial competition, in missionary enterprise. A world's series in baseball, or an intercollegiate football season, can work off the restless energies of many thousands who in earlier days would have lusted for war. The revival of the Olympic games was definitely planned as a substitute for war. And men must have not only excitements and rivalries, but real difficulties and dangers-something to try their courage and endurance and train them in hardihood. For this we have exploration and mountaineering, the prosecution of difficult engineering undertakings, the attacking of corruption and the achievement of political and social reforms. [Footnote: Cf. W. James, "The Moral Equivalent of War" (in Memories and Studies), p. 287: "We must make new energies and hardihood's continue the manliness to which the military mind so faithfully clings. Martial virtues must be the enduring cement, intrepidity, contempt of softness, surrender of private interest, obedience to command, must still remain the rock upon which states are built. The martial type of character can be bred without war. The only thing needed henceforward is to inflame the civic temper as past history has inflamed the military temper."]

(2) We may spread popular knowledge of the evils of war. It is incredible that this barbarous method of deciding disputes could be continued if the people generally had a lively realization of its cost in pain, money, and degradation. Already many societies exist for the diffusion of literature on the matter, [Footnote: And of course for other work in the direction of peace. The oldest such organization in this country is the American Peace Society. The Association for International Conciliation, founded in Paris by Baron d' Estournelles de Constant, in 1899, has branches now in all the important countries. Lately we have Mr. Carnegie's endowments for international peace] conscientious editors of journals and newspapers use their columns for peace propaganda, public schools teach children the evils

of war, ministers use their pulpits to denounce it. All this, effort must be pushed in greater degree until a general public sentiment is aroused that will insist on the peaceful settlement of all international difficulties.

(3) Indirectly, too, education and association can make war more and more unlikely. We can create a greater knowledge of and sympathy with other nations. We can to considerable extent train out pugnacity, quick temper, resentfulness, and train in sensitiveness to suffering, sympathy, breadth of view. All such moral progress helps in the war against war. We can encourage the interchange of professors and scientists between countries, increase the number of professional and industrial international organizations. The International Socialist party, with its threatened weapon of the general strike against war, may actually prove to be- whether we like it or not the most efficient of all forces. The International Federation of Students (Corda ratres), founded at Turin in 1898, with its branches in all civilized countries, may be of great use. A censorship of the press to exclude all jingoistic and inflammatory utterances may at times be necessary. It is even questionable whether uniforms and martial music ought not to be banished for a while, until the habit of peaceful settlement becomes fixed.

(4) Politically, we must make our public policies so high and unselfish that other nations cannot justly take offense. Most wars are provoked by national greed or selfishness, lack of manners, or the breaking of treaty obligations. The United States, it must be confessed, has to some extent lost the respect and trust of other nations for its high- handed methods and disregard of treaties. Congress is allowed to modify or abrogate any treaty without consultation with the other nation involved; and we have what many critics deem acts of grave dishonor upon our record. [Footnote: For example, the recent abrogation of our long-standing treaty with Russia, without her consent, which has forfeited her friendship; or what seemed to many the violation of our treaty-promise to England by Congress in its exemption, now repealed, of American coastwise shipping from canal tolls. It would be well to engrave over the entrance to the Capitol the Psalmist's words: "He that sweareth to his own hurt and changeth not."] ways we have needlessly offended and insulted other nations. The voter must watch the conduct of parties and work to elect men who, refraining from provoking other nations, will aim for peace.

(5) Practical steps in the direction of peace may be mentioned. Most important are arbitration treaties. They must be made binding, and made to apply to all matters; the loophole which permits a nation to refuse to arbitrate a matter which it believes to involve its "honor" practically invalidates the treaty altogether, as every matter in dispute may be so construed. Alliances in which one country agrees to help another if the

latter has agreed to arbitrate a matter and its enemy has refused, may be of great value. Treaties that guarantee existing boundaries and bind a nation not to extend its territory are useful, even if there is no adequate method as yet of enforcing such guaranties. The question whether we shall increase or decrease our army and navy is hotly disputed. The United States might well lead the way in disarmament, since the oceans that separate us from Europe and Asia are a better protection than forts or fleets, and no nation has enough to gain by fighting us to make it worth the cost. With the great European nations the case is different, and disarmament will probably have to come by mutual agreement. The only valid reason for an American army and navy lies in the power they give us to protect our citizens abroad, or to protect our weaker neighbors against foreign aggression. Perhaps until there is formed an international army and navy, it will be necessary for the most civilized and pacific nations to keep armed, since the less scrupulous nations would remain armed and acquire the balance of power. But the contention that a great armament is the best guaranty of peace is untrue, for two reasons: it is an inevitable provocation to other nations to match it with other great armaments; and the very existence of battleships and weapons creates a temptation to use them. The professional soldier is always eager to see active service, to prove his efficiency, have excitement, win glory and advancement. As the Odyssey puts it, "The steel blade itself often incites to deeds of violence."

(6) The ultimate solution for international difficulties must, of course, be world organization. The beginnings of an international court we have already, the outcome of the first two Hague Conferences, in 1899 and 1907. It must be given greater powers, and backed up by an international executive, legislature, and police. Perhaps the police will be the combined armies of the world put at the service of international justice. This "parliament of nations, federation of the world" is not a Utopian dream; it is hardly a greater step than that by which savage tribes, or the thirteen States of North America, or the South African and Australian States, became welded into nations. It is to be remembered that the wager of battle was the original method of settling private disputes; and even when trial by jury was authorized, the older form of settlement persisted long-being legally abolished in England only as late as 1819. Similarly, the peaceful settlement of international disputes will doubtless before many generations become so universal that it will be difficult for our grandchildren or great-grandchildren to realize that as late as early in the twentieth century the most civilized nations still had recourse to the old and barbarous wager of battle.

H. Spencer, "Patriotism,", " Rebarbarization" (in Facts and Comments). G. K. Chesterton, "Patriotism" (in The Defendant). G. Santayana, Reason in Society, chap. VII. Outlook, vol. 92, p. 317; vol. 90, p. 534. International Journal of Ethics, vol. 16, p. 472. The American Association for International Conciliation (Sub-Station 84, New York City) sends free literature on request. A bibliography of peace literature will be found in their pamphlet No. 64. E. L. Godkin, "Peace" (in Reflections and Comments). W. James, "Speech at the Peace Banquet," and "The Moral Equivalent of War" (in Memories and Studies'). Jane Addams, Newer Ideals of Peace, chaps. I, VII; The Arbiter in Council. J. Novicow, War and its Alleged Benefits. N. Angell, The Great Illusion. W. J. Tucker, The New Movement of Humanity. V. L. Kellogg, Beyond War, chap. I. D. S. Jordan, War and Waste. R. C. Morris, International Arbitration and Procedure. International Journal of Ethics, vol. 22, p. 127. World's Work, vol. 20, p. 13318; vol. 21, p. 14128. Independent, vol. 77, p. 396. Outlook, vol. 86, pp. 137, 145; vol. 83, p. 376; vol. 84, p. 29; vol. 98, p. 59. Hibbert Journal, vol. 12, p. 105.

CHAPTER XXIV
POLITICAL PURITY

AND EFFICIENCY THE attainment of a stable peace is the first public duty; the second is the achievement of an efficient government. Where politics are corrupt and inefficient all social progress is obstructed; and all such ideals of a reshaped human society as the Socialists yearn toward must be postponed until we have learned to run the machinery of government smoothly and effectively. The backward condition of peoples whose government is unintelligent needs no examples. The Russo-Japanese War brought into sharp contrast a nation of limitless resources and fine human stock handicapped and crippled by a selfish bureaucracy, and a much smaller nation, inexperienced and remote from the great world currents, but strengthened and made efficient by an intelligent and patriotic administration. In Persia and Mesopotamia we find poverty, ignorance, desert, where once flourished mighty empires: bad government is the cause. Greece and Italy and Egypt are struggling to recover from centuries of misgovernment. In this country government has been far wiser and more responsive to the community's needs; and yet the apathy of the intelligent public and the intrusion of private greed have distorted and obstructed legislation until social reformers throw up their hands in despair. But there are hopeful signs. The causes of this political mismanagement are being more generally recognized today, and it is probable that the next few decades will witness great strides toward improving the mechanism of American government and banishing corruption.

What are the forces making for corruption in politics?

(1) By one means or other, unscrupulous rulers and officeholders have always been able to replenish their private income by misuse of their official powers. Since popular government was first tried there has existed a class of professional politicians with little regard for the public welfare and ready to do anything to keep themselves in power and fatten their pocketbooks. We have in America the well-known phenomena of the "machine," the "ring," and the "boss," whose motto is "Politics is politics," and who are unashamed to put their interests above those of the people at large. Their control of the machinery of government enables them, unless ingenious provisions prevent, to wink at illegal voting and fraudulent counting of votes, to get the dregs of the population out to the polls, and perhaps intimidate their opponents from voting. The police power has often been misused for such purposes; the gerrymander is another clever method of manipulating the results of elections. Such means, together with the use as

bribe money of funds deflected from the public treasury, the blackmail of vice, and the acceptance of "contributions" from favored parties, create a vicious circle which tends to keep in power corrupt officials who have once got hold.

(2) But the power of unscrupulous politicians is made far greater by the support of those whose personal interests they make a business of furthering. Whole sections of the people are pleased and placated and bribed by special legislation in their favor, and as many individuals as possible are given positions. Behind every "boss" there are always hundreds of men who owe their "jobs" to him, and many others who cherish promises and hopes for personal favors. Jane Addams tells us that upon one occasion when the reformers in Chicago tried to oust a corrupt alderman they "soon discovered that approximately one out of every five voters in the nineteenth ward at that time held a job dependent upon the good will of the alderman." [Footnote: Twenty Years at Hull House, p. 316.]

(3) Of especial importance are the great "interests" that are always to be found behind a corrupt administration. These corporations are so dependent upon the good will of the Government for their prosperity, and even for their very existence, that from the primitive instinct of self-preservation as well as from the greed of exorbitant profits, they stand ready to give liberal bribes, or at least to back with money and moral support the party machine that promises to favor them. They control a large proportion of the newspapers and magazines, and are thus able to distort facts, protect themselves from attack, and even stir up a factitious distrust of would-be reformers. As every little contractor naturally favors the "ring" that awards contracts to him, so the great corporations publicly or secretly support it. The liquor trade and the vice caterers-the keepers of gambling dens, illegal "shows," and disorderly houses-back by their money and votes the "machine" that they know will let them alone. But, indeed, the most "respectable" trusts and public-service corporations are often most culpable, and the greatest power behind the throne. Their interest in the personnel of the Government is far keener than that of the average citizen; they can usually succeed, by cleverly specious presentations of the situation, in dividing the forces against them, and often, by "deals," in effecting secret alliances of the "rings" in control of supposedly opposing parties. The poor are right in supposing that these powerful "interests" are their greatest enemy; as that keen observer of our national life, Mr. Bryce, has put it, "the power of money is for popular governments the most constant source of danger."

(4) But, after all, this combination of forces in defiance of the common weal would not be effective but for the comparative indifference of the

people, which may thus be called a contributing factor. The average voter feels no stimulus of self-interest in the matter; "what is everybody's business is nobody's business," and the individual finds his personal influence so slight that it seems hardly worth his pains to do anything about it. Occasionally popular passions become aroused and reform movements make a clean sweep; but the result is usually temporary, and when the general attention is turned elsewhere the bosses creep back to power. Modern life has so many more personal interests in it than the ancient republics had, that public affairs seldom become so big and absorbing an interest. And the more public affairs become the concern of a special group of men with dubious reputations, the more politics are shunned by the average citizen. Home life and business, social life and amusements, aesthetic, intellectual, and religious interests, are so much more attractive to him, that he gives little heed to political conditions, lets himself be duped by newspaper talk, and votes blindly some party ticket, without realizing his gullibility and his poor citizenship.

What are the evil results of political corruption?

(1) The obvious result of these conditions is inefficiency of administration and waste of the public moneys. The real interests of city or State are neglected. Streets become filthy, unsanitary tenements are built, firetrap factories and theaters allowed; every effort to improve public health is sidetracked, and the will of the people is subordinated to the will of the gang. Officials are nominated or appointed not for their competence but for their subservience to the organization; the boss himself, inexpert in administration, responsible to no one, and usually bribable, dictates public policy. The public funds disappear as in a quicksand; extravagant prices are paid for building lots and contracts, in return for political support or a share of the loot. Philadelphia before the reform movement of 1911 borrowed fifty-one million dollars in four years, and at the end had practically nothing to show for it, with the city dirty, buildings out of repair, and everything important neglected. One contractor in the "ring" was paid $520,000 a year to remove the city garbage-a privilege which is actually paid for in some cities, the value of the garbage for fertilizer and the manufacture of other products making the collection of it a profitable business.

(2) Another evil result lies in the subordination of general to local interests. The scattered and ineffective "pork-barrel" appropriations of Congress are dictated not by intelligent consideration for the public weal, but by the desire to throw a sop to this and that section of the country, and thereby win votes. Costly buildings are authorized in many towns where they are not needed, river and harbor improvements proceed at a halting pace in a hundred places at once, unnecessary navy yards and custom houses are maintained at heavy cost, the army is scattered at many small and expensive

posts. Even the tariff is largely a deal between various manufacturing interests, rather than an instrument of the public good. Most officials consider themselves bound to exert all their influence in favor of their particular constituency's desires; if they cross those wishes they will probably not be reelected, while if they sacrifice the interests of the people as a whole they will be immune from punishment. Most of the state universities, normal schools, asylums, and other institutions have been located where they are as the result of a deal between different sections rather than with a view to the most advantageous site.

(3) To these grave evils we must add the moral harm of selfish and corrupt politics. Standards of honor are blurred, the spirit of public service is almost lost sight of, and the cheap materialism to which our prosperous age is too easily prone flourishes apace. The man who would succeed in politics-unless he is a man of extraordinary personality and favored by good fortune-must be disingenuous and a time-server, must truckle to bosses and do favors for the ring; he must appeal to prejudice and passion and put his personal advancement before his ideals. No one can estimate the evil effect that corruption in politics has had upon the national character. When we add the indirect effects- the distortion of the public news-service, the protection of vice, the insecurity of justice-the moral evils of political corruption are seen to be of gravest importance.

What is the political duty of the citizen?

(1) In the present chaotic state of our machinery of government, where corruption is so easy and efficiency so difficult to obtain, the burden must rest upon every conscientious voter to play his part with intelligence. He must study the situation, keep himself informed as to candidates and issues, watch the conduct of officials, vote at primaries and elections, however irksome and fruitless this effort may seem. Above all, he must use independence of judgment, and not let himself be duped by disingenuous appeals to "party loyalty"; where blind party voting is prevalent there is little stimulus to party managers to nominate able and honorable men or to promote needed legislation. Public opinion must be kept aroused, the sense of individual responsibility awakened, and political matters kept in the glare of publicity. At election times whoever can spare the time should, after learning the local situation, take some part in the campaign, by public speaking, personal soliciting of is a shame that the peaceable home-loving citizen should have to be dragged into this business of politics, which ought to be left to experts to manage; but at present there seems no help for it in most communities.

(2) An important service lies in joining or forming local branches of the leagues which now exist for the pushing of specific political measures, for

the investigation and publication of impartial records of candidates, or for the investigation of the expenditures and results of administrations. Under the first head we may classify, for example, the National Short Ballot Organization; under the second head the Good Government Association, that makes it its business to send to each voter in a community a printed statement of the past history of each candidate for office, including the record of his vote on important matters; under the third head there are the Bureaus of Municipal Research. The New York Bureau, incorporated in 1907, conducts a yearly budget exhibit that shows graphically what is being done with the money raised by taxation. Inefficiency and corruption are ferreted out, waste is demonstrated, suggestions are made for economy, for the improvement of administration in every detail, and the amelioration of evil social conditions. By its determined publicity it can do much to energize and modernize city government. [Footnote: Cf. World's Work, vol. 23, p. 683. National Municipal Review, vol. 2. p. 48.]

(3) The outlook for clean and public-spirited young men, with expert knowledge and ideals, who wish to enter a political career, is gradually becoming more encouraging. The reformer in politics must be not merely an idealist, but a man who can do things. He must show his constituents that reform government serves them better than the ringsters. Reform tactics have too often been negative; stopped, but no positive measures for social welfare have been passed. To be successful, a politician must show the people that he understands and is able to satisfy their needs. More effective than any moral house- cleaning in securing the tenure of an administration is its efficiency in promoting better living and working conditions, improving opportunities for recreation and education, or loosening the clutch of the predatory "interests." Moreover, the politician must be a good mixer, willing to work with those who do not share his idealism, good- natured and conciliatory, ready to postpone the accomplishment of much that he has at heart in order to get something done. As organization is in most matters necessary for effectiveness, he must usually work with a party, do a lot of distasteful detail work, and make compromises for the sake of agreements. Happily, the Progressive party has made an out- and-out stand for the application of morals to politics; and the growing movement in the cities toward seeking experts to manage their affairs gives hope that the way will soon be generally open for men of scientific training and high ideals in political life.

What legislative checks to corruption are possible?

It is, of course, an unnatural situation when the ordinary citizen has to spend a lot of time and effort if he would guard against being misgoverned. He ought to be able to tend to his own affairs and leave the machinery of government to those who have been trained to it and whose business it is.

And while no political mechanism will ever wholly run itself, without watchfulness on the part of the people, experience shows clearly that it is possible by a wise system to make corruption much more difficult and more easily checked. We Americans are beginning to awake from our complacent self-gratulation and realize that our political machinery is clumsy and antiquated and a standing invitation to inefficiency. The discussion of the relative advantages of legislative schemes belongs to the science of government rather than to ethics; but their bearing upon public morality is so important that certain typical movements must be explained. The stages by which the advanced form of popular government which we have now attained has been reached need not, for our purposes, be considered-the extension of suffrage to the masses, government by representatives, registration laws, the secret ballot, and the like. We need only discuss several reforms now being agitated and tried, whose aim is to make government more responsive to the real wishes and needs of the people, and more difficult of usurpation by selfish interests.

I. We may first speak of several reforms whose aim is to improve our mechanism of election, in order that merit, rather than "pull," shall lead to office, and that officials shall represent the people rather than the political rings. It is not generally true that good and able men are unwilling to accept public office; what they are unwilling to do is to truckle to bosses, to do all the questionable things that will keep them in with the ring, or to spend large sums of money in advertising their claims to the public. So thoroughly have political machines entrenched themselves that it is often practically useless for any one to oppose the machine candidate. Appointees receive their positions for "political services" rendered, or in return for a "campaign contribution" for which they may hope to recoup themselves when in office. To destroy utterly this political "graft" will be impossible until human nature becomes more generally moralized; but to render it more difficult and less common is the purpose of a number of measures, of which we may mention the following:

(1) CIVIL SERVICE LAWS. These require appointments to office, made by officials, to be made on the basis of competitive examinations which shall test the ability and knowledge of the applicants. By this means, within a generation, tens of thousands of positions have been put beyond the reach of spoilsmen, and men of worth have replaced political henchmen. Instead of a great overturn with every new political regime, the man who has now fairly won his position retains it for life, except in case of proved inefficiency. The quality of the public service has been immeasurably improved, the subservience of office-holders to political chiefs abolished. [Footnote: See Atlantic Monthly, vol. 113, p. 270. National Municipal Review, vol. 1, p. 654; vol. 3, p. 316.] But there are still many thousands of

offices that have not been brought within the civil service, and there are continual attempts on the part of politicians to withdraw from it this or that class of appointments, that they may have "plums" to offer their constituents. To the most important positions the civil service method is, however, inapplicable; imagine a President having to appoint as his Secretary of State the man who passed the best examination in diplomacy! So many other considerations affect the availability of a man for such posts that the elected officials must be given a free hand in their choice and held responsible therefore to the people. These important appointees will be enough in the public eye to make it usually expedient for the career of the appointers that they pick reasonably honest and able men-especially if the recall (of which we shall presently speak) is in operation.

(2) The short ballot. As our government has grown more and more complex, the number of officials for whom the citizen must vote has increased, with the result that he has to decide in many cases among rival candidates about none of whom he knows anything definitely. For four or five offices he can be fairly expected the merits of the candidates in the field; but to investigate or remember the relative merits and demerits of a score or more is more than the average voter will do. So he may "scratch" his party's candidate for governor or mayor, but usually votes the "straight ticket" for the minor officials. This works too well into the hands of the political machines. The obvious remedy is to give him only a few officers to vote for and to require the remaining offices to be filled by appointment instead of election.

By this method, not only is the voter saved from needless confusion and enabled to concentrate his attention upon the few big offices, but the responsibility for misgovernment is far more clearly fixed, and the possibility of remedying it made much easier. If a dozen state officials are elected, the average citizen is uncertain who is to blame for inefficiency; each official shoves the responsibility on to the others' shoulders, and it is not plain what can be done except to depose them all, one by one. If a governor only is elected, and is required to appoint his subordinates, the entire blame rests upon his shoulders. If dishonesty or misadministration is discovered, he must take the shame; he may be recalled from office if he is not quick enough in removing the guilty man and remedying the evil.

Further, the right to choose his own subordinates makes the work of the chief much easier, brings a unity of purpose into an administration which is likely to be absent when a number of different men, simultaneously elected, perhaps representing different parties, have to work together. The increased power and responsibility of the chief offices attract able men, men of ideals and training, who do not care for an office whose power is limited by that of various machine politicians who, they know, will hamper them on every side in their efforts for efficient administration. And, apart from this consideration, a man able enough to win election as governor is a far better judge of the men best fitted for the various technical duties that fall to his subordinates than is the general public. Experience shows that the men chosen by chiefs who are elected and held responsible to the people are generally abler than those elected to the same positions by popular vote.

The present movement toward a short ballot, with responsibility clearly denned and concentrated, will doubtless do away ultimately with the clumsy systems by which both States and cities in this country are now governed-the two-chambered legislatures, with their inevitable friction betwixt themselves and with the executive. This method of checks and counter-checks was thought necessary as a safeguard against tyranny, the bugbear of our forefathers, but is now the enemy of efficiency and the haunt of corruption. The much simpler commission form of government, which, originating in Galveston and Des Moines a few years ago, has already, at date of writing, been adopted by over three hundred cities, substitutes for the usual executive and legislative branches a small group of elected officials - commonly five-who, with the aid of appointed subordinates, carry on the whole business of the city. Some such plan may eventually be adopted for states, and even for the national government. [Footnote: R. S. Childs, Short Ballot Principles, Story of the Short Ballot Cities. C. A. Beard, Loose Leaf Digest of Short Ballot Charters. Free literature of the National Short Ballot Organization (383 Fourth Avenue, New York City). C. R. Woodruff, City Government by Commission. E. S. Bradford, Com- mission Government in American Cities. National Municipal Review, vol. 1, pp. 40, 170, 372, 562; vol. 2, p. 661. The American City, vol. 9, p. 236. Outlook, vol. 92, pp. 635, 829; vol. 99, p. 362. Forum, vol. 51, p. 354.]

(3) Direct primaries. Experience has conclusively shown that the caucus system of making nominations for office plays directly into the hands of the machine; its practical result has been that the voter is usually restricted in his nominees of the bosses and the "interests." The direct primary gives the independent candidate his opportunity, and makes it more practicable for honest citizens to determine between what candidates the final choice shall lie. It implies effort on the part of the candidate to make himself known to the voters; but such effort there must always be, unless the candidate is already a conspicuous figure, in order that the citizen may have grounds for his decision. It has in some places led to an exorbitant expenditure for self-advertisement; but this expenditure can be pretty well controlled by legislation. The argument that it does away with the deliberation possible in a caucus wears the aspect of a joke, in view of the sort of deliberation the caucus has in practice encouraged; and discussion does, of course, take place in the public press, which is the modern forum. It is possible,

however, that some modified form of the direct primary plan may be better still, such as the Hughes plan, which provided for the election at each primary of a party committee to present carefully discussed nominations for the following year's primary to approve or reject.[Footnote: See Outlook, vol. 90, p. 382; vol. 95, p: 507. North American Review, vol. 190, p. 1] Arena, vol. 35, p. 587; vol. 36, p. 52; vol. 41, p. 550. Forum, vol. 42, p. 493. Atlantic Monthly, vol. 110, p. 41.

(4) PREFERENTIAL VOTING. A more radical movement would abolish primaries altogether and settle elections upon one day by preferential voting. The voter indicates his second choices, and any further choices he may care to indicate. If no candidate receives a majority of first choices, the first and second choices are added together; if necessary, the third choices. In this way the danger, so often realized, of a split vote and the election of a minority candidate, will be banished; it will no longer be possible for a machine candidate, actually the least majority of the people, to win a plurality over the divided forces of opposition. The real wishes of the voter can be discovered and obeyed more readily than with our present troublesome and expensive system of double elections. [Footnote: National Municipal Review, vol. 1, p. 386; vol. 3, pp. 49, 83.]

(5) PROPORTIONAL REPRESENTATION. By means of preferential voting it is possible to make representative bodies a mirror not of the majority party, but of the real divisions of opinion in a community. One of the great evils in our present system of majority rule is the suppression of the wishes of the minority-which may amount to nearly half the community. [Footnote: Cf. Unpopular Review, vol. 1, p. 22.] Strong parties may go for many years without any representation, or with representation quite disproportionate to their numbers. By the method of proportional representation, every man's vote counts, and every considerable body of opinion can send its representative to council. Men of marked personality, who have aroused too great hostility to make them safe candidates as we vote today, because they would be unlikely to win a majority, can get a constituency sufficient to elect them, while the harmless nobody, elected today only to avoid a feared rival, will have less chance. The evil gerrymander will be abolished, and representative bodies will be divided along party lines in the very proportions in which the people are divided.

Moreover, since on this plan every vote counts, the greatest source of political apathy will be removed-that sense of hopelessness which paralyzes the efforts of the members of a minority party. Corruption will hardly pay; for whereas at present the boss has but to win the comparatively few votes necessary to swing the balance toward a bare majority, in order to have complete control, he will upon this plan secure control only in actual proportion to the number of votes he can secure.

Another advantage of the system lies in the stabler policy it will ensure. Our present system results in frequent sharp overturns, according as this party or that may get a temporary majority. But this battledore and shuttlecock of legislation does not represent the far more gradual changes in public opinion. A system whereby the number of representatives of each party is always directly proportioned to the number of votes cast for that party would make it possible to evolve a careful machinery of government, as is not possible with our periodic upheavals and reversals of personnel and policy.[Footnote: See publications of the American Proportional Representation League (Secretary C. G. Hoag, Haverford, Pennsylvania). National Municipal Review, vol. 3, p. 92. American City, vol. 10, p. 319. Thomas Hare, Representation. J. S. Mill, Representative Government, chap. VII. Political Science Quarterly, vol. 29, p. 111. Atlantic Monthly, vol. 112, p. 610.]

(6) THE SEPARATION OF NATIONAL, STATE, AND LOCAL ISSUES. The obtrusion of national party lines into state and municipal affairs has continually confused issues and blocked reforms in the narrower spheres. Masses of voters will support a candidate for governor or mayor simply because he is a Republican or Democrat, although the national party issues in no way enter into the campaign. Bosses skillfully play on this blind party allegiance, and many a scoundrel or incompetent has ridden into office under the party banner. The separation of local from national elections has proved itself a necessity; in the most advanced communities they are now put in different years, that the loyalties evoked by one campaign may not carry over blindly into another. The direct election of United States Senators has this great advantage, among others, of separating issues; in former days the alternative was often forced upon the citizen of voting for a state legislator who stood for measures of which he disapproved, or of voting for a better legislator who would not vote for the United States Senator he wished to see elected.

(7) Space forbids the further discussion of reforms that aim at improving the machinery of election. The value of anti-bribery laws is obvious, as of the laws that require publicity of campaign accounts, forbid campaign contributions by corporations, and limit the legal expenditures of individuals. [Footnote: Cf. Outlook, vol. 81, p. 549.] The publication at public expense and sending to every voter of a pamphlet giving in his own words the arguments on the strength of which each candidate seeks election has recently been tried in the West. But this is sure, that in one way or other the American people will evolve a mechanism which will make it easier for able and honest men to attain office than for the rogues and their incompetent henchmen.

II. A second set of reforms bears rather upon the quality of legislation than upon the selection of men for office. It is not enough that the way be made easy for good men to attain office; they must, when elected, be freed from needless temptations and given every inducement to work for the interests of the community they represent. Every possible pressure is valuable that can counteract the pull of sectional interests, party interests, or the interests of the great corporations, away from the general welfare. For even the best intentioned officials may yield to the insistence of local or partisan wishes, to the arguments of "big business," or to the lure of personal advantage.

(1) REPRESENTATION AT LARGE. The method of legislation by representatives of local districts leads inevitably to laws that are a compromise or bargain between the interests of the several districts, rather than the result of a desire to further the best interests of the entire community. Congressmen are continually beset by their constituents to secure special favors for them, aldermen are expected to push the interests of their respective wards. Each representative stands in danger of political suicide if he refuses to use his influence for these often improper ends; and legislation takes the form of a quid pro quo:-"You vote for this bill which my section desires, and I'll vote for the bill yours demands." This evil is so great that it may be necessary eventually to do away entirely with district representation.[Footnote: See Outlook, vol. 95, p. 759.]

(2) DELEGATED GOVERNMENT. Another plan, which evades the pressure of local interests while allowing district representation, also avoids the friction and deadlocks which result from government by a group of representatives of sharply opposed parties or principles. By this plan, a representative body is elected, by districts, or at large, by proportional representation; but this body, instead of itself deciding or executing the state or municipal policy, serves merely to select and watch experts, who carry on the various phases of government. These experts remain responsible to the representatives, who in turn are responsible to the people. This method promises to combine concentration of responsibility, efficiency, and business-like government, with democracy, that is, responsiveness to popular control. The national Congress may, for example, appoint a commission of experts on the tariff, agreeing to consider no tariff legislation except such as they recommend; in this way they are freed from all requests to propose this or that alteration in the interests of their State or one of its industries, while the commissioners, not being responsible to any localities, are under no pressure to yield to such requests. Similarly, the right to recommend-or even to enact-legislation on pensions, on river and harbor appropriations, or what not, may be delegated to an appointed body responsible only to the Congress at large; and all the "pork-barrel" legislation, which the better class of legislators

hate, but which is forced upon them by the threat of political ruin, may be obviated. [Footnote: Cf. the new (1914) Public Health Council of six members, in New York State, to whom has been delegated all power to make and enforce laws bearing upon the public health throughout the State (except in New York City). See World's Work, vol. 27, p. 495.] The plan of delegating power to appointed experts has very recently been winning approval in municipal government, where it is commonly called the "City Manager " plan. A small body of commissioners are elected and held responsible for the city government; these men may remain in their private vocations, and draw a comparatively small salary from the city. Their duty is to select an expert city manager who will receive a high salary, and conduct personally and through his appointees the whole business of the city. The commissioners may dismiss him if his work is not satisfactory and engage another to take his place. Responsibility is concentrated; mismanagement can be stopped at once, more readily even than by the recall; unity and continuity of policy become possible; in short, the same successful methods that have made American business the admiration of the world can be applied to politics. If this plan becomes widely adopted, as it bids fair to be, politics can become a trained profession, and we can be governed by experts instead of by politicians. [Footnote: See The City Manager Plan of Municipal Government (printed by the National Short Ballot Organization) National Municipal Review, vol. 1, pp. 33, 549; vol. 2, pp. 76, 639; vol. 3, p. 44. Outlook, vol. 104, p. 887.]

(3) THE RECALL. Many of the newer plans for government include a method by which an inefficient or dishonest official can be removed from office by the people, without the cumbersome process of an impeachment. It would not be wise to apply the recall to local representatives, who would then be still more at the mercy of local wishes; but with a short ballot and the concentration of responsibility upon executives or small commissions who represent the community as a whole, it is highly desirable to have a method available for quickly remedying mistakes. The danger of being recalled from office is a salutary influence upon a weak or a self-willed man. And the possibility of it allows the election of officials for longer terms, which are desirable from several points of view: they bring a more stable government, freed from too frequent breaks or reversals of policy; they permit the acquiring of a longer political experience, and stimulate abler men to run for office; they save the public the bother and expense of too frequent elections. [Footnote: See National Municipal Review, vol. 1, p. 204. Forum, vol. 47, p. 157. North American Review, vol. 198, p. 145.]

(4) THE REFERENDUM. A less drastic instrument of popular control over legislation is the referendum, which refers individual measures back to the people for approval or rejection. An official may be efficient and free

from corruption, yet opposed to the general wish on some particular matter. In this, then, he may be overruled by the referendum without being humiliated or required to resign his office. Thus not only the improper influence of the machine or the interests may be guarded against by the public, but the unconscious prejudices of generally efficient officials. Of course there is, in the case of both recall and referendum, the possibility that the official may be right and the people wrong. But that danger is inherent in democratic government. The best that can be done is to make government responsive to the sober judgment of the majority; if that is mistaken, nothing but time and education can correct it. [Footnote: See W. B. Munro, The Initiative, Referendum and Recall; The Government of American Cities, p. 321. Political Science Quarterly, vol. 26, p. 415; vol. 28, p. 207. National Municipal Review, vol. 1, p. 586. Nation, vol. 95, p. 324.]

The air is full of suggestions, and experiments are being tried in every direction. There is every hope that America may yet learn by her failures and evolve a system of government that shall be her pride rather than her shame. Our National Government has worked far better than our state and local government, but even that can be further freed from the pull of improper motives, made much more efficient and responsive to the general will. We are in a peculiar degree on trial to show what popular government can accomplish. The Old World looks to us with distrust, but with hope. And though the solution of our political problem involves many technical matters, it has deep underlying moral bearings, and affects profoundly the success of every great moral campaign.

R. C. Brooks, Corruption in American Politics and Life. L. Steffens, The Shame of the Cities. J. Bryce, The Hindrances to Good Government. W. E. Weyl, The New Democracy, chaps. VIII, IX. Jane Addams, Democracy
and Social Ethics, chap. VII. A. T. Hadley, Standards of Public Morality, chaps. IV, V. T. Roosevelt, American Ideals. C. R. Henderson, The Social Spirit in America, chap. XI. Edmond Kelly, Evolution and Effort, chap. IX. W. H. Taft, Four Aspects of Civic Duty. E. Root, The Citizen's Part in Government. D. F. Wilcox, Government by All the People. L. S. Rowe, Problems of City Government. H. E. Deming, The Government of American Cities. Publications of the National Municipal League (703 North American Building, Philadelphia). Political Science Quarterly, vol. 18, p. 188; vol. 19, p. 673;

CHAPTER XXV
SOCIAL ALLEVIATION

WHEN the security of peace and an efficient government are attained, the way lies open for the amelioration of social evils. Freedom from war and from political corruption are but the pre-conditions of social advance, which must consist in three things: the healing of existing ills, the reorganization of society to prevent the recurrence of similar ills, and the bringing of new opportunities and joys to the people. Our first step, then, is to consider social therapeutics-the palliation of present suffering, the redressing of existing wrongs; however we may seek, by radical readjustments, to strike at the roots of these evils, we must not fail to mitigate, as best we can, the lot of those who are the unfortunate victims of our still crude social organization. The detailed study of social ills and their remedies has come to be a science by itself, and a science that calls for close attention; for there is more good will than insight a field, and nothing demands more wisdom and experience than the permanent curing of social sores. But it falls to ethics to note the general duties and opportunities, to point out the responsibility of the individual citizen for wrongs which he is not helping to right, and to direct him to the great moral causes in one or more of which an increasing number of our educated men and women are enrolling themselves. A questionnaire recently sent out by the author of this book discloses the fact that over half the college graduates of this country have given time and money to one or more of the campaigns which are being waged for social betterment. [Footnote: Some of the results of this questionnaire were published in the Independent for August 5, 1913, vol. 75, p. 348.] These evils which it is the duty of the State to try to remedy we shall now consider.

What is the duty of the State in regard to:

I. SICKNESS AND PREVENTABLE DEATH? Physical ills are the unavoidable lot of the human race; but by no means to the extent to which they now prevail. A very large percentage of existing sickness and infirmity could have been prevented by a timely application of such knowledge as the intelligent already possess. It is the poverty, the crowded and unsanitary living conditions, the ignorance and helplessness of the masses, that perpetuate all this unnecessary suffering, this economic waste, this drag on human efficiency and happiness. Not only from humanitarian motives, but also from regard for national prosperity and virility, it behooves the State to wage war against preventable illness and safeguard the general health.

How shocking conditions are, in view of the sanitary and medical knowledge we now possess, we are not apt to realize. It is estimated that of the three million or so who are seriously ill in this country on any average day, more than half might have been kept well by the enforcement of proper precautions; that of the 1,500,000 deaths that occur annually in the United States, nearly half could have been postponed. Tuberculosis, for example, is not a highly contagious or rapid disease; it is absolutely preventable by measures now understood, and almost always curable in its earliest stages. Yet half a million people in our country are suffering from it, and about 130,000 die of it annually. Typhoid, which could readily be as nearly eradicated as smallpox has been, claims some 30,000 victims annually. It has been estimated by various statisticians that the nation could save a billion dollars a year through postponing deaths, and at least half as much again by preventing illness that does not result fatally. Tuberculosis alone is said to cost the country half a billion annually, typhoid over three hundred million, and so on. The cost in suffering, broken lives, and broken hearts is beyond computation.

There are many different ways in which the campaign for public health can be simultaneously waged:

(1) The enforcement of quarantine laws, vaccination, and fumigation, should be much stricter than it is in many parts of the nation. By such means the cholera, bubonic plague, and other terrible diseases have been practically kept out of the country, and smallpox has become, from one of the most dreaded scourges, an almost negligible peril. Experience shows strikingly the advantage of isolating patients suffering from contagious diseases; here at least the State, in the interest of the community as a whole, must sternly limit individual liberty. And it looks as if we were at the threshold of an era of "vaccination" for other diseases besides smallpox; typhoid is now absolutely preventable by that means, and the number of diseases amenable to prevention or mitigation by similar methods is yearly increasing. In some or all of these cases there is a slight risk to the patient, in view of which compulsory "vaccination" is in some quarters strenuously opposed. Leaving the discussion of the principle here involved to chapter XXVIII, we may confidently say, at least, that voluntary inoculation against diseases is an increasingly valuable safeguard not only for the individual in question but for the whole community.

(2) Apart from state action, voluntary organizations formed to attack specific diseases, by spreading popular knowledge of preventive measures, and pushing legislation for their enforcement, offer much promise. The Anti-Tuberculosis League can already point to a ten per cent decline in the death rate from that plague in the decade from 1900 to 1910. [Footnote: For methods and results consult the Secretary of the National Association

for the Study and Prevention of Tuberculosis, 105 East Twenty-second Street, New York City. Free literature is sent, and information furnished on request.] But while in New York City alone nearly thirty thousand fresh victims are seized by the disease every year, a voluntary organization cannot hope to cope with the situation; the power and resources of the State are needed. The congestion of population, and the lack of proper light and air, which are the greatest factors, perhaps, in the spread of the scourge, must be attacked by legislation. So typhoid must be fought not only by vaccination, but by legislation insuring a pure water supply, proper sewage disposal, and the protection of food from contamination. Measures necessary to eradicate that pest, the house fly, must be enforced, the mosquito must be as nearly as possible exterminated, streets and yards must be kept clean, the smoke nuisance abated, the slaughtering of animals and canning of food sharply regulated, sanitary conditions enforced in homes and factories. One of the prerequisites to any marked improvement will be the "taking out of politics" of the public health service and making it an expert profession.

(3) Another service that the community must eventually, in its own interests, provide, is free medical attendance, by really competent physicians, wherever there is need. Without referring to the suffering and anxiety spared, the expense of this service will far more than be saved the State in the prevention of illness and premature death. The most careful medical inspection of school children, including attention by experts to eyes, ears, and teeth, is of utmost importance; all sorts of ills can thus be averted which the parents are too ignorant or careless to forestall. [Footnote: Consult the literature of the American School Hygiene Association (Secretary T. A. Storey, College of the City of New York). L. D. Cruickshank, School Clinics at Home and Abroad. Outlook, vol. 84, p. 662.] It is earnestly to be hoped that the present chaos of medical education and practice will be soon reduced to a better order; that practitioners who prefer manipulation or mental healing, for example, will, instead of forming separate and antagonistic schools, unite their insight and experience with the main stream of scientific therapeutic effort. The quacks who delude and murder hordes of ignorant victims must be, so far as is practicable, severely punished; and adequate physiological and medical education should be required for all practicing healers, whatever methods they may then choose to employ.

(4) Besides free medical attendance, the State must pro- vide free hospitals for the sick, nurses for the poor, asylums for those who are incapacitated by infirmity from self-support. The care and treatment of the feeble-minded, the insane, the deaf, the blind, the crippled, should always be in the hands of experts; and, so far as possible, work that they can do must be provided.

With the enforcement of the measures we have enumerated, the need of such institutions will become much less; but at present they are inadequate in number and equipment, too often managed by incompetent officials, and not always free from scandal. [Footnote: Cf. C. R, Henderson, Social Spirit in America, chap. XV.]

(5) Most important of all, perhaps, is the work that must be done to save the babies. Approximately a third of the babies born in this country die before they are four years old; half or two thirds of these could be saved. Wonderful results in baby saving have followed strict control of the milk supply and the banishing of the fly. Besides this, mothers must in some way be given instruction in the very difficult and complicated art of rearing infants; for many of the deaths are due to simple ignorance.[Footnote: For methods and results in baby-saving, consult the Secretary of the National Association for the Study and Prevention of Infant Mortality, 1211 Cathedral Street, Baltimore, Maryland. Also Outlook, vol. 101, p. 190. J. S. Gibbon, Infant Welfare Centers.] Poverty, the necessity of self- support on the part of mothers, also plays a large part; we shall consider in chapter xxx the possibility of state care of mothers during the infancy of their children. II. Poverty and inadequate living conditions? If human illness can be in large measure averted by state action, poverty can be practically abolished. The poor we have always had with us, indeed; but we need not forever have them. There is no excuse for our tolerance of the suffering and degradation of the submerged classes; the causes of this wretchedness are in the main removable. The initial cost will be great, but in the long run the saving to the community will be enormous. Individual effort can only achieve a superficial and temporary relief; and even the two or three hundred charity organization societies in the country are impotent, for lack of funds and of power, to stem the forces that make for poverty. To dole out charity to this family and to that is unhappily necessary in our present crude social situation; but it is not a solution. It not only runs the continual risk of encouraging shiftlessness and dependence, but it does not go to the root of the matter. There will always be inequalities in wealth and room for personal gifts from the more to the less fortunate; but the State must not be content with such patching and palliating, but must strike at the roots of the evil. We will consider the chief causes of poverty and their cure.

(1) The cause that bulks largest is the inadequate wages of a considerable portion of the lowest class. It is obviously impossible to support the average family of five in decency, not to say in health, efficiency, or comfort, with an income of, say, less than a thousand dollars a year, as prices go at time of writing (1914). Yet great numbers of families at present have to exist somehow upon less, even much less. Five million adult male workers in this country receive less than six hundred dollars a year for their

work.[Footnote: Cf. Professor Fairchild's comments in Forum, vol. 52, p. 49 (July, 1914).] Even when mothers work who ought to be at home tending the children, even when children work who ought to be in school, the total income is often miserably inadequate. Yet there is ample wealth in the country, if it were better distributed, to pay a living wage to every laborer. By some one of the means which we shall presently discuss, the State must see that all laborers are well enough paid to enable them, while they work, to support in comfort a moderate family.

(2) Involuntary unemployment is the next source of poverty. This is due to many causes: the periodic depressions and failures of industries; the introduction of new machinery, throwing out whole classes of laborers; the enormous influx of immigrants and consequent congestion in the cities of unskilled labor; lack of education, or natural stupidity, which render some men too incompetent to retain positions. Ignorance can be overcome by proper compulsory education laws; all but the actually feeble-minded (who must be cared for in institutions) can, by skillful attention, be taught proficiency in some trade. And with a more widespread education the work that requires no skill can be left to the hopelessly stupid. The congestion of labor in the cities [Footnote: In February, 1914, there were reported to be 350,000 men out of work in New York City (Outlook, March 14, 1914).] can be largely remedied by free state employment bureaus which shall serve as distributing agencies; there is almost always work enough and to spare in some parts of the country, and usually not far away. But more than this is necessary; the State must see that work is offered every man who is able to work. All sorts of public works need unskilled laborers in every city of the country; there is digging to be done, shoveling and sweeping and carting. There are roads to be built, rivers to be dredged, parks to be graded, buildings to be erected, a thousand things to be done. It will be quite feasible, when wages are generally adequate, for the cities, by general agreement, to offer work to all applicants at a wage so low as not to attract men away from other employments, and yet to enable them to support their families decently. The low wages given will save the city much money directly, as well as saving it the care of the indigent. But it will be a feasible plan only when the city's jobs cease to be used as a means of vote-buying by politicians and are offered where they are needed. [Footnote: 1 See W.H. Beveridge, Unemployment. J.A. Hobson, The Problem of the Unemployed. Alden and Hayward, The Unemployable and the Unemployed. C. S. Loch, Methods of Social Advance, chap. IX. Quarterly Journal of Economics, vol. 8, pp. 168, 453, 499. Review of Reviews, vol. 9, pp. 29, 179. Charities Review, vol. 3, pp. 221, 323. Independent, vol. 77, p.363. National Municipal Review, vol. 3, p.366. The unemployment which is the result of laziness must be cured by compulsory work as in farmcolonies, which have

been successful in Europe. Cf. Edmond Kelly, The Elimination of the Tramp.]

(3) The third important cause of poverty is sickness and the death of wage earners. Here the way is clear. When the State has taken the measures we have enumerated for the public health, when it provides competent doctors and nurses, and bears the cost of illness, we shall have only the loss of wages during the illness or after the death of wage earners to consider. And here some form of universal insurance will probably be the solution; this is preferable to state care of dependents, as it carries no taint of charity. This solves every problem but the delicate one, which must be entrusted to expert diagnosticians, of determining to work is caused by physical weakness or mere laziness.

(4) The fourth great cause of poverty, drink, can and must be abolished in the near future, by the means already considered.

(5) There remain three personal causes which need be the only permanently troublesome factors- -laziness, self-indulgence, and the incontinence which results in over- large families. The laziness which prefers chronic inactivity to work is not normal to human nature, and will be largely banished by education, the improvement of health, and the improvement of the conditions and hours of labor. The obstinate cases of unwillingness to work must be cured by compulsory labor in farm colonies or on public works; most such cases respond to intelligent treatment and cease to be troublesome when some physical or moral twist has been remedied. The waste of income in self-indulgence of one form or other is more difficult to deal with; but the law can justly forbid the wage-earner from squandering upon himself money needed by wife and children, and direct that a due proportion of his wages be paid directly to the wife. If neither father nor mother will use their money for the proper welfare of the children, the State must take the children from them though that step should only be a last and desperate resort. Finally, there is the tendency, unfortunately most prevalent among the lowest classes, to have more children than can be decently cared for. To some extent this evil can be remedied by the dissemination of information concerning proper methods of preventing conception [Footnote: There is, however, a danger in the general dissemination of such information- the danger of increasing prostitution by lessening one of the chief deterrents there from.]; to some extent by moral training to self-control and a sense of responsibility. Or the State may undertake the countenance large families; if this is done (see chapter xxx), steps must of course be taken to prevent the marrying of the unfit-or, at least, their breeding. With our rapidly decreasing birth rate, and the spread of education, which will do away with "lower" classes and fit every one in some decent degree to be a parent, this will probably be the ultimate

solution. With the disappearance of poverty, the miserable living conditions of so large a proportion of our population will automatically improve. But much should be done directly by the State to prevent such housing conditions as make for physical or moral degeneration. We are far behind Europe in housing-legislation, and conditions in most of our cities are going from bad to worse. There is, however, no need whatever of unsanitary housing; it is merely the selfishness of owners and the apathy of the public that permits its existence. The crowding-which in New York City runs up to some thirteen hundred per acre-can be stopped by simple legislation. The lack of proper light or ventilation, of proper water supply, plumbing, or sewerage, of proper removal of ashes, garbage, or rubbish, is inexcusable. The results of living in the dark, foul-aired, unsanitary tenements of our slums are: a great increase in sickness and premature death; a stunting of growth, physical and mental, and an increase in numbers of backward and delinquent children; the spread of vicious and criminal habits through the lack of privacy and contagion of close contact with the vicious.

We are breeding in our slums a degenerate race,-boys who grow up used to vice, and girls that drift naturally into prostitution; we are allowing disease to spread from them, through the children that go to the public schools, the shop-girls we buy from in the stores, the servants that enter our houses, the men we rub elbows with on the street or in the street-cars. Very salutary are the laws that require the name of the owner to be placed on all buildings; shame before the public may wring improvements from many a landlord who now takes profits from tenements unfit for habitation. But it ought not to be left to the conscience of the individual owner; the State must exercise its primary right to forbid the crowding of tenants into houses which do not afford sanitary quarters and permit a decent degree of privacy.

III. COMMERCIALIZED VICE?

The duty of the State in regard to the vice caterers is obvious; the commercializing of vice must be strictly prohibited by law and enforced by whatever means experience proves most effective. We must learn to include in this class of enemies of society the manufacturers and sellers of alcoholic liquors, as well as of the less generally used arcotics; but this matter has been already discussed in connection]with our study of the individual's duty in relation to alcohol. Of the proprietors of gambling dens, indecent "shows," etc, we need not further speak, concentrating our attention instead upon the worst species of vice catering, the commercializing of prostitution. The extent to which the sale of woman's virtue prevails in our cities is scarcely believable. The recent commission of which Mr. Rockefeller was chairman actually counted 14,926 professional prostitutes in Manhattan alone, in 1912; while personal visitation established the existence of over sixteen hundred houses where the gratification of lust could be bought. Not all, certainly, were counted; and this list is, of course, entirely exclusive of the great number of girls occasionally and secretly selling themselves to friends, acquaintances, and employers. Many hundreds of men and women, keepers of houses, procurers, and the like, live on the proceeds of this great underground industry; and to some extent-though to what extent it is, of course, impossible to ascertain the forcible retention of young girls is exist in most of the world's cities. What is being done to abolish this ghastliest of evils? In most great cities, scarcely anything, for two reasons: the one being that so many men, perhaps the majority, secretly wish to retain an opportunity for purchasing sex gratification, the other that the police generally find the protection of illegal vice an easy source of revenue. If the police are honest, they break up a disorderly house-and let the inmates carry the lure of their trade elsewhere. The magistrates fine them, or give them sentences just long enough to bring them needed rest and nutrition, and send them back to their business. Or they drive them out of town-to swell the numbers in the next town. Attempts at legalization and localization are frank admissions of inability or lack of desire to fight the evil; their effect is to make the way of temptation easier for the youth. Compulsory medical inspection gives a promise of immunity from disease which is largely illusory, and entices men who are now restrained by prudential motives. There are, however, many promising lines of attack:

(1) When women gain the vote, they can be counted on to fight the evil. The prostitutes themselves, being mostly minors, and, in any case, anxious to conceal their identity, seldom vote; and the remaining women are almost

en masse bitterly opposed to the trade. With women voting, and an efficient political administration inaugurated in our cities, we shall hope to witness the end of the scandalous nonenforcement of existing laws.

(2) The abolishing of the liquor trade will take away the great political ally of the trade in girlhood; and without the demoralizing influence of alcohol fewer men will yield to their passions and fewer girls be pliant thereto.

(3) The Rockefeller Commission disclosed majority of prostitutes are almost wholly uneducated-about half of those questioned had not even gone through the primary school, and only seven per cent had finished the grammar-school work. Compulsory education, vigilantly enforced, will greatly lessen the number of girls who will be willing to take up the life of degradation, suffering, and premature death; especially will this be the case if sex hygiene is properly taught. Approximately a quarter of the girls studied were mentally defective; these should have been detected in the schools and removed to the proper institutions before they fell prey to the clever schemes of the procurer.[Footnote: Of 647 wayward girls recently at the Bedford Reformatory, over 300 were accounted mentally deficient.] For a falling-off in this alarming number of mental defectives we must await scientific eugenic laws to be discussed in chapter xxx.

(4) It is a shameful fact that thousands of girls, dependent upon their own earnings for support, receive less than enough to enable them to live in decent comfort, not to say with any enjoyment of life. Many, of course, waste their earnings on needlessly fine clothes, or at the "shows"; the American fashion of extravagant dress and the craving for amusement are factors of importance in the ruin of young girls. But five dollars, or even seven dollars, a week is not enough to live on in the cities; and many girls are paid no more, even less. The State, in framing its minimum wage laws, or other legislation, must take cognizance of this startling and intolerable situation.

(5) Provision should be made for the care of girls who come alone to the cities. Dormitories with clean and airy bedrooms at minimum cost, and attractive reading- and social-rooms, offering provision for normal social life and amusement, can do much to keep lonely and restless girls out of the clutches of the vicious provision for young men who live alone might avail to lessen to some extent their patronage of houses of vice.

(6) The model injunction acts of a few of our more advanced States "vest the power in any citizen, whether he or she is personally damaged by such establishment, to institute legal proceedings against all concerned; to secure the abatement of the nuisance, and perpetual injunction against its reestablishment." It is too early yet to speak with assurance of the practical working of this method; but it bids fair to make the brothel business more

precarious. If, in addition, laws against street soliciting are strictly enforced, the first steps of young men into vice will be made much less alluringly easy than at present.

(7) The most radical and effective measure of all will be to arrest the professional prostitutes, segregate them, and keep them segregated during the dangerous years, except as genuine signs of intention to reform appear, in which case they may be released upon probation. The expense will be, at the outset, considerable. But the girls will be taught trades, and kept at work which will in most cases more than pay for their support. Moreover, the community will, of course, save the vast sums now passed over by its lustful men to these women. The saving of health and life will be incalculable. The girls, although under restraint, will be infinitely better off than they were, and can in most cases, with patience and education, be made ultimately to realize their gain; as they grow older and forget their early years of shame, they can be set free again, with some skilled trade learned, and some accumulated earnings. Professional prostitution will, of course, still flourish to a degree underground; but it will be a highly risky business, attracting far fewer girls, and difficult for the uninitiated young man to discover. With this outlet for lust partially closed, there would no doubt tend to be an increase in solitary and homosexual vice, and in the seduction of innocent girls. But the latter outlet can be checked by raising the "age of consent" to twenty or twenty-one, and punishing the seduction of younger girls as rape. And the former evils, serious as they are, are far less of an evil than the creation of our present wretched class of professional prostitutes. As a matter of fact, there would, beyond all question, be a great diminution in sexual vice, the present amount of it being due by no means wholly to desire that is naturally imperious, but to the artificial fostering of that desire by those who hope to profit financially thereby.

IV. Crime?

The gravest of all social ills is-crime. Its treatment may be considered under the three heads of prevention, conviction, and the treatment of convicted criminals.

(1) To some extent, not yet clearly determined, the causes of crime are temperamental, due to congenital defects or overexcitable impulses. The inherited effects of insanity, alcoholism, and other pathological conditions, make self-control far more difficult for some unfortunates. Such baneful inheritances will some day be minimized by eugenic laws; and individuals whose abnormal mental condition makes them dangerous to society will be kept under permanent restraint. The causes of crime are, however, to a far greater degree environmental. Undernutrition, overwork, worry, and various other sources of poor health, create a condition of lowered

resistance to impulse. The herding of the poor into crowded tenements, the inability to find work, the lack of wholesome interests and excitements to provide a normal outlet for energy of body and mind, the daily sight of the luxury of the rich and the bitterness of its contrast with their own need, awaken dangerous passions and reckless defiance of law. The lack of education, contact with absorption of law-defying philosophies of life, tend to make crime appear natural and justified. All of these unhealthy conditions are being attacked under the spur of our new social conscience; and with every step in social alleviation crime diminishes. Criminals are, in general, just such men and women as we; in like situations we too should be tempted to crime. We might all repeat with Bunyan: "There, but for the grace of God, go I!" Give every man and woman a fair chance for happiness in normal ways, and the lure of crime will largely vanish.[Footnote: Cf. An Open Letter to Society from Convict 1776 (F. H. Revell Co.).] Yet human nature in its most favorable circumstances and in its most favored individuals has its twists and its anti-social impulses. For the potential criminal-and that means for every one of us-there must be elaborated also a system of moral or religious training which shall seek to develop the better nature that is in every man and enchain the brute. With such a discipline imposed upon each generation there would be a far greater hope for the repression of evil tendencies, whether due to temperamental perversion or provocative environment.

(2) If there is much to be done in the prevention of crime, there is also much to be done in insuring the prompt conviction of offenders. The legal delays and obtrusion of the technicalities which now so often obstruct the administration of justice, hold out a means to the criminal of escaping punishment, work hardship to the poor, who cannot afford to employ the sharpest lawyers, and needlessly retard the clearing of the reputation of the innocent. The overuse of the plea of insanity has become latterly a public scandal. In certain courts it has sometimes seemed impossible to convict a criminal who has plenty of money or strong political influence. In other cases such men have been set free on bail and proceeded to further may have to wait years for compensation; if they are poor, they may hesitate to set out on the long and dubious course of a lawsuit; or, if they embark upon it, it is only by an agreement wherein the speculator- lawyer takes the lion's share of the compensation. The result of all this friction in the machinery of the courts is an increase in crime, and an increase in the illegal punishment of crime. Lynching, which are such a disgrace to this country, are due primarily to indignation at crime which bids fair to be inadequately punished; they will occur, in spite of their injustice and brutality, until the penalties of the law are made universally prompt and sure and fair.[Footnote: See J. E. Cutler, Lynch Law. Outlook, vol. 99, p. 706.] A wholesome disregard of technicalities, and an interpretation of the law in

the line of equity, a rigid exclusion of irrelevant evidence and argument, the provision of an adequate number of courts to prevent the piling up of cases, and of a public defender, of skill and training, to look after the interests of the poor, the removal of judgeships from politics by the general improvement of our political system, and the adjudgment of insanity only by impartial, state-hired alienists-these are some of the reforms that ethical considerations suggest.[Footnote: Cf. W. H. Taft, Four Aspects of Civic Duty, II. Outlook, vol. 92, p. 359; vol. 98, p. 884.]

(3) The ends to be borne in mind in the treatment of the convicted Criminal are four: First, reparation to the injured party must be demanded of him, so far as money will constitute reparation; if he has not the money, his future work must go for its accumulation, so far as that is compatible with the support of his infant children. Secondly, he must be punished severely enough to serve as a warning to other potential offenders and, so far as they are amenable to such fears, deter them from similar crimes. Capital punishment for the worst crimes is shown deterrent than confinement; whether the danger of executing an innocent man is grave enough to offset this public gain is an open question.[Footnote: See A. J. Palm, The Death Penalty.] Thirdly, he must be prevented from doing any more harm; this means confinement just so long as expert criminologists deem him dangerous, whether not at all (unless to deter others) or for life. The old system of giving a fixed sentence is wholly unjustifiable; some are thereby kept imprisoned when there is every reason to believe them capable of living honorably and serving the community as free men, others are let loose, after a term, more dangerous to the community than ever. The habitual criminal, who alternates between periods of crime and periods of imprisonment, should be an unknown phenomenon. The judge should be obliged to pronounce an indeterminate sentence, and leave it to the expert prison officials to decide if, or when, it is safe to release the prisoner on parole. Experience has already shown that few mistakes are made (where prison management is kept out of machine politics); and as the released prisoner is under surveillance, and may be returned to the prison without trial for disorderliness, drunkenness, or other anti-social conduct, he is not likely to do much damage. A second offense would be likely to bring upon him imprisonment for life, which would be within the discretion of the prison officials. This method provides a spur to good behavior, and, when used in conjunction with the reforming influences we are about to consider, works admirably in abolishing the criminal class; whatever criminal class persists-those who cannot or will not reform are kept under restraint for life, where they can do no harm. Fourthly, and most important of all, a painstaking attempt must be made to reform the criminal, to make him a normal, socially useful man. At present our prisons are rather schools of corruption than of uplift; too often first offenders are thrown into

association with hardened criminals, and come out after their term of years with their minds full of criminal suggestions, and less able than before to live a normal life. The prison should be a training school for the morally perverted. First of all, the prisoner should be taught a trade, if he knows none, and made competent to earn an honest living. He should be kept at regular work, and his wages used partly to reimburse society for his keep, and partly to support his family, or, if he has none, to give him a new start when he leaves prison. Recent experience shows that the great majority of prisoners can be trusted to work outside the prison, at any ordinary labor, without guards-returning to the prison each evening.[Footnote: See Century, vol. 87, p. 746.] Regular hours, and wholesome living in every way, are, of course, enforced; sports are encouraged in leisure hours, and physical development ensured. Educational influences are brought to bear, through class-instruction, books, sermons, private talks. The individual's mind is studied and every effort made to supplant morbid and anti-social by normal and moral ideas. Few criminals but are amenable to skillful guidance; most of them, could, if pains were taken, be transformed into useful citizens. All this application of modern penological ideas means a greatly increased expense per capita; but this will be largely offset by the work required of all healthy prisoners, and in any case is the best sort of an investment. The prevention of crime is, in the long run, much less costly, even from a purely financial standpoint, than crime itself. On pathological social conditions in general: Smith, Social Pathology. E. T. Devine, Misery and its Causes. M. Conyngton, How to Help. C. Aronovici, Knowing One's Own Community. Jane Addams, Twenty Years at Hull House. S. Nearing, Social Adjustment. Charles Booth, Life and Labor of the People of London. Hall, Social Solutions. C. R. Henderson, Social Duties. W. Gladden, Social Salvation. Public health: H. Ellis, The Task of Social Hygiene, The Nationalization of Health. Outlook, vol. 98, p. 63; vol. 102, p. 764. Literature published by The Committee of One Hundred on National Health (105 East Twenty-second Street, New York City). C. R. Henderson, The Social Spirit in America, chap. V. World's Work, vol. 17, p. 11321; vol. 21, p. 13881; vol. 23, p. 692. W. H. Allen, Civics and Health. Poverty and living conditions: R. Hunter, Poverty. B. S. Rowntree, Poverty, A Study of Town Life. Adams and Sumner, Labor Problems, chap. V. A. S. Warner, American Charities. E. T. Devine, Principles of Relief. S. Webb, Prevention of Destitution. Literature of the American Association of Societies for Organizing Charity, and of the Charity Organization Department of the Russell Sage Foundation (both at 105 East Twenty-second Street, New York City). L. Veiller, Housing Reform. Deforest and Veiller, The Tenement-House Problem. J. Lee, Constructive and Preventive Philanthropy. Alden and Hayward, Housing. J. A. Riis, The Battle with the Slum. National Municipal Review, vol. 2, p. 210. Commercialized vice: Jane

Addams, A New Conscience and an Ancient Evil. Report of the Chicago Vice Commission: The Social Evil in Chicago. G. J. Kneeland, Commercialized Prostitution in New York City. Outlook, vol. 94, p. 303; vol. 101, p. 245; vol. 104, p. 101. Crime: F. H. Wines, Punishment and Reformation. E. A. Ross, Social Control, chap. XI. R. M. McConnell, Criminal Responsibility and Social Constraint. H. Ellis, The Criminal. A. H. Currier, The Present- Day Problem of Crime. P. A. Parsons, Responsibility for Crime. E. Ferri, The Positive School of Criminology. W. Tallack, Penological and Preventive Principles. E. Carpenter, Prisons, Police, and Punishment. Outlook, vol. 94, p. 252; vol. 97, p. 403. World's Work, vol. 21, p. 14254. North American Review, vol. 138, p. 254. International Journal of Ethics, vol. 20, p. 281.

CHAPTER XXVI
INDUSTRIAL WRONGS

WE have been discussing the treatment of recognized crime. But beyond the boundaries of conduct universally labeled as criminal, there is a whole realm of anti-social action to which the public conscience is only beginning to be sensitive, although it is often far more harmful to the general welfare than that for which men are imprisoned. Especially is this true of the wrongs connected with modern industry. As Professor Ross puts it, [Footnote: Sin and Society, p. 97.] "the master iniquities of our time are connected with money-making"; and so our "moral pace-setters," who are, for the most part, confining their attacks to the time-worn and familiar sins, "do not get into the big fight at all." The root of the trouble is that great power over the lives and happiness of others has been acquired by a small class of irresponsible men, many of whom fail to recognize their privileged position as a public trust and care only for enriching themselves. As we noted in chapter in, the complexification of our industrial life is making possible a whole new range of what must be branded as crimes; endless opportunities have been opened up of money-making at the cost of others' suffering. Often that suffering, or loss, is so remote from the path of the greedy business man that he does not see himself, and others fail to see him, as the predatory money-grabber that he is. The many who have been ruined by unscrupulous competitors are often embittered, the repressed capitalism; but the public as a whole has not been aroused to rebuke this "newer unrighteousness." We must proceed to note its commonest contemporary forms. In our present organization of industry, what are the duties of businessmen:

I. To the public?

(1) The first duty of businessmen is to supply honest goods, in honest measure. Underweight, undermeasure, double- bottomed berry-boxes, bottles so shaped as to appear to contain more than their actual contents, are obviously cheating. Misbranding of goods is now regulated, so far as interstate trade goes, by the Federal Pure Food and Drugs Act; and most States have similar legislation. Misrepresentation in advertisement should be severely punished; the selling of cold storage for fresh products, of part-cotton for all-wool clothing, of less for more expensive woods, and the thousand other ways of panning inferior goods upon an inexpert public for high-grade articles. At present there is little recourse but to carry distrust into all purchasing, learn to be canny, and to recognize differences in quality in all articles needed. But the average man cannot become an expert

purchaser; he buys furniture which breaks down prematurely; he pays a high price for clothing which proves to have no wearing quality; he buys patent medicines which promise to cure his physical ills, and is lucky if they do not leave him worse in health than before. Jerry- building, and the doing of fake jobs by contractors, especially for municipalities, is one of the scandals of our times. [Footnote: See Encyclopedia Britannica, article, "Adulteration." E. Kelly Twentieth Century Socialism, book ii, chap. i. For a notorious case of tampering with weights, see Outlook, vol. 92, p. 25; vol. 93, p. 811. For cases of adulteration, Good Housekeeping Magazine, vol. 54, p. 593. F. W. Taussig, Principles of Economics, chap. 45.]

(2) Another duty, less generally recognized by even the more honorable businessmen, is to sell their goods at fair prices. The strangulation of competition by mutual agreements or the formation of trusts, aided often by an iniquitously high tariff, has put many a business for a time on a par with those natural monopolies which, if unregulated, can always exact exorbitant prices for what the public needs. Rich profits have been made by the tucking of a few cents on to the price of gas, or coal, or steel, or oil, or telephone service. Enormous fortunes have been made, at the public expense, by the practical cornering of staple commodities. These hold-up prices should be clearly recognized for what they are-a form of modern piracy. No business man or corporation is entitled in justice to more than a moderate reward for the mental and physical labor expended; the excessive incomes of monopoly are largely at the expense of the public, who, by one means or other, are being compelled to pay more than a fair price for the article. [Footnote: For cases, see C. R. Van Hise, Concentration and Control, pp. 109,145, 149.]

(3) Finally, all business must be looked upon as a form of public service, and the convenience of customers scrupulously consulted. Where there is competition this tends to regulate itself; but our public- service monopolies have too often followed the "public- be-damned" policy. The long-suffering community puts up with inadequate and crowded streetcars, inconvenient train service, a bungled and high- handed telephone system. Railway managements have sometimes been criminally indifferent to public safety, finding it less expensive to lose occasional damage suits than to install safety appliances. Efficiency in serving the public has likewise been sacrificed to dividends; and courtesy, where it is not recognized to have a cash value, tends to disappear. Such indictments point to the widespread existence of the idea that men and corporations are in business for themselves only, and not as fulfilling a public need.[Footnote: For concrete illustrations, see Outlook, vol. 91, p. 861; vol. 95, p. 515. World's Work, vol. 23, p. 579.]

II. TO INVENTORS?

It has not been generally enough recognized that business men owe it to investors to do their best to see to it that they get fair returns on their money invested -and only fair returns. There are a number of ways in which, on the one hand, the investing public is "skinned," and, on the other hand, stock in a business, largely owned by the management itself, has been rewarded with undeserved dividends at the expense of the public.

(1) There are, in the first place, the get-rich-quick swindles, the out-and-out impostures, which have deceived the credulous into investments that never could pay. Bonanza mines, impractical inventions, town lots laid out on the prairie, orange groves that existed only on paper-such bogus hopes have enticed many an honest man and woman, who could ill afford to lose, into turning over their small earnings to the brazen exploiters.[Footnote: For cases, see World's Work, vol. 21, p. 14112.]

(2) But such arrant deception is not the commonest form of wrong. A more usual practice, and more dangerous- because it deceives even the intelligent- is to overcapitalize an honest business, to issue "watered" stock-that is, stock in excess of the actual value of plant, patents, and other assets. These stocks are issued merely to sell. If the business is very successful, its profits may pay a fair return on all this capital; if not, low dividends or none can be paid until the business slowly catches up with its overcapitalization. In all investment-as our industrial organization at present goes-there is risk; but to create a needless risk and deceive the public into taking it is plain dishonesty. The extra money thus sucked from the public goes sometimes to pay excessive salaries to the officials of the company, sometimes to pay excessive prices for patents or plants purchased; there are many subtle ways, known to "high finance," of misappropriating stockholders' money and diverting it to the pockets of the promoters. Many great fortunes have been made in this way; such exploitation is so new to society that it has not yet awakened to its essentially criminal nature. Even if the business is able to pay good dividends on watered stock, the crime of overcapitalization is not lessened, though the harm done is now not to the investor but to the public. Stocks should represent only the actual value of the property, so that dividends may be only a fair return for capital really invested in the business. Where there is sharp competition, the possibility of overcharging the public to make returns on watered stock is cut out, and the loss falls upon the investor. But in the case of monopolies, such as railways, or of combinations which practically stifle competition, the public may be charged enough to "pay a fair dividend to investors," although the money

upon which dividends are being made went not into improving the service, but into fattening the promoters' purses. [Footnote: On stock watering, see Dewey and Tufts, Ethics, pp. 561-64. Outlook, vol. 85, p. 562. Political Science Quarterly, vol. 26, p. 88. International Journal of Ethics, vol. 18, p. 151. C. R. Van Hise, Concentration and Control, pp. 115, 142, etc.]

(3) A third method of "fleecing" investors lies in skillful manipulation of the stock market. In ways which are known to the initiated, it is often possible artificially to raise or lower the market value of stocks. Unwary investors are lured in; timid investors are frightened out; through all ticker fluctuations the brokers win their commissions; the skilled financiers and organizers of combinations rake in unearned sums that are sometimes immense, while the losses fall mostly to the lot of the are honestly seeking to put their savings into solid investments. The ethics of the stock market has not yet been clearly decided, and the subject is too big to discuss here. It is mentioned only to point out one more form of social sinning, as yet inadequately punished or rebuked, whereby men of capital and brains have been able to pocket money for which they have given no return to society. [Footnote: For cases, see C. Norman Fay, Big Business and Government. Outlook, vol. 91, pp. 591, 636.]

III. TO COMPETITORS?

(1) The most conspicuous form of wrongdoing, perhaps, to be charged to modern business is the attempt to get monopoly by foul means. The story of too many of our great trusts is a story of competitors ruined by ruthless and unscrupulous methods. The competitor may be hurt by the circulation of falsehoods concerning his business, his right to patents, or the worth of his goods. He may be denied outlet to markets by control of the railway upon which he must depend. If the capital of the concern that is seeking monopoly permits, the price of the article manufactured may be lowered until rivals with less financial backing are forced out of business-after which the price can be raised and losses recouped. With skill and foresight worthy of a better cause, some of the great industrial leaders of our day have eliminated one rival after another and attained that unification of a business which has, indeed, its great economic advantages, but is not to be won at such a bitter cost. [Footnote: See, for example, I. Tarbell, History of the Standard Oil Company.]

(2) Even where monopoly is not sought, there are many unfair methods of competition-unfair to competitors and to the public that both should serve. One method, much discussed in recent years, is that of railway rebates. By this is meant favoritism in freight rates between shippers and between localities. One manufacturer, who is in a position to ship his goods by either of two railways, perhaps by a water route, is given a low rate to get

his freight; another manufacturer of similar goods, not so favorably situated, is made to pay a higher rate. Rates from seaboard or river cities, where water competition exists, have often been considerably lower than rates from inland towns on the same line, with a very much shorter haul. In such ways the railway squeezes those whom it can squeeze and is content with a bare profit where it can do no better. Where the railway is controlled by the same interests that control some industrial combination, the favoritism may go even farther, and the railway's profits be sacrificed entirely for the cheaper marketing of that particular trust's article. Against all such inequalities in the treatment of shippers the public conscience has lately protested; the railways are recognized as a public instrument of transportation, which should be open to use by all upon equal terms, at a price which will repay the cost of carriage plus a fair profit. [Footnote: On railway rebates, see H. R. Seager, Introduction to Economics, chap. XXIV, secs 260-63. F. W. Taussig, Principles of Economics, chap. 60, secs. 7, 8. Outlook, vol. 81, p. 803; vol. 85, p. 161.] IV. TO EMPLOYEES?

(1) The first duty of employers is to give to all employees a fair wage. If the business does not pay enough to allow this, it has no right to exist; if the owners are pocketing large salaries, or giving dividends to stockholders, this money should be used first for a proper payment of the workers. So many laborers are at the mercy of the employing class, because of their ignorance, their lack of capital and necessity of work at any wage, and often their unfamiliarity with the language and customs of the country, that it has become possible in many cases to treat them like animals and give them less than enough to sustain life in decency, not to say in comfort. Such a case as that of our benevolent Mr. Carnegie, who million dollars in one year's earnings of his steel trust, while many hundreds of his employees were getting but a miserable pittance and living in vile surroundings, is exceptionally glaring; but in lesser degree the same injustice is being wrought in many industries. Wages have, indeed, been raised gradually, here and there; but not usually by the free will of employers. The callousness of some of the privileged classes toward the underpayment of the lower classes is almost on a par with the attitude of the nobility before the French Revolution.[Footnote: See, for example, Outlook, vol. 101, p. 345.] Fortunately, the public is coming to see not only the wrong done to the helpless poor, but the cost to the community in breeding underfed, ill-housed, criminally tempted classes, and the danger that lies ahead if these classes realize their power before amelioration is effected from above. As a recent writer has put it, Addition Division=Revolution. [Footnote: S. Hearing, Wages in the United States; Social Adjustment, chap. IV. Ryan, A Living Wage.]

(2) Another phase of modern industrial injustice is the overlong hours of work still required in many industries. The race for cheapness of product has blinded manufacturers and the public to the cost in terms of human happiness. An eight-hour day is quite long enough to produce all that is necessary, with the aid of modern machinery; every man should be given a margin of leisure for education, recreation, and social life. And every man should be given the benefit of that one day's rest out of seven which is so precious a legacy to us from the Jewish religion.[Footnote: A joint legislative committee in Massachusetts in 1907 estimated that 222,000 persons in that State were working seven days in the week. Similar, or worse, conditions exist throughout the country.] Those industries that require continuous use of machinery should employ three complete shifts of workmen; and those that must be run every day in the week should have enough extra helpers man. This humanizing of hours cannot be done by individual action, where competition is sharp; but by legislation that bears equally upon all, a generous standard-the eight-hour day and six-day week - can be maintained, with hardship to none and a great increase in the health and happiness of the masses. Especially jealous should the law be for the welfare of women workers. In cotton mills in the South women work ten and twelve hours a day; in canneries in the North they work, during the short season, fifteen and eighteen hours a day, eighty or even ninety hours a week. Particularly should women be protected during the weeks before and after childbirth; as it is, women workers are often ruined in health for life, the rate of infant mortality is shockingly high, and the children that survive are usually subnormal. Girls through overwork are weakened too seriously to bear strong children- which, in any case, they have had no time or opportunity to learn how to nurture and rear. No doubt women should work, as well as men; if not in the home, then outside the home. But the contemporary economic pressure that bears so hard on so many girls and women must be eased not only for their sakes but for that of coming generations. [Footnote: Dorothy Richardson, The Long Day. S. Nearing, Social Adjustment, chap. X. J. Rae, Eight Hours for Work.]

(3) The most piteous form of industrial slavery is that of young children, who should be in school or out of doors, developing their minds and bodies into some measure of readiness for adult work and responsibility, instead of prematurely losing the joy of life and stunting their mental and physical growth. In 1910 some two million children under sixteen were earning their living in this country. Even many thousands of children of twelve years or less are set to work in our factories and canneries. These children get almost no development and wholesome recreation; in great numbers they die early, and if they live it is commonly to fall into some form of vice or crime, and to breed an inferior race. Nothing is more inhumane or more mad than for the community to permit cheapness of

goods at such a price. Indeed, child labor means, in the end, economic waste; the ultimate loss in efficiency on the part of these undeveloped, uneducated children, far more than overbalances the temporary industrial gain. The situation has been incredibly shocking; the employers who seek such an advantage over their humaner rivals, and the legislators who have winked at their inhumanity, deserve no mild reprobation. But legislation alone is not adequate to meet the situation; the underlying cause is the insufficient payment of adult workers, which practically necessitates supplementation by what the children can add to the family income. This is one illustration of the way in which all our social problems are tangled together so that it is impossible fully to solve any one without solving the others. When every adult receives wages enough to support a normal family-and when he is content to restrict his family to normal size; when the public schools are made efficient enough to show their evident worth to parents and to attract the children themselves, and a strict truant system takes care that the law is really obeyed; when the sick and defective and aged among the poor are cared for at public expense as a matter of course, there will be no need for children to work to help support the family; and we must endeavor, by the arousal of public opinion and by nationwide legislation, to keep children out of the factories, the shops, and the mines, till they are full-grown and educated. [Footnote: S. Nearing, The Solution of the Child-Labor Problem. J. Spargo, The Bitter Cry of the Children. E. N. Clopper, Child Labor in City Streets. Reports of Annual Meetings of the National Child Labor Committee. (Free literature. 105 East Twenty-second Street, New York City.)]

(4) A less appalling, but still sufficiently serious; aspect of industrial unrighteousness is the dirty, crowded, ugly, unsanitary, and sometimes indecent conditions under which many workers in our prosperous age have to carry on their work. Lack of proper lighting, space, and ventilation, unnecessary noises, and general untidiness, undermine the health and morals of laborers; while insufficient fire- protection causes intermittently one tragedy after another. Much has been done in many quarters to improve such conditions; not a few up-to- date factories are models of cleanliness and sanitation, spacious, reasonably quiet, and altogether pleasant places in which to spend the working day. They point the way which all must in time follow. In addition, the provision of reading-rooms, baths, rest- and recreation- rooms, lunch-rooms, athletic fields, and the like, give augury of that happy future when work shall be divorced from ugliness and free from unnecessary physical strain.[Footnote: Sir T. Oliver, Diseases of Occupation. W. H. Tolman, Social Engineering, chaps. III, X, XI. World's Work, vol. 15, p. 9534; vol. 23, p. 294. Outlook, vol. 97, p. 817; vol. 100, p. 353.]

(5) Finally, the callousness to injuries incurred by employees must be sharply checked. Well over a hundred thousand men, women, and children are killed or injured every year in the various industries of this country. Our proportion of accidents is far greater than in Europe; the great majority are preventable by the adoption of known safeguards. What stands in the way is, partly, ignorance and heedlessness on the part of employers, and, still more, the initial cost of installing safety appliances. It is often cheaper to lose an occasional damage suit than to forestall accidents. In coal mines alone we have let thirty thousand men be killed and seventy-five thousand be more or less seriously maimed, in a decade; proportionately about twice as many as in European mines-which are far from ideally safeguarded. There are two ways to check this waste and crippling of human life; one is to keep our legislation up to date, and require the installation of every effective safety device, no matter if the cost to the public has to be increased. The other is to make accidents so expensive to employers that they will have a greater interest in taking measures to prevent them.

Certainly all deaths or injuries in any industry where proper precautions have been neglected must be a criminal matter for the employer. [Footnote: Outlook, vol. 92, p. 171; vol. 93, p. 196; vol. 99, p. 202. World's Work, vol. 22, p. 13602; vol. 23, p. 713.] We must do entirely away with the system whereby accidents to workingmen bear so heavily upon their families. Though it is true that they are commonly due, in some measure, to the carelessness of the worker, his punishment, in the loss of life or limb, is great enough; and if he dies or is incapacitated from supporting wife and children, the burden should fall upon the community, which is able to bear it. It should not be necessary to bring a damage suit against the employer; that method is slow, dubious, and expensive; the corporation, with its expert lawyers, has too great an advantage over the helpless and sorrow-struck poor. In some form, automatic compensation for injuries is destined to become universal; the cost will fall upon the industry, where it belongs, bad feeling between employer and employee will cease, the courts will be freed from a good deal of work, and relief will follow injury with promptness and certainty. [Footnote: H. R. Seager, Social Insurance. Outlook, vol. 85, p. 508; vol. 92, p. 319; vol. 98, p. 49. S. Nearing, Social Adjustment, chap. XII.] What general remedies for industrial wrongs are feasible?

(1) The first step toward an amelioration of our crude and unjust industrial code is to awaken the public conscience to protest against the evils we have enumerated. Publicity, pitiless publicity, alone can lead to redress. These large- scale, impersonal sins must not be so nonchalantly tolerated; instead of applauding and envying the shrewd financier who rakes in unearned profits by clever manipulation, by unscrupulous use of inside information,

and disregard of the welfare of workers, competitors, and public, we must brand him as a selfish scoundrel, turn him out of the church, ostracize him in society. Such a man must not be looked upon as a successful businessman any more than a pirate is a successful trader; success must clearly imply obedience to the rules of the game. Taking all that one can grab without punishment is a reversion to barbarism; the unscrupulous magnate is morally no better than a pickpocket. And these men are, in general, responsive to public opinion; it has effected rapid improvement in some points in the past few years. Just so soon as the community conscience is aroused to the point of a general condemnation of industrial robbery, it will cease to flaunt itself so boldly, and lurk only underground with the other furtive sins.

(2) We cannot rely wholly upon the force of public opinion, however; the law must be ready to check those who are insensitive to moral restraints. One by one, the paths of evildoing must be blocked. Especially must the law learn how to punish corporations, which have been the greatest offenders. At present the stockholders throw responsibility upon the directors, the directors upon their managers, and they upon the subordinates who have personally carried through the evil practices. But to punish these subordinates is ineffective, because they have, in general, little money wherewith to pay fines, and will be ready to run the risk of imprisonment for the sake of pleasing their superiors and earning promotion. If they are imprisoned, others can readily be found to step into their places and higher up. It is these superiors who must be held responsible for acts done by their subordinates. If they realize the risk of punishment falling upon their own heads, they will see to it that illegal practices are discontinued. It will probably be necessary to hold directors responsible for the conduct of their managers, and stockholders for the character of their directors. It will then become the business of owners and directors to watch out for lawbreaking and to put men in control who will keep to fair dealing. This will put an end to the easy assumption of the directorship of several corporations at once by men whose names are wanted; directorship will be made to imply actual attention to the affairs of the business. And the stockholders will take pains to elect such directors as will not incur fines for the corporation that will lessen their dividends. [Footnote: For comment on this matter, see Outlook, vol. 88, p. 862.]

(3) Through these two means, public opinion and the law, we must work toward the ultimate solution, the establishment of codes of honor in the professions and industries. Canons of professional ethics have been adopted by lawyers and doctors; any member of these professions who is guilty of breaking these canons suffers loss of prestige and, almost inevitably, financial loss. So must it be in every industry; each must be

organized and must formulate for itself its code; so that pressure from within will supplement pressure from without. There is plenty of capacity for loyalty, self-denial, and discipline in men, even in captains of industry; it needs only to be aroused, crystallized, directed. "We may prevent certain specific practices by statutes which make them misdemeanors; but in so doing we have simply cut off one way of reaching an end. Men will get the same result by another route. obtaining money or office in certain specified ways. We must so shape their ambitions that they do not wish to obtain money or office by means that injure the community. We must get them to consider public selfishness as dishonorable a thing as we now consider private selfishness". If a man today crowds himself out of a theater, leaving behind him a trail of bruised women and children, the very newsboy in the street will hiss him when he gets to the door. Such a man will be despised by the public, and in his heart he will despise himself, for taking advantage of his strength to crush others. But if a man gets money or office by analogous processes, the world is inclined to admire the result and forgive the means; and the man, instead of despising himself for his selfishness, applauds himself for his success.[Footnote: A. T. Hadley, Standards of Public Morality, p. 8.] Certainly, unless in these peaceful ways we can transform our present system of grab-as-grab-can into a fair and rational industrial order, changes will come by violence and revolution. There are volcanic passions slumbering beneath the prosperity of our trade and manufacture; there is but a brief respite before society wherein to evolve a measure of social justice. The lower classes are awakening to their power; unless society and government grant them their fair share of the fruits of industry, they will take them through the wreck of society and government. There is no moral problem more pressing than the finding of peaceful remedies for industrial wrongs.

E. A. Ross, Sin and Society. H. R. Seager, Introduction to Economics, chap. XXII. C. R. Van Hise, Concentration and Control, chap. II. A. T. Hadley, Standards of Public Morality. H. C. Potter, The Citizen in his Relation to the Industrial Situation. W. Gladden, The New Idolatry. R. C. Brooks, Corruption in American Politics and Life. H. Jeffs, Concerning Conscience, chaps. XXII, XXIII. C. R. Henderson, The Social Spirit in America, chaps. VII, IX. J. S. Brooks, The Social Unrest. Jane Addams, Democracy and Social Ethics, chap. V. Buskin, Unto this Last. International Journal of Ethics, vol. 23, p. 455. [For specific references, see footnotes.]

CHAPTER XXVII
INDUSTRIAL RECONSTRUCTION

OUR modern industrial evils are so grave and so deep-rooted that it is highly questionable whether the pressure of public opinion, piecemeal legislation, and the development of codes of honor can strike deep enough to eradicate them. Is not, perhaps, the whole system morally wrong? Instead of these endless attempts to cure the natural results of the system, is there not need of a radical reconstruction? Various attempts have been made, divers proposals are offered, in the hope of curing the causes of present maladies and devising a juster system. Many of these are doubtless impracticable, or tend to work more hardship than amelioration. But each proposal, of any plausibility, has a right to a hearing if it offers to end the great wrongs of contemporary industry; we must be very confident that it will not work before we reject it. For some way must be found to right these wrongs, or our whole industrial order will go to smash. We must not condemn too hastily a method which has not had a thorough trial, or whose defects time and experience might remedy. For mistaken experiments can be discontinued; and great as is the danger in incautious radicalism, the danger in "standing pat" is greater.

Ought the trusts to be broken up or regulated?

The greatest sinners are, certainly, to speak generally, the great corporations that we call trusts-though the word "distrust" would better express contemporary feeling! So great has popular hostility to them become that the Democratic party platform of July, 1912, declared that "a private monopoly is indefensible and intolerable," and demanded "the enactment of such additional legislation as may be necessary to make it impossible for a private monopoly to exist in the United States," i.e., "the control by any one corporation of so large a proportion of any industry as to make it a menace to competitive conditions." But is it necessary to destroy this splendidly efficient concentration of industry in order to avoid its evils? The proposal to revert to the older competitive plan is reminiscent of the outcry against machine production a century earlier, and the earnest pleas then made to return to the hand-tool method. "Big business" constitutes one of the greatest advances in human industry, and therefore has surely come to stay. From the era of individual workers owning their tools, mankind advanced to the age of competition between small concerns using machines; no less marked an advance is that to the age of large-scale production and unified industry. Its advantages may be briefly summarized:

(1) The competitive system involves needless duplications of plant, machinery, and workers; clerks stand idly in rival stores, waiting for trade, drummers spend their time in getting trade away from one another, great sums have to be spent on advertising. Monopoly means a saving of all this wasted time, labor, and money.

(2) The competitive system means great fluctuations in industry, constant anxiety, forced cut prices, and frequent failures, with their financial ruin and heartbreak to employers and loss of work to employees. Monopoly means stability, comparative freedom from anxiety, and a saving of the economic confusion and loss of bankruptcies.

(3) The great scale of monopolistic production tends to still further economies. Raw ported in larger quantities, and so at lower cost; less need be kept on hand at a given time. The utilization of by-products, made feasible by large-scale production, has proved, in many cases, a striking addition to human wealth.

(4) Monopolistic production means that more money can be put into improved processes, into plant and machinery, into making factories sanitary, and working conditions pleasant. The conspicuousness of the plant makes it more open to public criticism and more likely to awaken a sense of pride in the owners. Conditions are seldom tolerated in the big concerns that go unheeded in the little shops.

Surely our attempt, then, must be to retain "big business," and cure its evils, rather than to turn the hands of the clock backward by reverting to the wasteful competitive system. If this proves possible, we should work for the organizing of the as yet unorganized industries. Half of human effort is still wasted, through lack of such organization. If the innumerable butcher shops, grocery stores, apothecary shops, dry goods stores, etc, throughout the country, were consolidated locally, and then for some considerable section of the country, we could have greatly reduced prices and greatly improved shops. Mr. Woolworth's chain of five- and ten-cent stores offers a familiar contemporary example of the efficiency and saving to the consumer of such consolidation.

What are the ethics of the following schemes:

I. TRADE UNIONS AND STRIKES? We must, then, consider what methods of regulating, without destroying, monopoly are efficient and morally defensible; and, first, the method into which the working classes have put most of their effort and enthusiasm. The labor-unions have, as a matter of fact, actually effected certain results, which we may rapidly review:-

(1) Their chief accomplishment, and indeed effort, has been the raising of wages and shortening of hours for labor. Their success, however, has fallen far short of their hopes; and it is impossible to say how much more they have accomplished in this direction than would have been effected by other causes without their efforts. As a whole, the employing class disbelieves in the unions and is strenuously disinclined to yield to their desires. And at present the employers are usually stronger than their employees, unless public opinion or legislation forces them to surrender their position.

(2) To some slight extent, but only to a slight extent, they have effected amelioration in other matters have freed labor from the tyranny of company stores, decreased child labor, secured the installation of safety appliances, sanitary conditions, and other needed improvements.

(3) Their social effect has been greatest. They have amalgamated our stream of heterogeneous immigrants and fired them with common understanding and purpose; they have taught the ignorant to cooperate, made them think, frowned to some degree upon vice, insured their members to. some extent against illness and death, and promoted general friendliness among the laboring classes.

On the other hand, their methods have been productive of much harm:

(1) The economic loss due to strikes has been enormous; the employers have suffered heavily, the public has suffered heavily; the laborers have suffered most of all. Social amelioration certainly ought not to have to come about through such wasteful methods and such bitter privation.

(2) The inconvenience caused the public by strikes has often been very great, especially where the coalmines or railways have been affected. Only a few years ago a veritable tragedy was barely averted, when President Roosevelt succeeded, after the most strenuous efforts, in ending the general coal strike in the winter season. A strike of locomotive engineers means obviously a great peril to the traveling public.

(3) The antagonisms and class hatreds engendered by this sort of industrial warfare do infinite moral harm, and retard heavily the peaceful solution of the problems. The class organs always denounce in bitterest terms the opposing class, and lawlessness always lurks in the background.

(4) Apart from their conduct of strikes, the labor unions must answer to many serious indictments. They have endeavored to restrict output, in order to raise prices. They have sought to restrict the number of apprentices in a trade, and have opposed trade schools, in order to keep down the competition for positions. They have insisted on a uniform wage without regard to efficiency. They have opposed scientific management and the increase of efficiency in various industries, in order to retain more workers

therein. They have insisted upon the retention of incompetent employees, thereby directly causing railway accidents and other evils. They have often antagonized such other ameliorative methods as profit sharing and government regulation, and have rejected overtures from employers, because these-to quote from a union pamphlet-"remove the scope and field of trade-unionism." They have at times been run in the interests of selfish leaders and seemed chiefly a moneymaking scheme of a few grafters.

There can be no question, on a dispassionate consideration, that the militant methods of the trade unions are an unfortunate and temporary expedient. The grievances which they have sought to remedy are very real and very bitter; and perhaps, on the whole, the unions have done more good than harm, and accomplished results that would not so soon have been effected in any other way. But they have been rather strikingly unsuccessful. After fifty years of propaganda, seventy per cent of all industrial workers remain non-unionized; and there has been a relative loss in their numbers during the past decade. They have never succeeded in cornering the labor market, and there seems to be no prospect of their succeeding. In all events, for a permanent and thoroughgoing solution of labor troubles we must turn to some other method.

II. PROFIT SHARING, COOPERATION, AND CONSUMERS' LEAGUES?

(1) The usual method of profit-sharing is for the employer to set aside voluntarily a certain proportion of the profits of successful years, to be distributed among the employees in addition to their regular wages, the distribution being made proportionate to the amount of each man's wages. It is thus properly called a dividend to wages, and is equivalent to a small ownership of the stock of the business by each worker. The advantage lies not only in the fairer distribution of the profits of a business, but in the interest, contentment, and increased efficiency of the employees. The self-interest of the laborers is enlisted to prevent strikes, and a feeling of good will tends to prevail. Not a few employers are giving a degree of profit sharing as a mere business proposition; and the results have been generally successful. But the method is only a sop. It touches only one of the evils above mentioned, that of underpayment of workers. And, for that matter, it is oftenest introduced where the workers are already well paid. It is possible only in successful and firmly established industries; and even in them, bad years may necessitate a temporary cessation of dividends to wages, and generate resentment in the minds of the laborers, who do not know the precise status of the business. Moreover, since the workers cannot be expected to reverse the procedure in lean years and contribute to the maintenance of the business, it is necessary, in most industries, to reserve a considerable sum from the profits of fat years to tide over possible periods of lean years. It might be possible to enforce by law the accumulation of such a reserve fund, and then the distribution of a fixed percentage of the net profits of the business to labor-instead of permitting all the profits to go into the pockets of owners or stockholders. But such a plan will probably be superseded by or incorporated into some more comprehensive solution for industrial evils, a scheme that can remedy other wrongs besides that of inadequate wages.

(2) Cooperation in production involves democratic management of a business as well as a more radical sharing of its profits. The workers themselves contribute the capital, elect the managers, and divide the profits. By their votes they can determine hours of work, and arrange conditions to suit themselves, so far as their capital allows. Cooperation-when fully carried out-is socialism on a small scale introduced into the midst of a capitalistic regime. Its defects are, first, that it is difficult while that regime lasts to find capital enough-since those who have capital to invest usually prefer to manage the business themselves or to entrust their money to a

business conducted on ordinary lines; secondly, that failure means the loss of the hard-earned savings of workingmen; thirdly, that it is difficult to retain skillful managers, since such men usually prefer the opportunities which individualistic business offers of making a larger income; and fourthly, that it is difficult for a democratically managed concern to compete successfully with autocratic business. Political democracies are at a disadvantage in a struggle with tyrannies, if the latter are governed by able men. A one- man policy is more stable, permits of quicker action and a more consistent policy than is possible to a democracy. Exactly so in business, our dictatorial captains of industry have an advantage over their usually less skilled and always less powerful heads, and their smaller capital. The millionaire can cut prices and stand losses which would ruin a cooperative body of workingmen. So that cooperative production has not generally proved successful. In any case, there seems to be no probability of societies of producers being able to supplant the capitalistic concerns; we must turn elsewhere for the solution of our problems.

(3) Consumers' cooperation has been more widely successful. On this plan a number of people contribute the capital of a business in equal small amounts and share the profits in proportion to their purchases. The possibility of excessive profits to a single owner or a small group of owners is thus abolished. But the other evils of autocratic industry remain; laborers are hired for current wages, as by the capitalists, and the temptations to unfair treatment of employees and of competitors remain.

(4) "Consumers' Leagues," so called, have made a business of ascertaining the conditions under which goods are produced, and exhorting their members to purchase only those which have involved fair treatment to the workers. The undertaking is praiseworthy, and has accomplished some good. But its effects are limited by obvious causes. It is extremely difficult in many cases for the consumer to discover the conditions of production of what he wishes to buy. It is a nuisance to have to burden himself with such perplexing considerations. And it is impossible to maintain public allegiance to a white list in face of the temptation of bargain sales. Evils must be attacked at their source; they cannot be effectively controlled from the consumer's end. III. Government regulation of prices, profits, and wages? There are two proposals that promise thoroughgoing cure for industrial evils government regulation of business, leaving it upon its present capitalistic basis, and socialism, the complete democratizing of industry. It seems that one or the other alternative must ultimately be accepted. According to the former, and less radical, plan, publicity of accounts would be required in every industry; and state or national commissions would have full power to supervise the conditions of production, to set a minimum standard below which wages must not fall, to fix maximum prices above

which the products must not be sold, to prevent stock- watering, to enforce standards of honesty and good workmanship in goods, to see to it that all competition is carried on fairly, and to forbid excessive salaries to managers. Equal standards would be exacted throughout an industry, and any increased cost of production would result in the raising of prices (except where profits had previously been exorbitant); thus there would be no real hardship upon employers. The minimum wage should not, of course, be set above the actual productive power of labor; and the inefficient laborers who would be thrown out of employment as not worth the standard wage must be looked after by the provision of free vocational education and state employment. Apprentices, cripples, defectives, and persons giving only part time, would be permitted to receive partial wages; and above the minimum wage, differences in stipend would still exist, as now, to stimulate industry and skill. With such provision for safe- guarding the rights of labor, of competitors, and of the public, profits would not be directly regulated; if they became excessive, they would be clipped by the requirement of a lower price for the product, or of more sanitary or safer conditions of production. But the initiative and energy of the owners would be retained by permitting a sliding scale of profits; the higher the wages paid, or the lower the price set upon products, the greater the profits they could be allowed. Thus a premium would still be set upon efficiency. Under this plan monopoly could be carried to any extent; strikes could be absolutely forbidden, and all dissatisfaction settled by the arbitration of the impartial government commission. Monopoly might even be legally maintained by a refusal of charters to would-be competitors, thus insuring to the public the advantages of a completely organized business without leaving the public at its mercy. The natural monopolies, such as railways, telephones, lighting-service, from which private fortunes have often been made at public expense, can easily be regulated by carefully considered and short-term franchises.

Up to date, the partial and tentative trials of this plan have been encouragingly successful. But there are obvious defects in it, which we must notice:

(1) The danger of failures in business would still exist. Some factors would tend to lessen this danger as, the prevention of stock- watering, misappropriation of funds, excessive salaries, and the unfair competition of rivals. But failures could no longer be averted by squeezing wages, neglecting conditions of production, or lowering the quality of goods. The employers may well ask, in bitterness, what right the Government has to close their chances of high profits when it leaves the chance of total loss. Private ownership of business, still retained on the plan we are considering, must involve risk of bankruptcy, with its economic waste and its suffering.

(2) The plant, capital, and management of a business would still be entirely at the disposal of the owner, and handed down in his family or to partners voluntarily taken in. The son of a capitalist, who inherits the business, may be by no means the most deserving or efficient person to carry it on. Industry is not democratic under this plan; justice is attained as a compromise between the interests of capitalists and laborers. Class antagonisms are still fostered; distrust of the impartiality of the government commission would continually be present, and might at any time lead to actual rebellion and violence.

(3) The temptations to corruption would be enormous. The capitalists, with their reserve funds, would be in a position to bribe or unfairly influence any susceptible members of the commissions; and with the danger of bankruptcy on the one hand, and the great prizes to be won on the other, there would inevitably result in the present state of the average human conscience-a great deal of foul play. Commissioners would have an unlimited opportunity of blackmailing employers. Labor members would pull in one direction, and upper-class members in another. The strain upon public morality would be severe.

IV. SOCIALISM? Socialism promises, according to its adherents, to accomplish all the good results of government regulation, while obviating its defects. It behooves us, then, to give it careful and unbiased attention. The movement toward it is, at least, one of the most significant and widespread movements of our times, evoking on the one hand extraordinary enthusiasm and loyalty, so that to millions of men it is almost a religion, and on the other hand deep distrust, impatient contempt, or bitter hostility. Moreover, the movement is steadily growing; we must recognize that it is not a fad, but a deep current, an international brotherhood that numbers in its ranks many able and intellectual men. We may here disregard the inadequate economic theories that have hampered its earlier years, and the Utopian dreams that have been published under its name, and consider it only as a practical program for remedying our acknowledged and serious industrial evils.

The gist of the socialist proposal is that all industry shall be made democratic, as government is now becoming democratic all over the earth. All plants and all capital are to be owned by the State, and all business run as the Post-Office is run, or as the Panama Canal was built. The managers of each industry are to be chosen from the ranks, according to their fitness, for proved efficiency and knowledge of the business. Everybody will be upon a salary, and the opportunity of increasing personal profits by lowering wages, cheating the public, neglecting evil conditions of production, or damaging rivals, will be absent. Thus, instead of trying by an elaborate system of checks to keep within due bounds the greed of man, the possibility of satisfying that greed is definitely removed, and all earnings made proportionate to industriousness and skill. We proceed to summarize the advantages that, it is urged, would follow the inauguration of this industrial democracy:

(1) All industries could be organized and centralized. A vast amount of human effort could be saved, and waste eliminated. Business would no longer, as so often now, be hampered for lack of funds to carry out plans. A special staff could be retained to invent and apply new ideas. In short, just as the trusts now are much more efficient and economical than the small concerns they have superseded, so the completely organized industries of a socialistic regime would be, we are told, in a position to double human efficiency. If the postal business were open to competition, there can be no doubt that we should be paying higher rates today for a much less efficient service. If it were a private monopoly, some one would probably be getting enormous profits out of it profits which now go back into extending the service. The labor saved by industrial unification would be available for a thousand other undertakings that cry to be carried out.

(2) All the industrial wrongs enumerated in the preceding chapter could, it is asserted, be remedied, and all problems adjusted, with comparatively little friction, because it would be to no one's particular advantage to retard such betterment. Those in control of every business, being upon a fixed salary, and having nothing to gain by squeezing laborers or public, would be amenable to a sense of pride in the honesty, cleanliness, and efficiency of their business, and the contentment of their employees. If they were too lazy or stupid to respond to such motives, they could quickly be superseded in office by men who were more ambitious for the fair showing of their branch of the public service.

(3) Opportunity to rise to the control of a business would be open to every laborer in it. The sons of rich men could no longer step easily into the soft berths, whether they were deserving or not. Proved efficiency, plus popularity, would be the road to success. With the higher wages paid to labor (made possible partly by the economic saving through organization, and partly by cutting out the private fortunes now made out of industry), every boy would be able to get a thorough vocational education, and be in a position to strive, if he is ambitious, for leadership. Industrial power would be conferred, directly or indirectly, by popular vote; business would be recognized as a public affair, and nepotism and hereditary advantage banished from it as they have been from politics.

(4) The risk of bankruptcies, with all their attendant evils, would be done away with entirely. Business would have a stability unknown to our present

individualistic industry, and businessmen would be freed from that anxiety that drives so many today to a premature grave.

(5) All speculation in stocks would be likewise eliminated. The necessary capital for any new undertaking would be provided by the industrial State, and the undeserved gains and losses of our present system of private investment would come to an end.

(6) Morally, there would be a probable gain in several ways. The elimination of private profit from business would give freer room for the development of a social spirit which is now choked out by the temptation that each owner of a business is under to grab all that he can for himself. There would be no motive, and no fortunes available, for, at least, the most striking forms of that corruption of the press which is such a grave problem today. Municipal theaters would be under no temptation to produce nasty plays. All this exploitation of human weakness and passion is done because it PAYS; if the men at the top were on a salary there would be no such inducement to cater to vicious instincts. The economic pressure that now pushes so many girls in the direction of prostitution would be relieved. The people generally would be dignified and educated by their participation in industrial, as now in political decisions. If some of the tougher strains of character, grit, push, endurance, etc. would be less fostered, the gentler and more social aspects of character would find better soil.

Whether all these advantages would actually accrue, in the degree hoped for, it is, of course, impossible to know. There are, however, at least two grave dangers in socialism which must be squarely faced:

(1) A certain degree of slackness and consequent inefficiency would almost inevitably result from the relaxing of the pressure of competition and the removal of the opportunity for unlimited personal profit. Employees and managers of state and municipal undertakings are apt to take things easily; and there have been usually waste and inertia and extravagance in such enterprises. The probable loss in grit, push, and endurance, mentioned above, might prove serious. We must admit that, on the whole, private business has been managed much better than public business, both in this country and abroad. To a considerable extent, however, the inefficiency of municipal and state undertakings has been due to the clumsiness and corruption of political systems, and can be cured by political reform. That public affairs can be managed as successfully as private business has been demonstrated on many occasions. The parcel post offers a much more economical service than the express companies ever gave. The most efficient and successful engineering undertaking ever accomplished by man the construction of the Panama Canal was a thoroughgoing socialistic achievement. Moreover, in our criticism of public undertakings, we are apt

to forget how slack and inefficient the great bulk of private business has been; our attention is caught by the few concerns that have made a striking success, and we overlook the vast numbers that have failed or barely kept alive. Looking at the matter psychologically, observation does not altogether confirm the statement that men need an unlimited possibility of financial reward to work hard. The vast majority of workers today are on salary; and on the whole they probably work as faithfully as the few at the top (continually becoming fewer) who have the spur of private profit.[Footnote: 1 Cf. this testimony in regard to former owners of stores in Minnesota and Wisconsin who have been bought out and retained as managers by cooperative societies: "they work for moderate salaries, and in almost all cases are working as ardently for success as they ever did for their own gain." N. O. Nelson, in Outlook, vol. 89, p. 527.] Not all capitalists are hard workers; much of the real work is done for them by salaried managers. It is very questionable if doctors and lawyers, who work for profits, give any more loyal service to the community than teachers, ministers, or nurses, who work on salary. There would still be the need of earning one's living, and the incentive of rising to positions of higher salary, greater authority, and wider interest. And, after all, most of the really good work of the world is done on honor, from the normal human pleasure in doing things well, and pride in being known to do things well. When freed from the private greed and antisocial class feelings which now inhibit it, this zest in efficient work and loyal service might receive a new impetus. A socialistic regime would surely make a business of inculcating in its public schools the conception of all work as public service; and the pressure of public opinion would bear more heavily upon workers-as there is today much freer criticism of public than of private undertakings. But even if there should be a considerable increase in slackness and a decrease in PER CAPITA production, that economic loss might be more than made up by the saving of labor through organization. And if not, it is true that efficiency is not the only good. Considerations of humanity should weigh with us as well as considerations of moneymaking; if socialism can cure the intolerable evils in our present selfish and chaotic system, a certain decrease in production might not be too great a price to pay.

(2) The running of the complicated socialistic machine would involve a great deal of friction, with consequent dissatisfaction and dissension. Problems would arise on all hands: On what basis should the wage-rate in this industry and in that be determined? How much of the public moneys should be put into this and how much into that undertaking? Was this department head fair in discharging this man and promoting that man? Suspicion of bribery and graft would continually recur. Bad seasons would be encountered, blunders would be made, overproduction would occur, men would be thrown out of employment in the work they had chosen,

floods, fires, plagues, and other disasters would sweep away profits; the adjustment of these losses would be an enormously delicate matter. At present, the poor are apt to feel that prosperity for them is hopeless; under a socialistic regime they would expect it, and be loath to see their incomes diminished when things went wrong. Socialism would require a great deal of good temper and willingness to submit to decisions which seemed unwise or unfair. It is highly doubtful if human nature is yet good enough to fit the system.

(3) A third objection to socialism, that corruption would be increased, is a much-debated point. There would be, as now, opportunity for falsification of accounts and embezzlement. Individual promotions would too often hinge upon personal friendship or favors received. The enormous administrative machinery would open up all sorts of new avenues to personal gain at the expense of others, which unprincipled men would be quick to take advantage of. But, on the other hand, no great private fortunes or wealthy corporations would exist to bribe, and no such money-prizes would exist to be won by bribery as are common in our present system. There would be no temptation to adulterate goods, and less of a temptation to award contracts or franchises to friends -since there would be no private profit in it. What supports our political rings today is, above all, the existence of the "interests" wealthy corporations that are making profits enough to spare large sums for "influencing" legislation; these "interests" would no longer exist. On the whole, then, the amount and direction of corruption under socialism is unpredictable; but its possibility should give us pause. The other general objections to socialism are probably less serious; some of them complete misapprehensions. It is certainly not anti-Christian; on the contrary, there are those who believe that it is the necessary the Christian spirit.[Footnote: Cf, for example, W. Rauschenbusch, Christianity and the Social Crisis.] It is not "materialistic" any more than any industrial system must necessarily be. It would not necessarily destroy private property or lessen human freedom, except in the one matter that it would prevent private ownership of the instruments of industrial production and destroy the freedom to conduct business to private advantage. But it is clear that it would involve us in all sorts of complicated and delicate problems of detail which would require generations for satisfactory solution and which might never be satisfactorily solved. And it might, of course, lead to other difficulties now unforeseen, graver and more difficult to meet than we now realize. Surely, then, it is not to be lightly undertaken, and not to be undertaken as a mere revolt of the lower classes against their industrial masters. It must be worked out in great detail, and contrasted with every possible alternative, before cautious statesmen will consent to its adoption. For it would mean a revolutionary change of enormous proportions; and it would not be easy to revert to the

earlier order. Our political machinery, under which the vast industrial system would come, must first be reconstructed and made efficient. Religion and public education must be strengthened to meet the new demands upon character and intelligence. It is earnestly to be hoped that if socialism comes, it will come not by revolution, as the result of a class struggle, but by evolution and a general consent, the result of long and careful public discussion. In the writer's opinion, present steps must be along the line of government regulation, with socialism as the possible, but as yet by no means certain, eventual outcome. In any case, there is no simple and sweeping panacea for our industrial ills; the patient thought and experimentation and effort of generations will be required before a satisfactory and stable equilibrium is attained.

Competition VS. concentration: C. R. Van Hise, CONCENTRATION AND
CONTROL, chap. I. J. W. Jenks, THE TRUST PROBLEM. E. von Halle, TRUSTS AND INDUSTRIAL COMBINATIONS. F. C. McVey, MODERN
INDUSTRIALISM. S. C. T. Dodd, COMBINATIONS, THEIR USE AND
ABUSE. R. T. Ely, MONOPOLIES AND TRUSTS. C. N. Fay, BIG BUSINESS AND GOVERNMENT. Edmond Kelly, TWENTIETH CENTURY
SOCIALISM, book II, chap, II; book III, chap. I. A. J. Eddy, THE NEW COMPETITION. Atlantic Monthly, vol. 79, p. 377. FORUM, vol. 8, p. 61. JOURNAL OF POLITICAL ECONOMY, vol. 20, p. 358. Labor unions and
strikes: J. R. Commons, TRADE-UNIONISM AND LABOR PROBLEMS.
Carlton, HISTORY AND PROBLEMS OF ORGANIZED LABOR. S. and
B. Webb, INDUSTRIAL DEMOCRACY; HISTORY OF TRADE UNIONISM. J. Mitchell, ORGANIZED LABOR. C. R. Henderson, SOCIAL
SPIRIT IN AMERICA, chap. ix. Jane Addams, NEWER IDEALS OF PEACE, chap. v. ATLANTIC MONTHLY, vol. 109, p. 758. H. R. Seager, I
NTRODUCTION TO ECONOMICS, chap. xxi. F. W. Taussig, PRINCIPLES
OF ECONOMICS, chap. 55. Profit sharing: W. H. Tolman, SOCIAL ENGINEERING, chap. vii. Seager, OP. CIT, chap, xxvi, sec. 281. Adams and Sumner, LABOR PROBLEMS, chap. X. N. P. Gilman, PROFIT SHARING; A DIVIDEND TO LABOR. Outlook, vol. 106, p. 627. QUARTERLY REVIEW, vol. 219, p. 509. Cooperation: G. J. Holyoake,

HISTORY OF COOPERATION. C. R. Fay, COOPERATION AT HOME
AND ABROAD. Adams and Sumner, LABOR PROBLEMS, chap. x. ARENA, vol. 36, p. 200; vol. 40, p. 632. H. R. Seager, OP. CIT, sec. 282. F. W. Taussig, OP. CIT, chap. 59. Consumers' leagues: Publications of the National Consumers' League (106 East Nineteenth Street, New York City). Government regulation: J. W. Jenks, OP. CIT, Appendices. C. R. Van Hise, OP. CIT, chaps, iii-v. F. W. Taussig, OP. CIT, chaps. 62,63. H. R. Seager, OP. CIT, chap. xxv. C. L. King, REGULATION OF MUNICIPAL UTILITIES. J. B. and J. M. Clark, CONTROL OF THE TRUSTS. E. M. Phelps, FEDERAL CONTROL OF INTERSTATE CORPORATIONS. ATLANTIC MONTHLY, vol. iii, p. 433. OUTLOOK,
vol. 99, p. 649; vol. 100, pp. 574, 690; vol. 101, p. 353; vol. 103, p. 476. NORTH AMERICAN REVIEW, vol. 197, pp. 62, 222, 350. INTERNATIONAL JOURNAL OF ETHICS, vol. 23, p. 158. JOURNAL OF POLITICAL ECONOMY, vol. 20, pp. 309, 574. Socialism: Edmond Kelly, TWENTIETH CENTURY SOCIALISM. H. G. Wells, NEW WORLDS FOR OLD. J. Spargo, SOCIALISM. M. Hillquit, SOCIALISM IN THEORY AND PRACTICE. A. Schaffle, THE QUINTESSENCE OF SOCIALISM. F. W. Taussig, OP. CIT, chaps. 64, 65. J. Rae, the roman numerals are both upper and lower case did not standardize PORARY SOCIALISM. R. T. Ely, SOCIALISM. W. G. Towler, SOCIALISM IN LOCAL GOIVERNEMNT. H. R. SEAGER,
OP. CIT, sec. 282. N. P. Gilman, SOCIALISM AND THE AMERICAN SPIRIT. R. Hunter, SOCIALISTS AT WORK. JOURNAL OF POLITICAL
ECONOMY, vol. 14, p. 257. OUTLOOK, vol. 91, pp. 618, 662; vol. 95, pp. 831, 876.

CHAPTER XXVIII
LIBERTY AND LAW

WE have spoken of the practical defects and dangers inherent in the various proposals that look to the rectification of industrial wrongs. But there is one source of opposition to these proposals that requires more extended consideration-the fear that they-and especially socialism-unduly threaten that ideal of personal liberty which our fathers so passionately served and we have come to look upon as the cornerstone of our prosperity. What is this ideal of liberty, and how should it affect our efforts at industrial regeneration? What are the essential aspects of the ideal of liberty? Throughout a long stretch of human history one of the most vexing obstacles to general happiness and progress has been the irresponsible power of sovereigns and oligarchies. To generations it has seemed that if freedom from selfish tyranny could but be won, the millennium would be at hand. Our heroes have been those who fought against despots for the rights of the people; we measure progress by such milestones as the Magna Charta, the French Revolution, the American Declaration of Independence. To this day we engrave the word "liberty" on our coins; and the converging multitudes from Europe look up eagerly to the great statue that welcomes them in New York Harbor and symbolizes for them the freedom that they have often suffered so much to gain. In Mrs. Hemans's hymn, in Patrick Henry's famous speech, in Mary Antin's wonderful autobiography, The Promised Land, we catch glimpses of that devotion to liberty which, it is now said, we are jeopardizing by our increasing mass of legislative restraints and propose to banish for good and all by an indefinite increase in the powers of the State. More than a generation ago Mill wrote: "There is in the world at large an increasing inclination to stretch unduly the powers of society over the individual, both by the force of opinion and even by that of legislation; and as the tendency of all the changes taking place in the world is to strengthen society, and diminish the power of the individual, this encroachment is not one of the evils which tend spontaneously to disappear, but, on the contrary, to grow more and more formidable."[Footnote: Essay on Liberty, Introductory.] Not a few observers today are reiterating this note of alarm with increasing emphasis. Are their fears well founded? We may at once agree in applauding the liberty worship of our fathers and of our contemporaries in the more backward countries. No secure steps in civilization can be taken until liberty of body, of movement, and of possession are guaranteed; there must be no fear of arbitrary execution, arrest, or confiscation. To this must be added liberty of conscience, of speech, and of worship; the right of free assembly, a free press, and that "freedom to worship God" that the Pilgrims sought. Wherever these rights, so fundamental to human happiness, are impugned, "Liberty!" is still the fitting rallying-cry.[Footnote: The exact limits within which freedom of speech must be allowed are debatable, (a) Speech which incites to crime, to lawbreaking, to sexual and other vice, must be prevented; and (b) slander, the public utterance of grossly disparaging statements concerning any person, without reasonable evidence of their truth. May we attempt to stifle the utterance of (c) such other untruths as are inexcusable in the light of our common knowledge? There are certainly many matters where there is no longer room for legitimate difference of opinion; and the general diffusion of correct knowledge is greatly retarded by the silly utterances of uninformed people. Yet to draw the line here is so difficult that we must probably tolerate this evil forever rather than run the risk of stifling some generally unsuspected truth.] rights are safely won; the danger now is rather of abusing them. We must not forget that liberty is only a means, not an end in itself, to be restricted in so far as may be necessary for the greatest happiness. From our discussion in Part II it should be clear that there are no "natural rights" which the community is bound to respect; liberty must be granted the individual so far, and only so far, as it does not impede the general welfare. We do not hesitate to end the liberty, or even to take the life, of those we deem dangerous to society. We do not hesitate to confiscate the land which we deem necessary for a highway or railroad or public building. Indeed, we hedge personal liberty about with a thousand restrictions by general consent, in the realization that public interests must come before private. We have no need to discuss the doctrine of anarchism [Footnote: For an eloquent defense of anarchism see Tolstoy's writings; here is a sample statement: "For a Christian to promise to subject himself to any government whatsoever-a subjection which may be considered the foundation of state life-is a direct negation of Christianity." (Kingdom of God, chap. IX.) Cf. this utterance of one of the Chicago anarchists of 1886. "Whoever prescribes a rule of action for another to obey is a tyrant: usurper, and an enemy of liberty."]- unrestricted liberty since the general chaos that would result there from, in the present stage of human nature, is sufficiently apparent. Liberty can never be absolute. Indeed, there has been a curious reversal of situation. The older cry of liberty that stirs us was a cry of the oppressed masses against their masters; now it is a slogan of the privileged upper classes against that increasing popular legislation which restricts their powers. Kings are now but figureheads, if they linger at all, in our modern democracies; governments are not irresponsible masters of the people, they are instruments for carrying out the popular will. The real tyrants now, those whose irresponsible authority is dangerous to the masses, are the kings of industry; if the cry of "liberty" is to be raised again, it should be raised, according to all historical precedent, in behalf of the slaves of modern industry rather than in behalf of the fortunate few who give up so grudgingly the practical powers they have usurped. There were those, indeed, who fought passionately for the divine right of kings, those who died to maintain the right of a white man to hold Negroes as slaves; there are those today who with a truly religious fervor uphold the right of the capitalistic class to manage the industries of the country at their own sweet will, unhampered by such legislative restrictions as the majority may deem expedient for the general welfare. But it is a travesty on the sacred word "liberty" that it should be thus invoked to uphold the prerogatives of the favored few. Liberty, in the sense in which it is properly an ideal for man, connotes the right to all such forms of activity as are consonant with the greatest general happiness, and to no others. It implies the right not to be oppressed, not the right to oppress. Mere freedom of contract is not real freedom, if the alternative be to starve; such formal freedom may be practical slavery. The real freedom is freedom to live as befits a man; and it is precisely because such freedom is beyond the grasp of multitudes today that our system of "free contract" is discredited; it offers the name of liberty without the reality. But apart from this questionable appeal to the ideal of liberty, there are not a few who sincerely believe, on grounds of practical expediency, that legislation ought not to interfere any more than proves absolutely necessary with the conduct of industry. This scheme of individualism we will now consider.

The ideal of individualism. The individualistic, or laissez-faire, ideal dates perhaps from Rousseau and the French doctrinaires; its best-known representatives in English speech are Mill and Spencer. Dewey and Tufts have pithily expressed it as follows: "The moral end of political institutions and measures is the maximum possible freedom of the individual consistent with his not interfering with like freedom on the part of other individuals."[Footnote: Ethics, p. 483.] Its leading arguments may be presented and answered, summarily, as follows:

(1) Legislation has so often been mischievous that it is well to have as little of it as possible. The masses are uneducated, the prey of impulse and passion; politics are corrupt; to submit the genius of free ENTREPRENEURS to the clumsy and ill-fitted yoke of a popularly wrought legal control is to stifle their enterprise and interfere with their chances of success. After all, every one knows his own needs best; and if we leave people alone, they will secure their own welfare better than if we try to dictate to them how they shall seek it. "Out of the fourteen thousand odd acts which, in our own country, have been repealed, from the date of the Statute of Merton down to 1872 . . . how many have been repealed because they were mischievous? . . . Suppose that only three thousand of

these acts were abolished after proved injuries had been caused, which is a low estimate. What shall we say of these three thousand acts which have been hindering human happiness and increasing human misery; now for years, now for generations, now for centuries?"[Footnote: H. Spencer, Principles of Ethics, part IV, sec. 131.] But to admit that much legislation has been blundering is not to admit that the principle of social control is wrong. Our political system must, indeed, be made must be placed in the way of overhasty and ill-considered lawmaking. But it is not always true that the individual is the best judge of his own ultimate interests; and it is demonstrably untrue that the pursuit by each of what he deems best for himself will bring the greatest happiness for all. The stronger and more favorably situated will take advantage of their position and resources; the weaker, though theoretically free, will in reality be under the handicap of poverty, ignorance, hunger. Such a system is inevitably vicious in its moral effects. To say that in a popular government legislation cannot properly standardize practice, cannot formulate a higher code of public morality than men can be depended upon to attain if unrestrained, is unwarrantably to discredit democracy. If the laws are bad, improve them. If the public is uneducated, educate it. If our system gives us poor lawmakers, change the system. But to give up the attempt at legal control, to leave things as they are or rather, to leave them to go from bad to worse, is unthinkable.

(2) Too much legislation stifles individuality, drags genius down to the dead level of average ideas, tends to produce an unprogressive uniformity of practice. It imposes the conceptions of the past upon the future. "If the measures have any effect at all, the effect must in part be that of causing some likeness among the individuals; to deny this is to deny that the process of molding is operative. But in so far as uniformity results advance is retarded. Every one who has studied the order of nature knows that without variety there can be no progress."[Footnote: H. Spencer, op. cit, sec. 138.] "Persons of genius, it is true, are, and are always likely to be, a small minority; but in order to have them it is necessary to preserve the soil in which they grow. Genius can only breathe freely in an atmosphere of freedom. ... It is important to give the freest scope possible to uncustomary things, in order that it may in time appear which of these are fit to be converted into customs." [Footnote: J. S. Mill, On Liberty, chap. III.] But the intention of social legislation is to check only such individual action as is demonstrably detrimental; the uniformity produced will be only a uniform absence of flagrant wrongs and adoption of such positive precautions as will make the detection and checking of these harmful acts easy. Beyond this minimum uniformity (which, however, must include an enormous number of details, so manifold have the possibilities of wrongdoing become) there will on any system be ample range for the development of new methods and processes. Whatever danger there once

was in choking individual initiative by needlessly paralyzing restrictions, will be, in the long run, negligible in an age of omnivorous reading and free discussion, and in a land whose conscious ideal is improvement, new invention, progress. As a matter of fact, it is chiefly through legislation that new methods of social practice become diffused. Each of our forty-eight States is experimenting in social guidance, trying to thwart this or that sin, to remedy this or that wrong, to work out a plan by which men can happily cooperate in our complex public life. The process of evolving an efficient and frictionless social machine, instead of being retarded by this activity of lawmaking, is actually accelerated thereby. Private business tends to fall into ruts; and one man's ideals are blocked by lack of cooperation from others. Legislation tends not only to preserve the best of past experiments; but, goaded by the zeal of reformers, and pushed by political parties, to drag complacent and inert individuals along new and untried paths. The greatest field for genius lies today in devising successful constructive legislation; and the greatest hope for progress in this era of mutual dependence lies in the winning of a majority for some social scheme that must be generally adopted if at all.

(3) Laws, however beneficent, which rise above the general conscience of the people are undesirable; character should precede legislation. "To conform to custom, merely as custom, does not educate or develop in [a man] any of the qualities which are the distinctive endowment of a human being. . . . He who does anything because it is the custom makes no choice. He gains no practice either in discerning or in desiring what is best. The mental and moral, like the muscular powers, are improved only by being used. . . . It is possible that he might be guided in some good path, and kept out of harm's way, without [using his own judgment, powers of decision, self control, etc.] But what will be his comparative worth as a human being? It really is of importance, not only what men do, but also what manner of men they are that do it." [Footnote: J. S. Mill, op. cit, chap. III.] A little common sense will show us, however, that there are, and always will be, plenty of occasions for exercising our moral muscle, however closely we hedge in the field of legitimate activity. Prone to temptation as men are, and beset by a thousand wrong impulses, we may well seek to block this and that path of possible wrongdoing without fear of turning them mechanically into saints. On the contrary, we should hasten to use the experience of the past to avert needless temptations from the men of the future.

Our experience has been costly enough; and if it has revealed its lessons too late to save contemporary social life, at least it should serve as warning for our sons. To sacrifice right conduct to moral gymnastics is to set up the means as more important than the end; every good act that can be lifted from the plane of moral struggle and put securely on the plane of habit is a step in human progress, and leaves men freer to grapple with the remaining temptations. If you wish to educate men up to a law, put it upon the statute books if you can, compel attention to it and discussion of the reasons pro and con, show its practical workings; it is far easier to educate conscience up to an existing law than beyond it. Moreover, it must be said that those who prefer to see men left to think things out anew for themselves, without the restraint and guidance of the law, show a singular callousness toward those whom their action, if they choose wrongly, will hurt. If we could trust men to choose aright-but we cannot; and men must be protected against their own stupidity and weakness, and that of others, by the collective wisdom and will.

(4) Individualism makes for prosperity. Offering a fair chance to all, it brings the best to the top; the fittest survive, and win the positions of power; the community as a whole is, then, in the end advantaged. "Free competition in profits coordinates industrial efficiency and industrial reward.This is equality of opportunity, through which every man is rewarded according to his worth to the consumer." [Footnote: F. Y. Gladney, in the Outlook, vol. 101, p. 261.] Unfortunately, however, it is those who are fittest to serve not the community but their own interests that have the best chance to survive-the clever, the privileged, the unscrupulous. Nor is there equality of opportunity where some will not play fair and others have a long start. The individualistic struggle makes for the selection of a type of greedy, self-centered man, with little sense of social responsibility. Even granted that the men who reach the top are the men best fitted to manage the industries of the country, this method of selection of leaders is too wasteful of strength, too hard on the unsuccessful, to be generally profitable. The prosperity of modern industry is due not primarily to its chaotic plan of individual effort and cross-purposes, but to the measure of cooperation we have nevertheless attained, with its consequent division and specialization of labor and large-scale production, aided by the extraordinary development of invention and machinery. The ideal of legal control. The epoch of ultra individualism, of what Huxley called "administrative nihilism," is rapidly passing. Jane Addams speaks of "the inadequacy of those eighteenth-century ideals the breakdown of the machinery which they provided," pointing out that "that worldly wisdom which counsels us to know life as it is" discounts the assumption "that if only the people had freedom they would walk continuously in the paths of justice and righteousness." [Footnote: Newer Ideals of Peace, pp. 31-32.] H. G. Wells remarks, "We do but emerge now from a period of deliberate happy- go-lucky and the influence of Herbert Spencer, who came near raising public shiftlessness to the dignity of a natural philosophy. Everything would adjust itself-if only it was left alone." [Footnote: Social Forces in England and America, p. 80.] It is becoming clear that we cannot

trust to education and the conscience of individuals to right matters, not only because as yet we provide no moral education of any consequence for our youth, but because, if we did, the temptations in a world where every man is free to grab for himself would still be almost irresistible. But there are two positive arguments for the extension of legal control that clinch the matter:

(1) Without the support of the law it is often impossible for the conscientious man to act in a purely social spirit. The competition of those who are less answerable to moral motives forces him to lower his own ideals if he would not see his business ruined. The employer of child labor in one factory cannot afford to hire adults, at their higher wage, until all the other factories give up the cheaper labor also. Where sweatshop labor produces cheap clothing for some manufacturers, the more scrupulous are undersold. One employer cannot, unless he is unusually prosperous, raise the wages of his employees or shorten their hours until his competitors do likewise. Improvement of conditions must take place all along the line or not at all. And since unanimous voluntary consent is practically impossible to obtain, and of precarious duration if obtained, the legal enforcement of common standards is necessitated.

(2) Men generally are willing to bind themselves by law to higher codes than they will live up to if not bound. In their reflective moments, when they are deciding how to vote, temptations are less insistent and ideals stronger than when they are confronting concrete situations. To vote for a law which will restrain others, and incidentally one's self, comes easier than to make a purely personal sacrifice that leaves general practice unaltered. To realize that this is true, we need but look at the remarkable ethical gains made now year by year through laws voted for by many of the very men whose practice had hitherto been upon a lower moral level. Very many evils that once seemed fastened upon society have been thus legislated out of existence.[Footnote: For a vivid picture of earlier industrial conditions which would not now be tolerated, see Charles Reade's Put Yourself in His Place.] And if the industrial situation still seems wretched, it is because, in our swift advance, new evils are arising about as fast as older evils are eradicated. The law necessarily lags behind the spread of abuses, so that "there will probably always be a running duel between anti-social action and legislation designed to check it. Novel methods of corruption will constantly require novel methods of correction . . But this constant development of the law should make corrupt practices increasingly difficult for the less gifted rascals who must always constitute the great majority of would-be offenders." [Footnote: R. C. Brooks, Corruption in American Politics and Life, p. 99.] The law can never, of course, cover the whole field of human conduct; it represents, in Stevenson's phrase," that modicum of

morality which can be squeezed out of the rock of mankind." Unnecessary extension of the law is cumbersome, expensive, and provocative of impatience and rebellion. Moreover, there is always some minimum of danger of injustice in attempting legal constraint; the law itself, as approved by the majority, may be unfair, or its application to the concrete case may be unfair. The individualists are right in feeling that men must be left alone, wherever the possible results are not too dangerous. But no hard-and-fast line can be drawn between activities that must be left free and those which must be regulated. Such apparently personal matters as the use of opium or alcohol must be checked because the general happiness is, in the end, greatly and obviously enhanced by such restraint. But there will always be, beyond the law, a wide field for the satisfaction of personal tastes and the practice of generosity. There is no double standard; if an act is legally right and morally wrong, that simply means that it lies beyond the boundaries of the limited field which the law covers. The extension of that field is a matter of practical expediency in each type of situation; beyond that field, but working to the same ends, the forces of education and public opinion are alone available. [Footnote: For a discussion of this point, see F. Paulsen, System of Ethics, book III, chap. IX, sec. 9. International Journal of Ethics, vol. 18, p. 18.] Should existing laws always be obeyed? Year by year we are extending our network of laws over human conduct; more and more pertinent becomes the them? and the further question, Are there times when the law may be rightly disobeyed? We shall discuss the second question first. It is obvious that our whole social structure rests upon the willingness of the people to obey the law. The watchword of republics should be, not "liberty," but "obedience"; their gravest danger now is not tyranny, but anarchy. We must individually submit with patience and good temper to the decisions of the majority, even if we disapprove those decisions. We must abide by the rules of the game until we can get the rules changed. And all changes must be effected according to the rules agreed upon for effecting changes. This law-abiding spirit is the great triumph of democracy; only so long as it exists can popular government stand. Though it be slower and exacting of greater effort and skill, evolution, not revolution, is the method of permanent progress. We must, then, band together against any groups that, in their impatience of reform or opposition to the common will, cast aside the restraints of law. However dearly we may long for woman's suffrage, we must sternly repress those excited suffragettes who would gain this end by defiance of law and destruction of property; even if they further their particular cause by their violence-which is highly doubtful-they do it at the expense of something still more precious, the preservation of the law-abiding spirit. Other organizations will not be slow to profit by the lesson of their success; and we shall have Heaven knows how many causes seeking to attain their ends by destructiveness and resistance. Similarly, the more serious and menacing rebellion of labor against law must be firmly controlled; much as we may sympathize with their grievances, we cannot countenance the attempt to remedy them by violence. The Industrial Workers of the World, with action, [Footnote: Cf, in a pamphlet issued by them: "The I.W.W. will get the results sought with the least expenditure of time and energy. The tactics used are determined solely by the power of the organization to make good in their use". The question of 'right' and 'wrong' does not concern us. In short, the I.W.W. advocates the use of militant 'direct action' tactics to the full extent of our power to make them." (Quoted in Atlantic Monthly, vol. 109, p. 703.)] have made themselves enemies of society. The advocates of "sabotage," the "reds" in the socialist camp, the preachers of practical anarchism, must be treated as among the most dangerous of criminals. On the other hand, the spread of the spirit of lawlessness among the lower classes should serve to warn the upper classes that present social conditions will not much longer be endured.[Footnote: Cf. Ettor (quoted in Outlook, vol. 101, p. 340): "They tell us to get what we want by the ballot. They want us to play the game according to the established rules. But the rules were made by the capitalists. THEY have laid down the laws of the game. THEY hold the pick of the cards. We never can win by political methods. The right of suffrage is the greatest hoax of history. Direct action is the only way."] There is a great deal of idealism among the advocates of violence;[Footnote: Cf, for example, Giovannitti's poem, The Cage, in the Atlantic Monthly, June, 1913.] there is a great deal of sympathy on the part of the public with lawless strikers, with the I.W.W. gangs that have recently invaded city churches, with all those under-dogs who are now determining to have a share in the good things of life. Unless the employing and governing classes meet their demands halfway, gunpowder and dynamite pretty surely lie ahead. Will the spirit of lawlessness spread? Ought we to slacken our process of lawmaking lest we make the yoke too hard to bear? As a matter of fact, it is through more laws, better laws, and a better mechanism for punishing infraction of laws, that we can hope to check lawlessness. Lynching-as we noted in chapter XXV-have been the product of inadequate legislation and judicial procedure; as our laws against the worst crimes become sharper, our police forces more efficient, and our court trials quicker and less hampered by technicalities, they decrease in number. As education on the liquor question spreads, violations of prohibition laws become fewer. The kind of lawlessness that is on the increase is that which exists as a protest against and a means of remedying evils that the laws have not yet properly dealt with. Give us by law an industrial code that will minimize the exploitation of the weak by the strong, bringing a good measure of security and comfort to all, and such outrages as those of the McNamara brothers will cease, or at worst will be merely sporadic and generally condemned. Allow present conditions to drift on without sharp legal guidance, and such outrages will certainly become more and more numerous. The alternative that confronts the modern world is plainly evolution by law or revolution by violence. Individualism: J. S. Mill, On Liberty. H. Spencer, Principles of Ethics, part iv, chaps, XXV-XXIX; Social Statics; and many other writings. J. H. Levy, The Outcome of Individualism. Various publications of the British Personal Rights Association. W. Donisthorpe, Individualism. W. Fite, Individualism, lect. IV. Legal control: Florence Kelley, Some Ethical Gains through Legislation. Jane Addams, Newer Ideals of Peace. E. A. Ross, Social Control, chap. XXXI. D. S. Ritchie, Principles of State Interference. J. W. Jenks, Government Action for Social Welfare. A. V. Dicey, Law and Opinion. J. Seth, Study of Ethical Principles, pp. 297-331. H. C. Potter, Relation of the Individual to the Industrial Situation, chap. VI. W. J. Brown, Underlying Principles of Modern Legislation. Journal of Philosophy, Psychology, and Scientific Methods, vol. 10, p. 113. A. T. Hadley, Freedom and Responsibility. J. W. Garner, Introduction to Political Science, chaps, IX, X. Edmond Kelly, Evolution and Effort. Lawlessness: Atlantic Monthly, vol. 109, p. 441. Outlook, vol. 98, p. 12; vol. 99, p. 901; vol. 100, p. 359. J. G. Brooks, American Syndicalism.

CHAPTER XXIX
EQUALITY AND PRIVILEGE

All men, our Declaration of Independence tells us, are created free and equal-that is, with a right to freedom and equality. They are not actually equal in natural gifts, but they ought, so far as possible, to be made equal in opportunity; equality is not a fact, but an ideal. And as an ideal it comes sometimes into conflict with its twin ideal of liberty; the freedom of the stronger must be curtailed when it robs the weaker of their fair share of happiness; but, on the other hand, a dead level of equality must not be sought at the sacrifice of the potentialities for the general good that lie in the free play of individuality. The various projects for securing a greater equality among men must be scrutinized with an eye to their total effects upon human happiness.

What flagrant forms of inequality exist in our society?

Equality is a modern ideal; in former times it was generally assumed that men inevitably belong to classes or castes; that some must have luxury and others poverty, some must rule and others obey. Plato, in constructing his ideal state, retains the walls between the small governing class, the warriors, and the mass of artisans, who are of no particular account but to get the work done. Castiglione, in his Book of the Courtier, declares that "there are many men who, although they are rational creatures, have only such share of reason as to recognize it, but not to possess or profit by it. These, therefore, are naturally slaves, and it is better and more profitable for them to obey than to command."

But the invention of the printing press brought ideas to the masses, the invention of gunpowder brought them power; the colonization of new continents leveled old distinctions of rank; the development of manufacture and commerce brought fortune and power to men of humble origin. The forces thus set in motion have resulted in our day in the general acceptance of political democracy witness in contemporary affairs the inception of the Portuguese Republic, the Chinese Republic, the abolition of the veto-power of the British House of Lords-and are creating a widespread belief in industrial democracy. So complete is our American acquiescence in the principle of equality in the abstract that it is difficult for us to realize the burning passions that underlay such familiar words as Don Quixote's, "Know, Sancho, that one man is no more than another unless he does more than another"; or Burns's "A man's a man for a' that"; or Tennyson's " 'Tis only noble to be good."

Yet, for all our abstract belief in equality, we have not become equal in opportunity, and in some ways are actually becoming less so. Land, for example, which was once to be had for the taking, is steadily rising in price, and is now, in most parts of the country, getting beyond the reach of the poor. Foreign observers agree that there is no other existing nation so plutocratic as our own; and wealth here is probably though the matter is in doubt becoming more and more concentrated. [Footnote: For a recent and cautious discussion of this point see F. W. Taussig, Principles of Economics, chap. 54, sec. 3. There is really no accurate information available to settle the question whether wealth is becoming more or less concentrated. Certainly the number of the rich has rapidly increased, and very many of the poor have risen into the class of the well to do. Wages and the scale of living of the poor have risen, but not in proportion to the total increase in wealth. The rich seem to be not only getting richer, but getting a larger SHARE of the national wealth.] It is estimated that one per cent of the inhabitants of our country now own more property than the remaining ninety-nine per cent.

The natural resources of the country have been to a considerable extent such natural monopolies as railways, telegraph and telephone service, gas and electric lighting, are controlled by, and largely in the interests of, a small owning class. The Astors have become enormously rich because one of their progenitors bought for an inconsiderable sum farm land on Manhattan Island which is now worth so many dollars a square foot. Others have made gigantic fortunes out of the country's forests, its coal deposits, its copper, its waterpower, its oil. A certain upper stratum of society is freed from the necessity of work, can exercise vast power over the lives of the poor, and use its great accumulations for personal luxury or at its caprice, in defiance of the general welfare. Such congestion of wealth involves poverty on the part of masses of the less fortunate. With no capital, the poor man cannot compete in the industrial game; he has no money to invest, no reserve to fall back upon; he must accept employers' terms or starve. He cannot pause to educate himself, to get the skill and knowledge that might enable him to work up the ladder. His power in politics is overshadowed by that of the great corporations with their funds and their control of legal skill. He cannot afford expert medical care, or proper hygienic conditions of life; he is lucky if he can get a measure of justice in the courts. To call such a situation one of equality is irony. It is certain that, far as we are yet from final solution of the problems of production, we are still farther from a solution of the problems of the distribution of wealth. "A new and fair division of the goods and rights of this world should be," De Tocqueville long ago declared, "the main object of all who conduct human affairs." What methods of equalizing opportunity are possible?

Three plans for a fairer distribution of wealth have been proposed. According to one, the profits from industry would be divided among the population on a basis of their NEEDS. This is, however, clearly impracticable; every one, would discover unlimited needs, and no one would be fit to make the apportionment. The second scheme is that all men should be paid alike for equal hours of work, or, rather, in proportion to the disagreeableness of the work, the amount of SACRIFICE made. This scheme is that usually advocated by Socialists. The objection to it is that equal pay for every man would take away the chief stimulus to initiative, skill, energy, efficiency; it would take the zest and excitement out of the game of life, make living too monotonous; there must be rewards for the ambitious youth, prizes to be won. The third plan proportions reward to efficiency. And on the whole, as men are constituted, it seems desirable to reward men financially according to their efficiency, so far as that can be measured.[Footnote: F. W. Taussig, Principles of Economics, chap. 64, sec. 3.] This does not mean to leave things as they are. For at present the shrewd, if also fortunate, are rewarded out of all proportion to their efficiency; and many who are not efficient at all, who even do no work at all that is socially useful, are among the wealthiest. Moreover, efficiency itself is only partly due to the individual's will and effort; it is due to the physique and gifts and fortune he has inherited, the education and environment that have molded him, the social situation in which he finds himself, the willingness of others to cooperate with him, and his good luck in early ventures. It seems unfair that to him that hath so much, so much more should be given. Or at least it seems fair that he that hath less should be given more favorable opportunity. It is not enough, as Professor Giddings says, to reward every man according to his performance; we must find a way to enable every man to achieve his potential performance. The plan of proportioning rewards to efficiency must be modified by mercy for the weak-minded and weak-bodied. It must be supplemented by earnest efforts to provide health, education, and favorable environment for all, and, by the limitation of the right of inheritance, that all may have, so far as possible, approximately equal opportunity. It must beware of judging efficiency by immediate and obvious results, must encourage inventions that ripen slowly, genius that stumbles and blunders before succeeding, work that contributes to others' results and makes no showing for itself. It must involve a restriction of the right to unearned incomes. To put these necessary corollaries to the efficiency-\ reward plan into concrete form:

(1) The handicap of ignorance must be removed by providing free education for all, to the point of enabling every one to develop efficiency in some vocation. Scholarships for the needy, the prohibition of child labor, and a high enough wage scale for adults to permit the youth of all classes to complete their education, are indispensable.

(2) The handicap of ill-health must be, so far as possible, removed by state support of mothers-so that children need not inherit a weakened constitution from overtired mothers, or suffer from want of care in infancy; by free medical aid to all; by strict legislation for sanitary housing, pure food, etc; by the provision of public parks and playgrounds.

(3) The possibility of exorbitant profits from industry (profits out of proportion to the actual contribution of the individual in skillful work, mental or manual) must be abolished, by one of the plans discussed in chapter XXVII.

(4) There must be abolition or sharp limitation of unearned incomes i.e., incomes for which a return to society in service has not been made by the getter. This is the step that is clearest of all theoretically, but the worst sticking point in practice. If we could persuade men that they should not reap where they have not sown, the gravest inequities of our present order would disappear. The sources of unearned incomes are, first, the "unearned increment" in land values; secondly, the "unearned increment" in the value of natural resources; thirdly, all interest on investment; fourthly, all wealth inherited or obtained by legacy or gift.

(a) Land in the heart of New York or London sells at fifteen million dollars or so an acre. The land value of Manhattan Island alone, the central part of New York City, is in the neighborhood of $3,500,000,000, and rapidly increasing. A few generations ago it was all bought from the Indians for $24. It is estimated that the "unearned increment" of land values in Berlin during fifty years has been between $500,000,000 and $750,000,000. What is true so strikingly in the case of these great cities is true, in lesser degree, of all cities and towns and villages that have grown in population. The total increase in land values in America since the days of the pioneers equals, of course, the present value of its land, since it was acquired by our forefathers without payment, or with only a nominal fee to the Indians. Almost all of this enormous increase in wealth has gone into the pockets of the fortunate individuals who got possession; very little into the public treasury. Our cities have remained terribly poor, always in debt, obliged to pass by many needed improvements and to impose heavy taxes on their citizens. Yet all this wealth (not counting improvements made by the possessor upon his land) has been socially created. Others have moved into the neighborhood, factories have been built near by, roads and railways and sewers and water systems and lighting-systems and police protection, and a hundred other things, have made the individual's land more and more salable. If our fathers had been wise enough to divert a large percentage of this increase in value into the public coffers, no one would have been wronged, but many private fortunes would today be smaller, and the entire population could have been free from taxation from the beginning, with plenty of money for all needed public works, including many that we can now only dream about.

It is easy to see what could have been done; to determine what should now be done is far more difficult. To try to regain for the public the unearned increments of past years would be an injustice to those who have purchased lands recently, at the increased prices, and even, perhaps, to those who have benefited by the increasing values, since they have regarded the increase as theirs and adjusted their expenditures to this added income. The best that could be done would be to take an inventory of all land values now, and provide for a recurrent reappraisal; then to take all, or a large percentage, of the increased value from now on. It would, indeed, be dangerous to attempt to take it all, on account of the extreme difficulty of drawing the line between earned and unearned increments; even the most painstaking and impartial decisions would be sometimes unjust. But to take half or two thirds of what should be deemed "unearned" would be practicable. Several modern States now take from ten to fifty per cent; and the percentage taken will doubtless increase. The objections to such a course are twofold. In the first place, it is pointed out that if the unearned increment of value is appropriated by the State, the State should recoup landowners for all undeserved decrements of value; it is not fair to take away the possibility of gain and leave the possibility of loss. So long, however, as our population grows, the State could afford to make good the comparatively few cases of decreased value and yet get a big income. The other objection is that the hope of winning the increased land values has been a great and needed incentive to the development of the country, and a legitimate compensation for the hardships of pioneering. But while this is true of the earlier days, it applies less and less to present conditions, and is hardly at all applicable to the profits made in city lands. On the whole, there seems little objection to the appropriation by the State henceforth of the unearned increments of land value. But the days of enormous increments are passing, and land will presently reach a comparatively stable value. So that this method of preventing inflated fortunes must be counted, on the whole except for new and rapidly growing communities a lost opportunity. [Footnote: H. J. Davenport, State and Local Taxation, pp. 294-303. F. C. Howe, European Cities at Work, pp. 189-207. Quarterly Journal of Economics, vol. 22, p. 83; vol. 25, p. 682; vol. 27, p. 539. Political Science Quarterly, vol. 27, p. 586. National Municipal Review, vol. 3, p. 354. F. W. Taussig, Principles of Economics, chap. 44, sec. 5.]

(b) What is true of land is true of the natural resources of the country-coal, minerals, oil, gas, waterpower, forests. These were seized, with a small payment or none, by the early comers, and sold later at a great advance, or worked for an increasing profit by the owner. Here, again, if the nation had maintained an inventory of these values and appropriated to itself all or a percentage of the increase in value (which results from the increasing public need of the resources and the limited supply, together with the increase in facilities for transportation, etc, rather than from the owner's labor or skill), many of our present gross inequalities in wealth would have been forestalled, and the community would be far richer in its common wealth. Add to the realization of this fact the sight of the reckless waste by private owners of such resources as can be wasted, and the present conservation movement is fully explained. The best that can now be done is to retain under government ownership such natural resources as have not yet passed into private hands, and to appropriate further increases in value of those that are privately owned. [Footnote: C. R. Van Hise, Concentration and Control, pp. 154-66. Outlook, vol. 85, p. 426; vol. 86, p. 716; vol. 93, p. 770; vol. 95, p. 21.]

(c) Practically all of the upper classes add to the incomes they earn by labor of hands or brain an "unearned" income derived from investment; i.e., from the willingness of others to pay for the use of their accumulated wealth or lands. A considerable class is thus enabled, if it chooses, to live without working. A great proportion of this wealth that draws interest was never itself earned by the possessors, in the stricter sense of the word "earned"; it has come to them by inheritance, by the increase of value of land or natural resources, or squeezed out of labor and the public by the unregulated profits of some autocratically managed industry or franchise. Is it expedient to allow this accumulated wealth to bring an income to its possessors? There are two possibilities: one goes with government control of private industry, the other with industrial socialism.

According to the first plan, income might still be derived from money in savings banks, from stocks and bonds, and from the rent of land and buildings. But it would cease to be a serious source of inequality. For if the unearned increment of land values and natural resources were deflected to the State, if none but moderate profits were allowed from industry; and if, in addition, the right of inheritance and gift were sharply curtailed, there would be, after a generation, no large fortunes left or thereafter possible. A man might receive by legacy a moderate amount of money, a little land or property; by working efficiently and living simply he might add continually to his investments and so come to have an income measurably beyond his earnings. But he could not get wealth enough for investment to be freed in perpetuity from the necessity of earning his living; and inequalities of wealth could not become very great; no greater, perhaps, than would be consistent with the greatest happiness.

According to the socialistic plan, since all industry would be run by the State, on state provided capital, there would be no demand for a man's savings except for purely personal uses, no stocks and no bonds, no savings banks, except for the safe deposit of money and valuables. All interest might then be forbidden; and a man would save merely for future use, or to pass on to others, not for the sake of drawing a further income from his savings. All rent must then in fairness be forbidden also, except such payments as would be a fair return for improvements made, buildings constructed, with the cost of repairs, insurance, etc. This would result in all land being owned by the users, and do away with landlordism. The unearned increment would be so widely distributed that it would be needless, for purposes of equalizing distribution, to bother with it, though it might still be appropriated by the State as a means of increasing its revenue. This scheme would make it impossible for any one to live without earning his livelihood, except during such periods as his accumulated earnings would tide him over. It would, indeed, lessen the incentive to saving; but if it were buttressed by the provision of fair salaries for all and by universal insurance against illness, accident, old age, and death, there would no longer be much need of saving. This social order would be eminently just, leaving only such inequalities in wealth as would result from the differences in productive efficiency of different men, coupled with a moderate right of inheritance. Its practicability, however, hinges upon the general practicability of socialism, which must remain for the present an open question. [Footnote: F. W. Taussig, Principles of Economics, chap. 46; chap. 66, sec. 5; chap. 64, radical change as this lies beyond the range of immediate possibilities]

(d) The right of inheritance and gift, which we have had to mention as aggravating other sources of inequality, needs, as matters are at present, drastic curtailment. The tax must not, indeed, be heavy enough to encourage spendthrift living and lessen thrift, or to cut too deeply into the capital necessary for carrying on business. But a carefully devised tax can escape these dangers; and it is plainly not best for society, or for the heirs themselves in most cases, that they should have irresponsible use of large sums of money which they have not earned in a world where millions are starving, physically, mentally, and spiritually, for lack of what money can provide. If, however, the plan last outlined is ever carried into effect, there will be no need of restricting the right of inheritance; even the alternative plan would require little attention to inheritance after present inequalities had been approximately leveled, as there would then be little opportunity for large accumulations. A sharply graded inheritance tax may therefore be looked upon as a now necessary but temporary expedient.[Footnote: F. W. Taussig, Principles of Economics, chap. 54, sec. 5; chap. 67. secs. 5, 6.] We may conclude with the consideration of four special problems that are related, in some aspect, to the conceptions of equality and privilege.

What are the ethics of:

I. The single tax? The single-tax idea is that all the public revenue should be raised by a land tax. The push behind the movement comes from the sight of the unearned fortunes that have been made out of land. The term is used loosely by some to mean merely the taking or taxing by the State, as we have already suggested, of all future unearned increments of land value, so far as they can be computed. But, this would not now provide enough revenue for most communities, and so would not really make possible a single tax. The real single tax would involve taking in taxation not only future INCREASES in values, but ALL the rental value of land. Even this would not always produce revenue enough, as the needs of public revenue bear no relation to the land values in a given area. But it would in most places produce considerably more than enough revenue. Land taxes in New York City, for example, if trebled, would supply all the revenue; they would have to be quintupled to absorb the entire rental value of the land the city stands on. The simplicity of the scheme appeals to many-especially to those who own no land. But it amounts to a confiscation of land values by the State, which would be unjust to land-owners, however advantageous to the rest of the community. It means charging everybody rent for the land he now owns. Present tenants would be no worse off, but present owners of the land they use, as well as landlords, would be hard hit. Let us consider each in turn.

A considerable proportion of the land is owned by the users, the majority of whom are members of the middle class and but moderately well to do. Upon them the burden of supporting our increasing public undertakings would largely fall. But why? THEY are not getting any unearned income. THEY have, in most cases, paid pretty nearly full value for their land, even though that land was originally acquired for little or nothing. They have put their earnings into land in good faith, when they might have put it into industry or enjoyed its use. The single tax would work grave injustice to them. It would also be practically inexpedient, in drawing the public revenue largely from a class that can less afford it, while leaving hardly touched most of the bigger fortunes, which consist seldom chiefly of land oldings. But even as to that part of the land that is bringing unearned income to landlords is it fair to stop that income unless we stop all other forms of income on investment? One man has put his fortune into stocks or bonds; he draws his five per cent in security with no further trouble than clipping coupons; another, having put an equal fortune into land, finds his five per cent income entirely confiscated. Not by such class legislation can justice be served or equality produced. The landlord class deserves no worse than the stockholder class or the investor in a savings bank. It is fair, as we suggested above, to put an end to ALL incomes from investment, and make every man live on his earnings; it is not fair to pick out landlords for exploitation.

II. Free trade and protection?

Free trade is undoubtedly the ultimate industrial ideal; not as a natural right, but as a matter of mutual advantage, that everything may be manufactured in the most economical place and way. The geographical division of labor is as generally advantageous as the assignment of highly specialized tasks within a community. Import duties result in diverting labor into less economical channels, and hence entail a loss to the community as a whole. The prosperity of the United States has been in considerable measure the result of its complete internal free trade. On this general truth the best economists are pretty universally agreed. The argument that a tariff wall is necessary to maintain our generally higher standard of wages and living is pure fallacy, as, indeed, can be seen in the fact that wages in free-trade England are higher than in protectionist Germany. The only legitimate economic question is whether special advantages may accrue from protecting certain industries under certain peculiar conditions. For example, a new industry, in the conduct of which skill has not yet been acquired, may need nursing while it is growing strong enough to produce as cheaply as foreign competitors. Again, when foreign nations impose a tax upon our products, it may be politically expedient to impose a counter-tariff, as a means toward reciprocity and eventual free trade. But the discussion of such situations involves no ethical principles, and may be left to the economists and statesmen.

The considerations that concern the moralist are rather such as these: Is it advisable to keep our own people self-sufficing, producing all they need to consume? Is it permissible to protect (by a subsidy, which is equivalent to an import duty in other matters) our foreign merchant marine, so as to have the satisfaction of seeing our flag flying in foreign ports and the assurance of plenty of transports, colliers, etc, in case of war? Or is it better for humanity that the nations should become mutually interdependent, requiring one another's products and somewhat at one another's mercy in case of war? There can be no doubt that the narrower, "patriotic" view retards the deepest interests of humanity, and that free trade is to be sought not only as a means toward economic prosperity, but as an avenue toward universal peace.

The other dominant ethical aspect of the situation lies in the fact that the tariff plays into the hands of certain monopolies, enables them to maintain high prices and make excessive profits, which international competition would reduce. As actually used, the American tariff is largely an instrument for favoring special classes of manufacturers at the general expense, and so is to be condemned.

On the other hand, where manufacturers are enabled by the tariff merely to make fair profits, and economic considerations would dictate a removal of the duty and the shifting of labor to industries where it could be more regard for vested interests should make us pause. To ruin an industry in which capitalists have invested their fortunes and laborers have acquired skill, although it would be in the end for the general good, would work unjust hardship to them; in such cases, then, a tariff should be lowered only with great caution, or some compensation should be made to the individuals who suffer loss thereby.

III. The control of immigration? Another contemporary question is whether discrimination may rightfully be exercised in the admission of aliens to residence in our country. Abstract considerations would suggest the desirability of equal treatment to all comers. But certain practical effects must be considered.

(1) The admission of hordes of ill-educated and ill-disciplined immigrants from countries lower in the scale of progress than our own is a serious menace to the ideals and standards of living that we have at great cost evolved. Our own morals and manners are not firmly enough fixed to be sure of withstanding the downward pull of more primitive conceptions and habits. Their willingness to work for small wages lowers the remuneration of Americans; their contentment with wretched living conditions blocks our attempts to raise the general standard of life. Many of them are unappreciative of American ideals, easily misled by corrupt politicians, and thus a deadweight against political and social advance. We may, perhaps, disregard the poverty of the immigrant, if he is in good health and able to work; we may even disregard his lack of education, if he is mentally sound and reasonably intelligent. But if some practicable method could be devised to lessen radically the incoming stream of those who are low in their standards of living, we should be spared the social indigestion from which we now suffer. One feasible suggestion is to limit the number of immigrants annually admitted from each country to a certain small percentage of the number of natives of that country already resident here. In that way the total number could be restricted without offense to any nation, and those peoples most easily assimilated would be admitted in greatest proportions. In addition, naturalization should be permitted only after a number of years, during which the immigrant would be in danger of deportation for proved criminality, vicious indulgence, intemperance, shiftlessness, troublesome agitation, and other undesirable traits.

(2) The admission of peoples of very alien race to residence side by side with our own inevitably gives rise to friction and unpleasantness. However irrational it may be, there are instinctive antipathies and distrusts between the different racial stocks. The importation of the Negroes brought us a terrible racial problem, one for which there seems no satisfactory solution. White men as a class dislike living side by side with them, and fiercely resent intermarriage, which might ultimately merge the races, as it seems to be doing in South America. A general feeling of brotherhood and social democracy is greatly retarded by this racial chasm.[Footnote: Cf. J. M. Mecklin, Democracy and Race Friction.] It is earnestly to be hoped that Chinese, Japanese, Hindus, and other non-European races may not be admitted to residence here in any great degree; similar antipathies and resentments would be added to our existing discords. It is not that these races are inferior to our own, they are simply different; and however superficial the differences, they are just the sort of differences that cause social friction. Precisely the same argument would apply to the exodus of Americans and Europeans to Asiatic countries. A certain amount of intermingling of students, travelers, missionaries, traders, is highly beneficial, in the exchange of ideas and manners it stimulates; that the main racial stocks should remain apart, on their several continents, in that mutual respect and brotherhood that the superficial repugnancies of too close contact tend to destroy. The plan suggested at the close of the preceding paragraph would sufficiently avert these undesirable racial migrations.

IV. The woman-movement? The demand of women for a larger life and a recognition from men of their full equality has found expression recently, not only in the hysterical and criminal acts of British suffragettes, but in many soberer revolts against the traditional assignment of duties and privileges. We may agree at once in deploring the exclusion of women from any rights and opportunities which are not inconsistent with a wise division of labor, and that patronizing air of superiority shown toward them by so many men-a condescension not incompatible with tenderness and chivalry. Theirs has been the repressed and petted sex. Yet there are no adequate grounds for supposing that men are, on an average, really abler or saner or more reasonable naturally than women; that they are, indeed, in any essential sense different, except for the results of their different education and life, and such divergences as the differentiation of sex itself involves including an average greater physical strength.[Footnote: But cf. Munsterberg, Psychology and Social Sanity, p. 195] Men and women are naturally equals; with equally good training they can contribute almost equally to the world's work; they have an equal right to education, a useful vocation, and the free pursuit of happiness. But equal rights do not necessarily imply identical duties; there is a certain division of labor laid down by nature. Women alone can bear children, mothers alone can properly rear them; no incubators and institutions can supply this fundamental need. If women, in their eagerness to compete with men in other occupations, neglect in any great numbers this most difficult and honorable of all vocations, there will be a dangerous decline in the numbers and the nurture of coming generations. Moreover, if homes are not to be supplanted by boarding houses and hotels, the great majority of women must stay at home and do the work which makes a home possible. Home making and child rearing are the duties that always have been and always will be the lot of most women; and they are duties too exacting to permit of being conjoined with any other vocation.

On the other hand, the woman who has servants and rears no children should be pushed by public opinion into some outside occupation; women have no more right to idle than men. All unmarried women, when past the years that may properly be devoted to education, should certainly enter upon some useful vocation; and there is no reason why (with a few obvious exceptions) any occupation save the more physically arduous should be closed to such. Every girl should be prepared for some remunerative work, in case she does not marry or her husband dies leaving her childless. Such economic independence would, further, have the inestimable value that she would be under no pressure to marry in order to be supported and have an honorable place in the world; if she is trained to earn her living she will be free to marry only for love. If she does marry, and gives up her prior vocation to be housekeeper and child-rearer, she should be legally entitled to half her husband's earnings. The grave difficulty is that a woman needs to prepare herself both for her probable duties as housekeeper and mother, and also for her possible need of earning a living otherwise. Education in the former duties, that must fall to the great majority of women, cannot safely be neglected, as it is so largely today; the only general solution will be for unmarried women to adopt, as a class, the vocations for which less careful preparation is necessary.

The question of the ballot is not practically of great importance, first, because equal suffrage is coming very fast, whatever we may say, and, secondly, because it will make no great difference when it comes. There is no natural right in the matter; the decision in political affairs might well be left to half the population-when that half cuts so completely through all classes and sections-if the saving in expense or trouble seemed to make it expedient. The interests of women are identical with those of men. Women are, in most parts of this country, as well off before the law as men; they do not need the ballot to remedy any unjust discriminations. Moreover, the ballot will mean the necessity of sharing the burden of political responsibility. The women who look upon the right to vote as a plum to be grasped for, a something which they want because men have it, with no conception of the training necessary to exercise that right responsibly, are not fit to be trusted with it. It often seems that it were better to restrict our present trustful and generous right of suffrage to those who can show evidence of intelligence and responsibility, rather than to double the number of shallow and untrained voters.

But, on the other hand, there is reason to suppose that women, through their greater interest in certain goods, will materially accelerate some reforms-as, the sanitation of cities, the improvement of education, child-welfare legislation, the warfare against alcohol and prostitution. The actual results already attained where women vote are, on the whole, important enough to warrant the extension of the right, as a matter of social expediency. Moreover, the very increase in the number of voters makes the securing of power through bribery more difficult; and the entrance of women into politics will probably hasten their purification in many places. At any rate, the necessity of voting will tend to develop a larger interest among women in public affairs, to fit them better for the education of their children, and to do away with the lingering sense of the inferiority of women. Certain it is, finally, that an increasing number of women want the vote, and will not rest till they get it.

General: F. W. Taussig, Principles of Economics, chap. 54. W. E. Weyl, The New Democracy, book I. Adams and Sumner, Labor Problems, chap. XIII. C. B. Spahr, The Present Distribution of Wealth in the United States. Dewey and Tufts, Ethics, chap. XXV, secs. 6, 7. Atlantic Monthly, vol. 112, pp. 480, 679. The single tax: Henry George, Progress and Poverty; Social Problems. R. C. Fillebrown, The A.B.C. of Taxation. Outlook, vol. 94, p. 311. Shearman, Natural Taxation. Atlantic Monthly, vol. 112, p. 737; vol. 113, pp. 27, 545. H. R. Seager, Introduction to Economics, chap, XXVI, secs. 283-88. F. W. Taussig, op. cit, chap. 42, sec. 7. Arena, vol. 34, p. 500; vol. 35, p. 366. New World, vol. 7, p. 87. Free trade: North American Review, vol. 189, p. 194. Quarterly Review, vol. 202, p. 250. H. Fawcett, Free Trade and Protection. W. J. Ashley, The Tariff Problem. H. R. Seager, op. cit, chap. XX, secs. 211-17. F. W. Taussig, op. cit, chaps. 36, 37. Immigration: Jenks and Lauck, The Immigration Problem. H. P. Fairchild, Immigration. Adams and Sumner, Labor Problems, chap. III. F. J. Warne, The Immigrant Invasion. A. Shaw, Political Problems, pp. 62-86. North American Review, vol. 199, p. 866. Nineteenth Century, vol. 57, p. 294. Educational Review, vol. 29, p. 245. Forum, vol. 42, p. 552. Charities, vol. 12, p. 129. Quarterly Journal of Economics, vol. 16, pp. 1, 141. The woman question: J. S. Mill, The Subjection of Women. C. P. Gilman, Women and Economics. O. Schreiner, Woman and Labor. K. Schirmacher, The Modern Woman's Rights Movement. Jane Addams, Newer Ideals of Peace, chap. VII. F. Kelley, Some Ethical Gains through Legislation, chap. V. Outlook, vol. 82, p. 167; vol. 91, pp. 780, 784, 836; vol. 95, p. 117; vol. 101, pp. 754, 767. Atlantic Monthly, vol. 112, pp. 48, 191, 721. Century, vol. 87, pp. 1, 663. National Municipal Review, vol. 1, p. 620.

CHAPTER XXX
THE FUTURE OF THE RACE

In proportion as fair means are found and utilized for remedying the gross inequalities in the present distribution of wealth, and big fortunes disappear, it will become necessary for the State to undertake more and more generally the functions that have, during the last few generations, been largely dependent upon private philanthropy. This will be an advantage not merely in putting this welfare work upon a securer basis, but in enlisting the loyalty of the masses to the Government. Much of the energy and devotion which are now given to the labor-unions, because in them alone the workers see hope of help, might be given to the State if it should take upon itself more adequately to minister to the people's needs. The rich can get health and beauty for themselves; but the poor are largely dependent upon public provision for a wholesome and cheerful existence. Laissez-faire individualism has provided them with saloons; in the new age the State must provide them with something better than saloons. "Flowers and sunshine for all," in Richard Jefferies' wistful phrase-the State should make a determined and thoroughgoing effort, not merely to repress, to punish, to palliate conditions, but in every positive way that expert thought can devise and the people will vote to support, to add to the worth of human life. We may consider these paternal functions of government under three heads: the improvement of human environment, to make it more beautiful and convenient; the development, through educational agencies, of the mental and moral life of the people; and the improvement, by various means, of the human stock itself.

In what ways should the State seek to better human environment?

(1) Municipal governments should supervise town and village planning. The riotous individualism of our American people has resulted in the haphazard growth of countless dreary towns and an architectural anarchy that resembles nothing more than an orchestra playing with every instrument tuned to a different key. The stamp of public control is to be seen, if at all, in an inconvenient and monotonous chessboard plan for streets. Congestion of traffic at the busy points; wide stretches of empty pavement on streets little used; houses of every style and no style, imbued with all the colors of the spectrum; weed-grown vacant lots, unkempt yards, some fenced, some unfenced; poster-bedecked billboards-verily, the average American town is not a thing of beauty. Matthew Arnold's judgment is corroborated by every traveler. "Evidently," he wrote, "this is that civilization's weak side. There is little to nourish and delight the sense of

beauty there." A certain crudeness is inevitable in a new country, and will be outgrown; age is a great artist. Man usually mars with his first strokes; and it is only when he has met his practical needs that he will dally with aesthetic considerations. Many of our older cities and villages have partly outgrown the awkward age, become dignified in the shade of spreading trees, and fallen somehow into a kind of unity; a few of them, especially near the Atlantic seaboard, where the stupid rectangularity of the towns farther west was never imposed, are among the loveliest in the world. But in general, in spite of many costly, and some really beautiful, buildings, and acknowledging the individual charm of many of the wide piazzaed shingled houses of the well-to-do, and the general effect of spaciousness, our towns and villages are shockingly, depressingly ugly. Money enough has been spent to create a beautiful effect; the failure lies in that unrestrained individualism that permits each owner to build any sort of a structure, and to color it any hue, that appeals to his fancy, without regard to its effect upon neighboring buildings or upon the eyes of passers-by. All sorts of architectural atrocities are committed-curious false fronts, fancy shingles, scroll-work balustrades, and the like;-in the town where these words are written, a builder of a number of houses has satisfied a whim to give eyebrows to his windows, in the shape of flat arches of alternate red and white bricks, with an extraordinarily grotesque and discomforting effect. But even where the buildings are good separately, the general effect is, unless by coincidence, a sad chaos.

In the more progressive countries of Europe matters are not left thus to the caprice of individuals; in some German towns, and the so-called garden cities of England, we have excellent examples of scientific town planning, conducing to homogeneity, convenience, and beauty. The awakening social sense in this country will surely lead soon to a general conviction of the duty of an oversight of street planning and building in the interests of the community as a whole. There is no reason why our towns should not be sensibly laid out, according to a prearranged and rational plan; they might have individuality, picturesqueness, charm; be full of interesting separate notes, yet harmonious in design, making a single composition, like a great mosaic. Such an environment would have its subconscious effects upon the morals of the people, would awaken a new sense of community loyalty, and drive home the lesson of the necessity and beauty of the cooperative spirit.

Among the features of this town planning are these:

Streets must be laid out in conformity with the topography of the neighborhood and the direction of traffic. Gentle curves, or frequent circles, as in Washington, must break the monotony of straight lines; the natural features of the landscape, hills, bluffs, a river, must be utilized to give character to the town. The height of buildings must be regulated in relation to the width of the streets, and the percentage of ground space that may be built upon determined. All designs for buildings must be approved by the community architects with consideration of their harmony with neighboring buildings. A public landscape architect should have supervision over and give expert advice for the planting of trees and shrubbery and the beautifying of yards back as well as front. Factories and shops should be confined to certain designated portions of a town (and the smoke nuisance strictly controlled); disfiguring billboards and overhead wires done away with; parks laid out and kept intact from intrusion of streets or buildings. Fortunately, the majority of our American houses, built of wood, are temporary in character; and most city buildings at present have a life of but a generation or two. In this evanescence of our contemporary architecture lies the hope for an eventual regeneration of American towns. In the city and village of the future, life will be so bosomed in beauty that there will be less need of artificial beauty-seeking and gaslight pleasures. A healthy local pride will be fostered and community life come into its own again.

(2) Municipalities should provide facilities for wholesome recreation out of doors. Children, in particular, ought not to be obliged, for lack of other space, to play upon city streets, where they impede traffic and run serious risks. [Footnote: On New York City streets two hundred and thirty-one children were killed in twenty-one months, according to recent figures.] Schoolyards should be larger than they generally are, and bedtime; in the big cities the roofs should be utilized also. Every neighborhood should have its ample playgrounds. For want of such provision children of the poor grow up pale and pinched, without the normalizing and educative influence of healthy play, and with no proper outlet for their energies, so that crime and vice flourish prematurely. With proper foresight open spaces can be retained as a city grows, without great expense; the economic gain, in a reduced death-rate, reduced cost for doctors and nurses, police, courts, and prisons, and increased efficiency of the next generation of workers, will easily balance the outlay, without weighing the gain in happiness and morality.[Footnote: See on this point, the literature of the Division of Recreation of the Russell Sage Foundation, and of the Playground and Recreation Association of America (1 Madison Avenue, New York City). Jane Addams, The Spirit of Youth and the City Streets. C. Zueblin, American Municipal Progress, chap IX. J. Lee, Constructive and Preventive Philanthropy, chaps. VIII-XII. Outlook, vol. 87, p. 775; vol. 95, p. 511; vol. 96, p. 443.] But, indeed, adults stand also in need of outdoor life. Grounds for ball games, bowls, and all sorts of sports should be generously provided if human life is not to lose one of its pleasantest and most useful aspects. For evenings there should be attractive social meeting-places, neighborhood clubs, supervised dance halls, and the like, such as the social settlements now to a slight extent provide, with notably beneficial results.

As the poorer classes come more and more into their inheritance of the fruits of industry, these desiderata may perhaps be again left to private initiative; but at present there is a large class too pressed by poverty to get for itself these necessities of a normal life; and the need of the people makes the duty of the State.[Footnote: Cf. C. R. Henderson, The Social Spirit in America, chap. XIV.]

(3) The States and the Nation must be careful to conserve the natural resources of the country from waste, and advantage of the people. The forests, still so recklessly felled, must be guarded, not only for the sake of the future timber supply, but to prevent floods, ensure a proper supply of water in times of drought, and preserve the soil from being washed away. The scientific practice of forestry, the maintenance of an efficient fire patrol, and the reforestation of denuded areas that can best be utilized for the growth of timber, must be undertaken or supervised by government experts. The very limited supplies of coal, oil, and natural gas must be protected from waste. Arid lands must be brought into use where irrigation is possible, swamp lands drained, waterways and harbors improved to their full usefulness.[Footnote: On national conservation, see C. R. Van Hise, The Conservation of Natural Resources. Outlook, vol. 93, p. 770. Atlantic Monthly, vol. 101, p. 694. Review of Reviews, vol. 37, p. 585. Chautauquan, vol. 55, pp. 21, 33, 112.] National and state highways must be built as object-lessons to the towns and counties that still leave their roads a stretch of mud or sand.[Footnote: It is estimated that ninety per cent of the public roads in the United States are still unimproved; that the average cost of hauling produce is twenty-five cents a mile-ton, as against twelve cents in France; that $300,000,000 a year would be saved in hauling expenses if our roads were as good as those of western Europe.] All of these material improvements have their civilizing influence, their moral significance; as Edmond Kelly put it, "By constructing our environment with intelligence we can determine the direction of our own development." So it is of no small consequence what sort of homes and cities we live in. During the next generation or so, while the State is slowly bestirring itself to undertake these duties, there will be great need of civic and village improvement associations, women's clubs, merchants' associations, etc, to arouse public interest, demonstrate possibilities, and stir up municipal holidays, Memorial Day, Independence Day, Arbor Day, Thanksgiving Day, etc, should be used to stimulate civic pride in these matters; pulpit and press should be brought into line. It will be a slow and discouraging, but necessary, task to awaken the people to a realization of the potentialities for a better civilization that lie in the utilization of government powers. What should be done in the way of public education? The principle of state support of education has, happily, been pretty fully accepted in this country, although in the East the universities still have to depend upon private benefactions.

The public-school system is excellent in plant and principle; the next step is to work out a rational curriculum. The average high-school graduate today has learned little of what he most needs to know how to earn his living, how to spend his money wisely, how to live. The average girl knows little of housekeeping, less of the duties of motherhood.[Footnote: Cf. H. Spencer, Education, chap. I: "Is it not an astonishing fact that though on the treatment of offspring depend their lives or deaths, and their moral value or ruin, yet not one word of instruction on the treatment of offspring is ever given to those who will hereafter be parents? Is it not monstrous that the fate of a new generation should be left to the chances of unreasoning custom, impulse, fancy . . . ?" The whole chapter is worth reading; the neglect of which Spencer complained still persists.] The dangers of sex indulgence-the greatest of all perils to youth, the poisonous effects of alcohol, the necessities of bodily hygiene, are seldom effectively taught. Moral and religious education is, owing to our sectarianism, almost absolutely neglected. The evils of political corruption and unscrupulousness in business, the social problems that so insistently beset us, are little discussed in school. Yet here is an enormous opportunity for the awakening of moral idealism and the social spirit. Boys and girls in their teens can be brought to an eager interest in moral and social problems; class after class could be sent out fired with enthusiasm to remedy wrongs and push for a higher civilization. The failure to awaken more of this dormant good will and energy, and to direct it for the elevation of community standards and the solution of community problems, is a grave indictment against our complacent "stand-pat" educational system. Religious instruction will be a delicate matter for the indefinite future; but inspirational talks on non-controversial themes should find place, and perhaps a presentation of different religious views in rotation by representatives of different communions. In some way, at least, recognition should be made of the important role played by religion in life. Besides the school system, other means of public education must be extended. The libraries and art museums must reach a wider public. The docent-work in the museums is a recent undertaking of considerable importance. Free public lectures, free mothers' schools, city kindergartens, municipal concerts, university extension courses-such enterprises will doubtless become universal. The work of the National Government in spreading knowledge of scientific methods of agriculture and of practicable methods of improving country life- information about the installation of plumbing systems, water supply, sewage systems, electric lights, etc.- is of wide educational value. In 1911 the average schooling of Americans was five years apiece. Such inadequate preparation for life is a disgrace to our prosperous age. Education should be universally compulsory until the late teens at least; it should be regarded not as a luxury, like kid gloves and caviar, but as the normal development of a human being and the common heritage. It ought not to be the exclusive privilege of "gentlemen"- of certain select, upper- class individuals; as economic conditions are straightened out, universal education will become practically feasible. It is not only as a matter of justice, but in the interests of public welfare, that education should be given to all. It will actually pay in dollars and cents, in increased efficiency, more intelligent voting, decreased crime, decreased commercial prostitution, and crazy propaganda of all sorts. The city of Boston was right in inscribing on its public library the motto: "The commonwealth requires the education of the people as the safeguard of order and liberty." What can be done by eugenics? Environment and education are of enormous importance in determining what the mature individual shall be. But the result is strictly limited by the material they have to work upon; the individual who is handicapped by heredity cannot expect to catch up with him who starts the race of life better equipped, if both have equally favorable influences and opportunities. These influences can effect little permanent improvement in the human stock; that can only be radically bettered by seeing to it that individuals of superior stock have children and those of inferior stock do not. We have "harnessed heredity" to produce better types of wheat and roses and cattle and horses and dogs; why not produce better types of men? The study of these possibilities constitutes the new science of eugenics, which its founder, Francis Galton, defined as the study of "those agencies which humanity through social control may use for the improvement or the impairment of the racial qualities of future generations." Dr. Kellogg defines it as "taking advantage of the facts of heredity to make the human race better." "Good breeding of the human species." We may first ask what duties the disclosures of this new science lay upon the individual.

(1) The constitutional health of children is partly deter parents at the time of conception and birth. Most deaths of newborn infants are due to prenatal influences. Overstrain, malnutrition, alcoholism, and all physical excesses tend to cause physical degeneracy in the offspring. It is obviously the duty of prospective parents- and that means practically all healthy young people-to keep themselves well and strong, so as to give a good endowment of health to their children.

(2) Feeble-mindedness, epilepsy, some forms of insanity, and some venereal diseases are inheritable defects; those who suffer from them must refrain from having children. Studies of the "Jukes" family and the "Kallikak" family, and others, show convincingly the spread of these defects where defectives marry. To bring children into the world to bear such burdens- and to cost the State, as they are almost sure to, for their support [Footnote: The descendants of the original degenerate couple of "Jukes" cost New York State in seventy-five years $1,300,000. See R. L. Dugdale,

The Jukes. H. H. Goddard, The Kallikak Family]-ought to be regarded as a grave sin.

(3) Little positive advice can yet be given as to those who are BEST fitted to have children, except in the matter of health and freedom from inheritable defects. According to Professor Boaz,[Footnote: F. Boaz, The Mind of Primitive Man.] one racial stock is about as good as another; so whatever selection is to be made may be between individual strains. But to breed the human stock for beauty, energy, mental ability, immunity to disease, sanity, or what not, is a task far beyond our present knowledge. Personal value and reproductive value are not closely correlative; and the factors that determine a good inheritance are highly complex. So that the choice of wife and husband may be left to those instinctive affinities and preferences which will in any case continue to be the deciding causes for the strong and educated and well-to-do to beget and rear children; the tendency to "race-suicide" among the upper classes is a matter for serious alarm. That portion of the population that is least able to give proper nurture to children, and to train them up to American ideals, is producing them in overwhelmingly greatest numbers. The older stocks in this country are dying out and being replaced by the large families of the east and south European immigrants. In England also, we are told, one sixth of the population, and this the least desirable sixth, is producing half of the coming generation. In 1790 the American family averaged 5.8 persons; in 1900 the average was 4.6. Among native Americans the average is lower still. College graduates are failing to reproduce their own numbers. Everywhere the Western peoples are breeding more and more slowly, while the Orientals, Negroes, and, in general, the less civilized peoples, are multiplying rapidly. Unless the upper classes in western Europe and America cease their selfish refusal to rear citizens, the earth will be inherited by the more backward peoples. This means, plainly, a perpetual clog upon progress. We may now ask what the State should demand in the interests of race- improvement.

(1) Health certificates may be required from both parties at marriage i.e., marriage may be prohibited without a guarantee from a licensed physician of freedom from communicable or inheritable disease, or inheritable defects. This seems the minimum of protection due the contracting parties themselves, as well as due the next generation.

(2) Marriage restrictions are easily evaded, however; unscrupulous physicians can usually be found to sign certificates. And where marriage is prohibited, illegitimacy is sure to flourish. Hence the segregation (with proper care) of those obviously unfit to become parents seems necessary. Great as would be the initial expense, the rapid reduction in the number of idiots, epileptics, etc, would in a generation or two counterbalance it and

greatly diminish the problem. It is estimated that there are some three hundred thousand feeble- minded persons in the United States, only twenty thousand of whom are segregated in institutions, the rest being free to propagate-which they do with notorious rapidity. Most of them can be made self-supporting; and real as the hardship to some of them may be in confining them from sex relations, the sacrifice seems demanded by the welfare of coming generations.

(3) An alternative to segregation (for inheritable, but not for communicable, diseases) is sterilization. The operation when performed on adults seems to have no effects upon character or the enjoyment of life, not even interfering with ordinary sex gratification. It is not painful, and perfectly harmless, to man; for women there is a risk, which is said, however, to be slight.[Footnote: Cf. Dr. E. C. Jones, in Woman's Medical Journal, December, 1912.] Sterilization permits the unfit to be entirely at liberty, to marry, if they can find mates, and to have all the pleasures of life except that of parenthood. A number of the American States have passed laws permitting the compulsory sterilization of certain very restricted classes of people undesirable as parents, at the discretion of the proper authorities; and this seems, on the whole, at least in the case of men, the best solution.

(4) Of an entirely different nature is the movement to secure state support for mothers; a movement, however, which is also eugenic in its intent. At present those parents who are zealous to maintain a high standard of living, those with talents which they are ambitious to develop, and those who realize keenly the care and expense that children need, are deterred from having many, or any; while the shiftless and happy-go-lucky propagate without scruple. There is, for all except the rich, a premium on childlessness, which the natural desire for parenthood cannot wholly discount. But this ought not to be so. Childbearing and rearing is a very necessary and arduous vocation, in which all the best women should be enlisted. In a socialistic regime the State would as a matter of course pay for this work as well as for all other productive work. But state endowment of motherhood, the payment of "maternity benefits," may be practiced apart from industrial socialism. It may be objected that the removal of economic pressure would bring an undue increase in population and the evils that Malthus feared. But the tendency of advancing civilization seems to be so strikingly toward a declining birth-rate-a phenomenon unrecognized in this country because of the tide of immigration, but apparent in western Europe-that the net outcome may be attained of a stationary population. Moreover, the scheme in question would not only tend to increase the number of children born to the prudent among the middle classes, it would enable mothers and prospective mothers to save themselves from that overwork which enfeebles so many children today; it would insure them the

means to care properly for the children. State inspectors would visit homes and examine the children of state supported mothers; the amount granted might vary in proportion to the care apparently given to the children, their cleanliness, health, progress in education, the clothing, food, air, and space provided for them; if the nurture of a child was judged too inadequate, it might, after warning, be removed to an institution and the parents punished.[Footnote: See, besides the books referred to later, H. G. Wells, "The Endowment of Motherhood" (in Social Forces in England and America); or, New Worlds for Old, chap. III. F. W. Taussig, Principles of Economics, chap. 65, sec. 1. Survey, vols. 29 and 30, many articles.] recruiting of coming generations from the diseased and feeble-minded, to prevent the handicapping of poor children through the overwork and poverty of their parents, and gradually to raise the level of inherited human nature. When coupled with improved environment and with universal and rational education, it will surely mean the existence of a happier race of men-which should be the ultimate goal of all human endeavor. What are the gravest moral dangers of our times? In conclusion, we may venture a judgment as to which, out of the many evils we have noted in contemporary life, are most serious, and where our moral energies should most earnestly be directed.

The most prominent of prevalent vices are certainly sex incontinence and the use of alcohol; the lure of wine and the lure of women have from time immemorial been man's undoing. Alcohol is being vigorously fought, and is probably doomed to general prohibition, together with opium and morphine and the other narcotics. The sex dangers are not to be so easily overcome, and we are probably in for an increase of license and its inevitable evils. There will be need for every farsighted and earnest man and woman to stand firm, in spite of enticing promises of liberty, for the great ideal of faithful marriage that makes in the end for man's deepest happiness.

The most prominent sins of today are, selfish moneymaking, selfish money spending, selfish idleness; the chief sinners we may label pirates, prodigals, parasites. By pirates are meant the dishonest dealers, the grafters, the vice caterers, the unscrupulous competitors, the pilers-up of exorbitant profits at the expense of employees and public; by prodigals, the spendthrift rich, the wasters of wealth, those who lavish in luxury or ostentation money that is sorely needed by others; by parasites, the idle rich, the lazy poor, the tramps, all who take, but do not give a return of honest work. There are also the jingoes, the preachers of lawlessness, the demagogues, and many less common types of sinners. But the particularly flagrant wrongs of our day have to do with the getting and spending of money; and the peril of the near future which looms now most menacingly on the horizon is the irritation of the wronged classes to the point of civil warfare and revolution. Such a calamity might, of course, be ultimately a means of great social advance; but it is a highly dangerous and uncertain method, involving great moral damage as well as great individual suffering, and to be averted by every possible means. The hope for averting it lies not only in the growth of public condemnation of lawlessness, but in the substitution of an ideal of service for the ideal of personal gain, and in the growing willingness of the community to check by progressive legislative measures the various means which resourceful men have discovered for advantaging themselves at the expense of society. Necessary initial steps are the securing of international peace and the construction of an efficient political system. When these ends have been attained and a just industrial order evolved, the citizens of the future will take pride in using the powers of the State to bring the greatest possible health and happiness to all.

Our forefathers had great wrongs to right-political tyranny to overthrow, human slavery to eradicate, civil and religious liberty to win, a system of popular education to inaugurate, and with it all the wilderness to tame and a new land to develop. For these ends they sacrificed much. It is for us to attack with equal courage the evils of the present. Life has outwardly become easy for many of us; our spiritual muscle easily becomes flabby. But there are new tasks equally importunate, equally worthy of our loyalty and sacrifice, hard enough to stir our blood. The times call for new idealism, new courage, new effort; the purpose of this book will not be attained unless the reader carries away from its perusal some new realization of the moral dangers that confront our civilization, and some new determination to have a hand in meeting them.

Environment: J. Nolen, Replanning Small Cities. T. C. Horsfelt, The Improvement of the Dwellings and Surroundings of the People. E. Howard, Garden Cities of To-Morrow. The City Beautiful (magazine). Literature of the National League of Improvement Associations, the American Civic Association (914 Union Trust Building, Washington, D.C.), the City Club of New York, Metropolitan Improvement League of Boston, etc. The Civic Federation of Chicago, What it has Accomplished (Hollister, Chicago, 1899). Atlantic Monthly, vol. 113, p. 823. World's Work, vol. 15, p. 10022. Outlook, vol. 92, p. 373; vol. 97, p. 393; vol. 103, p. 203. National Municipal Review, vol. 1, p. 236.

Education: H. Home, Idealism in Education. G. Spiller, Moral Education in Eighteen Countries. International Journal of Ethics, vol. 20, p. 454; vol. 22, pp. 146, 335. I. King, Social Aspects of Education. E. Boutroux, Education and Ethics. Proceedings of the National Education Association, Religious Education Association, International Moral Education Congresses. C. R. Henderson, The

Social Spirit in America, chap, xn, xm. S. Nearing, Social Adjustment, chaps, in, xv. World's Work, vol. 15, p. 10105. Outlook, vol. 85, pp. 664, 943; vol. 89, p. 789; vol. 94, p. 701.

Eugenics: C. B. Davenport, Eugenics; Heredity in Relation to Eugenics. W. D. McKim, Heredity and Human Progress. E. Schuster, Eugenics. C. W. Saleeby, Parenthood and Race Culture. H. G. Wells, Mankind in the Making, chap. in. New Tracts for the Times (various authors, Moffat, Yard Co.). Reports of International Eugenic Congresses. Atlantic Monthly, vol. 110, p. 801. Forum, vol. 51, p. 542. Quarterly Journal of Economics, vol. 26, p. 1.

Milton Keynes UK
Ingram Content Group UK Ltd.
UKHW040818051024
449151UK00004B/311

9 789362 518217